Bounded Integration

SUNY series in Comparative Politics

Gregory S. Mahler, editor

Bounded Integration

The Religion–State Relationship and
Democratic Performance in Turkey and Israel

Aviad Rubin

SUNY
PRESS

Published by State University of New York Press, Albany

For information, contact State University of New York Press, Albany, NY
www.sunypress.edu

Library of Congress Cataloging-in-Publication Data

Name: Rubin, Aviad, author.
Title: Bounded integration : the religion-state relationship and democratic
    performance in Turkey and Israel / Aviad Rubin.
Description: Albany : State University of New York, [2020] | Series: SUNY
    series in comparative politics | Includes bibliographical references and
    index.
Identifiers: LCCN 2020023191 (print) | LCCN 2020023192 (ebook) | ISBN
    9781438480770 (hardcover : alk. paper) | ISBN 9781438480787 (ebook)
Subjects: LCSH: Religion and state—Turkey—History. | Religion and state—Israel—
    History. | Islam and state—Turkey—History. | Judaism and state—Israel—
    History. | Democracy—Turkey—History. | Democracy—Israel—History. |
    Democracy—Religious aspects—Islam. | Democracy—Religious aspects—Judaism.
Classification: LCC BL65.S8 R83 2020 (print) | LCC BL65.S8 (ebook) | DDC
    322/.109561—dc23
LC record available at https://lccn.loc.gov/2020023191
LC ebook record available at https://lccn.loc.gov/2020023192

10 9 8 7 6 5 4 3 2 1

Contents

Illustrations

Figures

Tables

Acknowledgments

This book is the product of a challenging, decade-long journey. Along the way, I was assisted, guided, and inspired by many, to whom I am deeply thankful. First and foremost, I express my gratitude to Phil Oxhorn, a true mentor and an academic role model who guided me skillfully throughout this project and helped in crystallizing my ideas. I also thank Harold Waller and Juliet Johnson for providing thoughtful advice and support whenever needed. It is a particular honor to thank Michael Brecher, a scholar of rare quality who has been a source of inspiration since my studies at McGill University and to today. The Department of Political Science at McGill provided an unparalleled stimulating intellectual environment. In particular, I thank my peers in the department—Daniel Wolski, Francoise Montambault, and Kate Korycki, who were supportive, intellectually invigorating, and good company whenever the weight of the task became too heavy.

In my current academic home, the University of Haifa, I have been blessed with terrific colleagues. Special thanks go to my good friend Doron Navot, who read parts of this book and gracefully offered insights that were invaluable in improving the theoretical framework. I am also indebted to my colleagues at the School of Political Sciences, Daphna Canetti, Udi Eiran, As'ad Ghanem, Gal Gerson and Annabel Herzog, who provide a supportive scholarly environment.

The empirical part of this research was conducted in two countries that are a great deal more than simply case studies for me. Israel is my homeland, and this research was motivated by a personal commitment to make it a better and more just place. I was fortunate to be hosted at the Gilo Center for Democracy and Civic Education at the Hebrew University in Jerusalem, which provided a pleasant working environment during my field research.

During this research project, I came to know Turkey in an intimate way. Turkey is one of the most fascinating places in the world, and its welcoming people made my research there a unique and unforgettable experience. I express special thanks to Canan Aslan of the Middle East Technical University for her tireless help in organizing contacts and interviews, and to my dedicated friend and assistant Onur Kara for his invaluable work. I am also thankful to my friends Yusuf Sarfati, Sultan Tepe, and Gökçe Yurdakul, who helped me refine my understanding of contemporary trends in Turkish politics. It is hard for me to witness current affairs in Turkey. I wish this beautiful country and its courageous people better times soon.

This research would not have been possible without generous funding from the Steinberg Fellowship of the Jewish Federation in Montreal, the Rabin Scholarship from the Canadian Friends of the Hebrew University, the Süleyman Demirel Scholarship from the Moshe Dayan Center for Middle Eastern and African Studies, and the Azrieli Foundation's International Postdoctoral Fellowship. I thank them all. Special gratitude is due the Israel Institute, which generously supported the writing of this book by providing funding for visiting faculty positions at the University of Chicago and University of Toronto, and for providing a publication grant that helped bring this project to completion.

I am truly indebted to Meira Ben-Gad, a gifted editor, who often knew before me how best to elucidate my arguments and immensely enhanced the overall quality of this manuscript.

Finally, I thank my family. To my parents, who worked hard and showed me the way; my brothers, Ofir and Amir, and their families; my three adorable sons, Shai, Alon, and Omri, who are the chief source of joy in my life; and Shelly, my partner and dearest friend in the whole world, without whom this road would have been much harder. Shelly, this book is for you.

Introduction

This book has three main goals. First, it repudiates the commonly held assumption that the separation of religion from state affairs is a necessary condition for a well-functioning democracy. With a structured comparison of the experiences of Turkey and Israel, the chapters show that when popular preferences support the inclusion of religion in the regime, failing to do so may work against democratic performance. Conversely, the integration of religion in the state within certain bounds, if this policy accords with popular preferences, may have a positive influence on democratic governance.

Second, the analysis offered herein relies on a novel theoretical framework for explaining how varying levels of religious recognition by the state affect democratic performance. This framework provides a foundation for understanding the initial recognition given to religious content and actors in emerging regimes and changes in the state–religion relationship over time. Most important, it introduces conceptual boundaries within (or outside) which the state–religion relationship will support (or undermine) democratic performance. This is an important contribution to the literature on religion in politics—arena where, despite growing interest and the emergence of more nuanced postsecular perspectives, most research is still preoccupied with the belief that religious integration in politics negatively affects democratic regimes.

Third, this book aims to shed additional light on the nature of political modernization projects by assessing the applicability of lessons learned from Turkey and Israel to other polities seeking to democratize while confronting public demand for official recognition of religion. This question is most timely in Middle Eastern societies that seek formulas for sustainable governance following the Arab Spring, but it may prove helpful in other regions of the world and for other types of collective identity.

Background

Since the second half of the twentieth century, theories of modernization have adhered to the so-called secularization thesis: the belief that as societies advance, religion loses its societal functions, and consequently, religious values and institutions lose their authority. That is, based on the Western experience after the Enlightenment, theories in the social sciences have assumed that modernization and the ascent of reason would shrink religion's role in society, until it ultimately disappears. Contrary to all predictions, however, religion is far from its demise. Not only has religion not disappeared, but in many places, some of which are highly modernized, it has become even more central as a basis for political mobilization and as a core layer of identity. Although there has been a gradual shift in scholarly perspective toward a more nuanced understanding of religion's role in contemporary societies, the social sciences are still largely preoccupied with the notion of secularization (Karpov 2010, 233).

Recently, contemporary sociology has raised some doubts as to the accuracy of predictions about societal secularization and demonstrated that religion remains a potent social force in many societies across the globe (Berger 1999; Putnam and Campbell 2012; Stark 2015). Yet the application of the secularization thesis to the political realm—namely, the notion that religion and democracy are incompatible, and therefore that a secular political sphere is a condition for functioning democracy—largely remains the consensus view. This is mainly because religion and democracy are at odds: religion is about an ultimate divine truth, whose authority is rooted in the transcendental domain, whereas democracy emphasizes the peaceful coexistence of different truths, with authority rooted in human will. The policy prescription arising from this is straightforward: for democracy to flourish, politics should be isolated from religious influence. Even scholars who oppose a strict marginalization of religion from the public sphere embrace the view that the political domain should not be subject to religious influence. Casanova (2001, 1047) writes, "the relocation of the church to civil society implies not only voluntary disestablishment from the state . . . but also disengagement from political society proper . . . [T]his relocation is the very condition for the possibility of a modern public religion." Likewise, Habermas (2008, 28) notes that "the 'separation of church and state' calls for a filter between these two spheres—a filter through which only 'translated,' i.e., secular contributions may pass from the confused din of voices in the public sphere into the formal agendas of state institutions."

There is no doubt that some manifestations of religion stand in contradiction to democratic principles. In some societies, religious empowerment involves intolerance, violence, disrespect for civil rights, and systematic discrimination against women (Inglehart and Norris 2003)—a reality that seems to support the view that democracy and religion are inconsonant with one another. Nevertheless, to the degree that some present-day manifestations of political religion are irreconcilable with democratic principles, this book suggests that this is not necessarily because of unmitigated contradiction between religion and democratic values. At times, the causal arrow may run the other way. The centuries-long Western domination in the world and the strict imposition of a narrow, Western interpretation of democracy—which has strong liberal and secularist elements—on societies with large religious sectors, may be a cause of contemporary extremist manifestations of religion.

From this perspective, the varying experiences of Israel and Turkey, the only two modernist political projects in the Middle East that have exercised democratic practices through most of their political histories,[1] represent a paradox that begs explanation. Turkey emerged as a modernist political project that imitated the Western secular interpretation of democracy. Despite decades of constant attempts (some of them highly repressive) to marginalize religion from public and political life, the country has ended up less democratic and far from truly secular. Imposing strict secularism from above required authoritarian state-building during the first three decades after independence, recurrent military interventions in politics, and substantial violations of individual rights. If anything, the contemporary Turkish model—what we see in Turkish politics today—marks a slow departure from the original model and more openness to the presence of religion in the public sphere. Yet the initial policies toward religion have taken their toll on Turkish political culture. Today, the Turkish political system is plagued by polarization, distrust, and increasing authoritarian trends, all consequences of its past policies (Baran 2010; Dağı 2015; A. Rubin 2017). Also striking, state repression proved unable to eliminate the religious component from Turkish life, and religion in contemporary Turkish society and politics seems stronger and more irrepressible than ever.

Conversely, the state of Israel represents a modernist political project that deviated from the Western secular model of democracy, granted the Jewish religion a central official role, and has been able to maintain a stable democratic regime. In Israel, too, however, the state–religion relationship has not remained steady. After two decades of constructive relations, religious factions confronted the democratic state with extremist and abusive political behavior. One segment of the religious population, the religious Zionists, have turned from constructive collaboration with the state to a territorial-expansionist agenda in the Palestinian Occupied Territories and extraparliamentarian (often illegal) activities. The other segment of the religious population, the Haredim (ultraorthodox), have increased their leverage in Israel's fragmented political structure and exploited the democratic regime to obtain sectarian benefits at the expense of other groups in society. Yet despite the escalating encounters between the religious factions and the state in Israel, the Israeli regime has been quite successful in containing these challenges and preserving a stable democratic system.

The intricate history of the state-religion interaction in Turkey and Israel is marked by perplexing processes and outcomes for which existing explanations cannot adequately account. In turn, a close comparison of these two cases leads to some surprising and counterintuitive conclusions that challenge most of the existing scholarship on the impact of the state-religion relationship on democratic performance.

Of course, the state–religion relationship is not the sole influence on democratic performance. The rich corpus on democracy and democratization in recent decades suggested various structural, agential, and cultural influences on transitions from authoritarian regimes, the emergence of democratic regimes, and democratic performance. Important among them are power distribution among classes and sectors in the society (O'Donnell and Schmitter 1986; Huber, Rueschemeyer, and Stephens 1993), political development and institutional strength (Przeworski et al. 2000), the structure and performance of the economic sphere (Acemoglu and Robinson 2005), and the relative weight of liberal-constitutional ideas (Zakaria 1997). The current study does not underestimate the relevance of other factors to the development of democratic regimes and democratic performance. Rather, it aims to complement them by offering another prism—that of the state–religion relationship—through which we can gain better understanding of trends in democratic governance. This is why, wherever relevant, the analysis offered in this book acknowledges the influence of other factors (economic development, institutional strength, and the relative power of civil society) on democratic trends in the explored cases.

In these pages, I develop an analytical framework for explaining the impact of the state–religion interaction on democratic performance. I apply it through a structured comparison of Turkey's and Israel's religion–state dynamics and their impact on democratic governance. In the final stage, I assess the broader applicability of the findings beyond these cases.

A New Analytical Framework
for the State–Religion Relationship

As this book demonstrates in detail, the varying experiences of Israel and Turkey with regard to the state–religion interaction and its dynamic effect on democratic performance during different periods cannot be adequately explained by existing theories. I am referring primarily to the various short-comings of the secularization thesis (Stark 1999; Swatos and Christiano 1999), and to the problematic limitations of the inclusion-moderation thesis (Tezcür 2010; Schwedler 2011; Gurses 2014) and some minor fallacies of the twin tolerations thesis (Stepan 2001). Briefly, none of these theories offer a comprehensive analytical framework for understanding the full spectrum of interactions between religion and the state and their effect on democratic governance. The political element of the secularization thesis, with its premise that democratic governance mandates the isolation of religious inputs from the political sphere, does not conceive a religious presence in politics as an option (Bader 2010). It cannot serve to analyze cases where such interactions exist and produce diverse outcomes. The inclusion-moderation thesis, with its linear outlook (more inclusion is better), has three shortcomings. It falls short of providing a clear range for the constructive operation of religion in democratic settings; it draws its inferences mainly from nondemocratic Middle Eastern societies, which qualifies its applicability to democratic contexts; it fails to clearly distinguish between opportunistic and principled support for democracy (Tezcür 2010; Gurses 2014).

Alfred Stepan's (2000, 2001) twin tolerations is the most sophisticated existing framework for studying religion–state coexistence under democratic rule. However, it also suffers from several drawbacks, especially where the cases explored here are concerned. First, Stepan's conceptualization of democracy carries a considerable liberal component that borrows from his earlier work (Linz and Stepan 1996), which somewhat limits the applicability of his concept of democracy (Hashemi 2009). Second, although the twin tolera-tions thesis embraces a wide range of religious manifestations in the public and political spheres, it adheres to the secularization thesis's prohibition on religious veto powers in politics (Stepan 2000, 39)—something that may well happen, and indeed happened when religious parties became part of the government (Israel) or even led it (Turkey). Third, Stepan acknowledges the right of religious populations (agency) to participate in politics, but he does not discuss the presence and impact of religious content in the state, independent of religious political agency. Also important, he recommends sanctions against religious agents in politics if the latter violate democratic principles (Stepan 2000, 40), but the essence of such sanctions remains vague. For example, will these actors be suspended from politics permanently, temporarily, or at all?

A recent trend of "postsecular" literature remedies most of the shortcomings of earlier scholarship regarding the role of religion in politics. Specifically, the postsecular literature departs from the secularization thesis's sweeping negation of religion in politics, and allows—both normatively and analytically—the integration of religious actors, content, and argumentation into its analysis of the effect of religion in politics (Habermas 2008; Fererra 2009; Calhoun, Juergensmeyer, and VanAntwerpen 2011; Gorski et al. 2012; Nynäs, Lassander, and Utriainen 2012; Graham 2013; Stepan and Taylor 2014; Fox 2015). The perspective offered by this book joins to and complements the postsecular literature. It does not view the relationship between the state and religion as a static, unidirectional process that is simply either bottom-up or top-down and largely predetermined. The relationship is instead framed, in the tradition of Migdal's (2001) state-in-society theory, as reciprocal and dynamic. This perspective allows room for significant changes over time, following the political behavior of each actor—religious players and state organs—and their mutually constitutive effect on each other. In addition, it accounts for how structural and ideational changes in the surrounding environment might influence the phenomenon under investigation. Applying such an approach to the study of the state–religion relationship can help us understand the determinants of this relationship over time and reconsider deterministic conclusions about the ability of religion to peacefully coexist with and even reinforce democratically governed states.

More specifically, the analytical perspective I develop in chapter 2 has at least two substantive advantages where the analysis of religion in politics is considered. First, it implements a nondeterministic, open-ended approach that enables it to account for various outcomes in the relationship between the state and religious actors, ranging from mutual respect and support for democratic governance to clashes and attempts to undermine each other. Second, it has the capacity to explain the dynamic dimension of the state–religion interaction on the time axis, something that is overlooked by most existing theories of religion and state.

The analytical framework offered herein departs from the heavy emphasis on secularism that characterized previous theories and advances the political element of the postsecular literature in four important ways, which I present as four analytical propositions. The first is that religion and democracy may be compatible, meaning that they can peacefully coexist in a stable political system. The second is that the Western model of democracy, with its strong emphasis on secularization, is not the only viable option for democratic regimes. In other words, nonsecular variants of democracy are a conceivable option. The third proposition is that the state–religion interaction is dynamic and develops over time. Particularly crucial are the factors that shape new regimes' approach toward religion, because they set the starting point for the relationship and establish strong path-dependent arrangements and institutions that often will have enormous influence on how this relationship evolves over time (Mahoney 2000; Pierson 2004).

The last proposition relates to how religious actors should be perceived and analyzed in democratic society and politics. It holds that religious groups are social actors whose modes of behavior and engagement with the state are not random but are largely dependent on state policies toward them, which in turn leads to certain responses by these groups, and so on, creating a mutually constitutive interaction. The affiliation of religious actors is most important in this regard, namely, whether religious actors are integrated to the state apparatus and promote state policies or work mainly in civil society and challenge state policies (Huber, Rueschemeyer, and Stephens 1993, 74).

Case Selection: Why Compare Israel and Turkey?

Israel and Turkey are different in many respects, such as size, level of economic development, geographic position, and state traditions. Despite these differences, they are appropriate candidates for comparison because of their many relevant similarities (the most important of which I detail below) and chiefly because of two crucial points of difference. Let us start with the latter. First, from their origins, Israel and Turkey adopted opposite policies toward religion. For different historical and structural reasons, the Zionist nationalist movement and later the state of Israel gave Jewish religious content and actors (which I distinguish from the more amorphous and debatable "Jewishness" of the state that appears in Israel's declaration of independence and basic laws, which may be interpreted as primarily ethnic[2]) a positive official role in their ideologies and policies. In Turkey, the Kemalist nationalist movement and the Turkish state fought religious manifestations in the public and political spheres and repressed Islamic culture (although Republican Turkey's Diyanet, the directorate of religious affairs, acknowledged affiliation with Sunni Islam as an element of Turkish collective identity, thereby giving primacy in the secular system to one strand of Islamic identity; Keyman 2007, 225). These different strategies generated very different roles for religion as an identity and as a political instrument, which make these cases good candidates for study and a comparison between them telling.

Second, while neither state implemented a liberal democracy, they vary significantly in terms of their democratic performance. Israel has maintained a stable democratic regime despite considerable domestic and external challenges. In contrast, Turkey has endured frequent interruptions to democratic rule by unelected actors, including the security apparatus and the judiciary. Moreover, the legacy of hegemonic rule established by the previous Kemalist elite has been adopted by the incumbent religious elite and continues to undermine Turkish democracy. These striking differences, and the correlation between them, provide the theoretical puzzle of this study.

In terms of their similarities, the two states are located in the Middle East and have long been the only democratic (or partially democratic) polities in this region (Diamond 2010). This fact alone puts them in a unique position and makes a comparison interesting on the regional level. Moreover, Palestine was a province of the Ottoman Empire for more than 400 years, and despite varying legacies of their colonial pasts, the two countries share several related and relevant historical experiences. The most relevant point in this respect is that the British Mandate in Palestine, and later the state of Israel, retained the millet system, originally implemented in Palestine by the Ottoman Empire, which grants partial autonomy to each religious community in society.

In addition, the establishment of the two states was the accomplishment of two successful national projects—Zionism and Kemalism—that borrowed national and modern agendas around the same period of time (late nineteenth and early twentieth centuries) from European intellectual discourse (Avineri 1981; Mardin 1989). Similarly, these national movements benefited from an exceptional leadership manifested in the personalities and leadership skills of Kemal Atatürk in Turkey and David Ben-Gurion in Israel, two men of rare qualities who laid the foundations of their states and were central in dictating the initial arrangements of the state–religion relationship (Bar Zohar 1987; Mango 2008). Also significant is that the foundation of the two modern states was the ultimate outcome of long and costly wars of independence that consolidated the prominent status of their national leaderships and facilitated the latter's long-term rule.

The two countries are also comparable in domestic features. Despite a considerable difference in the overall size of their populations, Turkey and

Israel are both home to a significant majority group that identifies itself with one faith—Judaism in the Israeli case and Sunni Islam in the Turkish case. Both countries, since their establishment, have had to deal with a large minority of another ethnicity/nationality that has put forward demands for collective recognition by the state. Israel is home to an Arab minority making up approximately 20 percent of the population (1.8 million people out of 8.8 million), and Turkey has a Kurdish minority of roughly the same percentage (16 million people out of 80 million) (Central Intelligence Agency 2017). These countries have dealt with these large minorities in ways that debase their democratic systems, although using different methods in each case (Peled 1992; Smooha 2002; Peleg and Waxman 2007; Yavuz and Özcan 2015).

Furthermore, despite variations in the level of religion, the commonalities between Judaism and Islam offer good reasons to compare the state-religion relationship in Israel and Turkey. To begin with, Islam and Judaism are based on practice, not on faith. These religions require their adherents to follow a comprehensive code of behavior, as opposed to most strands of Christianity, according to which faith need not necessarily be manifested in particular behavior. Both have a very detailed religious legal code—the Islamic Sharia and the Jewish Halakha—that regulates every aspect of life, including the political realm. Both are characterized by the absence of a clear hierarchical order such as that found in Catholicism, and equally by the lack of a clear distinction between the political and spiritual spheres (Lazarus-Yafeh 2003). The religions share many practices, ceremonies, and traditions as well as doctrinal features. A partial list of similarities includes the following: strict monotheism; dietary laws (kashrut and halal); circumcision; and clergy (rabbis and ulema) who are scholars and theologians but not priests. Both revere the same figure—Avraham (in Hebrew) or Ibrahim (in Arabic)—as the father of the faith; the Jewish prophet Moses is seen in Islam as a role model for Muhammad. Both originally faced the same direction during prayer, toward Jerusalem (Bunzl 2004, 7).

Although the compatibility of Islam and democracy is generally doubted, an Islamic state need not necessarily reject democratic governance. This holds true in Muslim states such as Indonesia and Malaysia, and more recently Tunisia. Currently the Islamic Middle East is admittedly the region most resistant to democracy. But this is not necessarily because of Islam's ethos or doctrinal features (Bellin 2004; Stepan and Robertson 2004; Hinnebusch 2006; Diamond 2010; Esposito, Sonn, and Voll 2015). The dramatic mass protests, regime change, and democratic elections in several Arab countries since 2011 provide cautious signs of hope for the possibility of democratic progress. Likewise, there is no reason to assume that all strands of Judaism, even though conceived of as somehow Western (via the "Judeo-Christian tradition"), will be consistent in their support for democracy. Therefore, it is not the type of religion that determines its compatibility with democracy. Rather, this is determined by the specific circumstances and continuing dynamic interaction between the state and religious actors in different contexts (Schwedler 2001; Stepan 2001; Soper and Fetzer 2018). In Turkey and Israel, this relationship has changed significantly over time and produced different experiences with democracy. This is where a dynamic perspective can be an effective instrument of analysis to explain trends in the state–religion relationship and account for changes in the role of religion in transitions to democracy.

The cases of Turkey and Israel warrant a new dynamic approach to analyzing the state–religion relationship. In these countries the relationship between the modern state and religion began very differently before independence, witnessed considerable changes over time, and in many ways resulted in opposite outcomes. In the late Ottoman Empire, several factors pushed the leadership of the incoming elite to eliminate all possibility of religious influence in the new order. Following its establishment in 1923, the Republic of Turkey applied the common Western prescription—modernization and democracy require secularism—and tried to marginalize religion by imposing strict secularism through constitutional measures and military repression. Nevertheless, after nine decades of often coercively enforcing this policy, Turkey remained far from socially secular, with significant problems of democratic instability and a resilient authoritarian political culture. Unfortunately, a change of political elite from Kemalist to Islamist has failed to alter the century-old hegemonic political culture in Turkey, and the incumbent regime represses political opponents and restricts civil rights to retain power, a trend that worsened after the failed coup in July 2016 and the April 2017 referendum (see chapter 5).

In contrast, underlying structural and ideational conditions dictated the early integration of religious content into the Zionist ideology and religious actors into the ranks of the movement. Consequently, despite Zionism's secular orientation, postindependence Israel challenged the standard secularization thesis and chose to grant an official multidimensional role to religion in state affairs.

By integrating religion into the public and political spheres, Israel was able to develop a stable democratic regime and facilitate a relatively peaceful coexistence of secular and religious worldviews, at least during the first two decades after independence. Since 1967, however, the country's religious actors have endeavored to occupy disproportionate power in the political sphere and violate the principles of democracy by imposing their narrow worldview on different realms of state policy and social life. So far, Israeli democracy has been able to contain these challenges in an effective fashion and retain the democratic principles of the regime, but they have arguably eroded its performance, especially under Netanyahu's governments since 2009.

The lessons from these two cases challenge simplistic assumptions of existing theories about the conceptual relationship between democracy, modernization, and religion. The analytical framework offered in this book compares the dynamic relationship between the state and religion, its evolution over time, and its impact on democratization processes in Turkey and Israel. This can shed new light on our understanding of the state–religion relationship and its influence on democratization and democratic performance more generally.

Structure of the Book

The rest of this book is arranged as follows. In chapter 1 I develop the core premises of the analytical framework that I use throughout and show how it accounts for the state–religion relationship over time, the boundaries of civil society, and how it influences the development of a democratic regime. The remainder of the book applies the framework to Turkey and Israel. Each case is discussed in four consecutive chapters that correspond to four chronological periods. The chronological analysis emphasizes the dynamic element in the state–religion relationship and its corresponding influence on democratic performance in different periods.

Chapters 2 through 5 explore the Turkish experience. Chapter 2 presents the conditions in the prerepublican Ottoman Empire, which determined the role of the Islamic religion in the Turkish Republic. Chapter 3 discusses the nondemocratic phase of Turkish politics, which stretched between 1923 and 1950 and was largely a necessary product of the Kemalist program to impose secularism on society from above. Chapter 4 deals with the first democratic phase in Turkish politics, under Kemalist hegemony, between 1950 and 2000. It demonstrates how the Islamic religion was able to carve its place in Turkish politics, despite assertive attempts by the Kemalist establishment to contain its growing social and political power, and how this interaction changed religious actors' strategies of engagement with the state in recent years, bringing religious parties to political power in a formally secular regime. Chapter 5 discusses the most recent period of religion–state politics in Turkey under the AKP government (2002–2018). It demonstrates how religion served as an effective platform to pluralize the Turkish political discourse and at the same time exposes the influence of Turkey's initial treatment of religion on the country's current democratic downturn.

Chapters 6 through 9 discuss the evolving relationship between the state and religious actors in Israel. Chapter 6 covers the emergence of the Zionist movement in the late nineteenth century and the factors influencing the role this movement chose to grant the Jewish religion in its ideology and institutions, first in the Diaspora and later in the institutions of the Jewish community in Palestine (the Yishuv). In chapter 7 I investigate the arrangements that organized the role of religion in the new state of Israel and their positive impact on the sustainability of a stable democratic regime in the first two decades after independence. Chapter 8 demonstrates how modifications in the role of religion due to changing social, political, and security circumstances between the mid-1960s and mid-1980s subverted the constructive collaboration that characterized the previous state–religion interaction. Chapter 9 analyzes the mounting challenges by religious populations against the state from the 1980s to the present and how the latter has managed to effectively contain them in the boundaries of democracy.

Chapter 10, the concluding chapter, is divided into two sections. The first assesses the general applicability of the analytical framework as a tool of analysis and suggests some general lessons about the role of religion and other collective identities in emerging democracies as well as possible paths for future research. The second section discusses the applicability of the analytical framework offered in this book to emerging political regimes in the Middle East.

Chapter 1

Reconceptualizing the Role of Religion in Democratic Regimes

Any effort to explain the influence of the state–religion relationship on transitions to democracy and democratic performance means, first, articulating the complex interplay between religion and politics in democratic regimes. This is a bewildering task, because decades in which the secularization thesis has dominated the social sciences (Martin 1979, Casanova 1994; Berger 1999; Bruce 2011) have created a chasm between the study of politics, especially the study of democratic regimes, and the study of religion. Indeed, until the early 2000s, studies on religion in political science were almost completely absent (Wald and Wilcox 2006). In the twentieth century, the study of religion in the social sciences concentrated on religion's place in three related spheres: (1) individual life, seen through a psychological lens; (2) communal and cultural life, seen through an anthropological lens; and (3) social structures, seen through a sociological lens.

The third lens, sociology, carries the greatest relevance and potential to contribute to our understanding of religion in politics. Yet until the early 2000s, most sociological research was preoccupied with the secularization thesis, leading it to focus on the disappearance of religion from society, rather than its presence and influence.

The secularization thesis was an offshoot of modernization theory,[1] derived from the conviction that scientific and rationalist perspectives would triumph over religious affiliation in the modern era, leading religion to lose its social functions and eventually disappear from public life. Sociologist Peter Berger was probably the first to expose the deep ideological persuasion that governed this field of study, when he argued that "the ideological interest . . . *is the interest in quasiscientific legitimation of the avoidance of transcendence* . . . [which] serves to provide quasiscientific legitimations of a secularized world view" (1974, 128; emphasis in original). But back then, Berger was swimming upstream and by himself. Only much later was he joined by other sociologists who questioned the foundations and universal applicability of the secularization thesis (Juergensmeyer 1993; Stark 1999; Casanova 2006; Gorski and Altınordu 2008; Martin 2014).

As in many other instances, undeniable trends in the real world drove a change in scientific perspectives. The convergence of two parallel yet simultaneous processes—rapid modernization and the resurgence of religion throughout the globe—have produced social and political phenomena that the secularization thesis is unable to explain. Specifically, the multidimensional (individual, social, and political) renaissance of religion in contemporary societies in the face of sweeping assumptions about its eventual demise has brought prominent scholars to acknowledge the fallacy of the thesis and the need to reconceptualize the relationship between religion and the state in general, and in democratic settings in particular. For instance, Jürgen Habermas claimed that unprecedented diversity, immigration, and communication had brought the Western world into a postsecular era, requiring a new modus vivendi between Western societies and religious groups and doctrines (Habermas 2008).[2] Peter Berger noted that "the assumption that we live in a secularized world is false. . . . This means that the whole body of literature by historians and social scientists loosely labeled 'secularization theory' is essentially mistaken" (Berger 1999, 2). In the same fashion, Jean Bethke Elshtain, delivering the 2008 Seymour Martin Lipset Lecture on Democracy in the World,[3] concluded that "the secularization hypothesis has failed and failed spectacularly. We must now find a new paradigm that will help us to understand the complexities of the relationship between religion and democracy" (Elshtain 2009, 16). Tellingly, noted sociologist of religion Rodney Stark titled one of his articles "Secularization, R.I.P.," and concluded it by noting that "once and for all, let us declare an end to social scientific faith in the theory of secularization, recognizing that it was the product of wishful thinking" (Stark 1999, 269).

Certainly in non-Western contexts the secularization thesis has demonstrably failed as a framework of analysis for the interplay between religion and the state, as well as in its predictive capacity—especially when considering political transitions like those that took place in the post-Soviet bloc and more recently in the Middle East. Yet even in relation to Western countries—based on whose experience the secularization thesis was advanced—its applicability is now subject to serious scholarly debate, and critics outweigh supporters (Stepan 2001; Casanova 2006; Brubaker 2012; Davie 2013; Joppke 2013; Martin 2014). In particular, critics argue that the thesis's underlying assumptions about the relationships between societies, states, and religions are oversimplified, static, deterministic, and insensitive to contextual differences.

Recent sociological observation about the fallacy of the secularization thesis as an analytical and predictive tool for the role of religion in society spread to the study of politics. An increasing volume of scholarship in political science departed from the notion of political secularization (strict separation between religion and the political sphere) and sought new venues of research that integrate the role of religion in politics into analysis (more on this later). The goal of this chapter is to further advance the study of religion in politics by developing an analytical framework for understanding the impact of the interaction between religion and the state on democratizing and democratic societies. Such a framework will have potency only to the extent that it can overcome the deficiencies of existing theories of religion in politics.

The State, Politics, and Democracy

The modern state is the structure within which religion and politics interact, and its organs regulate the role of religion in various domains. Politics is a sphere of human activity concerned with mutually constitutive interactions with the state and society. Democracy is a kind of political regime or system of governance that regulates interactions and outcomes in the political sphere based on popular sovereignty. All three concepts are central to the investigation offered in this book and should be clearly defined before moving forward.

Modern states are a relatively young historical phenomenon,[4] but they soon became the primary form of social order in the contemporary world. The components of the state set forth in Westphalia included defined boundaries (territory), defined populations (subjects and later citizens), and legitimacy (internal and external). The development of the state in the nineteenth century fascinated social and political theorists such as Georg Hegel, Karl Marx, Émile Durkheim, and—more than anyone else—political sociologist Max Weber, who provided the most accepted definition of the modern state: a human community that successfully claims monopoly over the legitimate use of coercive capabilities in a given territory (Weber 2009, 78). After long neglect of the state and its institutional matrix as important variables in the study of politics in the twentieth century, there evolved renewed interest in the state machinery, with Huntington's "Political Development and Political Decay" (1965) and Evans, Rueschemeyer, and Skocpol's *Bringing The State Back In* (1985) being the most important contributors to this trend.[5]

Today the state is at the center of much political research, although the enormous diversity that characterizes states around the world makes it hard to apply a template definition of the state in all these studies (Migdal 2009). Research on the state identifies four types of definitions or perspectives. The first and most used perspective is the Weberian one, which takes coercion and the use of power from above as the founding element of states (Kelly 2003, chap. 3). The second perspective emphasizes the various functions of states as institutional matrices that define membership, regulate internal and external relationships, promote identity and cohesion, and distribute goods (Jordan 1985). The third perspective, the Marxist one, concentrates on the role of the state in the reproduction of resource distribution and in mitigating class struggles in modern societies (Jessop 1977; Piketty 2014). The fourth perspective emphasizes the dependence of the state on legitimacy from below, and hence the need for states to appease and win the support of their constituencies (Migdal 2009). The current research takes a combined approach, simultaneously investigating authority from above, dependence on voices from below, and the functions fulfilled by the state in a certain policy area. Although the analytical framework of this book does not deal directly with class struggles in the state, it does pay attention to how overlaps between class structure and religious affiliation influence the state.

Elemental to the definition of states is the definer's ontological approach toward the relationship between the state and society. Weberian (or statist) approaches see the state machinery as an autonomous political actor (Skocpol 1985). Conversely, liberal and Marxist approaches see state behavior as a mere vessel of either popular preferences (for liberals and pluralists; Dahl 2005) or distribution of material resources (for Marxists; Moore 1966; Jessop 1977). The most influential account of this relationship is offered by Migdal's state-in-society theory (Migdal 1988, 2001, 2009). In Migdal's conception, no clear causal arrow can be drawn between states and their respective societies. Rather, states and societies mutually constitute each other over time. The state both shapes society and is shaped by it. Migdal's account of the state focuses on longitudinal process tracing, historical critical junctures, and path dependency; it is sensitive to distinct social and historical contexts; and it highlights the evolving relationship between state and societies instead of a unidirectional effect of one on the other (Migdal 2009, 163). Given the enormous diversity among states, Migdal suggests paying less attention to what the state is and focusing instead on what the state does, namely, on state practices in specific domains (Migdal 2009, 168–78). Importantly, Migdal does not perceive the state as a unitary actor but advocates disintegrating "the state" to the specific actions of its organs—the executive, judicial, and legislative branches, the security apparatus, the bureaucracy, and so on (Migdal 2001, 2). This approach to the study of the state is particularly suited to exploring the ongoing interaction between religion and the state, and so I use it in this book.

The second concept that needs to be defined is politics. Harold Laswell defined politics as "who gets what, when, how?" (Lasswell 1936). Similarly, Easton's *Framework of Historical Analysis* defines politics as a system of authoritative allocation by the political system of values for society (Easton 1965, 96). Finally, Karl Deutsch defines politics as the pursuit of interests by particular individuals and groups; in his view, politics deals with the interplay of interests and with claiming and distributing rewards (Deutsch 1980, 11–12). Put simply, all these definitions share the notion that politics is an arena of interaction between individual and collective human agents seeking political power—that is, the authoritative capacity to control or to participate in controlling the state apparatus, to design state policies, and to determine preferences for resource allocation.

Finally, democracy needs to be defined. Democracy is one of the most complicated, multifaceted, and disputed terms in the discipline. The complexity of the concept and its contested meaning have led to considerable confusion regarding its definition and application. To complicate things further, in today's world the label "democracy" provides a stamp of legitimacy for political regimes and is often exploited by authoritarian leaders to legitimate political regimes that in fact display very little democratic governance (Diamond 1996; Collier and Levitsky 1997; Zakaria 1997).

What is the basis on which democracy should be defined? Huntington (1991) argues that scholarship offers three alternative foundations for defining democratic regimes: (1) as an accepted set of procedures, (2) according to its desired goals, and (3) according to its source of authority. The second and third alternatives (definition by goals and definition by authority) raise serious difficulties,[6] because they depend on unique historical-cultural contexts and particular sets of values. Both are used only in the margins of scholarly research, whereas the procedural definition is the most accepted and consequently employed most frequently (Hungtington 1991).

Robert Dahl was the first to provide a sound definition of procedural democracy, which he based on the following components: "freedom to form and join organizations; freedom of expression; right to vote; eligibility for public office; right of political leaders to compete for votes and support; alternative sources of information; free and fair elections; institutions for making government policies depend on votes and other expressions of preference" (Dahl 1971, 3). Later on, Schmitter and Karl (1991) added two fundamental conditions to Dahl's list: internal autonomy, meaning that elected leaders should be free from intervention by nonelected functions in the decision-making process; and external autonomy, meaning that democracy should guarantee the independence of domestic political regimes from extra-territorial influences. These additions are crucial when religion is considered because of the tendency of some religious actors to seek undemocratic veto powers not aligned with public preferences and because of their potential susceptibility to extraterritorial demands and preferences stemming from transnational religious interests, which might not be in line with the results of the democratic process.

Finally, a crucial distinguishing element of democracy is a high level of uncertainty regarding the results of the political process, what Przeworski (1986) calls "institutional uncertainty." According to Przeworski, democracies allow open-ended political results, and all political actors collaborate with and respect this notion of uncertainty. Conversely, in nondemocratic regimes, the political result is either fixed or strictly limited without public deliberation, and the electoral process is an inefficient vehicle for political change. Przeworski's conceptualization of democracy is important because it rejects any predetermined substantive content that limits the capacity of the political process to facilitate an open-ended result.

With these considerations in mind, the concept of democracy used throughout this book consists three components: (1) Dahlian principles, (2) the autonomy of elected politicians, and (3) an open-ended game characterized by institutional uncertainty.[7] This conceptualization has considerable advantages. It is widely used, it is applicable in different social and cultural contexts, and it provides a universal standard for assessing the level of democratization in society (O'Donnell and Schmitter 1986; Plattner 1998). As such, it is applicable to almost every political context, allowing for comparison across cases and generalizable conclusions. Moreover, although this definition is mainly procedural, its conditions imply important substantive rights, such as equality, freedom of speech, freedom of association, and more, that reflect some of the liberal elements of democratic governance. At the same time, this definition avoids the trap of conflating democracy as a procedural system of governance with liberalism as ideology. Even in it is narrowest form, democracy contains some liberal elements, while other elements of a liberal worldview—secularism, equal treatment of different cultures and collective identities, and wide acceptance of different conceptions of the good may be others—are not perceived here an inherent part of democracy. What is striking is that this widely accepted conceptualization (and similar ones) does not emphasize or even mention secularism as a necessary component of democracy.[8] This brings me to the discussion of religion in politics.

Religion in Politics

Up to about 2000, research in political science refrained from exploring the relationship between religion and politics (Madeley 2009, 174), mainly because of the dominance of the rationalist, modernist, and developmental approaches that governed the study of politics in the second half of the twentieth century (Lipset 1959; Deutsch 1961; Almond and Powell 1966). Consequently, scholarly knowledge about the interaction between religion and politics was generated mainly in sociological research. Most of this research concentrated on the Western Christian world, was directed by the logic of the secularization thesis, and focused on the social sphere, often treating the dynamics of religion in politics as a mere reflection or consequence of social trends (Martin 1979; Casanova 1994; Bruce 2011).

Notwithstanding its limitations, sociological research has provided valuable insights into the interaction of religion and the state throughout history and created categories for the examination of trends in this relationship that are highly relevant to politics. Berger, in his classic work *The Sacred Canopy* (1967), focused on the role of religion as a unifying value system that governs social and political life, while Martin (1979, 2014) emphasized the influence of critical junctures in history on evolution or revolution in relationships between societies, states, and religions. Casanova (1994, 2006), addressing secularization, defined it as a multidimensional change encompassing three processes: (1) a decline in belief and observance at the individual level, (2) differentiation of secular from religious responsibilities at the societal level, and (3) privatization of religion and its detachment from the public sphere at the political and institutional levels (according to Casanova, this third point was the thesis's most debatable element). The sociological literature also introduced an important distinction between substantive definitions of religion, which address what religion is, and functional definitions, which address how it manifests itself in society (Berger 1974; Hamilton 2001).

Finally, sociologists distinguished between "belonging" and "believing," and showed that even in Western Europe, the heartland of secularism, the decline of institutionalized religious authority was not accompanied by a decline in religious-based value systems (Davie 1990, 2006; Chaves 1994). Davie's (2006) concept of "vicarious religion" captures the idea that in much of the Western world, many citizens are content to delegate day-to-day religious practice and belief to a small group of professional and lay religious leaders.

The recent resurgence of religion throughout the world (Juergensmeyer 1993; Berger 1999; Cesari 2014; Stark 2015), including its deepening effect on international and domestic conflicts (Juergensmeyer 2003; Fox and Sandler 2004; Hassner 2009; Toft, Philpott, and Shah 2011), has generated new interest among political scientists in the political roles of religion. A few works by political scientists still resemble sociological research in focusing on societal dynamics from below and through the lens of the secularization thesis, such as Norris and Inglehart's (2004) exploration of the connection between material security and religiosity throughout the world, Gill's (2001) work on how the structure of the market for religions affects the relative prosperity of religious denominations, or Ben Porat's (2013) research on secularizing entrepreneurship at the grassroots level. But the majority of political studies on religion take a different perspective, one highlighting the political manifestations of religion and its multifaceted interactions with the state.

Various terms are employed in the literature on the interaction between religion and politics. These include "religion" or "religious" and such combinations as "religion and state," "the state–religion relationship," "church and state," and "religion in politics." These terms are rarely defined, and indeed, according to some, are impossible to define (Grzymala-Busse 2016). I proceed by summarizing how political science generally treats this relationship before offering my own definition of religion in politics.

First is the ontological perspective. Religion in political studies is implicitly conceptualized in one of two ways, or sometimes both: as doctrine (i.e., religious content) (Brubaker 2012; Almond, Appleby, and Sivan 2003) or as agency (i.e., religious actors) (Juergensmeyer 2008; Künkler and Leininger 2009; Haynes and Hennig 2011). Second is the unit of analysis. In contrast to psychological or strands of sociological and anthropological research, which inquire into practices and beliefs at the individual level, the political study of religion is concerned with collective interactions at the group level of analysis (Wald, Owen, and Hill 1988; Haynes 1998, 5).

Both aspects of the concept "religion in politics" are straightforward. Less so is a third and final aspect, the factors shaping the interaction. Studies in political science tend to concentrate either on top-down treatment of religion(s) by the state (Fox 2008, 2015, 2016; Monsma and Soper 2009), on bottom-up behavior of religious actors in politics (Künkler and Leininger 2009; Haynes and Hennig 2011), or on how structural conditions influence the interaction (Norris and Inglehart 2004). However, a number of scholars—notably Haynes (1998), Hibbard (2010), and Grzymala-Busse (2012, 2015, 2016)—conceptualize the interaction between religion and the state in a more dynamic and mutually constitutive way. As Haynes puts it (1998, 5), "the relationship between religion and politics is both dialectical and interactive: each shapes and influences the other. Both causal directions need to be held in view." This approach is more sophisticated in acknowledging the effect of both sides of the equation (state and religion) on the outcome and is sensitive to changes in this interaction over time. Fox (2015) suggested that the relationship between religious actors and the state over the role of religion in the state is characterized by what he calls "the competition approach," an ongoing push and pull between the two poles.

Building on the important insights already provided in the literature, religion in politics is understood here as the multifaceted interaction over time between religious actors and state organs over the extent to which religious populations and religious content are granted recognition in the polity. Within this interaction, the state and religious actors have distinct inputs. Religious actors engage in politics to promote theocratic demands, sectarian demands, or both. Theocratic demands aim to shape the character of the entire public sphere in accordance with religious doctrine, including things like state symbols; days of rest; issues of personal status such as marriage, divorce, adoption, or custody; moral questions such as abortion; religious curricula in the education system; and so on. Sectarian demands refer to selective benefits for religious populations, such as allocation of specific funding for religious purposes or particular exemptions from universal civil duties, such as taxation or conscription to the military.[9]

For its part, the state can grant different levels of recognition to religious actors and religious content in the polity. Such recognition falls into four domains: symbolic, political, institutional, and economic. Symbolic recognition occurs when the state acknowledges (e.g., by affording constitutional status to) religion and religious content in objects, actions, or practices with ceremonial value in the public sphere (e.g., public holidays, the state flag or emblem, the national anthem, prayers at official events). Recognition in the political arena, or political recognition, exists when the state sanctions faith-based political associations, including the participation of religious-based parties in elections and in government. Institutional recognition reflects the existence of official state institutions that implement religious doctrine, such as religious courts, religious education systems, and the like. Finally, economic recognition covers the allocation of state resources for religious purposes in all three of the other domains, as well as for special sectarian needs.

The definition of religion in politics employed in this book has considerable advantages. It breaks down the all-encompassing phenomenon of religion in politics into identifiable categories and facilitates longitudinal examination of trends in these categories over time. In addition, it takes a reciprocal approach that considers the distinct effect of each side on the overall dynamics. Finally, it takes account of the dual face of religion in the public sphere—as content and as agency—thus allowing a more refined analysis of the role of religion in the state.

Foundations of a New Analytical Framework for the Religion–State Interaction

Here I outline the elements of a new analytical framework for explaining the relationship between religion and the state. The framework is based on four related propositions, each of which touches on a different aspect of the religion–state relationship in contemporary societies. The first two propositions are as follows. (I) Religion and democracy are not inherently incompatible. (II) Western variants of democracy are not the only viable option. If either proposition I or II cannot be established (as assumed, for example, by the secularization thesis), further discussion on the subject is unnecessary, because without the word "not," neither proposition can translate into policies that acknowledge, let alone tolerate or embrace, some role for religion in politics.

The second two propositions are as follows. (III) The role of religion in the state depends on structural and ideational factors, is largely shaped prior to regime or state formation, and is incorporated in the state's institutional matrix during the critical juncture of state formation. (IV) Religious actors are potential members of civil society. With respect to proposition IV, the current research suggests that religious actors should be viewed as social actors who can be either accommodated in or excluded from civil society. Their participation in civil society is not entirely voluntary and autonomous, but is largely dependent on state policies toward religious content and agency, the responses of religious communities, and the evolving nature of this relationship. The state is viewed here as pivotal in shaping the boundaries of civil society. In return, the strength and vibrancy of civil society are important expediters of democratic governance.

I address each proposition in detail.

I: Religion and Democracy Are Not Inherently Incompatible

Secularization was a product of modernization and the Enlightenment in Western Europe during the eighteenth and nineteenth centuries, and it emerged at the same time as the first wave of democratization (Huntington 1991). The simultaneity of the two processes led prominent scholars to argue that the presence of religion in the public sphere is a barrier to democracy (Lipset 1959, 1994; Deutsch 1961; D. E. Smith 1970; Huntington 1996). In his canonical text *Political Man*, Lipset argued that one of the most important facilitators of democracy is an ability to develop what he calls "a secular political culture" (1959, 89). Further, he suggests that with the exception of Protestantism,[10] "as long as religious ties reinforce secular political alignments, the chances for democratic give-and-take, and compromise, are weak" (1959, 93). More recent studies echo this view in suggesting a strong empirical correlation between societal secularization, material modernization, and democratic governance (Norris and Inglehart 2004; Inglehart and Welzel 2005).

In this context, Islam is thought of by many to be the religion most resistant to democracy. This is for the simple reason that historically, unlike the case with the Catholic Church in Europe, there was no separation between the political and spiritual leadership in the Islamic tradition, from the Prophet Muhammad onward (Najjar 1958; Zartman 1992; Lewis 2002). However, other major religions, including Catholicism and Hinduism, were perceived in the past to be largely incompatible with democracy and modernity (D. E. Smith 1970; Madan 1997; Nandy 1997).

Indeed, some principled tension does exist between religion and democracy. Democracy assumes the coexistence of competing truths and the ultimate authority of the people in determining the common good. It requires equality, tolerance, acceptance of diverse perspectives toward life, and a continuous pluralistic bargaining process between different groups in society. In contrast, all religions (especially the monotheistic ones) assume an ultimate, preordained truth, manifested in a religious legal code[11] and a set of absolute divine imperatives that are not open to bargaining or compromise. As opposed to political practices, religious doctrine is not dependent on the contemporary will of the people but is determined by God and interpreted by religious scholars in a manner that isolates it almost entirely from public deliberation. Indeed, "religion, at least the religion of the Abrahamic traditions (Judaism, Christianity and Islam), stresses moral absolutes. But politics is all about compromise" (Zakaria 2004, 13).

However, the historical record shows that this tension can be mitigated in practice. Around the world, countries with majorities from all three Abrahamic religions—from Italy, Britain, and Chile to Israel, Bangladesh, Indonesia, and Tunisia—have been able to develop a framework to accommodate religion with political tolerance, civility, and democratic governance. The same is true for countries whose populations adhere in large numbers to nonmonotheistic religions, India being a prime example. This reality suggests that various religions can peacefully coexist in plural societies under democratic governance and are by no means strictly incompatible with democracy.

Perhaps the best empirical evidence of a shift toward democracy within a religion comes from Catholicism in Latin America. The Catholic Church was generally a conservative political force and a barrier to democratization in the region, but since the 1960s it has played a pivotal role in the transition to democracy and resistance against authoritarian regimes in Central and South America (Cleary 1985; G. Cook 1994; Oxhorn 1995; Fleet and Smith 1997). Similar evidence exists for other religions. For instance, one study found that impressive majorities in Middle Eastern (and largely Muslim) states rated democracy as a good or the best type of governance (Tessler and Gao 2005). In Indonesia, Islamic parties play a peaceful and cooperative role in the country's nearly two-decades-old democratic regime (Horowitz 2013; Menchik 2016). The crucial role played by the Islamic Ennahda party in Tunisia's transition to democracy inspires new optimism about the prospects for democracy in the Arab Middle East (Filali-Ansary 2016; Ghannouchi 2016).

Furthermore, both political theorists and theologians have suggested that religious doctrines are multivocal (Stepan 2001) and thus can be interpreted in a way that does not reject democratic governance but complements and supports it (Abou El Fadl 2001; Gülen 2001; Hanafi 2002; Masmoudi 2003; J. Anderson 2004; Ibrahim 2007; Ghannouchi 2016). Over time, common interpretations of different religions may change and make these religions more (or less) receptive to pluralism and democracy (J. Anderson 2004).

In conclusion, since 2000 or so there has been a significant shift from complete negation of the idea that democracy and religion are compatible toward a more nuanced approach, one that recognizes a variety of possible teachings in every religion, some of which are compatible with democracy. Consequently, the emerging theoretical frontier is no longer how to limit and reduce the power of religion in democracies, but how to promote those voices within religion that might support this regime type. Religious support for or opposition to democracy is not predetermined but is dependent largely on the dynamic and evolving interaction between the state and religious segments in society. This also suggests that in exploring the dynamics of the state–religion relationship in different contexts, the specific doctrinal content of each religion is less important than the political and social circumstances determining the political give and take between the state and its institutions on one hand and the representatives of religion on the other (Schwedler 2001; Stepan 2001).

II. Western Variants of Democracy Are Not the Only Viable Option

If secularization is not based on democratic theory, how can we account for it being commonly accepted as a core principle of democracy? The answer is rooted in what can be referred to as European exceptionalism (Eisenstadt 2000; Casanova 2006). The unique historical exchange between states in the West and Christianity led to a common yet misleading acceptance of secularization as a core element of democracy. The emphasis on secularization unjustifiably narrowed the conceptual boundaries of democracy and reduced the applicability of democratic governance to societies in which religion plays an important social role. In some cases, attempts to impose a secular variant of democracy led to considerable problems in the implementation of democracy, generating resentment toward this system of governance and alienating significant segments in society from active participation in civil society and the democratic process (Nandy 1997; Stepan 2001; Tilly 2004).

In the West, secularization and democratization emerged out of recurrent struggles involving the state, the religious establishment, elites, and the masses. The development of Western democracy was slow and gradual, and it coincided with significant trends toward modernization—industrialization, nationalism, higher levels of education, economic development, urbanization, and the emergence of a solid middle class, as well as secularization of the populace (Moore 1966; Tilly 1998, 2004; Norris and Inglehart 2004). Despite slight variations among the countries of the West (especially in terms of their electoral systems, constitutional content, and institutional designs) the institutional basis of Western democracy is quite similar in all these nations (Diamond 1996; Carothers 1997; Zakaria 1997). Political secularism—the institutionalized separation of politics and religion—is considered a key component of state formation in the West. The Treaty of Westphalia in 1648 signified a shift of political and social dominance from the Church establishment to the secular elite and culminated with the formation of the secular nation-state. This unique sociopolitical development led European societies to amalgamate secularism into their understanding of democratic governance. For them, democracy meant secular democracy.

Non-Western societies did not take the same path when setting up their political regimes. In many regions, particularly in North Africa and the Middle East, newly liberated or newly constituted states in the postcolonial era did not become de facto independent in managing their internal affairs. The great powers of the time still exercised their influence and intervened in local politics in accordance with their political interests. European countries did not let their former colonies develop their own systems of government or types of democracy but insisted on strict emulation of the Western model, including its embedded secularist agenda, as the only viable democratic model. As Tilly argues, "Northwest powers did not simply provide prestigious models of democratization; they often imposed those models. . . . Regimes did not simply choose the most attractive forms of democratic government, but responded to strong international pressure" (Tilly 2004, 246–47). Consequently, non-Western societies were forced to either adopt the Western model without adjusting it to fit their specific cultural and historical attributes or give up on democracy and develop undemocratic types of government as an expression of their independence. This is true for many aspects of these societies, but especially with regard to religion. In several Middle Eastern countries, including Egypt, Iran, and Algeria, the struggle to furnish religion with a role in the state was tied to the struggle against Western domination and neocolonialism (K. Armstrong 2014).

This specific historical record does not mean that Western secular variants of democracy are the only viable option. For instance, Bell (2006) argues that in South Asia, Confucian values can reasonably underpin political regimes that are not inferior to Western democracy. Likewise, Tessler and Gao's study on support for democracy in the Middle East found that although a solid majority of Middle Easterners support democratic governance, about half would like to see an "Islamic democracy"—a democratic regime in which religion plays a significant formal role (2005, 91). Similarly, Hefner found that most Muslims in Indonesia, a young democracy and the largest Muslim country in the world, "continue to look to their religion for principles of public order" (2001, 493).

Even in the Western world, the birthplace of secular democracy, the majority of countries do not adhere sternly to secularism. Strict separation of state and religion is present as a constitutional principle in the US and French systems. In Portugal, religiously based political parties are prohibited. But these are the exceptions rather than the rule. In most of Europe, religion is accepted to varying degrees in the public sphere and the state. Six Western European states—Denmark, Finland, Greece, Norway, Sweden, and the United Kingdom—have an established state religion. In other countries, such as the Netherlands, Austria, and Germany, religiously based political parties are allowed and religious education programs are substantially funded by the state (Stepan 2001, 219–20; Neuberger 2002; Monsma and Soper 2009). With the notable exception of the United States, most Western countries allocate funding for religious education, collect religious taxes, fund the clergy, and operate a government department of religious affairs (Fox 2008, 107). Indeed, aggregating data about the separation of religion and state (SRAS) from 152 states between 1990 and 2002, Fox identified SRAS in only 22.3 percent of the cases examined even when employing the most lenient definition of SRAS. In the rest of the world, there was some form of engagement between the state and religion, and government involvement in religion was found to be substantial throughout the world (Fox 2008, 101).

A growing volume of empirical and normative works discuss the tension in Western democracies between liberal principles—primarily freedom of and from religion and state commitment to cultural neutrality—and manifestations of the dominant religion in the public sphere. This tension has surfaced in response to several controversial decisions by Western governments to sanction the presence of Christian symbols in public spaces, such as schools in Italy in the *Lautsi v. Italy* case (European Court of Human Rights 2011), keep a crucifix in the Parliament hall in Quebec despite a recommendation by a public commission on diversity to remove it (Recommendation G3, 271; Bouchard and Taylor 2008), or prohibit the erection of minarets in Switzerland by a federal referendum (Cumming-Bruce and Erlanger 2009). These cases and scholarly responses to them further challenged the primacy and even adequacy of separation models. Miller (2014) argued that the minarets ban in Switzerland should not be opposed on grounds of infringement of human rights or the state commitment to the neutrality principle. In contrast, the individual right to equality should be balanced with the right of the majority group to express its collective identity, which in many cases includes religious symbols in public spaces. Following this line of argument,

Weiler (2013) suggested that religious–state relationships are the product of specific circumstances and that separation models are not superior to nonseparation ones. Joppke (2013) analyzed the *Lautsi* case and argued that acknowledging the embeddedness of Christianity in European history and public culture may facilitate better accommodation of minority rights than the liberal claim to universal neutrality. Finally, Perez, Fox, and McClure (2017) demonstrate that despite the commonsense appeal of the equality and neutrality arguments often made by liberals, favoring the dominant religion does not produce higher resentment of other religious minorities toward the state, compared with religious minorities in religiously neutral states.

This all suggests that democracy is a set of general principles that can be modified in any society as long as the specific model does not violate the definition of democracy presented above. In turn, this requires that the discussion shift from societies' compliance with an artificially implemented fixed model toward understanding how the basic procedural model and its principles can be adapted to particular contexts.

Figure 1.1 illustrates the difference between the two conceptions of democracy. In the upper box, the Western model of democracy is seen as being narrow, rigid, and insensitive to contextual specificity. It requires disparate societies to adopt a single model of democracy, one that imposes secularization in the public sphere. This conception follows the reasoning of modernization theory, according to which there is one universal path toward development and democratization, and the only way to achieve it is by strictly following the experience of those who have already succeeded (i.e., the Western countries). In contrast, the lower box defines democracy as a more abstract, general, and transferable method of governance that respects the procedural and normative foundations of the concept. It adopts a framework of core principles (in accordance with the definition suggested above) that must be adapted to fit different contexts. It assumes that there is more than one single path toward development and democracy. In short, in the upper box society must adjust to the model. In the lower box, the model adjusts to society.

One possible adjustment permitted by the conception offered in the lower box of figure 1.1 is to allow some role for religion in the regime, namely, accepting a nonsecular form of democracy. That is, this conception allows for a specific design of the relationship between state and religion in a way that can best support the democratic regime, without violating the basic requirements of democracy. This suggests that in certain societies

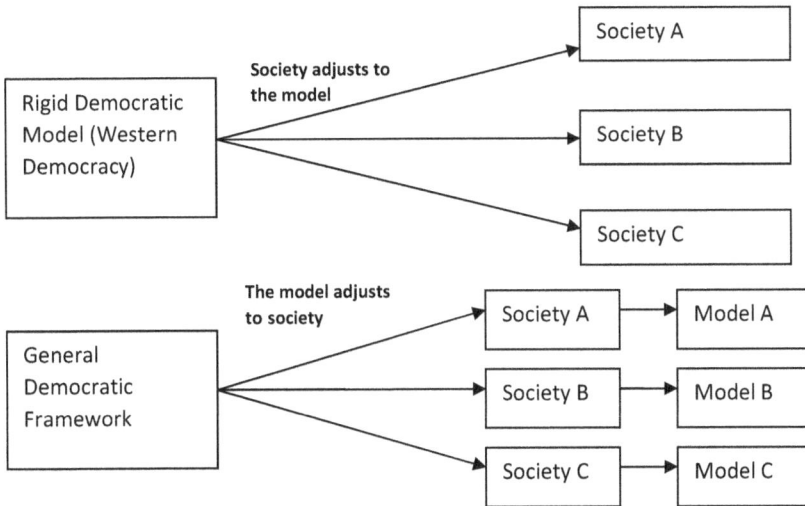

Figure 1.1. The two conceptions of adjustment to democracy.

it may be not only possible but perhaps desirable to construct rules and policies for a democratic political system in which religion plays a formal and significant role in the state.

III. The Role of Religion in the State Depends on Structural and Ideational Factors Rooted Prior to Regime or State Formation

Not much has been written about the determinants of religion's place in emerging regimes.[12] Studies dealing with state policies toward religion have primarily discussed changes in policy toward religion while disregarding the initial role granted to religion following independence or regime formation (Gill 1998; Monsma and Soper 2009; Fox 2016). Two comparative studies, however, inquire into how preregime processes influence the state–religion relationship. Kuru (2007, 2009) examines why political regimes develop distinct types of secularism. He argues that the type of secularism adopted in the state (passive or assertive) is determined by the formal category of the former regime and the balance of power among groups that supported or opposed the incorporation of religion in the state prior to independence. But Kuru's argument is incomplete in that it overlooks the possibility of nonsecular regime types. He fails to account for the whole spectrum of possibilities regarding the role of religion in the state. Grzymala-Busse (2015) investigates the effect of the relationship between religion and the nation before independence on the relative influence of the religion in policy making after independence. She finds that religions that defend the nation before independence enjoy greater leverage in policy making in the new regime. Her study, however, investigates only Christian churches in Europe and North America (i.e., the Western world).

The study of nationalism offers the most developed insights into nation and state building. This literature likewise has little to say about the construction and content of national ideologies, especially the role of religious content in them. This is particularly true for two of the four approaches in the field: primordialism (J. A. Armstrong 2000; Grosby 2000; Gat 2012) and constructivism (B. Anderson 1991; Hobsbawm 2000). The instrumentalist and ethnosymbolic approaches offer more refined arguments with added theoretical insights. The approaches converge in the notion that the spectrum of symbols, "histories," and values from which the elites choose is limited and depends on the nation's cultural and religious history (Hastings 1997; Marx 2003; A. D. Smith 2008). "Usable pasts" that are more central in the collective memory of the masses are more likely to be incorporated into the national ideology because they serve as bases of support and recruitment (A. D. Smith 2000; Kaufman 2001; Kubik 2003). This is exactly why many national movements anchor their national ideology in the nation's "golden age"—a perceived glorious epoch during which the nation prospered in territorial, economic, or cultural terms (A. D. Smith 1997).

In many nationalities, religion is an integral part of national identity and sometimes even the primary source of national identity (Hastings 1997; A. D. Smith 2008; Brubaker 2012; Abulof 2014). Some nationalist elites choose to incorporate religion into their national agenda, whereas others disregard or marginalize it. Their decision on a certain role for religion depends on contextually specific structural and ideational variables, which make the incorporation of religion more or less supportive to the political goals of the emerging elite.

Figure 1.2 outlines four interrelated elements, three of them structural-ideational and the fourth temporal-historical, which determine the initial role of religion in the regime. These are (1) prevalence of religion in the outgoing regime, (2) extent of overlap between religious and other elements of national identity, (3) demographic realities, and (4) regime formation as a critical juncture.

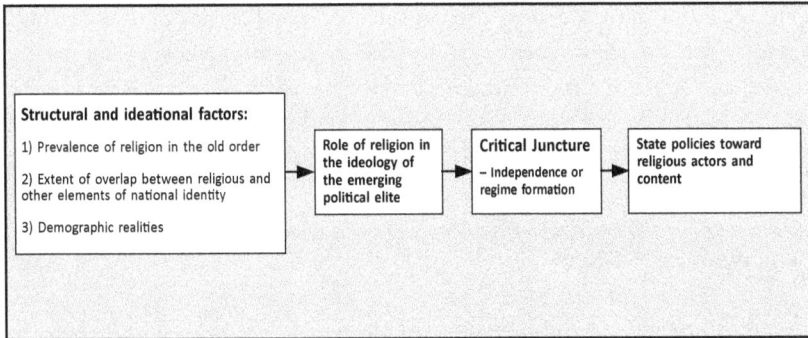

Figure 1.2. Factors that determine the status of religion in the state.

Prevalence of Religion in the Outgoing Regime

Borrowing from Kuru's argument, the stronger religion in the old regime, the greater the challenge it represents to the new order—and the more likely it is to be downplayed in the ideology of the emerging national elite. In contrast, if religion is not entrenched in the old, contested regime, it can be tolerated and even used as a recruitment tool without risking political challenge to the incipient order. Importantly, unlike Kuru, this work does not focus solely on the formal character of the outgoing regime. Rather, it takes notice of the multifaceted status of religion in the old order, which includes institutional, political-societal, cultural, and ideational features.

Extent of Overlap between Religious and Other Elements
of National Identity

National identity is a mix of various ingredients, including ethnic ties, language, religious identification, a common culture, tradition, and territorial affiliation, that interplay differently in different contexts. In Quebec, the national identity is primarily linguistic and cultural; in Rwanda, it is based on race and tribe; in Ireland and Bosnia, it is mostly the religious element that is emphasized. The more these different elements of national identity overlap, the harder it is to ignore or dismiss one component without compromising the whole. In contrast, when these elements are self-sufficient, it is possible to choose among them without threatening the construction of a new, robust, and appealing national identity. For example, the Spanish language and Catholicism in Latin America or the Arabic language and Islam in the Middle East are not indispensable to the formation of a national identity, because these attributes are shared by multiple societies in the region and are not unique to one national project. When states in these regions sought to construct new identities as distinct nation-states, for the most part they chose to emphasize those ingredients of national identity that defined their populations as unique.

Demographic Realities

The role of religion in the emergence of a new political order is influenced by demographic factors as well. This variable brings together two elements. First, it is only possible to construct a unified collective identity around religion in cases where a majority (or at least a critical mass) of the population identifies with one religion (Rustow 1970; Juergensmeyer 1995). Accordingly, religion might be recruited by the political elite for constructing a national identity in a place like Egypt, where a majority of the population subscribes to one religious denomination (Sunni Islam). Conversely, in a place like Lebanon, which has no dominant ethnoreligious group, efforts to build a national identity around religion are likely to fail. Second, religion can serve as an effective recruitment tool for the national project when the population is spread thinly through the designated national territory, especially when people within the borders have little else in common. On the other hand, it can be pointless or even counterproductive to employ religion in the national project when the people are territorially concentrated and share the same social attributes (language, culture, and history), even more so when other populations outside the national borders have the same religious affiliation.

Regime Formation as a Critical Juncture

The conditions in place at the moment of regime formation are of crucial importance to the future status of religion in the state—a point that echoes the vast literature in the field of historical institutionalism on path dependency, institutional legacies, and critical junctures (Mahoney 2000; Pierson 2004; Capoccia and Kelemen 2007). Following the establishment of the new regime, the emerging political elite is likely to implement the fundamentals of its political agenda, including the role of religion, in the public, political, and socioeconomic institutions of the state. After being solidified in institutional and constitutional arrangements, the initial structure can remain resilient for many years despite significant social and political changes.

IV. Religious Actors Are Potential Members of Civil Society

How should we conceptualize the relationship between religious populations and democratic performance? More specifically, what perspective will serve best to analyze and predict the circumstances under which the state–religion relationship will reinforce democracy and those under which it will challenge and erode the democratic system? Religious groups and movements are part of the social fabric. They represent a coherent perspective on life and a code of moral and practical behavior. In their various activities, they engage with a wide spectrum of social issues, such as education, welfare, and youth organizations, as well as worship services. The legitimacy of the regime and the quality of its democratic governance are somewhat dependent on whether religious groups are accommodated into civil society or marginalized from it (Walzer 1992; Pell 2004). Hence religious populations should be treated as social actors and potential partners in civil society. This argument first requires clarification of the definition and nature of civil society.

There are two main scholarly outlooks on civil society. The (until recently) dominant outlook views civil society as a voluntary realm, independent of state influence, in which high levels of trust, strong social networks, and a similar set of values among members of society facilitate political stability and democracy. According to this view, those who belong to civil society agree on the fundamentals of the society and thus can cooperate in harmony. In addition, civil society works to curtail state power, and thus its relationship with the state is viewed as a zero-sum game—the stronger civil society is, the weaker the state becomes (Almond and Verba 1963; R. Putnam 1993; Fukuyama 1996, 2002). These premises are irreconcilable with state recognition of religion and its representatives. This is because religion represents a set of (often illiberal) values and beliefs shared only by some members of society, and thus it exposes the public sphere to fundamental disagreement. When translated into restrictive policies, this approach toward civil society is likely to generate friction between the state and religious segments of the population, narrow the regime's base of support, and result in endemic political instability.

The 1990s saw the emergence of an alternative outlook on civil society, one that sees it as an arena of conflict and disagreement. According to this perspective, members of society do not share a "thick" consensus but a "thin" consensus that relates only to acceptable forms of expression and peaceful conflict resolution in the political arena (Oxhorn 2006). Civil society is "the setting of settings" that provides space for deliberation without

advocating particular ideological content (Walzer 1992). This conceptualization includes several elements that make it better suited for grasping how
the complex relationship between religious actors and the state influences
democratic performance. First, in the new conceptualization, the unit of
analysis is not free and equal individuals but groups, collectivities. Also
important, the realm of civil society is not seen as detached from the state.
On the contrary, the state is held responsible for defending, promoting, and
expanding the boundaries of civil society (Skocpol 1996; Oxhorn 2006).
That is, "the challenge of making civil society relevant is also a challenge
of the state" (Oxhorn 2003, 2).

This conceptualization integrates religious groups in analyses of civil
society while recognizing the crucial role of the state in shaping religious
behavior within its borders. It is more realistic than the traditional view in
that it does not wish to flatten ideological disagreements. It sets a framework
for peaceful coexistence of different ideological sectors in society. Finally, this
approach emphasizes dynamic interaction over rigid structure, a perspective
that conforms with mine in this book.

This conceptualization carries considerable advantages when implemented as policy. State recognition of religion permits space for religion in
the public and political spheres, including granting an official role to religion
in the state as a possible outcome of the political process. Such treatment
provides religious actors with a stronger incentive to support and identify
with the regime and is likely to promote cooperation between the state
and religious groups in a way that endorses pluralism and political stability.
Moreover, such an inclusive policy may produce broader commitment to
democratic principles among religious groups, greater legitimation from
below for the regime, and better democratic governance.

Based on the foregoing discussion, it is now possible to introduce a
novel explanatory framework for the effect of the state–religion relationship
on democratic performance. A graphic presentation of its components can
be found in figure 1.3.

First, the roots of the state–religion relationship should be sought in
the preindependence era or, more specifically, in the role of religion in the
ideology of the incoming political elite before the new regime is established.
This role is not determined arbitrarily but is shaped by structural and ideational circumstances. Second, the role of religion is translated into state
policies once the new regime is established. In this respect, the moment of
independence is critically important because it shapes the state's institutional
design, including its policies toward religion, and creates resilient path

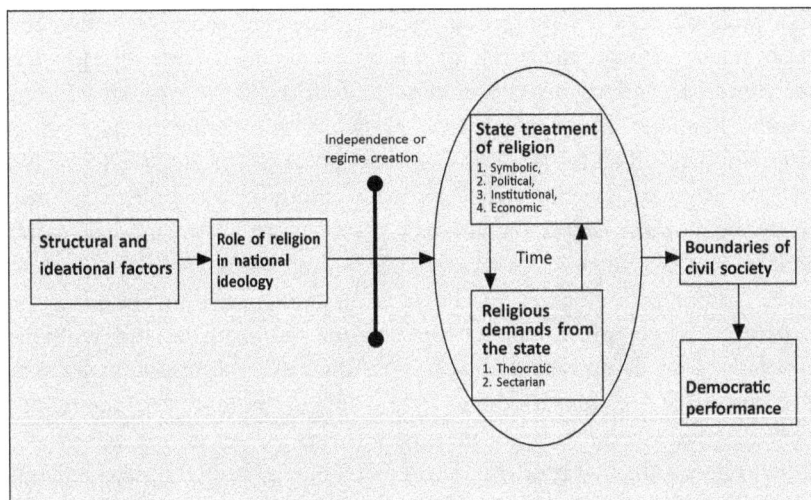

Figure 1.3. The elements of the state–religion relationship.

dependency with enormous influence on the evolution of the religion–state relationship over time.

Third, following the establishment of the regime, a mutually constitutive process begins between the state and religious actors within it. State policies toward religion condition whether religious groups will be included in civil society. These policies generate and are subject to responses from below and thus change over time. This reciprocal process shapes the behavior of each party toward the other and the relationship as a whole. Acknowledging the dynamic element in the state–religion relationship carries the most analytical value. The relationship is anything but static or linear. Changes in the distribution of political power and structural developments may lead to changes in state policies toward religion from above. New interpretations of religious doctrines, as a consequence of ideational and domestic social changes or external events, may alter the behavior of religious organizations and their strategies of engagement with the state from below (A. Rubin 2014). Fourth, changing the boundaries of civil society by including or excluding religious sectors in or from participation in the public and political spheres has an impact on democratic performance.

Before delving into the empirical inquiry, it is important to acknowledge the partial capacity of this framework in explaining the range of influences on democratic performance. This book, and the framework it introduces and employs, does not pretend to explain the entire realm of democratic performance through the prism of the state–religion relationship. On the contrary, it recognizes the effects of other factors already suggested in the existing literature as shaping a society's democratic performance, such as international influences on the domestic political system, demographic realities, economic trends, level of institutionalization, and political culture. Analyzing all these factors and assessing their relative impact on democratic performance is a huge task that stretches beyond the scope of the current work. The contribution of this book is more modest—underscoring the impact of the ongoing relationship between state organs and religious populations on democracy and offering analytical lenses through which to investigate this question. It does so by providing a more sophisticate framework that extends the range of possible roles for religion in the democratic polity; offers a thick, path-dependent explanation to how the state–religion relationship form and evolve; and breaks the phrase "religion in politics" into identifiable elements that can provide a more accurate picture of the explored phenomenon.

Over the next four chapters, I turn to the first of my case studies—the Republic of Turkey. In chapter 2, I examine how structural and ideational factors in the years prior to the establishment of the republic led to a policy of coercive secularization in the new polity, which opened the door to later negative consequences of that policy for Turkey's democratic performance.

Chapter 2

Religion and State in
Turkey's Prerepublican Era

Following the establishment of the Turkish Republic in 1923, the Kemal Atatürk–led nationalist government took extensive measures to uproot Islam from the public and political spheres. As this book suggests, the roots of this policy should be sought in the interplay between structural and ideational factors in Ottoman society that predated the foundation of the republic and their influence on the agenda of the revolutionary elite at the time of independence. Indeed, it is now broadly accepted that the postindependence political and social reforms in Turkey should not be understood as divorced from earlier Ottoman history. On the contrary: it could be argued that Kemalist policies toward religion signified merely another stage in the development of Ottoman society and politics. These policies did not come out of thin air but were preceded by recurrent (largely unsuccessful) attempts to modernize and secularize the Ottoman Empire beginning in the late eighteenth century.

As this chapter elaborates, the waning vitality of the Ottoman Empire generated strain between the masses and traditional elites who identified with Islam on one hand, and an emerging Western-inspired elite on the other about the proper role of religion in the social and political order. This strain ended with the victory of the Westernizers following the eventual collapse of the empire during World War I. The interplay of structural and ideational factors—specifically, the strength of religion in the old order and the nationalist movement's desire to distinguish the Turkish state from the rest of the Muslim world and detach the Turkish people from cultural affiliation with Islam—drove Atatürk's regime to conceive both folk religion and institutionalized religion as challenges to the Kemalist project. Consequently, the regime endorsed an outlook that equated modernity with secular and scientific perspectives and sought to free Turkey of its backwardness by ridding society of its traditional elements.

Before I delve into the specifics of how the relationship between religion and state played out in the prerepublic era, a brief overview of Ottoman history may be helpful. Noted Turkish historian Sina Akşin divides the history of the Ottoman Empire into four periods. The first, foundational period begins around 1299 with the emergence of the Ottoman principality under Osman Bey, founder of the Ottoman dynasty, and continues with a series of conquests that gradually expanded the principality's territory through the mid-fifteenth century. The second period begins in 1453 with the conquest of Istanbul (Byzantine Constantinople) by Sultan Mehmet II (known in Turkish as Fatih Mehmet, or Mehmet the Conqueror), continues with more victories that extended the Ottomans' land from Crimea to North Africa and Eastern Europe, and includes the Golden Age of Süleyman the Magnificent (Kanuni Sultan Süleyman; r. 1520–1566). Importantly, during this period the Ottomans conquered Egypt by defeating the Mamluks, after which the head of the dynasty assumed the role of caliph, head of the Ummah, the Muslim community of believers. The second period ends with the assassination of the Grand Vizier Sokullu Mehmet in 1579.

The third period, from 1579 to 1699, is a time of stagnation, during which the empire was governed by a series of unskilled rulers. The last period, between 1700 and 1922, is a period of decline, territorial losses, a deteriorating economic situation, political instability, and the eventual disintegration of the empire (Akşin 2007, 7–8).

Taking a broad view, between the thirteenth and sixteenth centuries, the Ottoman dynasty consolidated and maintained a prosperous empire that stretched from Persia in the east to Vienna in the west and southward to Egypt. Its armies were the might of Europe, and its economy flourished. The pinnacle of the empire was the reign of Süleyman the Magnificent, who established a legal code based on Sharia and expanded the territory of the empire to its maximum limits. During the second half of the sixteenth century, the Ottoman Empire changed course and began to decline. A detailed account of the reasons for this decline is beyond the scope of this work, but the main factors included a combination of European military advances, especially by Portuguese marine forces and Russian and Austro-Hungarian land forces; a debilitated economy in the wake of European imports of natural resources and goods from the Americas; and a fall in the quality of the Ottoman civil service, which brought administrative inefficiency and rampant corruption. This process was exacerbated by an Islamic "superiority complex" that impeded borrowing new knowledge and technologies from the European empires (Lewis 2002).

The long decline of the Ottoman Empire motivated elites with a Western orientation to pursue efforts to reform the state and society and make them more efficient and modern. However, their attempts were opposed by a powerful antireformist alliance that sought to preserve its preferred status. Subsequent reforms were characterized by an inability to replace the religious order with a secular system of institutions. The result, from the end of the eighteenth century onward, was an incoherent system of "dual institutionalism," where parallel systems of secular and religious institutions operated in various administrative domains. This institutional character persisted until the foundation of the republic in 1923 and is key to understanding the treatment of religion by the Kemalist regime after independence (Berkes 1964; Mardin 1997).

The Role of Islam in the Ottoman Order

From the foundation of the Ottoman Empire, Islam occupied a pivotal role in its political and social affairs. Islam was introduced to the Turks around the tenth century, three centuries before the establishment of the empire, by nomads from other Muslim territories. Importantly, in contrast with the experience of other Muslim societies, Islam was not imposed on the Turkic people but was accepted voluntarily. When the Ottoman Empire was established, Islam was already well ingrained throughout the territories under its rule. From its very emergence the Ottoman Empire was devoted to the defense and promotion of Islam (Lewis 2000, 10–11).

The entrenched role of Islam in the empire was reflected in every realm of social and political life. Islamic scholars enjoyed a unique status that protected them from persecution without trial or confiscation of their property by the sultan (Akşin 2007, 13), as well as broad autonomy in law and education. The empire applied Sharia law in every aspect of life, more than any other Muslim society in history (Lewis 2000, 11). Also, throughout the Ottoman era Islam functioned as a principal ingredient in culture and politics and was a primary source of identity for the subjects of the empire. Indeed, until the mid-nineteenth century, the Turkish subjects of the Ottoman Empire regarded themselves primarily as Muslims, rather than as Turks (Toprak 1981, 27; Ahmad 1991, 3; Kushner 2006, 163).

The Islamic faith also had a stronghold in the institutional and administrative systems of the empire. The head of the empire carried both secular and spiritual-religious positions. He was simultaneously sultan, or secular ruler of the empire, and caliph, leader of the Ummah. The legal code of the empire and its education system were based on Islamic doctrine, drawn from the Quran and Sharia. The *sheikh-ul-Islam*, the most senior religious scholar, was second only to the sultan in the administration. The *ulema* (religious sages) enjoyed extensive involvement in state institutions, and "assumed many of the functions that state institutions perform in administrative set-ups of a more differentiated character" (Toprak 1981, 29).

The official institutional role of religion in the empire was complemented by two additional social functions. First, religion served as a conceptual bridge or source of common discourse between the elite and masses and as a mechanism for solidarity among Muslim subjects throughout the empire. Second, in addition to the existence of "high" religion, which occupied formal roles in state institutions, there existed popular, mystical manifestations of Islam, which operated for centuries in the form of Tarikats, or Sufi dervish orders. Historically, these two religious realms (institutional and folkloristic) often clashed, but toward the end of the empire the two became closely intertwined, a process that resulted in a significant presence of Tarikat members in the structure of government (Mardin 1971, 203–6).

Early Reforms (1789–1839)

As I argued in the opening to this chapter, the Kemalist reforms of the republican period did not come out of thin air but were preceded by recurrent efforts to modernize and secularize the Ottoman Empire over the previous century and a quarter (at least). Let us now look more closely at these failed efforts.

It is common to relate the beginning of the reform era to the reign of Sultan Selim III (r. 1789–1807) (Davison 1968, 67; Zürcher 2005, 39; Akşin 2007, 20). Selim III was fascinated with Western progress long before he became sultan. In 1792, he initiated a broad reform program, the Nizam-i Cedid (New Order), as a means to overcome the empire's stagnation and decline. In particular, Selim III sought to Westernize the empire's military and education system, increase its efficiency, and reduce the levels of corruption in the bureaucracy. In an attempt to bring in Western knowledge, he hired the services of foreign officers, especially French military men, to guide the reforms (Lewis 2000, 48).

Selim III failed to complete his reforms because of strong opposition by three interest groups, which proved very influential in the reform era. These were the Ayans, a group of semi-independent nobles in the periphery of the empire who resisted centralizing reforms that might have diminished their autonomous status; the Yeni-çeri (Janissaries), the old guard of military personnel, who opposed the sultan's intention to replace them with modernized troops; and the ulema, religious scholars who enjoyed preferred status and institutional influence in the sultan's administration (Findley 2008, 12). The two latter groups, in particular, formed a powerful alliance that enabled them to play an active conservative and antireformist role. For instance, when the Janissaries revolted against the sultan in 1807, it was with the support of the highest religious authority in the Ottoman Empire, the sheikh-ul-Islam, who issued a *fetva* (religious decree) stating that the new reforms contradicted the principles of religion and thus were void (Zürcher 2005, 43). Selim III lacked the coercive capability and political backing needed to stand against the rebellious troops and was removed from office shortly thereafter. The ulema and Janissaries reversed most of Selim III's reforms and crowned his cousin, Mustafa IV, as the new sultan. The Nizam-i Cedid initiative thus had very limited impact. Its main achievement lay in creating new channels of interaction with the Western world and making a first break with the traditional order, after which more profound attempts followed.

The next major reform took place a year after the removal of Selim III, and paradoxically was triggered by the Ayans. The Ayans' approach to reform was complex. On one hand, they rejected Selim III's ambition to tighten the empire's control over their territories. On the other hand, they opposed the conservative coalition between the ulema and the Janissaries. In July 1808, fearing the growing power of the Russian empire in the East, one of the strongest Ayans, Mustafa Pasha Bayraktar, took Istanbul by force with the intention to recrown Selim III. Those holding Selim III assassinated him before he could be released, but Mustafa Pasha succeeded in saving and then crowning Mahmut II, a cousin of Selim III and a supporter of reforms (Zürcher 2005, 46). Mustafa Pasha was appointed grand vizier and became the de facto ruler of Istanbul before dying in a Janissary attack just four months later, but during this short time in power he was responsible for two important developments. First, he organized a modern military force, the Segban. Second and more important, he convened the leading Ayans in Istanbul and made them sign the Sened-i Ittifak (Document of Agreement), in which they committed to just rule, fair collection of taxes, loyalty to the sultan, support for economic and bureaucratic reforms, and establishment of a modern military. This document, commonly referred to as the "Ottoman Magna Carta," was a turning point in the relationship between the nobles and the sultanate (Akşin 2007, 22–23).

A month after the Sened-i Ittifak was signed, the Janissary–ulema alliance revolted again and conquered the capital. To strengthen his position, Mahmut II killed his brother Mustafa, his only male relative (and hence only legitimate rival as heir of the Ottoman dynasty). After some bargaining, the parties reached an agreement whereby Mahmut II would remain sultan but would freeze all intended reforms. The impasse between Mahmut II and the antireformist alliance lasted two more decades before the former was able to initiate a new wave of reforms. Mahmut II waited patiently for an opportune time to break the stalemate imposed on him by the ulema and Janissaries, and in the meantime he built his military capabilities. In June 1826 the Janissaries rebelled in protest at the growing power of the new army, but this time the sultan's troops massacred several thousand Janissaries. Immediately thereafter, Mahmut II formally abolished the Janissary corps. This move, referred to in Turkey as the Auspicious Event, eliminated the main opposition to the sultan and cleared the way for new reform initiatives (Davison 1968, 74–75; Findley 2008, 12).

During the 1830s, facing only weak opposition, Mahmut II was able to accelerate the pace of modernizing reforms, which served as preparatory steps for the later Tanzimat (see below). Mahmut II built a modern army with the active assistance of Prussian officers and structured a modern navy, the third biggest in Europe, with British and US guidance. Military officers and civil servants were sent for training and education in Western countries and later became agents of Westernization in the empire. The sultan also eliminated various administrative positions that had existed for centuries and transformed them into modern ministries, such as foreign affairs, the interior, and the treasury. The Council of Ministers acted as a cabinet and the grand vizier as prime minister, instead of his traditional role as deputy of the sultan. This era also saw the creation of the first Ottoman newspaper, the founding of a formal translation chamber, and the first Western-type schools of medicine, civil service, and the military (Davison 1968, 75; Akşin 2007, 25).

The Tanzimat Period (1839–1876)

The next major reform, the Tanzimat (Reordering or Reorganization), took place under Mahmut II's successor, Abdülmecit, and his reformist mentor Mustafa Reşit Pasha. Recognizing the decaying situation of the empire and the rising power of European countries, Abdülmecit feared that European powers would intervene in Ottoman territories to protect the Christian minorities of the empire from discrimination. In addition, the Ottoman administration was desperate to boost its collapsing economy with financial assistance from European countries. The rationale behind the Tanzimat was that formal adoption of Western values (suitably adapted to the Turkish context) might facilitate deliberation with Western countries, prevent European aggression or interference in the domestic affairs of the empire, and increase the chances for much-needed economic assistance.

The Tanzimat was proclaimed on November 3, 1839, and from the outset it was a combination of old and new. On the declarative level, it blamed the decline of the empire on the nonobservance of Quranic precepts, thereby reasserting the palace's commitment to an Islamic-based order. On the practical level, it initiated a series of secular and modernizing reforms, especially in the realms of property rights, equality before the law, individual rights, secular reforms in government, and the separation of powers (Davison 1968, 78–82; İnalcık 1973).

Although the Tanzimat reformers sought to ease the path to reform by paying lip service to traditional religious values, they failed to diminish the influence of religious doctrines, check the power of religious actors, or reform religious institutions. The reformers developed new secular state institutions, but did not alter or abolish the old religious ones. The result was an institutional dualism that characterized the Ottoman regime until its eventual collapse and replacement by the republic. Indeed, institutional dualism was perceived as a primary reason for the failure of the reforms. More specifically, this dualism thwarted comprehensive reform in the bureaucracy, created two sets of laws, courts, and education systems, and preserved the power of the ulema. It stood in the way of cohesive governance and the exercise of a coherent and unitary modus operandi for the state. A century later, these failures prompted the Kemalist movement to take harsh measures against anything related to religion once the republic was founded (Toprak 1981, 32–33).

The most notable cases of dual institutionalism and its ramifications were found in the two most important indoctrinating systems—education and the law. In education, the government established a new Western-oriented school system, introduced modern secular curricula, and placed the secular education system under control of a modern Ministry of Education, officially divorcing it from ulema supervision (Findley 2008, 22–23). At the same time, the vested interest of the ulema in traditional education made the old system untouchable. The government kept operating the *mekteb* and *medrese* systems (elementary and higher religious schools, respectively) with their traditional religious content (Berkes 1964, 106–10). Educational dualism was instrumental in creating and widening a gap between the relatively traditional rural population, where religious education preserved its primacy, and the urban population, which was more receptive to modern, secular ideas. Certainly, such a rural–urban schism was not unique to the Ottoman Empire (Huntington 1965; Moore 1966), but when complemented and amplified by an overlapping religious–secular schism, it created a significant cultural and perceptual disparity between the urban Western-oriented youth, who enjoyed advanced education, and the villagers, who received a traditional religious education.

A similar bifurcated development took place in the legal domain. The Tanzimat reformers approved new, Western-oriented penal, land, and commercial law codes, but they were politically unable to dislodge Sharia religious law, which remained in place alongside the new legislation. The court system was divided into two parallel subsystems, with Sharia courts supervised by the sheikh-ul-Islam and state courts by the secular Ministry of Justice. Moreover, the ulema continued to serve in the new courts and eroded what otherwise would have been substantial secularizing reforms (Findley 2008, 20–21). That division preserved significant pockets of backward-looking practices, such as gender discrimination, unfair economic practices, and ethnic discrimination.

Moreover, the intention of the Tanzimat reforms to reduce the leverage of Islamic actors was a source of social and political unrest. In contrast to the developmental experience of European countries (Huntington 1965; Almond and Powell 1966), the Tanzimat was not a response to or accommodation of mass demands. Instead, the reforms were forced on society from above by the sultan's administration and therefore never enjoyed wide popular support. To the contrary: the elitist and secular nature of the reforms stimulated opposition by the Muslim majority and was central in triggering violent reactionary riots in 1859, 1860, and the 1870s. Even among the reformist elite there were loud voices criticizing what they perceived as a dishonorable attempt to imitate Europe and its values at all costs, including giving up Islamic traditions and values that had served for centuries as core elements of Ottoman culture (Zürcher 2005, 87–89).

The Hamidian Era (1876–1908)

As described, the Tanzimat stimulated considerable criticism and the development of new ideas in the reform movement. Central in this trend were the

Yeni Osmanlilar (the Young Ottomans). The Young Ottomans criticized the Tanzimat's superficial imitation of Western culture, advocated the employment of Islamic doctrine as a foundation for modernization and liberal ideas, and called for restoring the role of the ulema in the empire. The most important thinker in this group was Namik Kemal, a translator and journalist whose writings based liberal and constitutional values on Islamic foundations, with the aim of allowing all subjects, Muslim and non-Muslim alike, to identify with the empire and be loyal to it (Kadioğlu 1996, 180; Uzer 2016, 21).[1]

The Young Ottomans consolidated their power in the Ottoman cabinet and succeeded in removing the inefficient and corrupt Sultan Abdülaziz and crowning Murad V (r. May–August 1876), who supported the promulgation of a written constitution. Unfortunately, Murad suffered from mental illness, and on September 1, 1876, he was replaced by his younger brother, Abdülhamid II (r. 1876–1909).

With respect to Abdülhamid II's attitudes toward reform, contemporary scholars are divided. Some regard his rule as a time of regression in the process of modernization, whereas others argue that many of his policies were a continuation of the Tanzimat. There is no doubt, though, that Abdülhamid II endowed the Islamic religion and identity with a centrality that it had not enjoyed for some time. After almost a century of recurrent attempts to downgrade religious influence in the empire, Abdülhamid II restored Islam's role as the main source of meaning for the Ottoman state and society. As we will see, this policy heightened the tension between traditionalists and modernists and was responsible for the formation of the Young Turk movement and their eventual triumph over traditional forces (Fortna 2008, 38–39).

At the beginning of his reign, however, Abdülhamid II had no alternative but to pursue constitutional reforms. In December 1876, the empire's first constitution was promulgated, and general elections took place for the first Ottoman parliament. The constitution was based on the Belgian and German constitutions and promised a series of individual rights, changes in the tax system, and limits on the power of the ruler. But the constitution and the parliament were both short-lived. A series of decrees by Abdülhamid restored power to the hands of the sultan (Zürcher 2005, 99); and in February 1878, in the wake of a disastrous war with Russia, Abdülhamid II suspended the constitution, and the Tanzimat period and the Young Ottoman movement came to an end. From that point on, Abdülhamid II consolidated his rule, which was characterized primarily by a return to religion.

Throughout his kingship, Abdülhamid II manipulated religious symbols, played out his spiritual role as caliph, and promoted Islamic solidarity and identity (Davison 1968, 95). He surrounded himself with conservative sheikhs and ulema and took active measures that reflected the return of the empire to the Islamic world at the expense of its relations with the West.[2] One step in this direction was the construction of a railway between Damascus and the holy city of Medina in Saudi Arabia. Another was restoring a pan-Islamist ideology as a source of identity for Muslim inhabitants in the empire as well as for Muslim minorities in non-Muslim countries (this is discussed in more detail later in this chapter). A third policy was the advancement of the medrese school system and multiplication of the Tarikat orders. Increasing numbers of ulema were positioned in the education system, and the curricula emphasized Islamic content.

Was Abdülhamid's religious fervor real? It seems likely. According to Fortna (2008, 41), "his religiosity seems to have been genuine, and appears to have sustained him through the most trying of times. More importantly, Islam and its history provided him with an important political and social compass." But Abdülhamid's proreligious policies were also shaped, at least partly, by political calculus. Significant territorial losses in European lands under Ottoman rule (particularly the Balkans) during the nineteenth century turned the remaining population of the empire more Asian and Islamic. In consequence, Islam united most of its inhabitants more than ever. In addition, this policy provided the sultan with considerable leverage among Muslim minorities outside the empire—minorities that could be mobilized as a political tool against neighboring countries should the latter decide to intervene in the empire's affairs (Landau 2004, 21–29; Fortna 2008, 46–53). But the sultan's dictatorial and reactionary behavior also generated substantial opposition to his regime. The dissidents—mainly non-Muslim subjects, liberal intellectuals, and army officers—perceived Abdülhamid's rule as both a regression from what had been achieved in the Tanzimat era and a primary reason for the empire's apparent decline and territorial shrinkage (Hanioğlu 2008, 64). This opposition eventually brought Abdülhamid's rule and its religious tendencies to an end.

The Young Turks and the Second Constitution (1908–1918)

The period between 1908 and 1918 was the concluding chapter of the Ottoman Empire. In many respects, political and ideological circumstances in this decade powerfully shaped the nationalist movement and the policies it exercised following the foundation of the republic in 1923.

The opposition group that removed Abdülhamid II from office in 1908 and served as a prototype to the Kemalist movement had emerged two decades earlier. It was established in 1889 by a group of cadets in the military medical school in Istanbul, and before long it gained wide support among students in other institutions around the empire. The group had a second headquarters in Paris, where they became familiar with European positivist philosophy, and where members published several newspapers critical of Abdülhamid's regime. This group called itself the Committee of Union and Progress (CUP), but they were popularly known as the Young Turks (Hanioğlu 2001).[3]

It took the CUP more than a decade of failed attempts (1896–1908) to topple Abdülhamid's regime, during which time their ideas expanded among the Ottoman military's field troops. In 1906, a group of officers, among them Mustafa Kemal (later Kemal Atatürk), founded a cell of Young Turks in Damascus (Rustow 1959, 522). Similar cells were formed in Salonika, Palestine, Macedonia, and other provinces of the empire. In 1907, the Paris-based leadership merged with the Salonican Association of Ottoman Officers, expanding the CUP's base of support.

In July 1908, the time was deemed opportune for a revolution. Following several violent riots in different provinces, the Young Turks demanded that the sultan reinstate the constitution of 1876. Shortly thereafter the sultan was forced to comply, and the CUP seized de facto control over the empire (Lewis 1983, 165–68).

The CUP was not a popular revolutionary movement from below in the fashion of earlier European revolutions,[4] and the ideas it advocated were not shared by the conservative masses. Although the CUP was genuinely committed to the advancement of scientific, modern, and constitutional ideas and to equality for non-Muslim citizens of the empire, the group lacked political status and wide political support. With this in mind, the CUP judged that it made sense to maintain the old political order and exploit it as a platform for gradual reforms. However, the irreconcilable conflict between the CUP's reliance on the old order and its commitment to far-reaching reforms resulted in indecisive policies, with the CUP sometimes zigzagging between two or more conflicting policies on various issues. Such a pattern characterized the CUP's treatment of religion (Ahmad 1968, 35; Hanioğlu 2008, 111).

The CUP included radical secular and materialist factions that conceived of religion as a barrier to development and modernization, opposed any role for it in the public and political spheres, and embraced the Protestant ethic and Lutheran reforms as examples of how religion and the state ought to interact. Indeed, one of the CUP's founders, Dr. Abdullah Cevdet, was leader of the Garbcılık (Westernization) movement, whose members promulgated an ardent secularist and Western-oriented ideology (Hanioğlu 1997). The CUP's executive was particularly suspicious of pan-Islamism, the official ideology of the Hamidian sultanate, which they perceived as a threat to the unity of the empire and as discriminating against non-Muslim subjects. Accordingly, the CUP introduced a number of profound secularizing reforms, especially in law and education. The curriculum in the medrese system was revised and new, Western-oriented civil and family codes were introduced. The sheikh-ul-Islam was removed from the cabinet. The Sharia court system was subjected to the secular Ministry of Justice, and women were granted more legal privileges (Zürcher 2005, 147–48; Hanioğlu 2008, 104).

This situation did not last. Despite its initial progressive intentions, before long the CUP was forced to adopt dictatorial methods to sustain its rule. This led to the emergence of an organized opposition of both religious factions and liberal forces who opposed the undemocratic ruling style of the CUP. An important section of this opposition was the militant Ittihadi Muhammedi (Muhammadan Union), which opposed modernization and advocated full reimplementation of Sharia law. Along with resistance to restoring the constitutional order, the opposition opposed efforts to grant equal rights to the empire's non-Muslim inhabitants. Riots against non-Muslim communities were sparked in different places throughout the empire and even approached Istanbul (Ahmad 1968, 28; Farhi 1971, 279–82).[5]

On April 13, 1909, a coalition comprising the Muhammadan Union, religious soldiers, and students of religious schools (*softas*) revolted against the CUP,[6] demanding the restoration of Sharia law. In the short run, the revolt was successful. Sultan Abdülhamid II, who was officially still head of state, accepted most of the rebels' demands, and the CUP leadership fled Istanbul. Yet within ten days, the military order was reinstated under the CUP's leadership, Abdülhamid II was deposed, and the rebel leaders—including Sheikh Vahdeti, head of the Muhammadan Union—were arrested and later executed.

Although the CUP retook control, the uprising shocked it, because it patently demonstrated the power of religious forces in Ottoman society and the fragility of the CUP's government. From that point on, the CUP treated religion with kid gloves and avoided new confrontations with religious actors. Even the removal of Abdülhamid II, a necessary step given his support for the rebellion, was authorized by a fetva signed by the sheikh-ul-Islam (now restored to the cabinet) to give it religious legitimacy (Ahmad 1968, 34; Farhi 1971, 285; Zürcher 2005, 124). The Young Turks acceded to a variety of more prosaic demands that restored the Islamic character of the state. For instance, they declared Sharia to be the normative source of the constitutional regime and the basis of Ottoman law. They also closed theaters and drinking places and required women to wear a veil in public (Farhi 1971, 279). They instituted censorship against anti-Islamic publications (including *Ictihad*, the mouthpiece of the Garbcilik movement) and confiscated translations of antireligious European books (Hanioğlu 1997, 139; Zürcher 2005, 157).

When the empire entered World War I on the side of Germany and Austria, the CUP sought to assure the loyalty of their Arab and Muslim subjects by declaring jihad (holy war) against the Entente Powers. Nonetheless, the CUP regime began to crumble around the beginning of the war, as the Ottoman forces found themselves suffering defeats on the battlefield. The end of the war left the empire beaten and devastated. In Anatolia alone, the Ottomans suffered three to four million casualties, three quarters of them civilians. The empire lost its provinces in the Arab world, Asia Minor, Mesopotamia, and the Balkans, and the British army occupied Istanbul and the Bosporus Straits. The CUP leadership lost its grip on government and fled to Europe. An Ottoman delegation was forced to sign a humiliating ceasefire agreement with the victorious powers in Mudros on October 30, 1918 (Kayali 2008, 112–25). These consequences hastened a fundamental crisis of legitimacy in the torn country and facilitated the rise to power of Mustafa Kemal's nationalist movement.

To conclude, the Young Turks' decade in power signified yet another round of indecisive policies toward religion which proved unsuccessful in uprooting religion from the imperial order. Hanioğlu summarizes the situation nicely: "The CUP leaders resembled the Tanzimat statesmen who, promoting the new while preserving the old, fostered an ambiguous dualism. They kept the Sultan, but introduced the Committee; maintained the Islamic identity of the regime, yet endorsed secularism . . . It was up to a younger generation of revolutionaries, no longer burdened by the responsibilities of Empire and the challenge of nationalism, to abandon the Ottoman past and build something radically new" (2008, 111).

Ideational Factors: The Burden of Islam

As long as Islam served as a principal source of identification among Otto-man subjects, attempts to replace it were doomed to failure. Until the late eighteenth century, the reference community for Turks was the Ummah; other concepts with more secular meanings such as *devlet* (state) or *vatan* (motherland) were rarely used or discussed. Toward the end of the Ottoman era, identity substitutes began to emerge, and these crystallized in a new nationalistic form following the shift to a republican order.

Three main ideological alternatives, each with its own political agenda, emerged during this period: (1) pan-Islamism; (2) Ottomanism (or pan-Ottomanism); and (3) Turkism (or pan-Turkism) (Landau 2004). By the end of the nineteenth century, the Turkish nationalist ideology had the upper hand, and this was instrumental in shaping Kemalist ideology (Uzer 2016). In what follows, I discuss the three ideologies and the interactions between them, which brought Turkism to the fore.

Pan-Islamism. As described throughout this chapter, an Islamic iden-tity was deeply embedded in Ottoman society from the foundation of the empire and was shared by the masses and elites alike. Beginning in the mid-nineteenth century, the emergence of nationalist awareness among non-Muslim subjects of the empire, mainly in the Balkans and Eastern Europe, sent pan-Islamism as an organizing principle into retreat, until it was brought back to the fore during the reign of Abdülhamid II at the century's end. Pan-Islamism served the Muslim elite as an important legitimizing tool, but at the same time it generated local accusations of discrimination and aspirations for independence in non-Muslim provinces, such as Macedonia and Serbia. In addition, by appearing to threaten the rights of the empire's non-Muslim (predominantly Christian) inhabitants, pan-Islamism risked legitimizing European involvement in the domestic affairs of the empire.

Ottomanism. (Pan-)Ottomanism emerged in response to the inability of the pan-Islamist worldview to address the new nationalism arising in the empire's non-Muslim territories. Proponents of Ottomanism aimed to gain the loyalty of these non-Muslim populations by establishing a constitutional political order that would grant equal rights to all subjects of the empire, regardless of ethnicity, religion, or language. Ottomanism first appeared toward the end of the Tanzimat period and reached its peak in 1876, when the first constitution was approved. After a period of conservative regression during the reign of Abdülhamid II, Ottomanism was revived by the Young

Turks and served as the formal ideology of the regime until its final collapse in 1918 (Kushner 2006, 162).

Pan-Ottomanism faced strong opposition from the empire's Muslim majority, who perceived it—correctly—as undermining the latter's preferential status and the predominantly Islamic character of the state. This conflict between competing interests led to recurrent violent riots against non-Muslims and to what can only be described as ridiculous political situations. The deposition ceremony of Sultan Abdülhamid II in 1909 nicely reflects the problematic nature and inherent inconsistency of pan-Ottomanism: "While giving the Sultan's deposition the semblance of a step taken under the Şeriat [Sharia], it [the CUP] had to place the matter in the hands of the *Evliya-yi umur* [secular authorities[7]], who consisted in part of Christians and Jews. The crowning indignity was that a deputation consisting of two Moslems, an Armenian and a Jew came to present the Caliph, 'God's shadow on earth,' with the fetva confirming his deposition" (Farhi 1971, 294).

Turkism. The third ideological alternative developed much later, in response to the relative failure of the other two ideologies.[8] It took two forms: pan-Turkism and a more local, specifically Turkish version. The pan-Turkist version developed first. While pan-Islamism was based on religion and pan-Ottomanism on West European civic nationalism, pan-Turkism was based primarily on East European ethnic nationalism; it embraced the Turkic peoples, a broad ethnolinguistic group of various peoples and societies throughout Eurasia who speak Turkic languages or dialects (Uzer 2016). Paradoxically, pan-Turkism was not a manifestation of a genuine and spontaneous nationalist sentiment among Turks, but a response to the emergence of militant nationalism among the non-Turkish and non-Muslim minorities in the empire. Growing nationalist sentiments among different peoples across the empire left its Turkish-Muslim subjects the sole remaining loyal community.

Gradually, pan-Turkism was replaced by a local Turkish patriotic version (Lewis 1983, 275–76), as scholars and public figures published books and articles that "rediscovered" the pre-Ottoman and pre-Islamic history of the Turkish people and emphasized its richness and glory. Turkist thinkers mythologized the history of the nation and linked it to the ancient Hittite people, who had ruled Anatolia three millennia before. The Hittite past was exploited to instill a sense of ethnic pride and identification among the Turkish people and to serve as proof that the Turkish people had existed long before the birth of Islam in the seventh century. Turkish intellectuals also argued that Turks as an ethnic group shared their origins with European ethnicities, an assumption that strengthened the link between Turkey and Western civilization (Kushner 2006, 164–67). However, it is noteworthy that this identity discourse was elitist and failed to penetrate the Ottoman masses, who remained "largely indifferent" (Landau 2004, 24).

Toward the end of the nineteenth century, the national discourse—at least among the elite—became increasingly secular. Islam as a source of identity was attacked by Young Turk intellectuals, who perceived it as a barrier to development and prosperity and sought to replace it with positivist, materialist, and scientific principles. Consider, for instance, the following well-known comment of Abdullah Cevdet, the leader of the Garbcılar: "Religion is the science of the masses, [whereas] science is the religion of the elite. The science, which is the religion of the elite, has been continuously expanding and elevating, whereas religion, which is the science of the masses, cannot be expanded and elevated in accordance with science, and this is the most important illness of the Islamic World and Turkey" (in Hanioğlu 1997, 140).

Likewise, the Turkish intellectuals cast doubt on whether Islam was a sufficient bond among the people of the empire. At the same time, the shrinking size of the empire and the fact that it remained mostly Turkish and Muslim made pan-Ottomanism less appealing. Therefore, most intellectuals favored a "Turkist" strand of nationalism that involved the promotion of a primarily secular interpretation of Turkish history, language, and culture (Landau 2004, 29). Ziya Gökalp was a leading figure among these Turkish-nationalist thinkers. Gökalp was influenced by Durkheim's ideas about the superiority of the nation over the individual, and adapted Durkheim's theories to call for the merger of Turkey's ancient culture with the developed civilization of the West. Another important nationalist intellectual was Yusuf Akçura, whose ideas overlapped with Gökalp's, except for his greater emphasis on Turkish ethnicity as the founding principle of the nation. Later, Gökalp's and Akçura's writings greatly influenced Atatürk's nation-building policies (Berkes 1954; Uzer 2016).[9]

The simultaneous growing distaste for the Islamic religion and the promotion of a Turkish ethnic identity facilitated the creation of an alternative national ideology, one that emphasized relatively narrow secular ethnicity at the expense of imperial and religious sentiments. Young Turk intellectuals understood that Westernization required much more than administrative and institutional reform. For them it was "fundamentally a trans-valuation of values, a transformation of one's view of oneself, of one's history, and of one's place in the body politic. . . . According to European political theory this indispensable feeling of solidarity existed at its strongest only in nation-states, where it was nationality and language, not so much religion or loyalty to a dynasty, which bound men together" (Kedourie 1968, 21–22).

The development of a distinct secular Turkish nationalism coincided with and served a desire among some Turks to break their political, cultural, and territorial attachment with the rest of the Muslim world, particularly its Arab component. Economically, many of the empire's Arab territories, including Palestine, Syria, and Iraq, remained relatively underdeveloped after centuries of Ottoman rule. While the Turkish leadership promoted modern development, the Arab world preserved its traditional values and premodern market structures (Hershlag 1980), which put a heavy burden on the crumbling economy of the empire. In addition, culturally, Arab societies had always been perceived as inferior by the Ottomans. Modernization mandated affiliation with the values of highly developed Western nations and detachment from the backwardness of the Arab world. Preserving a bond of identity with the Arab world risked generating new demands and expectations by the latter regarding the responsibility of the republic toward its former provinces. The only way to avoid this and distance the two societies was by downgrading the Islamic component in Turkish identity.

From Empire to Republic: The War of Independence

The transition from empire to republic continued between 1918 and 1923 and represented a critical juncture for the formation of a certain type of a state–religion relationship. During that time a combination of factors—a devastating political situation, a severe crisis of legitimacy in what was left of the Ottoman government, and an intellectual discourse that blamed religion for this dire situation—led to the emergence of a nationalist movement that eventually founded a sovereign Turkish nation-state on the ashes of the Ottoman Empire.

It took almost a year between the signing of the Armistice of Modrus in October 1918, which formally ended hostilities between the Allied Powers and the Ottoman Empire, and the emergence of the nationalist movement under Mustafa Kemal. During that time, the devastating situation in the defeated empire invited recurrent aggressions by Western powers, neighboring states, and former provinces. To defend the attacked regions, between 1918 and 1919 the Muslim population and former CUP officers established local "associations for the protection of rights" (AFPRs) throughout what later became Turkey: in Izmir, Trakya (Thrace), Edirne, Kars, Erzurum, Trabzon, and Urfa (Lewis 2000; Aksakal 2008).[10]

The spark that ignited the Turkish struggle for independence was the Greek invasion of Izmir in May 1919, which was an attempt to occupy and annex western Anatolia. Although the Turkish people had become used to frequent violations of their sovereignty, this assault by a former Ottoman province was too humiliating. The AFPR and remnants of the Ottoman army organized to fight the Greeks under the leadership of General Mustafa Kemal, who was appointed general inspector of the Samson region. From that moment, Mustafa Kemal devoted himself to building a Turkish nationalist movement, preserving Turkish lands, and founding an independent Turkish state.

Mustafa Kemal's exceptional leadership and military skills enabled him to form a nationalist army by reorganizing scattered Ottoman troops under his command.[11] When reports of his independent activities against the Greeks arrived in Istanbul, the sultan ordered Mustafa Kemal back to the city. In response, he resigned from the army, removed his uniform, and led the nationalist movement as a civilian (Lewis 2000, 200). Kemal joined the AFPR in eastern Anatolia, which served as an institutional platform for the activities of the nationalist movement. In July and September 1919, the association organized two conferences, in Erzurum and Sivas, in which a National Congress was formed, Kemal was officially elected chairman, and a National Convention was approved. Ankara, a small Anatolian city, became the movement's headquarters in December 1919 (and later became Turkey's capital). From this point on, two rival governments operated in Turkey—a formal but ineffective one in Istanbul, and a nationalist one, led by Kemal, in Ankara. While the formal government tried to appease the European powers and save whatever parts of the Ottoman Empire they could, the nationalist movement concentrated its efforts on defending the territories of Turkey from foreign invasion and later on replacing the incapable government in Istanbul.

The disparity of goals between the nationalist movement and the formal government escalated following the latter's signing of a humiliating treaty in Sèvres on August 10, 1920, which permitted the Western powers to annex various Anatolian territories. This agreement hastened the transfer of power and popular support from Istanbul to Ankara. Between December 1920 and September 1922, the nationalist forces conducted successful battles against Greek troops in Inönü and Skarya; against Armenian and French troops;

and against the Caliphate Army, Ottoman troops who remained loyal to the sultan (Lewis 1983, 550). The successful military outcomes led to the Treaty of Lausanne in July 1923, which restored Turkish territorial integrity and national pride. It further boosted the legitimacy and political leadership of the nationalist movement and Mustafa Kemal and legitimated the establishment of the Turkish Republic on October 29, 1923 (Lewis 1983, 204–6).

Importantly, in the early stages of the war of independence, the nationalist movement repeatedly declared its loyalty to the sultan-caliph and refrained from any antireligious rhetoric. While accusing the official government of corruption and treason, the nationalist movement declared its main goal to be protection of the caliph. This policy changed in April 1920 after the serving sheikh-ul-Islam issued a fetva making killing the rebels (i.e., the nationalists) in the name of the caliph a religious obligation. Surprisingly, instead of disregarding or denouncing the manipulation of religious authorities for political aims, the nationalist movement used the same strategy. In May 1920, the mufti of Ankara, supported by more than 150 Islamic scholars, issued a counter-fetva, according to which religious decrees written and published under external pressures were declared void and Muslim soldiers were commanded to assist the nationalist movement in freeing the caliph from political imprisonment. Likewise, when Mustafa Kemal consolidated his rule over Turkish lands in 1922 and abolished the sultanate, he was careful not to touch the sultan's other title of caliph, knowing the great meaning it symbolized for Turks. The caliphate was abolished just two years later, after the republic was founded (Lewis 2000, 203–4). However, months before the inauguration of the republic, Kemal provided a clue regarding his plans for the caliphate and religion in general in a press conference on January 16, 1923: "This state has no relationship with the Caliphate anymore. . . . We cannot go one step forward if we leave the people to themselves. . . . The law of revolution is superior to other existing laws and rules."[12] Several months later, following the beginning of the republic, the long-term political and ideational processes described above came to full expression, and the implementation of a new radical and comprehensive policy toward religion was unleashed.

Conclusion

From the larger perspective of this book, the preindependence period is notable in two respects. First, it serves as a chronological link between the

Ottoman and republican regimes and as the beginning of a critical juncture with path-dependent consequences in the Kemalist movement, with crucial impact on the state–religion relationship after independence. In particular, the central role of Islamic institutions in the Ottoman state machinery, a series of failing attempts to diminish the religious element in the empire, and the embeddedness of Islamic identity in Ottoman society all shaped the aggressive stance of the Kemalist movement toward religion in the Turkish republic. Second, in striking contrast to the republican era, during the war of independence the nationalist movement respected the traditional role of religion and did not launch reforms like those that were later so identified with the Kemalist project. The nationalists acknowledged the power of religion as a recruitment tool and a legitimizing mechanism and did their best to avoid confrontation with such a strong social and political force when broad support for the national struggle was needed. They even occasionally manipulated the Islamic religion in accordance with their needs. How these two seemingly opposed perspectives can coexist—that is, the preindependence period as a period of relative concord with religion, and as a founding moment with crucial effect on the Kemalist antipathy toward religion—will become clearer in the next chapter.

Chapter 3

Turkey's Authoritarian Laicism, 1923–1950

The early years of the Turkish republic, between 1923 and 1950, were pivotal for the modern Turkish state in many respects, including in modeling the character of the state–religion relationship and its impact on democratic governance in decades to come. This period shaped what followed in two respects. First, the nationalist movement reengineered the sociopolitical structure of Turkish society by initiating a radical secularizing campaign that set the foundations for the state–religion relationship in Turkey. Second, without popular support for the movement's ambitious vision, its initial plans to institute democratic practices were quickly abandoned. The result was a long undemocratic phase that shaped the relationship between Turkish society and the state in a profound way. In particular, this phase was characterized by a strong alliance between the Kemalist leadership, the armed forces, and the bureaucracy that enforced an intolerant secularist social transformation on Turkish society while repressing deviating groups and worldviews. Imposed secularism from above undermined pluralism in Turkish politics, worked against the development of civil society, and led to persistent conflict between the state apparatus and religious actors. Responses from religious actors—whether characterized by violence or peaceful dissent—were met with similarly harsh measures on the part of the state, creating a vicious circle of dissent and repression throughout the one-party period, working against the establishment of democratic governance.

Revolutionary Transformation

Following the successful outcome of the war of independence, the nationalist movement established itself as the unchallenged political elite of Turkey.

As discussed in chapter 3, this elite perceived religion as a key reason for the backwardness and eventual disintegration of the Ottoman Empire and thus an obstacle to achieving modernization and Westernization. It therefore sought to deprive the Islamic religion of any public and political influence (Ahmad 1988, 1991a; Lewis 2000; Shmuelevitz 2006). But Kemalism was far more ambitious than just an attempt to restrict religion to the private sphere. The goal of the movement's social project was to comprehensively transform Turkish society from one civilization (Islamic) to another (Western) by engineering new social values and behavior. For Mustafa Kemal and his followers, becoming "civilized" was the crucial task facing Turkey and the key to securing the nation's future. Kemal's enthusiasm for this civilizing project is reflected in one of his most well-known speeches, given in Kastamonu on August 24, 1925: "Our thinking and mentality will have to become civilized. And we will be proud of this civilization. Take a look at the entire Turkish and Islamic world. Because they failed to adapt to the conditions and rise, they found themselves in such a catastrophe and suffering. We cannot afford to hesitate any more. We have to move forward . . . Civilization is such a fire that it burns and destroys those who ignore it" (in Kasaba 1997, 27–28).

This transformation, this hyperengineering of society, was perceived as so essential that realizing it justified extreme measures to remove old habits and social conventions and establish new ones (Scott 1998).[1] The new republican elites wanted complete adoption of Western behavior, identity construction, and values: "The ideal attributes of a progressive and 'civilized' Republican individual included wearing neckties, shaving beards and moustaches, going to the theater, eating with a fork, husband and wife walking hand in hand in the streets, dancing at balls, shaking hands, wearing hats in the street, writing from left to right, and listening to classical western music" (Göle 1996, 23). Secularism was seen as part and parcel of the modernization project, under which scientific rationalism would replace religious beliefs and practices. Indeed, "Turkey was made secular because secularism and rationalism went hand in hand" (Ahmad 1988, 754).

The process of shaping the state–religion relationship was not autonomous from structural (especially socioeconomic) conditions in Turkish society. Despite the comprehensive rhetoric of the Kemalist leadership, the modernization project was essentially elitist and limited. It was aimed chiefly at the urban centers, especially at the already Western-oriented elite. In other words, the Kemalist elite focused its social reengineering on selected portions of society, leaving the Turkish masses alone (Ahmad 1988, 755; Kadioğlu

1996).[2] In the absence of the uniting force of religion, this process facilitated the creation of a center–periphery cleavage (Mardin 1997).

Most important, the Kemalist-led modernization process was superficial in the sense that it only achieved behavioral and structural changes while neglecting the social, political, and moral elements of modernization—the Enlightenment values of social mobilization, pluralistic public discourse, and acknowledgment of basic civil rights.[3] In embracing the (in my view misleading) idea that the transition to modernization required marginalizing religion from the public sphere, the Kemalists found themselves in direct conflict with adherence to public preferences and respect for citizenship rights and freedoms—in other words, with democracy. In essence, the Kemalists had to choose between two costly alternatives: putting time and effort into a campaign of persuasion directed at the populace and risking failure; or abandoning (at least temporarily) democratic principles and imposing what they believed to be necessary steps toward deep social change. The Kemalists chose the second option as likely to be more effective, but as this chapter shows, the long-term social and political costs were higher than expected. In retrospect, not only did the Kemalist regime fail in consolidating its worldview, especially with regard to uprooting religion as a source of identification and social organization, but undemocratic practices, hegemonic tendencies, and a weak civil society became and remain important features of contemporary Turkish politics (A. Rubin 2016).

The clear ideological preference for secular modernization over democracy is reflected nicely in the absence of democracy among the six guiding principles of Kemalism—republicanism, populism, secularism, revolutionism, nationalism, and statism.[4] Indeed, whenever any of these precepts conflicted with democratic principles, the Kemalist regime preferred the implementation of the former at the expense of democracy.

The Kemalist Alliance

As just described, the Kemalist transformative project was elitist and top-down. Unlike other famous revolutions (French, American, Russian), it was not generated from below by grassroots activists or forces in civil society, and thus lacked popular support (Mardin 1971, 199; Heper 1991). This had two related political consequences. First, because the Kemalist elite failed to penetrate the periphery of the state and mobilize the masses in support of its political goals, it could not risk establishing multiparty democracy, which would have required it to compete against political actors and ideas with better capacities for mass mobilization. Hence, the Kemalist party—the Republican People's Party (RPP; Cumhuriyet Halk Partısı in Turkish)—began its rule by prohibiting political opposition (Penner-Angrist 2005; Kiris 2012, 398). Second, the absence of mass political support forced the RPP to look for alternative allies to support its modernizing project and secure it from political challenges. These circumstances created a strong alliance between the RPP, the military, and the bureaucracy, with intellectual backing from the intelligentsia, the legal profession, and the media (Lewis 2000, 370). The formation of this alliance took place during the war of independence and was further strengthened after the establishment of the republic. It created a committed elitist circle that imposed its hegemonic worldview on Turkish politics and society from the foundation of the republic and retained a strong grip on certain realms of state power and politics in contemporary Turkey until recent years.

The armed forces had been the political cornerstone of the regime throughout the life of the Ottoman Empire. Indeed, "the state model in this polity essentially came from the military" (Heper 1991, 46). During the war of independence, the military became Atatürk's strongest ally and supporter of reforms. Atatürk and his second-in-command, İsmet İnönü, were highly regarded military generals, and the same was true of their closest confederates and advisers. Atatürk was part of the Young Turk group of military officers, and he participated in their activities from 1906 onward. When the government in Istanbul removed him from his military position in 1919, a majority of high-ranking military officers remained loyal to him (Zürcher 2005, 186). In fact, "for every top-ranking front commander who remained in Istanbul until the end, there were two who joined the Anatolian cause" (Rustow 1959, 533). These officers' formal education in military schools during the CUP regime (1908–1918) and the military experience they acquired trying to curb nationalist revolts among the non-Turkish minorities of the empire generated strong nationalist feelings among them. Finally, Atatürk's leadership skills, displayed in his troops' successes against Greek aggression during the war of independence, were strongly admired by the military (Rustow 1959).

Atatürk did take some measures to isolate the military from politics, especially as a response to potential political challenges from this direction, but the close relationship between the two realms continued through the history of modern Turkey. There is solid evidence for strong ties between military officers and civil politics. For instance, twenty of the twenty-five generals who served during the war of independence left the military, entered politics, and were recruited to the cabinet and parliament. Between 1920 and 1943, the ratio of former military officers in the Grand National Assembly (GNA)—the unicameral Turkish legislature—was between one-sixth and one-eighth (Rustow 1959). This historical alliance created a perception among the commanders of the Turkish Armed Forces (TAF) that the military was the guardian of Turkey's social transformation. As Ümit Cizre puts it (2008, 303): "TAF's legitimization of its dominant role lies in its identification of its 'interests' with those of the nation; it sees its mission as a continuing transformation of the country's values in the direction of modernity. Secularism is the pillar, the principle and the proof of its role."

Atatürk's reliance on political backing from the military led him to consult with the higher echelons of the TAF before executing important political moves, including the decision to disestablish Islam in the republic. There is evidence, for example, that before embarking on his first important secularizing reform, abolishing the caliphate in March 1924, Atatürk met in person with military commanders to confirm that the military supported the move (Weiker 1981, 101). This long-lasting alliance came at the expense of forming broad civil coalitions in support of reforms in the early years of the republic. It also consolidated the political role of the TAF in the republic, with long-term consequences (Rustow 1959; Weiker 1981; Yavuz 2009).

The other partners in the Kemalist alliance were the Turkish bureaucracy, the intelligentsia, the legal profession, and the media. To begin with the bureaucracy, during the nineteenth century, a new generation of bureaucrats replaced the old Ottoman bureaucracy and embraced a new "operational code," which was responsible for the formation of new state institutions under secular administrative law, "all of which had a tacit background of positivist rationality" (Mardin 2006, 12). The tendency to empower the state at the expense of individual freedom and initiative was strengthened in the republican era, especially when statism was made one of the constitutionally protected pillars of Kemalism. The bureaucracy was a tool and a partner in the Kemalist transformation of Turkey, and the bureaucrats saw Kemalism as the only possible path toward national prosperity. This vision dictated a strict and intolerant attitude toward what was and was not in the service of the nation, one that did not welcome civic participation or civil spheres of operation outside the realm of the state (Weiker 1973, 14–16). Like the alliance with the military, this legacy had a long-term effect on Turkish society and politics, with "an over-empowering bureaucracy which leaves little room for individual initiative and collective pursuit of interests within autonomous domains, free from state interference" (Toprak 1996, 91).

The role of the intelligentsia in developing modern nationalist ideas and its influence on the thinking of the Young Turks and later Atatürk were detailed in chapter 2. The legal profession and the media became new professional domains only in the late Ottoman Empire, the former because until the nineteenth century the legal system rested on the principles of Sharia, and the latter because of the empire's very low literacy rates. Nevertheless, these professions played an important part in Turkey's transformation. The legal profession was responsible for replacing the old religious legal system with modern continental law codes. For its part, the media became a tool for spreading Kemalist ideology and reforms. From 1923 to 1950, the government kept strict reins on the media and prevented the development of a free press. The only daily newspaper that operated throughout the period was *Cumhuriyet* (Republic), which effectively served as the regime's mouthpiece. All newspapers not under government control were closed down in 1925, except for one liberal newspaper, *Yarin* (Tomorrow), which belonged to a friend of Atatürk and so was allowed to operate until 1931 (Zürcher 2005, 212).

To conclude this point, in the absence of mass support, Atatürk recruited and allied with social sectors that accepted the vision of the Kemalist movement. This alliance made a powerful coalition that controlled the state machinery for decades and created a path-dependent power structure in Turkish politics with long-lasting consequences. Moreover, the power of this group was responsible for the creation in Turkey of a resilient political duality, an important characteristic of Turkish politics until recently. As Yayla explained to me, "In Turkey there are two governments. One is a democratically elected government. . . . It is expected to act within the limits of the constitution and it is accountable. . . . The other is a bureaucratic government. It is not accountable but it limits democracy and it limits the democratically elected government."[5]

I shall now describe this coalition's policies toward religion, the responses it generated from religious populations and the consequences of this interaction on Turkish political culture and democratic governance.

Secular Reforms

Immediately after the proclamation establishing the Republic of Turkey on October 29, 1923, the state introduced comprehensive policies aimed at uprooting religion from social and political life. Most of these reforms were proclaimed during the formative years of the regime—the first five years of the republic, 1924 to 1928. A second wave of reforms took place in the mid-1930s. These reforms defined the relationship between the state and religion in a way that has determined the evolution of this relationship to the present.

Two models of secularism presented themselves to the Kemalist leadership. The US model, which Ahmet Kuru calls "passive secularism," maintains a strict separation of religion from the political sphere but still respects the right of religious groups to conduct their rituals in public. The French model offers a more assertive and repressive form of secularism called laicism (*laïcité* in French, or *laiklik* in Turkish). The goal of laicism, which was established by the Jacobins during the French Third Republic, is to restrict religious content and actors by subjecting the religious establishment to state control and supervision (Kadıoğlu 1996; Yilmaz 2005, 387; Kuru 2007; White 2008, 357). Mindful of Islam's entrenched position in the life of the general populace, the Kemalists chose the French model. Repressive supervision, rather than separation, became the guiding principle of the alliance's policy toward religion.

Secularizing reforms began less than five months after the foundation of the state and reversed previous policies that had acknowledged Islam in the Ottoman order. They included measures against manifestations of Islam in the state; against folk Islam, namely, the popular Sufi dervish orders (Tarikats), which served as important socializing institutions among the lower classes; and against cultural and social aspects of Islamic identification (Toprak 1996; Zürcher 2005).

The first step was to eliminate political recognition of Islam to curtail potential contenders for political power and consolidate the hegemony of the national movement. On March 3, 1924, the GNA passed an act abolishing the caliphate (the complementary religious role of the Ottoman sultan as head of the Ummah) and sent the remaining members of the sultan's family into exile. This act followed the abolition of the sultanate in 1922 and the declaration of a republic in 1923, which together signified the construction of a new political system in Turkey (Akşin 2007, 192). Abolishing the caliphate generated significant dissatisfaction even among ardent supporters of secular reforms. After all, the caliphate was an institution five centuries old, and it symbolized the Islamic nature of Turkish society and its ties with the rest of the Ummah. But this was exactly why the reformers saw dissolving it as essential: "An institution which had its theoretical base in a supra-national concept of solidarity was, of course, inimical to the interests of the nationalist movement" (Toprak 1981, 45).

On the same day, the GNA passed two other laws that launched a broad series of secularizing reforms at the institutional level. The first unified the education system under the Ministry of Education, outlawed the old system of medreses, and even prohibited any teaching of the Quran outside the public education system. The second act abolished the Ministry of Religious Affairs, establishing instead the Diyanet (Directorate of Religious Affairs) as a bureaucratic unit in the prime minister's office. The logic of this act was to eliminate the autonomous political influence of religion in the government and subject it to the prime minister's authority (Yilmaz 2005, 388).

Despite the secularist rhetoric of the Kemalist alliance, the Diyanet supervised religious according to the Sunni strand of Islam, thus giving Sunni Islam differentiated status than that of other strands of Islam (Alevi, Shiite, etc.) or other religions (Christian, Jewish, etc.). Some scholars argued that the Diyanet's modus operandi reflected a favorable treatment to Sunni Islam, which emphasized the Sunni element in Turkish nationalism. Another explanation holds that Sunni Islam was perceived as the most salient challenge to Kemalist ideology, so governmental supervision concentrated in it, not because of concrete preference to this strand of religion (Keyman 2007).

A month later, in April 1924, the state enacted another major institutional reform, closing down the religious Sharia court system and abolishing the position of sheikh-ul-Islam, the highest Islamic authority in the state. By that time the religious courts were responsible only for matters of personal status, but this act ended the duality that had characterized the Ottoman legal system and subjected the entire structure to a secular Ministry of Justice. This act was followed by the adoption of Western-oriented civil and criminal codes in 1926. On February 25, 1925, the GNA passed a law that prohibited any use of religion in politics and treated such uses as treason against the nation.[6]

The next phase involved a full-scale attack on various symbolic manifestations of Islam. In November 1925, the state outlawed the wearing of the fez, a hat that had been common in the Ottoman Empire. All civil servants were required to wear Western-type hats. Ironically, the fez was not an authentic Islamic symbol but an import from Europe at the beginning of the nineteenth century, brought to Turkey as part of Sultan Mahmut II's modernizing reforms. Nevertheless, as far as the state was concerned, this symbol had become too closely identified with the religious face of the old regime and thus had to be abandoned. Wearing religious garments such as the abaya and caftan were also prohibited in public. The state outlawed the use of epithets or titles with religious identification such as "dervish" and "sheikh."[7]

Other reforms of a symbolic nature were aimed at "closing the door on the Islamic-Ottoman cultural heritage" (Toprak 1981, 42) while making new connections with the West. These included adopting the Gregorian calendar in place of the Islamic lunar calendar in December 1925;[8] the Western way of organizing time in place of the Islamic system, built around prayer times, in 1926; and Western systems of weights, measures, and numerals in place of the old Ottoman systems in 1928 (Kuru 2007). Another very important symbolic reform was the adoption in November 1928 of the Latin alphabet for the written Turkish language in place of the Arabic script. Although not aimed directly against Islam, this reform symbolized Turkey's turn from Islamic to Western civilization. Adopting the Latin script brought Turkey closer to the Western world and away from its Arab neighbors and Middle Eastern past. The next phase in this direction was purging Persian and Arabic vocabulary from Turkish, followed in 1929 by a prohibition on teaching these languages in Turkish high schools.

As mentioned earlier, a particularly aggressive aspect of repression against folk Islam was the abolition of the Tarikats, Sufi orders that were very popular among the masses throughout the country. These institutions came from a nomadic culture and combined Islamic practices with pagan ceremonies and mystical forms of worship. They were key elements in the Ottoman social matrix and provided a socialization framework for many subjects of the empire. The most well-known among them were the Mevlevi, Bektashi, Nakshibandi, and Suleimanci orders, all of which had established strong ties (both formal and informal) with the central administration of the empire (Mardin 2006). Although the primary target of reforms was institutionalized Islam, the Kemalist regime soon realized that the real danger might come from these spiritual orders, which were not submissive to state authority and opposed secular reforms. Consequently, in 1925 the state issued laws that closed down the orders, their lodges (*tekke*), and places of worship (*zaviye*) and forbade entrance to the tombs of saints that were used by the orders for rituals (Lewis 1983, 328).

Another aspect of social transformation related to religion, with arguably positive consequences, was a significant change in the status of women in Turkish society. Reforms in this realm were also perceived as antireligious because they challenged the patriarchal tendencies of the Islamic faith. This change was achieved in part by abolishing the religious legal code and court system, which systematically discriminated based on gender. The state pushed women to pursue careers in professions traditionally regarded as masculine, such as academia, law, the media, and even aviation (Kandiyoti 1991). (One of Atatürk's adopted children, Sabiha Gökçen, became the first female combat pilot in the republic and perhaps the world.) In March 1929, the first beauty contest in Turkey took place.[9] That same year, the minister of Internal Affairs declared that women would soon be given the right to vote and stand for election.[10] Turkish women obtained the right to vote in local elections in 1930 and achieved full universal suffrage in 1934. Women were first elected to the GNA in 1935.

The first round of reforms ended with the removal of two articles from the constitution of 1924, completing the divorce of the Turkish Republic from the Islamic religion: the second article, which established Islam as the state religion in Turkey, and the twenty-sixth article, which made the application of Sharia one of the responsibilities of the GNA. In 1924 the Kemalist state had faced stronger opposition, felt politically insecure, and did not dare erase Islam from the constitution. After five years in power and considerable success in imposing its reforms, Atatürk's government felt secure enough to go this extra mile. This change completed the disestablishment and marginalization of Islam from Turkish society and politics.

A second wave of reforms began in the early 1930s, after a few years without significant new legislation on religious issues. In 1934 the GNA passed a law that mandated the adoption of family names by all citizens;[11] at this time, Mustafa Kemal was granted the surname Atatürk ("Father of the Turks"). Another symbolically important reform was changing the official day of rest from Friday, the Islamic holy day, to Sunday, a move that improved commercial connections with the West but was foreign to most Turks. The reform that generated most opposition from the public in the 1930s was a state initiative to create an artificial Turkish variant of Islam by requiring Quran recitations and the call for prayer (*ezan*) to be conducted in Turkish. As the language of the Quran, Arabic maintained the population's link with Islam and their Ottoman foundations. By preventing the masses from reading the Quran in Arabic, the Kemalist state disconnected them from their cultural and religious roots and facilitated the Kemalist program of indoctrination. This new attempt to isolate Muslim Turks from their religious foundations was accompanied by a reversal of economic recognition. The few remaining public religious schools were weaned off state resources, and by 1932 there remained no allocation of state funding to religious schools (Toprak 1981, 49).

At first glance, the various secularizing reforms painted Turkey in bright colors and raised excitement among European scholars about the ability of traditional societies to transform and modernize. On closer observation, the success of these reforms was very limited, primarily because of their inability to penetrate all sectors and regions of the country. Although the urban centers experienced a revolutionary transformation in people's values and habits, the peasant population of Turkey was not much influenced by the reforms. Penetration of the new secular education system to villages was limited, literacy rates remained low, and many people rejected modern innovations such as family names in their daily life. In this respect, the Kemalist modernization project was partial and selective (Zürcher 2005, 227).

After Atatürk's death on November 10, 1938, no significant new reforms were launched. Nevertheless, the state's politically manipulative treatment of religion in the 1940s until the end of single-party rule deepened the cleavage and tension between the state and religious segments in society. I discuss this in more detail later, but first I explore societal responses to the secularization reforms and the patterns that developed in the relationship between religion and state throughout this period.

A Vicious Circle: Societal Responses to Coercive Secularism

This section describes the responses of religious populations to the laicist policies of the Kemalist regime. The full-scale attack on the practices and beliefs of Muslim Turks and the significant multidimensional downgrading of religion were not welcomed by Turkish society. Although antireligious acts enjoyed the status of law, they were foreign to the lifestyle of most Turkish people, especially in rural areas and in the small and medium-sized cities in the periphery.

The response of the religious populace was diverse but can generally be divided into three categories: (1) peaceful individual dissent; (2) peaceful collective dissent; and (3) violent dissent. The authoritarian regime treated all three types of protest and manifestations of belief in the same repressive way. Wearing a fez or calling for the restoration of Sharia were considered an offense against the state and its modernizing project and were treated in the same manner as armed revolts or violent acts. The chronology of events demonstrates that this extreme and insensitive state response polarized religious populations, escalated the tension between the state and society, and generated harsher state measures as well as more extreme manifestations of dissent.

State–society interactions around antireligious reforms started with the foundation of the republic and continued until the Menemen Incident in late 1930, which symbolized an important turning point in the relationship between the two factions. The first documented case of peaceful individual dissent took place in January 1924, before the reforms were even formally under way. A religious man, Hafiz Ibrahim Effendi, was sentenced to 1,000 years (!) in prison for distributing pamphlets claiming that morality should derive from Islamic doctrine and that women should keep themselves covered.[12] In two other documented cases several years later, individuals who advocated a return to religious principles and nonviolent opposition to the reforms were immediately arrested.[13] In another incident in 1930, several activists in the city of Adana unfurled a flag covered with antirepublic and anti-RPP slogans; in their efforts to reach the perpetrators, the police arrested thirty people.[14] In short, the state tolerated no expressions of opposition or advocacy of religious content, and its disproportionate reactions reflected the regime's resolve to repress any manifestation of religion that might challenge its rule.

Other peaceful expressions of dissent came in the form of collective action, which can be seen as a spontaneous and unorganized type of civil society activity. The most well-known example came in response to the November 1925 legislation prohibiting the fez—for the masses, a basic symbol of Muslim culture. In the wake of this legislation, mass demonstrations of fez-wearing men gathered spontaneously in the cities of Sivas, Keyseri, Erzurum, Rize, Maras, and Giresun. Admittedly, the population was less concerned about the formal role of religion in the state than they were about restrictions on everyday practices. Nonetheless, everywhere these protests were repressed in ruthless ways. *Cumhuriyet* mentions the following state responses. In Sivas the leader of the protest, Imamzade Mehmet Effendi, was sentenced to death and others were imprisoned;[15] in Erzurum thirteen protesters were sentenced to death;[16] and in Rize eight protesters were sentenced to death.[17] Notably, *Cumhuriyet* was the regime's mouthpiece, and thus it most likely did not report the full scale of state actions against protesters.

Although most of the opposition was peaceful, the reforms also generated a number of violent incidents. Three had particular importance. The first was a revolt launched in the territory of Kurdistan on February

13, 1925. This revolt was organized and headed by Sheikh Said, a Kurdish member of the Nakshibendi order. One of its triggers was the repression of Kurdish identity by the state, but most scholars agree that the primary motivation for this revolt was religious—an effort to restore the caliphate and Sharia law in the republic. Certainly, the peasants who supported the revolt did so solely on religious terms (Ahmad 1991a, 7; Kadioğlu 1996, 187; Akşin 2007, 201; Zürcher 2005, 202).

The Sheikh Said revolt was put down in May 1925, only three months after it started, following the capture and execution of Said and forty-six other leading rebels in April. But it gave the government a persuasive excuse to take further authoritarian and repressive measures. During the struggle against the rebels, the state passed a Law for the Maintenance of Order, which granted it dictatorial powers. Acting in accordance with these powers, the state established so-called independence tribunals,[18] which did not show much respect for civil rights. According to Zürcher (2005, 204), the number of people imprisoned by these courts reached 7,500, of whom 660 were executed. Also in accordance with this law, the state closed down all media not under government control[19] and outlawed the Tarikats, forcing Sufi orders adherents underground. The suppression of the dervish orders radicalized their followers, who kept practicing underground. In addition, the state shut down the very short-lived (November 1924–June 1925) Progressive Republican Party, which was a first attempt at opening the political scene to opposition views. The state prosecutor argued that this party had supported the rebellion and used religion for political purposes (Ahmad 1991b; Zürcher 1991).

The second violent incident was a plot to assassinate Atatürk in Izmir in 1926. The plotters were headed by Ziya Hurshid, a former member of the GNA who opposed the abolition of the caliphate. Their plan to hide a bomb in Atatürk's car during an organized visit to the city of Izmir was uncovered by the police, and the plotters were tried and executed by the independence tribunal in Izmir. This incident unleashed another wave of state repression, with massive arrests and trials, including of former military generals, members of the Young Turk movement, and even personal friends of Atatürk who had become his political opponents. This wave of repression all but eliminated any possible opposition to the regime—military, religious, or political (Lewis, 2000, 222).

Between 1927 and 1930, unrest among rebels with both Kurdish and religious grievances continued, punctuated by a number of particularly violent incidents.[20] Against this backdrop, toward the end of 1930 the Kemalist elite confronted the boldest religious-based attack on its authority yet in the city of Menemen. On December 23, 1930, Dervish Mehmet, a sheikh of the Nakshibendi order, led a group of followers in a demonstration against the republic. Calling for the restoration of the caliphate and Sharia, they waved a green flag (the color of Islam) from a nearby mosque.[21] The protest quickly escalated into a riot: "Reserve Officer Fehmi Kubilay, on arriving at the scene, tried to intervene but was shot dead by reactionaries who cut off his head, stuck in on a pole and displayed it to the crowd. Two watch men were also killed. Repression followed and martial law was declared. A military court was established, which condemned twenty eight people to death" (Akşin 2007, 210).

According to *Cumhuriyet*, in the wake of this incident about 200 people were arrested, and 37 were sentenced to death.[22] According to Zürcher, the number of arrestees in the incident approached 2,000 (Zürcher 2005, 179). Determined to demonstrate its strong hand, the state closed down the mosque from which the riot had started and erected a memorial to the slain officer in the center of Menemen.[23] Immediately after the incident the state closed down a newly established opposition party, the Free Republican Party, which had been inaugurated only three months earlier, in August 1930; this was to be the last short experiment in democratic practices in the single-party period. The excuse for the unlimited suspension of any political opposition was the alleged exploitation of religion by the opposition parties, first in 1925 and then in 1930. The conclusion of the state was that "the multi-party system could not work until the revolution was better established" (Akşin 2007, 210).

The Menemen event traumatized the Kemalist elite. It challenged and embarrassed the state, confirmed the opposition of the masses toward efforts to move the country forward, and forced the Kemalists to the bitter realization that the secular reforms had not taken root in society (Kadioğlu 1996, 187). The following passage by Yakub Kadri, a Kemalist author and diplomat, captures this realization nicely: "It's as though nothing has happened all these years, as though . . . the idea of any of our radical reforms has [not] altered anything in this country. . . . Who were the passive, silent observers of this tragedy? Citizens of this secular, contemporary Republic of Turkey. That is the true calamity" (Ahmad 1991a, 8). Yet instead of sober reassessment of the ramifications of its antireligious policies, the state elected to impose an even more militant version of secularism, which became the official policy of the 1930s. For this reason, the Menemen Incident was an important milestone in the evolution of state policies toward Islam.

In particular, in the wake of the Menemen riot the state intensified its efforts to institute an artificial Turkish type of Islam. This was done in several ways. First, in 1932 the state introduced a translated version of the Quran and required that prayers (including readings from the Quran) be conducted in Turkish.[24] Of course this generated spontaneous and organized opposition, which was repressed harshly by the state. Laypeople and imams (Islamic clerics) who insisted on conducting prayers in Arabic were arrested around the country.[25] Second, the use of epithets with religious connotations was proscribed, including titles like *hoca, hafiz,* and *molla*—honorific titles or terms of respect that were derived from Islamic tradition but were commonly used in everyday speech. The state reinforced the prohibition on wearing religious attire outside of mosques.[26] Finally, the security apparatus hardened its persecution of the dervish orders, which continued their worship practices underground. Yet this direct attack strategy on the foundations of Islamic identification and practices failed to achieve the marginalization of Islam and facilitated the use of religion for political mobilization by opposition groups and further alienated the state elite from its subordinate masses (Zürcher 2005, 225).

End of an Era: Atatürk's Death
and the Transition to a Multiparty System

Atatürk had been the leader of the nationalist movement since its foundation and was the engine behind the radical social and cultural transformation the Kemalist state imposed on Turkish society. With his death on November 10, 1938, the reform era came to an end. In 1937, the RPP had inserted into the Turkish constitution the six principles of Kemalism—republicanism, populism, secularism, revolutionism, nationalism, and statism—which had guided Atatürk's reform project. This act celebrated Atatürk's political legacy and gave the Kemalist principles constitutional status, establishing them as the ideological core of the Turkish political system (Kili 1980).

Between 1938 and 1945, the Kemalist elite did not launch significant new reforms with regard to religion. Rather, they aimed to consolidate the earlier reforms and strengthen their rule over the country. The Kemalist alliance formed during the war of independence backed İsmet İnönü as Atatürk's successor, and he became the second president of Turkey and the new chairman of the RPP. Notably, the military was instrumental in securing İnönü's appointment, manifesting its political power (Akşin 2007, 233).

During World War II, which broke out less than a year after İnönü took office, Turkey maintained neutrality. Nonetheless, through the war years the Turkish state and population were more concerned about external threats and economic burdens than about internal politics, and very few religion–state incidents took place in this period. Shortly after the war's end, in September 1945, the Turkish cabinet approved the establishment of the National Development Party, headed by Nuri Demirdağ, and this ended the one-party regime.[27] In January 1946 came the establishment of the Democratic Party (DP, Democrat Partısı), which won the election in 1950.[28]

The dramatic decision to open the Turkish political system to elections and multiparty competition—to democracy—was not influenced primarily by trends in the state–religious relationship. Rather, it was influenced by personal, organizational, socioeconomic, and external factors. On the personal level, Akşin emphasizes İnönü's pluralist and democratic attitudes and his expressed intention to make the political system more inclusive even before he formally became head of state (Akşin 2007, 234). Regarding organizational influence, Penner-Angrist highlights changes in the political discourse in Turkey that facilitated a new willingness within the RPP to tolerate political opposition to its rule. In particular, Penner-Angrist suggests that during İnönü's presidency, the RPP improved its ability to mobilize the masses by increasing its penetration in Turkish society compared with earlier decades. Also, all new parties had to commit to keeping their political agendas within the ideological boundaries set by the six Kemalist principles. This depolarized the political discourse, because new opposition parties could not really challenge the foundations of the Kemalist project (Penner-Angrist 2005).[29] A third factor was related to conflict among the elites. According to Waldner, conflict among Turkish elites, especially between state elites and the business sector, around the state's illiberal tendencies and growing grip over the economy had diminished the business sector's support for the state. This required the ruling Kemalist elite to seek a broad political base among the general population (Waldner 1999, 56–59).

In addition, international pressures indubitably played a role in compelling İnönü to pluralize and democratize the political arena. By the end of World War II, Turkey feared the growing power of the Soviet Union on its Eastern border and wished to join both the United Nations and NATO, as well as to receive much needed economic and technological aid from the United States to protect itself from the Soviet threat. The United States conditioned its support on Turkey's willingness to adopt a more democratic and plural political system, which persuaded İnönü to open the system to multiparty participation (Zürcher 2005, 243–45).

The formation and presence of political opposition required tactical changes by the RPP as it sought to maintain its control over power. These included populist reforms, especially in the realm of religious recognition, as well as political manipulation, which included both lawful and unlawful actions. More specifically, the RPP understood that it must increase its popularity among the general public. Thus it became the first party to systematically manipulate religion for political purposes in the Kemalist era. Between 1947 and 1950, the RPP underwent a significant attitudinal change toward religion, primarily in education. In January 1947, at its party congress, the RPP decided that a certain degree of personal religious education outside the public school system would be permitted.[30] Within weeks, the Ministry of National Education announced that parents were free to teach their children about religion and religious values outside the classroom.[31] In July 1947, the Education Ministry permitted the opening of formal courses and seminars on religion.[32] Another surprising policy was allowing, for the first time, the reading of Quran verses by a religious scholar, in a mosque, on Atatürk Memorial Day.[33]

Between 1948 and 1950, the RPP introduced a plethora of proreligious policies. At the party congress in February 1948, the RPP voted to allow teaching of the Quran in public elementary schools.[34] In May 1948, the party decided that the Imam Hatip religious schools would be reopened; the Education Ministry executed this decision in January 1949.[35] A law passed in June allowed the opening of a faculty of theology,[36] and in February 1950, the cabinet agreed to reopen historical tombs throughout the state, primarily those of the Ottoman sultans Yavuz and Fatih.[37] In this respect, one ardent follower of Atatürk's philosophy was correct to note that "of course, after the death of Atatürk, Kemalism witnessed some erosion."[38] These policies, however, were insufficient for recruiting the political support of those whose basic cultural and religious identification had been repressed for such a long time.

The RPP also tried to block the growing power of the opposition through political maneuvering. In June 1946, the party announced that general elections scheduled to take place in July 1947 would in fact be held one year earlier, in July 1946, only six months after the establishment of the DP. This act, clearly aimed at lowering the DP's chance of building an effective political organization before the election, was met with considerable criticism by the opposition, but the DP resolved to compete in the election and won 62 out of 465 seats in the GNA. After publication of the results, it became clear that the ruling party had also been involved in electoral fraud on a large scale, including widespread irregularities in vote counting. Celal Bayar, one of the DP's leaders, argued in the assembly that based on the party's investigation, the DP was entitled to 279 seats in the GNA (Zürcher 2005, 248). These tactics kept the RPP in power for three more years.

Ultimately, however, such tactics were unable to halt the growing popularity of the opposition. In the elections of May 14, 1950, the DP won an overwhelming majority of seats in the GNA and took the reins of government after three decades of the RPP being the sole political power in Turkey. This transformation marked the beginning of a democratic phase in Turkish politics, which considerably changed the dynamics of interaction between the (unelected) Kemalist alliance, the (elected) government, and religious factions in society.

Conclusion

This chapter investigated state policies toward religion during the first, one-party phase of the Turkish Republic, and the evolving patterns of the state–religion relationship over this time. The Turkish experience supports the assumption of continuity between attitudes toward religion before and after formation of the state and the transformation of prestate agendas into state policies after the state is established. The Kemalist state made considerable efforts to impose an assertive type of secularism on Turkish society. In the absence of popular support for this ambitious project, the Kemalist elite chose to forgo any democratic ideals they might have held, leaving democracy to be introduced only when the goals of the revolution were completely achieved—something that could never actually happen. The Turkish experience reveals the problematic one-size-fits-all prescription of modernization theory, which the Kemalist elite fully adopted and tried to implement. In contrast to the assumptions of modernization theory, secularization was never achieved. But the logic of modernization justified the undemocratic nature of the secularizing reforms until Turkish society was "ready" for political democracy.

Second, in the absence of popular support, the Kemalist elite needed an alternative political alliance in the state apparatus to support its radical policies. The alliance that emerged included the Kemalist political platform (the RPP), the armed forces, the bureaucracy, and the recruited media. During the one-party period, this alliance provided solid political support for the Kemalist project. Because it did not succeed—or perhaps even really try—to spread its worldview in the public arena, this alliance developed an illiberal, intolerant, and undemocratic approach toward politics. This shared worldview maintained the Kemalist alliance intact, kept it in power for a long time, and has had considerable negative effect on how politics has evolved in Turkey in recent decades.

Finally, as long as the Kemalist elite ruled the country with no political opposition, it felt free to act repressively against religion. Once the political climate changed, the ruling elite was forced to make concessions to religion in return for political support. At that point it began to appeal to the general public by presenting a new and more lenient approach. This behavior demonstrates what happens when the treatment of religion fails to reflect public preferences and democratic practice. It also reveals that when religion is deeply embedded, even decades of constant repression will fail to uproot it from society and will generate destructive rather than constructive state–society interaction. If religion cannot be dismissed, modernization projects must acknowledge it and take measures to integrate it and in return may enjoy the support of religious members of society.

Chapter 4

Religion and Democracy under Kemalist Hegemony, 1950-2000

The account in this chapter explores the evolving nature of the state–religion relationship in Turkey during the second half of the twentieth century and substantiates the proposition made earlier about the dynamic nature of the state–religion relationship. Indeed, the opening of the Turkish political arena to multiparty competition in the late 1940s substantially altered the relationship between elected governments and religious actors. First and foremost, it compelled political parties to recruit support from the electorate by manipulating religion in politics in various ways, a trend that eroded the state's initial assertive secularism policy. Second, the transition to democratic governance put some restraints on the arbitrary powers of unelected institutions and facilitated the emergence of faith-based civic activity, which in turn demanded further recognition of religious content and actors by the state. At the same time, the debate over secularism deepened the societal cleavage between elected governments, religious actors, and the Kemalist establishment, with the latter blocking democratic challenges to the secular political order. In this period, recurrent challenges to Kemalist hegemony by religious actors largely failed to achieve institutional or legal recognition of religion.

Modernization was another trend that influenced the state–religion relationship during this time. Following limited and partial modernization under one-party rule, Turkey experienced rapid and more comprehensive modernization starting in the 1950s, coming to full fruition in the 1980s. One expression of this modernization was mass migration from rural settlements to urban centers. As shown in table 4.1, Turkey's urban population increased from 18.5 percent of the total population in 1950 to 28.2 percent in 1965, 40.6 percent in 1980, and 59 percent in 1990. In

Table 4.1. Population growth in Turkey, 1940s–1990s

Year	Population	Urban Area (10001+)	Rural Area	Istanbul	Ankara	Izmir
1945	18,790,174	3,475,046 (18.5 percent)	15,315,128 (81.5 percent)	860,558	226,712	198,396
1950	20,947,188	3,894,708 (18.6 percent)	17,052,480 (81.4 percent)	983,041	288,536	227,578
1965	31,391,421	8,859,417 (28.2 percent)	22,532,004 (71.8 percent)	1,742,978	905,660	411,626
1980	44,736,957	18,167,495 (40.6 percent)	26,569,462 (59.4 percent)	2,772,708	1,877,755	757,854
1985	50,664,458	25,889,750 (51.1 percent)	24,774,708 (48.9 percent)	5,475,982	2,235,035	1,489,772
1990	56,473,035	33,326,351 (59.01 percent)	23,146,684 (40.99 percent)	6,748,435	2,553,209	1,762,849

Source: (Shmuelevitz, Urbanization and Voting for the Turkish Parliament 1996, 163).

Istanbul alone, the population grew from 2.77 million inhabitants in 1980 to 6.75 million in 1990, mostly through in-migration by newcomers from rural regions, who settled in shantytowns around the city. Massive waves of internal migration were responsible for more intense encounters between the Kemalist urban and secular center and the traditional, rural, and more religious periphery. Also important, diffusion f modernization to the entire population furnished religious actors with better exposure to politics and improved their mobilizing capacities. They learned to make use of modern instruments such as the media and the economy for recruiting popular support and formed civic associations that disseminated proreligious ideas at the grassroots level. Consequently, there emerged a capable conservative counterhegemonic leadership that introduced new challenges to the Kemalist establishment's worldview and hegemonic control.

Equally important, the period explored in this chapter exemplifies the longtime negative consequences of the initial restrictive treatment of religion and the barriers it put in the way of democratic advancement. As long as religious demands were not perceived as threatening their hegemony, the

Kemalists acted with restraint or sought to coopt the religious sectors. In contrast, whenever religious demands posed a serious threat to the establishment's grip on power, the latter responded in an undemocratic way, including military interventions and restrictive judicial decisions.

The relatively long era of Kemalist hegemony can be divided into two main periods. The first period extends from the transfer of power in 1950 to the military coup in 1980. The second stretches from the period after the 1980 coup to the Adalet ve Kalkinma Partisi (AKP, the Justice and Development Party)'s ascendance to power at the turn of the century.

Start of the First Democratic Period, 1950–1960: Easing Treatment of Religion

Single-party rule in Turkish politics ended in 1950 with the transfer of government from the Kemalist Republican People's Party (RPP) to the Democratic Party (DP). But this transition did not affect the legacy of a strong state forged by the Kemalists. In the absence of civic discourse, the debate about the role of religion in the state remained mainly at the elite level and produced significant animosity between the elected government and the Kemalist establishment (Heper 1991; Toprak 1996). The Kemalist alliance, now in opposition, believed that the DP was doing all it could to marginalize the RPP and reverse the achievements of Kemalism. Similarly, the DP feared the RPP was doing everything in its power to delegitimize the DP's rule and replace it by undemocratic means (Harris 1970; Karpat 1972, 355). Despite ongoing mutual criticism, the new ruling party remained generally loyal to Kemalist principles, an unsurprising development given that the DP's two senior leaders, President Celal Bayar and Prime Minister Adnan Menderes, had served for many years as deputies in the RPP before they split off to form the DP.

The DP policy on religion should be viewed not in isolation but as part of a larger political agenda. The DP's two immediate concerns were improving the economy and widening the party's political support base. In the economic realm, the first five years of DP rule showed positive signs for economic growth. Turkey strengthened its economic relationships with Western countries, and the government allocated significant resources to industry and agriculture that helped in modernizing these sectors. But this relatively short-lived economic prosperity was not enough to secure sustainable growth. First, massive politically motivated but economically unjustified government investment in different realms helped trigger the 1955 eruption of a severe economic crisis (Simpson 1965, 147). Then, toward the end of the 1950s, the government's initial emphasis on private enterprise gave way to more statist-centralist policies, like those of the RPP. Exacerbating these trends, structural modernization, especially literacy and urbanization, remained limited and did not reach many parts of Turkey's vast territory. Narrow modernization was also responsible for the relatively low mobilizing capacities of the religious segments in society.

The DP's other concern was securing and expanding its constituency. Their support base consisted of farmers and peasants from the Anatolian periphery who were, on average, more religious and traditional than the urban masses, and certainly more so than the secular, Western-oriented, professional voters who formed much of the core constituency of the RPP. The DP leadership realized that in the countryside, where the Kemalist reforms had failed to penetrate, religion remained a powerful social and political force. In fact, "the more remote a village from the capital or from any large urban center, the more likely were its inhabitants to be hardly aware of the secularization laws" (Landau 2004, 133). Lifting some restrictions on private religious observance was seen as an effective way to secure the support of the rural population. For the DP, the resurgence of religion was not an ideological goal but an efficient recruitment tool (Reed 1954, 271; Cizre-Sakallioğlu 1996, 237). The government was well aware of its delicate relationship with the Kemalist establishment and was genuinely committed to the principles of Kemalism. The resulting policies of the DP government toward religion throughout the 1950s thus reflect an attempt to maneuver between these opposing poles—winning the support of religious Turks by acknowledging the role of religion, while adhering to Kemalist principles (Toprak 1981, 75; Margulies and Yildizoğlu 1988, 13–14).

As part of this balancing act, the DP eased various state restrictions on religious content in the public sphere. Immediately after gaining power, the new government lifted the ban on calling the *ezan* (call for prayer) in Arabic.[1] Three months later, the cabinet approved compulsory religious lessons in elementary schools.[2] Parents who did not want their children to participate in those lessons had to request an exemption in advance. The new policy contradicted the previous government's policy of prohibiting religious content in the public education system. To balance the proreligious change, responsibility for the curriculum to be used in religion classes was not given to the Diyanet but to the Ministry of Education, which was controlled by ardent Kemalists.[3] Other proreligion policies included inserting Quran readings into the state radio program and de facto tolerance of religious garb in public. The state also expanded the Imam Hatip religious school system (designed to train preachers and prayer leaders) by opening fifteen new schools. The number of students attending Imam Hatip schools rose from 876 in 1951 to 3,377 in 1960. Finally, the state launched a training program aimed at supplying imams to 1,000 Turkish villages (Reed 1954, 274; Weiker 1981, 109).

Although its constituency was satisfied with the proreligion reforms, some DP initiatives disturbed the delicate balance between religion and Kemalist principles. In May 1951, several DP deputies from Konya proposed a bill that would have reversed many of Atatürk's reforms, restoring permission to wear the fez, mandating head coverings for women, forbidding the erection of statues (considered a form of idolatry under Islam), and most important, decreeing a return to the Arabic alphabet and the reestablishment of Sharia law.[4] This initiative destabilized the equilibrium between the proreligious actors and the Kemalist establishment and provoked criticism in the media, in Parliament, and among parts of the general public. The turmoil came to an end only after the Konya deputies dropped the proposed bill and expressed their loyalty to Atatürk and adherence to Kemalist reforms.[5]

In many instances, however, the DP repressed religious activity. In the 1950s, many raids were launched against religious orders and movements, especially the Ticani, Nurcu, and Bektaşi.[6] The DP leadership used secular rhetoric and supported expelling party members who advocated a return to religious rule and the reestablishment of the caliphate.[7] The government outlawed the manipulation of religion for political gain[8] and sanctioned the abolition of the short-lived Millet Partisi (Nation Party), which was accused of doing so.[9] Another law prohibited criticism against Atatürk and the Kemalist ideology (Cizre-Sakallioğlu 1996, 237).

Following the beginning of the economic crisis in 1955, the turn toward religion became more apparent. The DP lost the support of the business sector and to compensate for this loss, it sought to establish a covert political alliance with the religious sector by softening its activities against the religious orders and social religious movement. This change increased the political leverage of these organizations. The most popular movement at the time, the Nurculuk, was headed by Saidi Nursi, an Anatolian Kurdish sheikh. In 1959, feeling secure in his popularity and political power base, Sheikh Nursi put forward an explicit political demand: namely, that the Hağia Sofia in Istanbul—originally a Byzantine church that was made a mosque after the city's defeat by the Ottomans and then turned into a museum by Atatürk—would be restored to its status as a mosque. In the published letter setting forth this demand, Nursi argued that he could ensure support for the DP from some 600,000 followers and students.[10] This was the first demonstration of religious intervention in the democratic political game that fully made use of the power of mass support. Given the legal restrictions then in place on religious interference in politics, the government's response was surprising. The government did not open an investigation against Nursi or detain him for this obvious manipulation of religion for political gain. Instead, he was invited to Ankara by DP deputies to refute accusations against him made by the opposition about his reactionary activities and political relationship with the DP,[11] and Prime Minister Menderes openly defended Nursi and rejected the opposition claims.[12]

Overall, compared with the RPP's draconian restrictions on religious expression, the DP government was perceived by its constituents as more respectful of its citizens' cultural and religious practices. This policy had a positive impact on the behavior of religious actors. Throughout the 1950s, there is no record of religious-based violence or attempts by religious groups to act unlawfully against the government. Antisecular incidents that led to a response from the authorities were few and scattered and included wearing religious garb in public,[13] selling calendars in Arabic,[14] and establishing an underground school for teaching Arabic and the Quran.[15] In addition, religious actors destroyed a number of statues of Atatürk, although this probably had more to do with the Islamic prohibition against what were perceived as idolatrous images than with anti-Atatürkist sentiment per se.[16]

In short, as one scholar notes, "Prime Minister Menderes can be credited with having prevented the splintering-off or radicalization of religious groups and with expanding the state's social legitimacy through its liberal stance vis-à-vis Islam" (Karakas 2007, ii). Despite the peaceful interaction between the government and the religious populace, the Kemalist alliance[17] perceived the relaxation of Atatürk's secularizing reforms as a treacherous trend. Mounting criticism by Kemalists and deteriorating economic circumstances propelled the DP government into increasingly antidemocratic policies, such as restrictions on the freedoms of expression and association and limits on political opposition. These only made the political atmosphere more unstable and provided justification for more authoritarian intervention (Weiker 1963; Harris 1970).

In April 1960, Inönü declared in the legislature that "when conditions are complete, revolution becomes a legitimate right for the nation, for the citizen begins to think that no other institution or way exists to defend his rights" (Karpat 1972, 356). This was an explicit warning that the Kemalist coalition intended to topple the government and bring Turkey back to secular modernization, which Kemalists believed was the only route to progress. On May 27, 1960, the military intervened for the first time in Turkish democracy in the name of Kemalist ideology. This pattern of events was recurred in different versions every decade into the 2000s and reflected the bifurcated nature of the Turkish state, one that pitted an elected government with limited powers against a powerful Kemalist alliance that directed important state systems without popular support.

Crucially, this relationship between Turkey's democratic governments and the Kemalist alliance pivoted around the role of religion in the state, in relation to the 1960 coup and later. As one of Turkey's senior political scientists put it, "the politicians' utilization of religion for political ends became the most contentious issue. This was the single most important justification the military advanced when they intervened in 1960–1961 and later" (Heper 1991, 49; see also Weiker 1963). During the 1950s, the DP government reached an implicit modus vivendi between religion and politics, which offered toleration of private worship and at the same time the enforcement of public and political secularism. The unruffled behavior of religious actors in that decade demonstrates acceptance of this understanding regarding the role of religion in the state. However, the Kemalist coalition did not accept this arrangement and imposed its nonpluralistic worldview on society in complete disregard of the will of the people and in violation of the basic tenets of democracy.

The 1960 Coup and Its Aftermath

The 1960 coup marked a clear break in Turkish democracy. Immediately following the coup, the Turkish Armed Forces (TAF) appointed former Chief of Staff General Cemal Gürsel as head of state, banned all political parties, imprisoned the DP leadership,[18] and founded a Committee of National Unity (CNU)—composed mainly of military officers, with a few appointed civilians—to rule Turkey. Compared with other military interventions, such as those seen in Latin American countries, the Turkish 1960 coup was mild. The military seized power for a relatively short term and exercised little violence against the populace. The TAF quickly appointed a group of intellectuals to write a new constitution with improved checks and balances and better protection of civil rights. This was meant to overcome the deficiencies of the 1924 constitution, which had enabled the authoritarian tendencies of the former government toward the end of its term (Weiker 1963).

Interestingly, the TAF did not impose a hard-core Kemalist stance toward religion. Instead, it embraced a combination of strict laicism along with respect for the cultural role of religion in society. This policy was intended to gain legitimacy and prevent opposition to its rule by either Islamist or radical leftist groups (Cizre-Sakallioğlu 1996, 237). Indeed, immediately after the coup, the CNU announced that it had no intention of interfering in people's religious beliefs and practices. At the same time, it stated that political parties and individuals would be punished severely if they brought religion into politics.[19] Indeed, the generals did not hesitate to act decisively against what they perceived as religious provocations. For instance, in December 1960 the military dealt with fifty-five sheikhs and *aghas* (religious leaders) who had voiced support for an Islamic politics by exiling them from their homes in the more religious eastern regions of Turkey to the more secular western part of the country, where their power would be diluted.[20]

This dual approach was maintained in the wording of the 1961 constitution. Article 2 deliberately coupled Kemalist principles with reference to democracy and an acknowledgment of human rights: "The Turkish Republic is a nationalistic, democratic, secular, and social state governed by the rule of law, based on human rights and the fundamental tenets set forth in the preamble."[21] Article 19 followed the dual treatment of religion. It granted citizens freedom of and from religion, forbade any use of religion for political gain, and gave the constitutional court authority to close down associations and parties that violated this restriction.

The 1961 constitution also contained an elaborate chapter on human rights, reordered the structure of government, and provided more checks on the arbitrary powers of the executive branch. On the whole, it was more supportive of democracy and liberal principles than the one it replaced, and facilitated the emergence of Turkish civil society. As a result, in the 1960s and 1970s, Turkey witnessed considerable growth in the number of political parties, interest groups, and civil associations, including religious ones (Toprak 1996, 91; Özçetin et al. 2014, 7). At the same time, the new constitution endowed the state with the power to abolish collective activity centered around religion or even identified with religion. Of course, given that the line between cultural manifestations of religion and manipulation of religion for political gain is inherently blurry, this laid the ground for recurrent disputes between the Kemalist establishment and religious actors in years to come (Landau 2004, 137).

The CNU transferred the government back into the hands of civilian politicians following national elections in October 1961. But it did not retreat entirely from the political scene. The elections positioned the RPP as the biggest party, with 37 percent of the vote, while the Justice Party (JP, Adalet Partisi), a newly formed party that took the place politically of the banned DP, came second with 35 percent. Two smaller parties each won 15 percent of the vote. This result was a clear sign that a majority of the public did not want to see the Kemalist RPP in power. Nevertheless, the military insisted that RPP leader İsmet İnönü become prime minister. Consequently, between 1961 and 1964 the RPP led several shaky coalition governments. While in power, the RPP reversed some of the DP's proreligion policies and hardened its stance on civil expressions of religion. Among other sanctions, it resumed raids and criminal investigations against followers of religious orders and reactionary sheikhs and halted the construction of new Imam Hatip schools despite growing demand by the public for this type of education.[22] The most restrictive policy the RPP came out with, however, was imposing a weekly state-sanctioned sermon that all imams were required to read during Friday prayers, which eliminated the imams' autonomous authority to preach.[23] These policies were by no means popular and were largely responsible for steady erosion of political support for the RPP until its resounding defeat in the 1965 elections.

The 1965 elections brought the JP to power. Here, too, the treatment of religion alone does not explain the JP's popularity. As with its predecessor, the DP, the JP's electoral success relied on a combination of appealing policies on the economy and religion and the political skills of its leader, Süleyman Demirel. A third reason, unique to the JP, was its strategy of operating a broad platform of grassroots activity in the party's political campaigns, mainly through clientelism. The JP had built a network of services for new migrants from the countryside (*gecekondu*), who were concentrated in slums on the outskirts of the large urban centers. These services ranged from employment to marriage registration and were operated by local party activists. The party's political base was in the same segments in Turkish society that had formerly supported the DP—peasants and urban laborers as well as a small commercial and industrial sector, which together represented an alternative to the old elite (Sherwood 1967; Özler 2000, 44).

The JP lacked a strong ideological core and instead developed a pragmatist and flexible political agenda. This was particularly true with regard to religion. The party's policies in this realm reflected its recognition of the power of religion in Turkish society, as well as an attempt to appeal to its traditional electoral base. As Sherwood argued: "The Justice Party's attitude toward religion cannot be separated from its public appeal to the peasantry. . . . The peasants simply list[ed] mosques along with water, roads, educational opportunity for their children, and government support of agricultural prices as the things they expect[ed] from any government or party soliciting their votes" (Sherwood 1967, 58–59).

Some of the party's public religious gestures could be understood as provocative. Most controversial was Demirel's regular participation in Friday prayers along with the top party echelon and his close advisers (Cizre-Sakallioğlu 1996, 240). However, Demirel was a believer and observant Muslim long before he became prime minister, making it unlikely that this was just an opportunistic political act. Likewise, before the elections Demirel was known to use religious rhetoric and emphasize his connections with the leadership of the Nurculuk movement. Other proreligious acts included the foundation of four new Islamic institutes of higher education in 1966,[24] and, in 1968, the government's participation in a pan-Islamic conference in Morocco.[25] This latter was in clear contradiction with ongoing Kemalist efforts to isolate Turkish society from the rest of the Muslim world.

These policies were opposed by the Kemalist camp. Shortly after the JP formed its 1965 government, a group of scholars from faculties of law and political science throughout the country submitted a petition affirming secularism as the most important principle of the republic and criticizing the allegedly antisecular intentions of the new government.[26] A similar petition was signed by the Kemalist-oriented Federation of Turkish Teachers' Associations (TÖDEF).[27] In addition to frequent critiques by the parliamentarian opposition, there were many expressions of antireligious sentiment by high-ranking, supposedly apolitical public servants, such as President Cevdet Sunay (another former chief of staff),[28] incumbent chief of the General Staff Cemal Tural,[29] president of the Court of Appeals İmran Öktem,[30] and the rector of Istanbul University.[31] Their statements reflected the nonpluralistic perceptions of this group and its qualified respect for democratic principles.

By the end of the 1960s, mass migration from the village to the city and the formation of new spaces for religion in society made circumstances opportune for two intertwined developments. In contradiction to the assumptions of modernization theory, this migration did not secularize the formerly rural population. Instead, the latter brought their cultural foundations to the urban centers and intensified the secular–religious divide in Turkey's big metropolises. In the social realm, the empowerment of religion generated more activities by Islamic civil society associations. Religious actors came to realize the power of civic engagement in the public sphere and exploited it on various occasions. Examples of this trend, by individuals and collectivities, included demonstrations by religious students against Ankara University's expulsion of two women students who refused to remove their headscarves,[32] a woman lawyer's insistence on covering her hair during court sessions,[33] and the demand by a religiously affiliated trade union, Hak İş, that workers should be allowed one hour a day for worship.[34] One must add the growing number of faith-based civil society associations, especially in the domains of philanthropy and education; by 1968, these reached an impressive number of 10,730 registered associations, making up 28.4 percent of all associations in Turkey. The increasing popularity of religious orders despite being formally illegal, especially the powerful Nurcu and Nakşibendi orders, contributed to enhancing the place of religion in society. This entire social matrix benefited from supportive coverage by religiously affiliated media, which included several newspapers and periodicals (Landau 1976, 8–9).

The other equally significant development was the foundation in 1970 of a political party, theNational Order Party (NOP; Milli Nizam Partisi), which placed religious concerns at the core of its agenda. Although this party was abolished in May 1971 by the constitutional court, it "played a key role in the re-politicization of Islam by enlarging the channels of political representation" (Yildiz 2003, 187). The NOP served as an archetype for a series of subsequent religious parties with the generic name Milli Görüş (the Parties of National Outlook), which—despite being periodically shut down by the constitutional court—demonstrated resilience and durability in their manpower, religious rhetoric, and electoral base.[35]

While religious civil society activities represented a resurgence of religion from below, the formation of religious political parties was aimed at transforming from above the cultural role of religion in Turkish society into a political one while benefiting from the broad social power base provided by religious civil society associations. The closeness of these developments is apparent in the vibrant connections forged between religious orders and religious politicians. In fact, the NOP was formed with the approval and blessing of the influential Sheikh Kotku, leader of the Nakşibendi order. Since then, the Milli Görüş parties have been dependent to some extent on the support of this order (Mardin 2006, 15).

With the advent of religious political parties, the engagement of religious actors in the secular state became more intensive. This was especially true after the National Salvation Party (NSP, Milli Selamet Partisi), succeeded in winning 11.8 percent of the vote in the 1973 elections and became a minor

partner in the RPP government. The RPP was compelled to accept the NSP
in the coalition due to cold political calculation: without the support of the
NSP, the RPP would not have been able to recapture the government. The
RPP-NSP partnership provided the religious camp real political leverage for
the first time. The founder of the Milli Görüş, Necmettin Erbakan, became
deputy prime minister, and other party members were put in charge of seven
portfolios in the cabinet, including the important ministries of State, Justice,
the Interior, and Commerce (Landau 1976, 31–34). Even more important
was the fact that the Kemalist RPP was willing to join in coalition with a
religious faction, thereby providing the NSP, its followers, and its ideology
further legitimacy in Turkish politics.

To protect itself from being dissolved by the constitutional court (like
the NOP), the NSP refrained from basing itself unequivocally on Islam.
Nevertheless, various written documents and public speeches by party leaders
suggest that the NSP was Islamist in all but name. Their official agenda proclaimed that Turkey must remain loyal to its glorious (i.e., Islamic) heritage
instead of imitating other civilizations. It distinguished itself from capitalism
and socialism as materialist and amoral ideologies, in contrast to the party's
strong moral (i.e., Islamic) foundations. Finally, it maintained that secularism
should be interpreted in a way that was not hostile to religion and that the
state should protect the right of individuals to observe their religion and allocate
significant resources to moral (i.e., Islamic) education (Landau 1976, 13–15).[36]

Recognizing the political leverage that came with participation in
government, the NSP joined every coalition government between 1973
and 1980, whether led by the RPP on the left or the JP on the right. This
participation generated a momentous change in the public role of religion. Religious demands were put forward explicitly, and partnership with
mainstream parties provided the NSP with legitimacy and strong political
backing. Three weeks after the elections of 1973, Erbakan announced that
the government would build eighty-four new Imam Hatip schools in the
coming year.[37] In quick succession, the NSP minister of State, Suleiman
Arif Emre, announced that public TV and radio would devote more time to
religion and morals,[38] and the Ministry of Tourism produced and distributed
an Islamic map of Turkey featuring religious destinations.[39] The NSP leadership emphasized religious sentiments in their behavior and rhetoric. For
instance, Erbakan's first foreign visit in office was to Saudi Arabia, a clear
expression of Turkey's natural ties with the Islamic Arab world.[40] Likewise,
in 1976, the NSP pushed the JP-led government to become a full member
in the Organisation of Islamic Cooperation.[41] The party also led a campaign

for enforcing Islamic values in society that included restrictions on alcohol consumption and more severe punishments against obscenity and pornography (Landau 1976, 40–42).[42]

The ability of the NSP to achieve many of its political demands was rooted in the balancing role it held in the political system. The two big parties (the JP and RPP) were willing to make far-reaching concessions to win its support—a situation similar to that of the Haredi parties in Israel after 1977 (see chapter 8). Furthermore, the NSP exploited its position in government to strengthen its political power base by putting party followers in the administration, as well as through indoctrination in the education system, again in similarity to state penetration tactics by the religious-Zionist settler movement in Israel (more on that in chapters 8 and 9). The party dismissed many senior civil servants from ministries under its control and appointed party supporters in their place. This was accompanied by demands to expand the Diyanet by 25,000 new positions, the appointment of 5,000 new imams in less than a year, and the massive construction of new mosques throughout the country (Landau 1976, 43).[43] Likewise, the party understood that students of religious schools were more likely to become party followers in the future (Sarfati 2014). Hence, party leadership publicly encouraged the populace to participate in religious education and funneled state resources toward this goal.[44]

These measures fortified the religious camp but also raised anxiety in the secular camp that Turkey would fall into extremist hands and lose its Kemalist character. In response, Kemalists employed myriad tactics to block the increasing power of the religious actors, including the law and the courts. Erbakan was accused by the state prosecutor of manipulating religion for political gain and violating the constitutional principle of secularism and the laws banning the use of religion by political parties.[45] This is notable because a public servant, in service of Kemalist ideas, felt secure enough to raise public allegations against an incumbent deputy prime minister. Other measures included the use of presidential veto power to block proreligious legislation;[46] the legislature's rejection of bills that gave Imam Hatip graduates the same accreditation as graduates from public high schools; and the imprisonment of religious functionaries in the media and the bureaucracy for alleged antisecular activities.[47] Intolerance toward religious political activity included occasional violence whose perpetrators remained unknown, particularly the 1970 bombing of the NOP's local branch in Eskişehir.[48]

Despite repressive activities by the Kemalist strongholds, religious actors refrained from violent and antidemocratic responses. Until the late

1970s, there are no records of violence or extralegal challenges against the regime by religious groups. This reality demonstrates that extending the boundaries of civil society above a minimum bound of acceptance and accommodating social groups (religious or otherwise) into a more pluralist system is likely to produce a more democratic and peaceful society and concentrate efforts to promote group interests through legal parliamentarian channels. Also important, NSP presence in government, in cooperation with religious groups in civil society, promoted pluralism and the inclusiveness of Turkish democracy. The common goals and achievements of religious political parties that took part in government and civil society organizations that worked from below challenge scholarly estimates according to which religious associations promote democracy, whereas religious groups that ally with the state work against democratic governance (Huber, Rueschemeyer, and Stephens 1993).

The End of the First Democratic Period and the Growth of Religious Militancy

The relatively constructive collaboration between the ruling parties and religious segments in society did not last long. It fell victim to the comprehensive instability that plagued Turkish society and politics in the late 1970s. Starting in the 1960s, Turkish politics witnessed the emergence of radical left-wing movements that advocated Maoist and Marxist ideas and competed with right-wing and religious factions for the support of the *gecekondu* (Özler 2000). This competition radicalized all sides, quickly deteriorated to large-scale violence, and brought Turkey to the verge of civil war by the end of the 1970s. Only within this context can one understand the relative radicalization in rhetoric and behavior of religious actors during this time, which stands in palpable contrast to their moderation following their accommodation into politics.

Leftist ideas became popular among labor unions and were also adopted by intellectuals, academicians, and students, who spread them through public debates and publications in left-wing journals (Zürcher 2005, 297–98). In 1968, a group of extreme leftist intellectuals formed the National Democratic Revolution (NDR, Milli Demokratik Devrim)—a radical movement founded on the presumption that only violent struggle could bring revolutionary change to Turkey. The NDR instigated urban guerilla warfare throughout Turkey, intending to destabilize society and eventually alter the political order.

The primary right-wing platform was the Milliyetçi Hareket Partisi (MHP, Party of Nationalist Action).[49] This party was headed by the nationalistic Colonel Alparslan Turkeş, whose militant ideas had led to his expulsion from the military in the 1960 coup. The MHP advocated an anticommunist and radical nationalistic agenda. It formed an extreme youth group, the Bozkurtlar (Grey Wolves), which engaged in paramilitary training, terrorized the streets, and assaulted leftist politicians, media figures, and students (Ahmad 1993, 163).

Each political faction was involved in two simultaneous struggles, one against the political center and state institutions and another against its ideological rivals. Beginning in 1968, radicalization on both sides deteriorated into recurrent violent clashes between the factions and with state security forces. Both the left- and right-wing factions shifted their political weight from parliamentarian politics to "street politics," and the government seemed paralyzed and unable to control the violence.

In 1971, the political stalemate stimulated the military to intervene in politics for the second time. On March 12, 1971, the TAF forwarded an ultimatum to Prime Minister Demirel threatening seizure of the government should the civil authorities fail to bring stability to the country. Demirel resigned, and the generals appointed a technocratic government. Several parties, including the religious NOP,[50] were outlawed by the constitutional court, and the TAF cracked down on various forms of perceived political opposition, including the religious orders. Over the next few years, the armed forces amended the 1961 constitution and made it more restrictive, while expanding the powers of the military-controlled National Security Council.

Government was transferred back to civil politicians in January 1974, but the polarization and levels of violence did not decrease. To make things worse, Turkey's invasion of northern Cyprus in July 1974, prompted by a Cypriot coup that sought to annex the island to Greece, generated considerable international criticism against the new Turkish government and consumed considerable efforts from the already occupied Turkish security apparatus. Toward the end of the 1970s, violence became rampant, with daily street fights and more than 1,000 political assassinations a year. The period between 1978 and 1980 saw a daily average of 20 fatalities and a total death toll of 5,241 people from terrorism (Akşin 2007, 279).

The religious parties were ideologically closer to the political right and occasionally joined it in specific social or political campaigns, especially after MHP leader Turkeş abandoned his initial Kemalist stance and began emphasizing the role of Islam in Turkish identity (Zürcher 2005, 300).

Importantly, through most of the 1970s, religious groups were less involved in physical violence compared with the left- and right-wing movements (Landau 2004, 160)—a fact that can be explained only when we consider the accommodation of religious actors in formal politics during this time and their significant achievements in government, which created a strong incentive to play by the rules. But toward the late 1970s, the political behavior of religious actors changed dramatically. The radicalizing trends in Turkish society and, no less important, the empowering impact of the Islamic Revolution in Iran in 1979 pushed religious actors to extremism and led to a series of events that challenged the state and hastened the military takeover in 1980.

The first of these incidents happened in the city of Kahranmaraş in December 1978, when a group of Sunni Muslims calling for Turkey to become an Islamic state attacked Alevi supporters of the RPP.[51] More than 100 people were killed in these riots, which only ended when the authorities placed the city under martial law.[52] This was followed by assassinations of secularist figures, beginning with the journalist Abdi İpekçi, editor of the daily *Milliyet*, in February 1979;[53] other notable figures presumably killed by religious militants included Kemalist intellectuals Cavit Orhan Tütengil and Ümit Kaftancıoğlu. The rhetoric of the religious leadership became more revolutionary and provocative. In September 1980, the entire NSP leadership led a rally in Konya, where demonstrators carried banners and shouted slogans in Arabic advocating a return to theocracy and Sharia law.[54]

The events in Konya and the revolution in Iran were used as justifications for another military coup. On September 12, 1980, three days after the Konya rally, the military seized control of the government for the third time in twenty years. Thus began the longest period of direct military rule in Turkish history. Interestingly, despite the relative moderation of religious actors compared with the leftist and rightist factions, the armed forces' formal statement justifying the coup stressed the need to contain the threat of religious fundamentalism (Ahmad 1981; Sunar and Toprak 1983).

Start of the Second Democratic Period (1980–2000): Illiberal Religious Empowerment

The TAF banned all political parties in 1981 and authored a new constitution in 1982. The constitution reaffirmed the nationalistic tendencies of the Kemalist establishment and reversed the civil orientation of the 1961 constitution. The new constitution was approved by referendum in October 1982, though the prereferendum campaign was decidedly one-sided, with opponents prevented from making their case. The TAF also restricted organs of civil society such as trade unions, professional guilds, religious associations, and the like and sought to consolidate central control at the expense of autonomous associational activity (Yeşilada 1988, 352–54).

Interestingly, on the issue of secularism, the 1982 constitution was marked with deliberate ambiguity. On one hand, the character of the Turkish Republic, including the guiding principle of secularism, is secured in Articles 1–4 with no possibility of amendment.[55] On the other hand, the preamble to the constitution prohibits any worldview that deviates from "Turkish historical and moral values"—wording that deliberately departs from Atatürk's focus on rationality and science and potentially opens the door to integration of religious values into state policies (Heper 1991, 49). Also, Article 24 mandates the instruction of religious culture and moral education in the curricula of primary and secondary schools.

The nuanced approach of the new constitution toward religion was only one manifestation of a more comprehensive change toward religion during the 1980s, with long-term and partially unexpected outcomes. Until 1980, efforts to integrate religion into Turkish public culture were carried forward mainly by religious associations and parties. In contrast, the postcoup period was marked by intentional empowerment of religion from above. The military and its civilian allies leaned toward the conservative right and perceived the left as the major threat against the Turkish republic. After the coup these actors sought to give more recognition to religion as a check against the left. This policy resulted in an unprecedented expansion of Islam into politics and culminated in 1996 with the foundation of a short-lived coalition government led by the religious Welfare Party (WP, Refah Partisi).

As in earlier decades, the pace of modernization also had an effect on the state–religion interaction. Yet contrary to mainstream modernist predictions, modernization empowered religion in Turkish society. Turgut Özal's governments during the 1980s were successful in bringing unprecedented levels of development that penetrated all segments of society. Modernization also affected the religious factions in what might be considered a superficial manner. While exploiting the material advantages of modernization, religious actors chose not to adopt a pluralist worldview or seek peaceful coexistence with the secular elements in society. Encouraged by the successful experience of Islamists in Iran and the recent empowerment of religion on the domestic Turkish scene, the religious leadership adopted a militant and illiberal goal—to replace the Kemalist hegemony with an Islamic one.

During this time, the Kemalist and Islamist factions conceived the ideological disagreements between them as a zero-sum game interaction with clear losers and winners. It was not integration that religious actors sought but the formation of a wholly new system. In reaction, the Kemalist establishment used its coercive capabilities to secure its hegemonic status. In the absence of efficient pluralistic mechanisms to resolve intergroup disputes, this phase, like the preceding one, ended in 1997 with military intervention and the reinstallation of a coercive secular order.

The Turkish Islamic Synthesis and Ascendance of Religion in Politics

In the aftermath of the 1980 coup, the generals sought an ideological counterforce to leftist ideologies that would appeal to the populace and provide the state with an effective social control mechanism. They found what they were looking for in the Turkish Islamic synthesis (TIS, Turk Islam Sentezi)—an ideology that was developed in the 1960s by the Aydınlar Ocağı (Hearth of Intellectuals), a group of nationalist intellectuals who sought to forge a new social order by drawing on elements of the country's pre-Islamic Turkic heritage and cultural Islam. The TIS envisioned a union between religion and state, a society built on the foundations of Islam, and a coalition between the military and civil government. Adherents of this ideology also identified groups of enemies that must be controlled or eliminated by the state, including atheists, communists, materialists, separatists, Western humanists, minority religions, and progressive intellectuals (Akin and Karasapan 1988, 18; Yeşilada 1988, 365; Çetinsaya 1999, 373–74). The TIS served as Turkey's leading ideological platform well into the 1990s.

The adoption of the TIS by pivotal partners in the Kemalist alliance was a deviation from the original teachings of Atatürk and his vision of republican Turkey. In this regard, one scholar has rightly noted that "indeed, under the laws which the secular governments propagated during the 1980s, Atatürk himself would no doubt have been arrested for insulting the Prophet and hurting the feelings of the religious population" (Lapidot 1996, 68). The adoption of the TIS by the TAF thus generated tensions in the Kemalist alliance. In particular, the generals, who had always perceived themselves as guardians of the republic and the Kemalist ideology, were accused by intellectuals of betraying the legacy of Mustafa Kemal. Alparslan İsikli, deputy president of the Atatürk Thought Association, told me how Kemalist intellectuals perceived the generals following the 1980 coup: "The generals who issued the 12 September coup did some things that were bad for Turkey but represented themselves as Kemalists. That is, they implemented a policy that was exactly in contradiction of Kemalist principles, but they still represented themselves as Kemalists."[56]

In foreign policy, adoption of the TIS meant ending Turkey's tendency to isolate itself from the rest of the Islamic world. During this time, Turkey became an active member in the community of Islamic nations, hosted Islamic conferences,[57] participated in a peace commission of Islamic countries aimed at ending the Iran–Iraq war,[58] and expressed its solidarity with Islamic countries.[59] In the domestic arena, the government introduced compulsory religious courses in public education, erected numerous mosques, founded new Islamic institutes of higher education, published a book on Atatürk's attitude toward Islam, and expanded the authority of the Diyanet. To be sure, these measures were not intended to fully "set religion free" in the Turkish public sphere. Rather, they were designed to exploit Turks' religious identity and meld it with national feelings as a common denominator for social identity and public order. At least formally, the military sought to preserve political secularism, but the relative resurgence of religion soon confronted the Kemalist elite with new challenges.

Military rule ended with the approval of the 1982 constitution and national elections in 1983. Before handing the reins of government back to civilian politicians, the military took three important measures in an attempt to stabilize the political scene. First, the new constitution set an entry threshold of 10 percent for parties competing for seats in the GNA. The rationale was to make it impossible for relatively small political interest groups—essentially leftist, Kurdish, and religious parties—to obtain parliamentary representation. Second, in an effort to prevent a return to the populism and radicalization that had characterized politics before 1980, the military prohibited the participation of old (i.e., pre-1980) politicians and parties in the 1983 elections. Third, the military imposed the creation of large electoral blocs by approving only three new political parties. Two of these, the Halki Partisi (People's Party) and Miliyetçi Demokrasi Partisi (Nationalist Democracy Party), were established with the backing of the TAF, and the third—the Anavatan Partisi (ANAP, Motherland Party)—was formed independently by Turgut Özal and other figures.

To the surprise of many, ANAP obtained 45 percent of the vote, which gave it a majority of seats in the GNA and the ability to form a single-party government. ANAP's popularity can be credited first and foremost to the charismatic appeal of its leader, Turgut Özal, his proven economic skills as the minister in charge of financial reconstruction under the military government, and his political shrewdness and good relationship with the TAF's high command. Also important, many Turks were attracted to ANAP's traditional agenda and endorsement of the TIS. Özal himself was an observant Muslim and a former member of the religious NSP, and he maintained overt connections with the Nakşibendi religious order, of which his brother was a leading activist.

Özal became the most prominent politician in Turkey until his death in 1993. He served as prime minister between 1983 and 1989 and president from 1989 to 1993. His political agenda rested on four somewhat contradictory pillars—conservative Islam, nationalism, economic liberalism, and social democracy. In practice, this agenda meant "a social structure that will still be dependent upon moral-religious (Sunni) values of the past, while simultaneously proposing dramatic changes to the economy and prosperity of the country" (Kalaycıoğlu 2002, 46).

During Özal's leadership, modernization in Turkey reached new levels, with massive industrialization and urbanization throughout the country. The business sector applauded his economic measures, and a new group of Anatolian businessmen emerged from district cities such as Keysari, Konya, and Gaziantep. This group, commonly known as the "Anatolian bourgeoisie" or "Anatolian tigers," consisted of entrepreneurs and small business owners who, despite their prosperity and influence on the Turkish economy, preserved a traditional religious culture and way of life (Karakas 2007, 20).

Özal also promoted the TIS and skillfully exploited his personal faith for political gain—for instance, publicizing his participation in the Hajj, the pilgrimage to Mecca (for which he was accused by his opponents of manipulating religion for politics). His government granted the religious orders semi-legal status, and it approved the construction of a mosque in the legislature building in Ankara, an act with important symbolic meaning.[60] Islam's influence in Özal's government came to the fore in a scandal known as the Rabita Affair, when an investigative journalist, Uğur Mumcu, revealed that the Turkish government was secretly accepting large amounts of money from the Saudi-based Rabitat al-'Alam al-Islami (Muslim World League), for various religious purposes. Indeed, the mosque in the legislature building and the Arabic studies program at the Middle East Technical

University in Ankara were both funded by the Saudis. These connections revealed the mingling of Saudi money with Turkish politics and exposed the hidden relations between the Saudi donors and Özal and his family (Lapidot 1995, 15–16).

The exploitation of people's religious identity from above resulted in a growing volume of religious activities from below. The proreligious measures taken first by the military and later by Özal's governments, enabled an unprecedented presence of the Islamic religion in public life in the Turkish Republic. As Margulies and Yildizoğlu noted: "No one who spends even a few days in Turkey can fail to notice the larger crowd in mosques, the greater number of people wearing religious dress, the atmosphere during the holy month of Ramadan. The activities of the religious orders, particularly the Süleymanci and the Nakşibendi, cover a whole range of areas" (Margulies and Yildizoğlu 1988, 17). The impact of the Tarikats on the revival of religion also grew as the orders exploited modern recruitment techniques. The orders provided social services such as dormitories and Quran classes for poor students, established a popular TV channel, and published numerous books and the widely circulated daily newspapers *Zaman* and *Milli Gazette*. These measures were complemented by more traditional activities, such as gatherings in mosques, home visits, and discussion groups. The more these orders grew in autonomy and reach, the stronger they became in terms of political power and ability to lobby the government (Ayata 1996, 49–50).

Importantly, the 1980s saw the ascendance to power of the Gülen movement, an Islamic socioreligious movement led by Fethullah Gülen, a student of the late Saidi Nursi, the former head of the Nurculuk movement. The Gülen movement soon became the most powerful Islamic movement in Turkey, with branches in the Balkans, the Central Asian republics, Middle Eastern countries, and centers of Turkish immigration in the European Union, such as Germany. The movement operated a network of social services, known as the Hizmet, which included schools, Quran courses, and various welfare services. These provided the order with a large clientele and advanced its influence in Turkish society and beyond (Yavuz and Esposito 2003; Hendrick 2013; Marty 2015) (more on this later).

The End of the Second Democratic Period

The broad resurgence of religion brought the so-called holy alliance, a religious faction within the ANAP, to adopt a more radical proreligious stance that no longer fit with the pragmatist line of the party. In the late 1980s, this group withdrew its support from the ANAP and joined the WP, which was founded in July 1983 as a substitute for the dissolved NSP. In 1987, Necmettin Erbakan was allowed back into politics after being tried and acquitted on charges of antisecular activities, and he became head of the WP.

The WP embodied a new type of religious political representation. First, instead of being run by a small elitist group, it was first and foremost a social movement that concentrated on grassroots activity, which was translated to the national political level. The party expanded its political power base by developing and training a sophisticated network of local activists with good familiarity with their potential electorate and initiated activities that won the sympathy of the street, such as paying visits to mourning families or assisting poor families with food and money (Ayata 1996; Yavuz 1997; White 2002).

Second, the party offered an innovative political agenda—one that combined traditional communitarian values with economic development and technological progress and was flexible enough to attract people from different regions and socioeconomic strata. Public support for the party came from four segments in Turkish society: Islamic intellectuals, Sunni Kurds, squatter town dwellers, and the new Anatolian bourgeoisie. For each of these groups, the party tailored a distinct political agenda with fine-tuned emphases. This flexibility, together with the relative autonomy of local branches to design their own policies in accordance with the needs of their communities, provided the party with much electoral appeal (Yavuz 1997, 79–80).

Third, the WP harnessed the economic hardships of the lower strata to its religious agenda. The party exploited the resentment of the general populace against the negative effects of Turkey's integration into world markets, especially the growing gap between the haves and have-nots. The party positioned itself as supporting the Siyah Türkler (literally, Black Turks), referring to all Turks who had been sidelined by the Kemalist state since its foundation, against the Beyaz Türkler (White Turks). This polarized description of society was a powerful recruitment tool for citizens who felt alienated from the Turkish state for cultural and economic reasons (Sumer 2003; Demiralp 2012). By this means, the WP leadership sought to challenge the Kemalist coalition with an alternative paradigm or social vision led by its emerging counterelite and backed by three key social players—women, engineers, and Islamic intellectuals. Educated Muslim women were an important component in the rhetoric of the new elite. Their ability to fuse a modern lifestyle, higher education, and careers with adherence to a traditional, religious-based worldview visibly discredited the Kemalist perception of an embedded inequality toward women in traditional Islamic culture. Islamist leaders with engineering degrees, including Erbakan, were important in proving that Islamist worldviews did not stand in opposition to modernity, higher education, and technological progress. Finally, the religious elite benefited from the intellectual backing of Islamic thinkers such as Ali Bulaç, Ismet Özal, Abdurrahman Dilipak, and Ahmet Davutoğlu, who developed nonapologetic arguments and sophisticated critiques of Turkey's sweeping adoption of Western culture (Göle 1997; Karasipahi 2009).

Religious actors did not reject modernization altogether. Quite the opposite: they adopted and used modern tools to expand their penetration into society and politics. In fact, the Turkish case suggests once more that, contrary to the arguments of modernization theory, modernization was a key factor in the reappearance of religion in Turkey from the 1980s. Indeed, the resurgence of religion and its new methods of engagement with the state and society should be understood as a consequence and manifestation of modernization rather than as antithetical to it.

The WP demonstrated impressive growth in electoral support over a relatively short time span. In 1987, the first election in which the WP competed, it garnered 7.2 percent of the total vote. This was lower than the 10 percent threshold and did not grant it seats in the legislature. In the 1991 election, to secure representation in the GNA, the WP ran in alliance with the nationalist MHP; the two parties together won 16.2 percent of the vote, which translated into 62 seats in the GNA. In the local elections of 1994, the party made considerable progress, winning 19.7 percent of the total vote and mayoral positions in twenty-nine large cities, including Istanbul and Ankara, which had until then been considered bedrocks of Kemalism in Turkey. In the national elections in December 1995, the WP ran on its own and won a convincing victory with 21.4 percent of the total vote, making it the biggest party in the GNA with 158 seats. On June 28, 1996, after half a year in which the center-right parties ANAP and the Doğru Yol Partisi (True Path Party), struggled and failed to form a stable government without the WP, the True Path Party agreed to join a coalition with the WP and Erbakan became the first Islamist prime minister in Republican Turkey.[61]

The ascent of Erbakan and the WP seemed to mark a new beginning in Turkish politics. Indeed, for some political analysts, the rise to power of a religious party was thought to reflect the final stage of democratic consolidation in Turkey (Özbudun 1996). However, this hope proved too

optimistic. The expanding political influence of the religious camp intimi-
dated the Kemalist elite and spurred it to act decisively against the emerging
challenge. On June 17, 1997, in the face of pressure from the TAF, Erbakan's
government fell and he resigned, less than a year after taking office.

The demise of this short-lived experiment in religious empowerment
at the helm of government can be attributed to hegemonic tendencies and a
disrespect for pluralism in the Kemalist and religious camps. On the Kemalist
side, by the late 1980s the military and its partners began to realize that
their initial intentions to empower religion through the TIS while keeping
it "civilized" and under state control had gotten out of hand. In response,
the TIS was abandoned and the Kemalist alliance turned their efforts to
containing the expanding power of Islam. Beginning in 1986, the legal system
and security forces resumed their assaults against the religious orders and
other religious associations, including arresting activists. These were accompanied by decisive statements from the military and legal apparatus about
the republic's commitment to secularism.[62] The military higher command
initiated a twice-yearly procedure of discharging officers involved in religious
activity. In addition, the heated debate over headscarves in public spaces
and especially in the education system resumed, climaxing in a decision by
the constitutional court to overrule new legislation that allowed women to
cover their heads in universities. Like the hat reform more than sixty years
earlier, this issue generated significant resentment that took expression in
rallies, demonstrations, and legal appeals.[63]

The WP did not embrace a pluralist worldview either. Although the
party was very effective in exploiting modern means of obtaining mass
support, it failed to adopt pluralist elements of democracy. The party's leadership demonstrated intolerance toward other identities and worldviews and
dismissed progressive values such as gender equality and religious diversity.
That is, while embracing procedural or electoral democracy as "the only
game in town," the WP did not adopt what Fareed Zakaria (1997, 2004)
calls the legacy of constitutional liberalism. This approach positioned them
in opposition to both Kemalism and democracy and exacerbated the tension
between the two camps. In addition, with the exception of a few leading
liberal figures in the party (such as Bahri Zengin, Ali Bulaç, and Abdullah
Gül) the mainstream leadership was strict and conservative—a mind-set that
may have been an outgrowth of their longtime conflictual interaction with
the Kemalist state. As Hakan Yavuz describes it: "Having been socialized
by the rather authoritarian Kemalist tradition, the conservative core leadership of the party, which includes Necmettin Erbakan, Oğuzhan Aşilturk

and Şevket Kazan, reacted negatively to this openness and insisted on the subordination of cultural and political cleavages in Turkish society to a single ideology, state-centric Islam. Clearly there are several ambiguous trends within the WP and the current leadership represents the least democratic characteristics" (Yavuz 1997, 76).

Undemocratic tendencies were reflected in the WP's rhetoric and behavior before the party won the 1995 election, especially by Erbakan. For instance, in January 1987, he took part in a protest against the headscarf ban, during which demonstrators shouted in favor of Sharia and jihad and clashed with the armed forces.[64] In March 1988, Erbakan spoke before 25,000 people at a violent demonstration against Ankara's ties with Israel, in which protesters burned Israeli flags.[65] On another occasion, he provoked the secularists and intensified hostility by promising to build a mosque in the middle of Taksim Square, the central square of Istanbul and a symbol of the Kemalist revolution.[66] Other statements, while not antidemocratic, provoked the Kemalist establishment and raised its anxiety levels. For instance, a WP deputy argued that "the official regime in Turkey is Kemalist secular dictatorship,"[67] and other party deputies suggested that the TAF's restriction of worship in its ranks be declared hostile to Islam,[68] statements that were undoubtedly perceived by the Kemalist establishment as a direct attack on its values and legitimacy.

The WP's intolerant worldview spread to its grassroots and resulted in fanatical behavior by some religious activists. Jenny White's account of an interview with a WP activist is very telling in this regard:

> Perhaps I was the first to bring it up, when I tried to explain why Welfare scared many secularist Turks, that people thought that Welfare wanted *Sharia* law, not democracy. Much to my surprise, instead of taking the opportunity to demur, Halil fired into a heated defense of *Sharia*. "We have to follow Allah's design." Referring to our previous conversation, I asked him whether Allah's design was democracy. He was momentarily flustered but soon caught up again in sloganlike exclamations about the requirement to follow Allah's will. His voice was hard and almost spitting, his eyes steely, his back arched as if daring me to disagree. (White 2002, 12)

Nonpluralistic sentiments spread widely and included decisions by directors of religious schools that students who did not fast during Ramadan would be disqualified for scholarships or would be given failing grades in a Quran course,[69] threats to judges who conducted court cases against religious activists,[70] and physical violence in university facilities against nonobserving students.[71] Most serious were deadly attacks against intellectuals and political figures with differing viewpoints and against religious minorities. The prosecular journalists Bahriye Uçok, Turan Dursun, and Çetin Emeç were assassinated in 1990, and Uğur Mumcu—who had exposed the Rabita Affair—was assassinated in January 1993.[72] The Neve Shalom Synagogue in Istanbul was bombed twice, first in 1986 and again in 1992, causing casualties and damage both times.[73] In June 1995, religious extremists assaulted the head of the Jewish congregation in Ankara.[74] In July 1993, a raging Sunni crowd attacked a hotel in Sivas where members of the Alevi sect were holding a convention; they set the hotel on fire and caused the death of thirty-nine Alevi intellectuals and artists.[75] In another incident, gunmen in Istanbul fired on members of the Alevi community; two Alevis were killed and sixteen were injured.[76] These acts of violence were attributed to fanatical Islamic groups such as Hizballah, Islamic Jihad, and Hizb-ut-Tahrir, which were founded in the late 1980s and aggravated the anxiety of Kemalist circles in the state apparatus about the possible consequences of the rising power of militant Islam in Turkey.

Levels of distrust and hostility between the two camps increased following the formation of Erbakan's government. The religious leadership saw itself as committed to revolutionizing Turkey on the domestic and international fronts, leading to fears that the government would abuse the democratic process to install in Turkey a theocratic regime similar to that of Iran. Numerous government actions and statements seemed to vindicate this anxiety. Two weeks after the formation of the new government, Recep Tayyip Erdoğan, then a member of the WP and mayor of Istanbul, argued in an interview that democracy is not an end in itself but only a means.[77] In quick succession, İsmail Kahraman, the new minister of Culture, reiterated the WP's preelection promise to build a mosque in Taksim Square;[78] Şevket Kazan, the new minister of Justice, proposed a bill that would have given preferential treatment to criminals who memorized the Quran;[79] Minister of State Lütfü Esengün announced huge funding increases for Imam Hatip schools;[80] and the minister of Education proposed to bring in graduates of the Al-Azhar Islamic Institute in Egypt as teachers in Turkish schools.[81] Erbakan's actions were a source of uncertainty and fear for secularists, especially the armed forces. On the foreign policy front, the new prime minister strengthened Turkey's relationships with Middle Eastern countries, particularly Iran and Saudi Arabia, at the expense of relations with the West. At home, he built up personal relationships with leaders of the religious orders even though their activity was formally illegal. Most provocatively, Erbakan arranged a special meal to mark the end of the Ramadan fast and invited leading figures of the religious orders.[82]

The straw that broke the Kemalist back came in February 1997 at a rally in Sincan, a suburb of Ankara, where the mayor had organized a "Jerusalem night" in support of the Palestinian cause. During the rally, which was attended by the Iranian ambassador, religious extremists called for forcing Sharia law on Turkish society.[83] The military's response was aggressive. On February 4, tanks rolled onto Sincan's main boulevard. On February 28, the generals handed the government a list of eighteen directives, setting off three months of political stalemate. Erbakan's government resigned on June 17. In January 1998, the constitutional court abolished the WP and suspended Erbakan from political activity for five years.

Following the fall of the WP government, a new center-right government led by the ANAP's Mesut Yilmaz formally held power until the 1999 election, after which a secular coalition was established. Nonetheless, the military and the bureaucracy became the true rulers and policy makers in Turkey until 2002 (Cizre-Sakallioğlu and Çinar 2003, 319–22).

Conclusion

This chapter covered the first half-century in Turkey's democratic history. The covered time period provides relevant lessons about the dynamic nature of the interaction between the state and religious populations and its impact on democratic performance. Throughout this era, Turkish politics experienced ups and downs and was subject to undemocratic interventions. Nevertheless, in regard to religion, it is safe to argue that at the turn of the century, the Kemalist treatment of religion had failed to achieve its goals. Indeed, secularization in Turkey failed at the individual, societal, and political levels. Despite the Kemalists' efforts to secularize society, religion remained central to the average Turk. Turkish citizens increased their consumption of religious services, demanded more mosques and religious education, and developed a distinctly Muslim culture. In addition, the religious orders, local mosques, and religious associations continued to serve as important social institutions. Religion proved to be a powerful recruitment tool in politics, with more and more people choosing to give their vote first to proreligion secular parties, such as the DP, JP, and ANAP, and later to religious parties like the NSP and WP.

The 1980s and 1990s were characterized by increasing recognition of religion from above, and exploitation of this relative accommodation by religious actors from below. The two most important religious players during this period were the religious orders, with their broad networks of social services, and the WP, a powerful religious party with a solid infrastructure in civil society. Yet a process that seemed at first to be an important step toward consolidating pluralist democracy ended with yet another undemocratic interference by the armed forces, once again reinforcing the hegemonic tendencies of the Kemalist coalition. Path dependency played a crucial role in limiting the boundaries of political discourse and the ability of the state apparatus to accept far-reaching modifications to the formal secular structure of the state. The Kemalist foundations of Turkey imposed strict ideological restraints as well as a biased distribution of power that was very hard to break or modify.

At the same time, the behavior of religious actors was also responsible for the disruptive relationship that evolved. Instead of embracing a more pluralist vision for Turkish society and politics, religious actors continued to view Turkish politics as a zero-sum game and expressed intolerance toward differing worldviews in the public and political spheres. The WP's aspiration to replace one hegemonic worldview with another was no better than the Kemalist alliance's intention to preserve its hegemonic status, and the growing clash between these hegemonic tendencies had an obstructive effect on Turkish democracy.

Finally, the account of this period reveals the complex and nonlinear nature of the relationship between modernization and religious empowerment in society and politics. Specifically, the strong and positive correlation between modernization trends and the increasing role of religion in Turkey stands in stark contradiction to the postulate of modernization theory that religion will fade away as modernization progresses. Also, the dynamism that characterized the state–religion relationship in Turkey cannot be adequately explained by static theories of civil society. Changing behaviors and patterns of engagement by the state and religious actors should be understood as part of an ongoing reciprocal constitutive process. External influences and new strategies of engagement from below and above altered the dynamics of the interaction between the state and religious publics and the distribution of power among social and political actors. This in turn had an effect on levels of pluralism and openness in society, which was directly correlated with the stability and quality of democratic governance.

Chapter 5

Religion, Democracy, and the Prevalence of Hegemonic Tendencies, 2000–2017

The most recent phase in Turkish democracy began at the turn of the millennium, with the formation of a new religious party in 2001—the Adalet ve Kalkinma Partisi (AKP, Justice and Development Party)—by Recep Tayyip Erdoğan, a Welfare Party member who had been mayor of Istanbul from 1994 to 1998. Since then, the AKP has established itself as the predominant political force in Turkey, winning five consecutive national elections with 34.2 percent of the vote in 2002, 46.6 percent in 2007, 49.9 percent in 2011, 40.9 percent in June 2015, 49.5 percent in November 2015, and 42.56 percent in June 2018. In addition, Erdoğan won two consecutive presidential elections, with 51.8 percent of the vote in August 2014 and 52.6 percent in June 2018 (from the Turkish Republic Supreme Election Council website).[1] As of this writing, the AKP has controlled the executive and legislative branches of Turkey's government since 2007. Furthermore, the AKP and Erdoğan have become increasingly authoritarian, using legal and constitutional mechanisms to ensure their continued hegemony and dispossessing the military of its relative autonomy and function as guardian of the republic. First, in 2007 the AKP-led legislature amended the 1982 constitution to introduce a direct popular vote for president (previously elected by the GNA), thus enabling Erdoğan's ascent to the presidency in 2014. More recently, following a failed coup attempt in summer 2016, another amendment changed the country's system of government from parliamentarian to presidential, concentrated unchecked power in the hands of Erdoğan, and placed a serious question mark over Turkey's democratic character (Sezgin 2017). This amendment was put to referendum in April 2017 and approved by a narrow margin.

In terms of this book's perspective, the years since the AKP took power in 2002 demonstrate the dynamism of the religion–state interaction in Turkey and the perils of a political system built on hegemonic and restrictive foundations. The first phase of AKP rule, between 2002 and 2007, strengthened Turkish democracy even as religion took a greater public role. The AKP joined with other anti-Kemalist groups to challenge Kemalist hegemony by borrowing a Western-liberal discourse, embracing a pluralistic vision for Turkish society and politics, and demanding more religious freedom in the name of this pluralism. The AKP's political success in this time should be credited largely to its ability to build broad power bases in civil society—including myriad youth groups and other associations, both religious and secular—that supported the party's political claims.

After the AKP consolidated its grip on political power, Turkey's hegemonic and nonpluralistic political culture resurfaced. Since 2007, and especially after 2011, Erdoğan's government has placed harsh restrictions on the media, promoted antiliberal policies, harassed political opponents, stifled mass protests, and been accused of large-scale corruption. As a leading scholar of Turkish politics has argued, the AKP "drift[ed] toward an excessively majoritarian conception of democracy, or even an electoral authoritarianism of a more markedly Islamic character" (Özbudun 2014, 155). These trends intensified after Erdoğan became president in August 2014 and culminated after the failed coup in summer 2016. With deteriorating rights and freedoms, repression of free media and political opposition, emergency laws that circumvent regular state legislation, and the breakdown of institutional checks and balances, democracy in contemporary Turkey lost its most fundamental components.

Did increased religious recognition by the state produce this outcome, as many scholars suggest? I believe the answer is largely no. In fact, as I indicated already (and will show here), democratization and pluralization increased during the AKP's early years in power. The AKP's moderate and inclusive policies facilitated new interpretations of religious doctrines and Atatürk's philosophy in ways that made them more compatible and less hostile to each other (Turam 2007). What ultimately thwarted democratic consolidation in Turkey was not religious recognition by the state but hegemonic tendencies that were formed during the one-party period and took precedence over pluralism and democratic principles once the AKP established itself as Turkey's predominant political force (A. Rubin 2016).

The AKP's Road to Political Power, 2001–2007

The military's intervention in politics in 1998—its fourth such intervention since the establishment of the Turkish Republic—led to a period of paralysis in Turkish politics. Although it abolished the Welfare Party (WP), the military had no interest in governing the country directly. It forced the government's resignation but did not suspend the constitution or dissolve the legislature. The next few years were characterized by weakness and decline in the Turkish party system, with none of the existing political parties offering any clear vision for solving the pressing political problems (Cizre-Sakallioğlu and Çinar 2003, 317).

The conservative religious elite did not wait long to establish a substitute for the WP: the Virtue Party (VP, Fazilet Partisi), founded in December 1998. The party made a serious effort to avoid the militant rhetoric of the WP and thereby avoid its predecessor's fate, but it retained the WP's fundamentalist worldview. The VP was formally headed by conservative Recai Kutan, though Necmettin Erbakan remained the leader behind the scenes. The party's lack of vision, its continued adherence to radical nonpluralistic ideas, and its nontransparent internal structure provoked division in the ranks between traditionalists and reformists (Mecham 2004). The traditionalists saw their camp as the direct successor of the Milli Görüş parties, whose ideas and ideology they espoused. The other camp, the reformists, included a group of leading figures from the ranks of the Milli Görüş, including Bulent Arinç, Abdullah Gül, and Cemil Çiçek, under the leadership of Recep Tayyip Erdoğan. This group challenged the traditional camp by promoting more liberal and pluralistic ideas, along with a more democratic and transparent internal party structure. After the VP was dissolved by the constitutional court in 2001 for expressing antisecular ideas, the party split. The traditionalist camp founded yet another radical Islamist party, the Saadet Partisi (SP, Felicity Party), and the reformists formed the AKP.

The new AKP faced two immediate challenges. First, it had only one year to develop an effective political infrastructure before the next national elections. Second, its charismatic leader, Erdoğan, had been imprisoned and banned from politics by the constitutional court after reading a poem with Islamic connotations in a public speech in December 1997 (Heper and Toktaş 2003). The first challenge was dealt with in three ways. First, the AKP used the same methods of recruitment and campaigning as did the former WP. As part of this strategy, it exploited its then-good relationship with the Gülen movement, which had not previously sought to influence politics, to garner the latter's support. The election of 2002 was the first occasion in which a majority of Gülen followers voted for an Islamic party (Turam 2007, 136). Second, the party formed political alliances with groups in society that, despite holding very different worldviews, believed that the AKP would serve as an effective platform to do away with Kemalist hegemony once and for all. In particular, the AKP recruited the support of liberal intellectuals and the Kurdish population (more on this later), creating a broad base of support that compensated for the relative short time until the election. Third, the party opened its ranks to deputies from other center-right and right-wing parties. In addition to a core group from the dissolved VP, the new party included experienced politicians from the Milliyetçi Hareket Partisi (MHP) and Anavatan Partisi (ANAP).

To address the second challenge (Erdoğan's formal exclusion from politics), the party made Abdullah Gül its formal frontrunner, with Erdoğan the de facto leader. This arrangement was based on the (accurate) expectation that if the AKP won the election, Erdoğan would be pardoned and eligible to become the official party leader and prime minister.

During its first half-decade in power, the AKP continued on the path it had laid out at its inception. Three features characterize the party's strategy and policies until 2007. These are its ability to form (and its reliance on) broad coalitions in society, its use of deliberately conciliatory language with regard to religion, and its promotion of policies with broad appeal in the economic and foreign policy fronts. Although the three features overlap, it is helpful to focus on each one in turn.

Forming broad coalitions. Although most people in Turkey identify with Islamic tradition, modernity and exposure to democratic values had led many to oppose the authoritarian nature of the religious parties in the decades prior to 2002. Consequently, only hard-core Islamists voted for the Milli Görüş parties, while mainstream conservatives preferred center-right parties such as the Democratic Party, Justice Party, and ANAP. This made the potential electorate of the religious parties relatively limited. The religious parties also suffered the electoral consequences of a sturdy competition between the powerful Nakşibendi order and the Nurculuk and Gülen movements. As long as the leadership of the Milli Görüş was affiliated with the Nakşibendi, followers of the other two refrained from casting their ballots for religious parties (Yeşilada 2002, 67).

As seen in figure 5.1, the Milli Görüş saw its best performance in the 1995 election, when the WP won 21.4 percent of the total vote. Before and

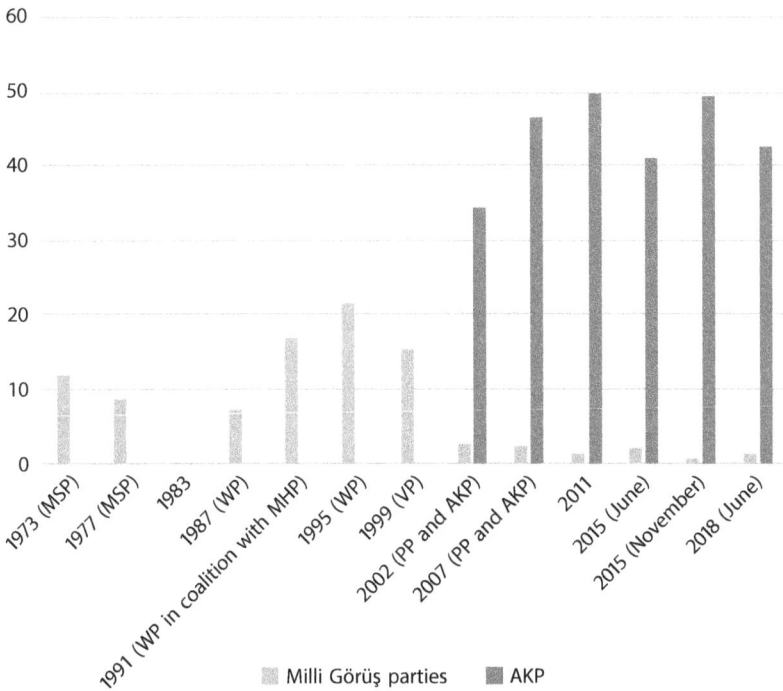

Figure 5.1. Share (percent) of the vote won by religious parties in Turkish National Elections, 1973–2018. *Source:* http://www.ysk.gov.tr (Supreme Election Council website).

after 1995, religious parties achieved significantly lower results. In contrast, the AKP's share of the vote ranged from 34.43 percent to 42.56 percent between 2002 and 2018. More than anything else, these much higher figures reflect the AKP's ability to extend the boundaries of its natural constituency, most notably by attracting the liberal camp and the Kurdish minority.

Let us start with the liberal camp. Turkish society has always been home to a vibrant liberal intellectual movement whose roots trace back to the Young Ottomans. This movement opposes any type of political authoritarianism and traditionally avoided siding with either Kemalists or Islamists. After the 1960 coup, this group took the name İkinci Cumhuriyetciler (Second Republicans). Its members claimed that Kemalism (the First Republic) had fulfilled its ideological role after the consolidation of the republic and that Turkey should now develop more open and pluralistic societal and political arenas. Attempts to form a political party based on a liberal agenda did not fare well, and individuals in this group voted for center-left parties by default. After the 1997 military intervention, liberals came to realize that the unchecked power of the military in politics was the main impediment to democratization, much more so than the presence of the Islamic elements in politics. Thus, they sought to join forces with a political faction that might form an effective opposition against the illiberal hegemonic tendencies of the Kemalist establishment. The only existing such political force in Turkey at the time was the AKP.

For its part, the AKP understood the electoral potential of using liberal terminology in the domestic arena, as well as the sympathy it might garner from Western countries for doing so. The converging needs of both sides pushed the liberals and the AKP to form a political alliance and led to the AKP's adoption of liberal human rights–oriented language. Instead of advocating the abolition of secularism, the party declared its intention to interpret secularism to protect individuals' rights to express their religiosity in the public sphere. Thus, in place of the old secularism-fundamentalism schism the Kemalist establishment had marketed successfully for decades, the AKP skillfully altered the dispute to one between secularism and democracy, with the AKP as the leader of the democratic camp. Ironically, a religious party that labeled itself conservative became the most liberal faction in Turkish politics. This terminological shift brought leading secular liberal thinkers to support the party, including Attila Yayla, founder and chairman of the Liberal Düşünce Topluluğu (Association of Liberal Thinking),[2] Ihsan Dağı of the Middle East Technical University, sociologist and journalist Ali Bulaç, and Islamic-liberal columnist and writer Mustafa Akyol. The AKP also attracted the support of many liberal-oriented civil society associations, including the Young Civilians (YC, Genç Siviller),[3] the Siyaset, Ekonomi ve Toplum Araştırmaları Vakfı (SETA, Foundation for Political, Economical, and Social Research),[4] and the Başkent Kadın Platformu (BKP, Capital City Women's Platform),[5] as well as many others. Although these associations are formally politically independent, in practice many party figures were drawn from their leadership. For example, BKP director Fatma Bostan Ünsal was a founding member of the AKP, and her husband, Faruk Ünsal, represented the party in the GNA. Likewise, Dr. Nezir Akyeşilmen, director of the YC, served as a political advisor for the AKP Member of Parliament Zeynep Dağı (who also happens to be the wife of Professor Ihsan Dağı). This intimate and somewhat tangled network of connections between the AKP and civil society actors suggested tight multifaceted connections between the party and its civil supporters. Indeed, a significant chunk of AKP delegates in the

GNA were secular people with modern liberal orientations. The fact that the AKP integrated these people into its ranks in various positions reflected the party's commitment in its early stages to reach out to different segments in society and expand its electoral potential.

The religious-liberal alliance posed a real challenge to the Kemalists, whose worldview was based on a set of dichotomies (modern vs. traditional, secular vs. fundamentalist) that were upended by the new alliance. Kemalists had a hard time digesting the fact that people who identified with their modern rational principles and lived as they did could support the AKP. As Professor Yayla told me: "It is very easy for the Kemalists to brush off conservative religious people as being old, outdated, uneducated, primitive. But it is not so easy with us. Because when I make a speech I make references to John Locke, to David Hume, not to the Quran. That makes them very angry. They can't fight back . . . They were not able to understand us. We drink alcohol, we have girlfriends, we live a modern life, etc., but we defend these bloody conservative people."[6]

The liberal stream was also instrumental in redefining the AKP, in accordance with accepted Western terminology, as a "conservative democratic party" (rather than simply "conservative party"); in fact, the phrase was introduced by Erdoğan in a speech at Harvard University in January 2004.[7] This had the effect of lessening the animosity of the Kemalists toward the AKP. Although some in the Kemalist camp accused the AKP of *takkiye* (dissimulation or hypocrisy), the new liberal language was less threatening to the Kemalist elite than were the absolute religious demands Erbakan expressed in the past.

Notwithstanding the advantages of the liberal-religious alliance, party members with truly liberal worldviews never reflected the average AKP supporter. The party's liberal members tended to be highly educated, with graduate degrees often earned in Western countries or at top-tier Turkish universities such as Boğaziçi, METU, or Bilkent. They constituted an elite group rather than an authentic development from grassroots activists. The average AKP supporter did not necessarily support a pluralist and liberal agenda. Party leaders were shrewd enough to use liberal language selectively, employing a liberal discourse in "high politics" contexts, domestically and abroad, and more traditional language in daily interactions with their electorate and mass organized events. Liberals who supported the party were aware of this opportunistic element in the AKP's discourse, but they believed that continuous use of liberal language would eventually change attitudes: they would come to believe what they were saying (Dağı 2006).

Consider the response of a former AKP delegate when I asked him (in 2009) how he could explain the contradiction between the AKP's liberal discourse and its religious foundations: "There is no contradiction. It is a kind of opportunism but when you use liberal discourse as an instrument you also change. You cannot stop yourself from changing because you use this as an instrument."[8]

The AKP's other important ally during its first decade in power was the Kurdish population in eastern Turkey. Since the foundation of the republic, the Kemalist establishment had persecuted Kurds and prevented them from expressing their distinct national identity. In 1978 a group of Kurdish nationalists with a Marxist credo formed the Parti Karkerani Kurdistan (PKK, Kurdish Workers Party, and launched a struggle against the Turkish state, including violent attacks against state and civil targets across Turkey. The Turkish government responded harshly to the uprising, sending the armed forces and (from the 1980s) local militias on raids against Kurdish communities and prohibiting all expressions of Kurdish culture or language. Over the next decade, mutual violence claimed the lives of tens of thousands of people on both sides (Ergil 2000; Saracoğlu 2009; Aydin and Emrence 2015). After a few years of relative quiet following the capture of PKK leader Abdullah Öcalan in 1999, the collapse of the Iraqi regime in 2003 reignited violence between the Kurdish national movement and the Turkish state (Kingsley 2017).

Before the AKP, Turkey's religious parties had turned a blind eye to Kurdish claims. Although Erbakan argued that Kurds and Turks were united by Islamic bonds, he did not wish to upset the WP's Turkish electorate and thus never acknowledged the Kurds' distinct collective identity. Moreover, although the Kurdish population voted in significant numbers for religious parties, the latter rarely included Kurdish figures in their ranks. In contrast, while the AKP—mindful of strident Kemalist resistance[9] and nationalist sentiment among many of its followers—avoided all-encompassing reform on the Kurdish issue, its approach to Kurdish nationalism in its early days was at least partially accommodative. The party nominated Kurdish delegates to the GNA and enacted reforms easing restrictions on the Kurdish population. For instance, the AKP approved a state-funded television channel for the Kurds and allowed them to resume the use of Kurdish names.[10] Consequently, in the 2007 elections the AKP won a majority of votes in Kurdish cities, most notably in Diyarbakir, the Kurdish capital of Eastern Anatolia, which had been a focal point of Kurdish nationalism.

It would be a mistake to naively perceive the AKP's relationship with the Kurdish population as motivated solely by idealism. According to former AKP deputy Faruk Ünsal, this was no more than "a marriage of interests."[11] The AKP used its alliance with the Kurds for political gain, and the Kurds realized that cooperation with the AKP might benefit them more than supporting the PKK. Moreover, easing restrictions on the Kurdish people, culture, and language was aimed partly at complying with the human rights element of the Copenhagen criteria, part of Turkey's efforts to meet the conditions for accession to the EU (a major goal of the AKP; more on this below). Nevertheless, the important point is that the demands and terminology of AKP allies, Kurds as well as liberals, were being expressed in public. This language penetrated into the public discourse and resonated in Turkish society.

The linguistic front. As should be clear by now, before the AKP, interactions between Kemalists and Islamists were mostly hostile, with each side questioning the legitimacy of the other. This dynamic generated a winner-take-all political culture, wherein efforts are made to eliminate political opponents instead of accepting their right to exist in the public sphere and compete for public support (A. Rubin 2016). During its first few years, the AKP endeavored to alter this dynamic to secure the party against charges of antisecularism and at the same time lay the foundations for at least minimal cooperation with the Kemalist establishment over their common political interests, such as economic growth and political stability. Rather than exploiting rhetorical clashes with the Kemalist establishment, a tactic used by the earlier religious parties that only invited aggressive repression, the AKP adopted nonconfrontational language and refrained from criticizing the core elements of Kemalist ideology. This strategy served three purposes. First, it protected the AKP from the fate met by all previous religious parties—being banned by the constitutional court. Second, it alleviated mistrust and anxiety and supported cooperation between the AKP and the state apparatus. Third, abrogating the traditional view of Kemalism and religion as rigidly dichotomous convinced many traditional Turks with Kemalist convictions to vote for the AKP. Erdoğan's words in 2004 illustrate this approach nicely:

> We are against the employment of discourses and organizational approaches that create divisions of Us and Them and make one specific fact—ideology, political identity, ethnic element, or religious thought—the center of the polity, thereby antagonizing all

> other choices. . . . While attaching importance to religion as a
> social value, we do not think it right to conduct politics through
> religion, to attempt to transform government ideologically by
> using religion, or to resort to organizational activities based on
> religious symbols. To make religion an instrument of politics and
> to adopt exclusive approaches to politics in the name of religion
> harms not only political pluralism but also religion itself.[12]

Erdoğan's words imply a deep change in the worldview of religious actors in politics. Under this new perspective, the role of religion in the state becomes just one of many things the government needs to address, rather than a prism through which every political concern must be considered. Likewise, Sharia law not only ceases to be seen as a panacea for all societal ills but is no longer even desired as a formal element in the political order. This turned out to be a shrewd move. The NSP and WP advocated Sharia for political purposes. But as one noted scholar of religion in Turkey told me: "No one wants Sharia law in Turkey."[13] Likewise, Ibrahim Kalin, Erdoğan's current spokesperson and a former chairman of SETA, told me that polls conducted by SETA consistently show only a tiny fraction of Turkey's citizens favoring the reinstallation of Sharia law.[14] Cognizant of the lack of popular support for Sharia and its explosive potential vis-à-vis the Kemalist establishment, the AKP completely abandoned the concept.

One of the party's electoral advantages in the early stages was its ability to "secularize" issues that until then were considered sacred in the Turkish public sphere, while keeping Islam in the background (Tepe 2006, 109; 2008). Even political debates with a religious core, such as the wearing of headscarves in public facilities, were presented as questions of human rights and individual welfare, as matters of conscience and free choice (Kortweg and Yurdakul 2014, chap. 3). In the same manner, the debate over giving graduates of Imam Hatip schools access to universities or the public service was approached as relating to equality of opportunities and freedom of occupation rather than religion (Sarfati 2016).

To further reduce animosity and open channels of collaboration with the Kemalists, the AKP publicly embraced Kemal Atatürk (the person) and Kemalism (the ideology) as common Turkish values. The party's formal gatherings routinely featured pictures of Atatürk and commemorated his legacy, gestures that were unthinkable for the former religious parties. Although not all Kemalists accepted the sincerity of these acts, they gained the sympathy of the general public and helped boost the party's popularity.

These actions on the linguistic and symbolic fronts created a resemblance between the AKP and Christian democratic parties in Europe—a goal implicit in the AKP's new self-definition as a conservative democratic party. As Hale noted: "There are intriguing similarities between their party [the AKP] and the Christian democrat parties of Western Europe in terms of policies, especially on moral, cultural, and educational issues; international attitudes; and support structures" (2006, 83).

The policy front. Following its 2002 electoral victory, the AKP refrained from dealing with religious issues and chose to concentrate on two policy domains for which there was broad consensus in Turkey: economic reconstruction and accession to the European Union. Between 2002 and 2007, the AKP was relatively successful in managing both issues. It is true that advocacy for both economic reform and accession to the EU predated the AKP. Joining the EU was a longtime desire of Turkey and had been on the table for many years. Nevertheless, the AKP can be credited with taking concrete steps in an effort (eventually unsuccessful) to achieve this aspiration by improving the human rights situation and weakening the army's influence on politics. The party became an enthusiastic supporter of accession to the EU, and its government approved comprehensive reforms to promote it (Öniş 2006b). The AKP's pro-EU policy pushed the Kemalist state apparatus into a corner. On one hand, the Kemalists supported accession to the EU as a reaffirmation of Turkey's legitimate membership in the West, as well as on economic grounds. Joining the EU would generate significant growth for the Turkish economy, and for this reason it was supported by Turkey's business elite and by the electorate generally. On the other hand, the secular establishment suspected that the EU process disguised the Islamists' true intentions—using EU reforms to weaken the military and turn Turkey into an authoritarian theocracy. Eventually, the RPP and the armed forces, fearful of losing their hegemonic status, declared themselves opposed to joining the EU. This enabled AKP members to present themselves as the advocates of globalization and progress, as against the nationalism and isolationism advocated by the Kemalist establishment, and this garnered it additional support from Turkey's business sector (Öniş 2006a, 214). The EU accession process has been stalled since 2005, but at least at first this was due largely to intra-European disagreements over Turkey's accession rather than to Turkish policies.

The party also performed well on the economic front. Despite fears among many that it would pursue a populist path to appease the electorate, the AKP exercised disciplined economic policies in cooperation with the

International Monetary Fund and without flouting budgetary constraints. This enabled the government to bring inflation down to its lowest point in three decades and achieve an impressive growth rate. Indeed, Turkey's economy grew significantly under the AKP by almost every measure: between 2002 and 2013 GDP rose from US$233 billion to $820 billion; GDP per capita increased from $4,500 to over $10,700; imports rose from $70 billion to $242 billion; and exports grew from $47 billion to $157 billion (data from Kutlay 2015). The government allocated significant resources to infrastructure in both urban centers and rural areas and elevated the standard of living in the country. The most significant change took place in Istanbul, where the government initiated large-scale road-building and public transportation projects, including modern subway and tram lines.

The AKP's strategies of engagement with the secular state in its first term, along with its notable successes in various policy fields, altered the dynamics of interaction between Kemalists and Islamic actors and the political division of power in Turkey. For the first time in Turkish history, the Islamic camp became a leading political force at the expense of the fading Kemalist establishment. However, the latter continued to oppose any formal acknowledgment of religious actors and content beyond what was specified in the 1982 constitution. Even as the AKP introduced more informal integration and toleration of religion into Turkey between 2002 and 2007, the Kemalist alliance fought to preserve the core elements of the old political order. This political reality is nicely captured in the 2007 Freedom House special report on Turkey, whose opening words are "Turkey presents an ever-shifting dichotomy between democratic progress and resistance to reform" (Reppuchi 2007, 711).

Changing Winds: The Elections of 2007

The balance of power shifted dramatically in the summer of 2007. Under Turkey's 1982 constitution, the country's president was elected by members of the GNA instead of directly by the voters. Toward the end of President Ahmet Necdet Sezer's term in office (2000–2007), the AKP named moderate Deputy PM Abdullah Gül as its candidate for president. Nominating Gül over the other two party leaders—Speaker of the GNA Bülent Arinç and Prime Minister Tayyip Erdoğan—was partly intended to appease the secular public and prevent further polarization in Turkish society. Nevertheless, the secular apparatus opposed any candidate with a clear religious affiliation. The announcement of Gül's candidacy sparked a massive wave of protest throughout Turkey by the Kemalist establishment and its remaining supporters. Marches and rallies were organized in major urban centers, including Izmir, Ankara, Istanbul, Antalya, and Mersin.[15] The goal of the rallying secularists was not developing a more inclusive political sphere or further democratic reforms, but maintaining the old status quo and the marginalization of religion from the public space.

The protests also received backing from the armed forces. Over the years, military officials had become adept at speaking out on civil and political themes in a way that would produce broad exposure in the mass media.[16] Two weeks before the AKP announced Gül's candidacy, Chief of Staff General Yaşar Büyükanıt made this statement: "Recently, the main issue emerging in connection with the presidential elections has focused on the debate over secularism. This is viewed with concern by the Turkish Armed Forces" (quoted in Bülent and Vural 2009). This seemingly innocuous comment was an implicit promise of more aggressive interference in the election process by the army and the constitutional court down the road, should the AKP insist on putting forward Gül's candidacy. This was indeed the case. Because the AKP enjoyed a solid majority in the legislature, Gül was elected on April 27, with most opposition legislators boycotting the election. However, the constitutional court annulled the vote, ruling that a quorum had not been present. For its part, close to midnight on the April 27, the military published on its website a short memorandum that contained the following statement: "It should not be forgotten that the Turkish Armed Forces are a side in this debate and are a staunch defender of secularism. The Turkish Armed Forces are against those debates . . . and will display its position and attitudes when it becomes necessary. No one should doubt that" (Bülent and Vural 2009). This memo, later nicknamed the e-coup, signaled clearly the military's intention to intervene in the election process if Gül was declared president.[17] Like in 1997, the military did not take control over civil politics directly, but its aggressive interference effectively removed power from the elected politicians. Under this pressure, Gül was compelled to withdraw. The AKP then called a snap election, moving the ballot scheduled for November 2007 to July.

The intervention of the armed forces in the political process generated rage and frustration in the general public, as well as among intellectuals and media circles. Bülent Keneş, a well-known columnist for *Today's Zaman*, captured the public's feelings: "By taking an unexpected step toward midnight on Friday that could never be encountered in any contemporary democracy,

the General Staff has not only intervened in, and thereby insulted, democratic politics, but has also insulted the Turkish people's dignity, honor,
mind and will by making this statement. . . . Those people [Turkish citi-
zens] have never forgiven and will never forgive those using against them
the threatening and dissuading power of the arms provided by their taxes
and self-sacrifices" (Keneş 2007).

Recognizing and exploiting the unprecedented antimilitary sentiment,
Erdoğan directly confronted the army chiefs: "It is unthinkable that in a
state governed by the rule of law the Turkish general staff—as an institution under the Prime Minister—would speak against the government" (in
Filkins 2012). By casting the episode in the framework of democracy versus
authoritarianism, Erdoğan's audacious reaction marked a significant turning
point in the civil–military relationship in Turkey and reaffirmed the AKP's
status as leader of the democratic camp.[18] As a result, the AKP gained
the support of all Turks who opposed undemocratic military intervention
in politics, and it emerged victorious in the July 2007 election with 46.6
percent of the total vote, against just over 20 percent of the total for the
Kemalist RPP. In the aftermath of the election, Gül was nominated for the
presidency again, and on August 26, 2007, he became the first religious
president of Turkey. In a symbolic act, the chiefs of staff did not participate
in his inauguration ceremony.

To summarize, in the spring and summer of 2007 the Kemalist
establishment once again violated democratic principles for the sake of
preserving its hegemonic status. Meanwhile, the growing power of pro-
democratic forces in Turkey, both religious and secular, under the AKP's
leadership translated into unprecedented demands to pluralize the system
and allow non-Kemalist voices to be represented. Although the Kemalists
remained sufficiently powerful in 2007 to block formal institutional and
constitutional changes in the Turkish regime, their defeat in Gül's election
reflected a step in a new direction.

Indeed, in 2007 it seemed that Turkey was on track to overcoming its
authoritarian tendencies and consolidating its democratic system. Scholars at
the time went so far as to suggest that the AKP's political conduct reflected
a shift toward a more inclusive and pluralistic politics in Turkey (Turam
2007; Yavuz 2009; Akyol 2011), and even that the dawn of a democratic
post-Kemalist era was on the horizon (Dağı 2008). But following the second
electoral victory of the AKP, the hegemonic features of Turkish political
culture resurfaced, this time under the incumbent religious party.

The Prevalence of Hegemonic Tendencies, 2007–2018

As of 2018, Turkey's democratic regime is in serious retreat. According to *The Economist*'s Democracy Index, Turkey's score (on a 1–10 scale where 10 is most democratic) dropped from an average of 5.72 for 2006–2012 to 5.04 in 2016 to 4.37 in 2018.[19] Likewise, the Freedom House freedom rating for Turkey (on a 1–7 scale where 1 is most free) went from 3 between 2007 and 2012 to 4.5 in 2017.[20] Since 2011, Turkey's government has grossly violated civil rights and liberties, restricted the media, and repressed potential contenders for political power. This trend accelerated in the summer of 2016 after an attempted coup, following which Turkey's government enacted a state of emergency, conducted mass arrests and detentions, fired more than 150,000 employees in the public sector, and closed down newspapers and social media platforms. In April 2017, a referendum vote approved a constitutional amendment that modified Turkey's regime to a presidential one, concentrated power in the hands of the president, and seriously weakened checks and balances in the system.

The first disquieting signal of the AKP's emerging authoritarian inclination came in the mass arrests and trials in relation to the Ergenekon and Sledgehammer cases, involving alleged attempts by the military to destabilize Turkey as an excuse to stage a coup.[21] Although such plots had indeed previously occurred in Turkey, and thus were not inconceivable, these cases had a number of suspicious features. From the start, much of the evidence appeared fabricated and unconvincing, and in other ways the judicial process failed to adhere to accepted standards of due process. Moreover, accusations relating to the cases were filed against hundreds of high-ranking officers in what appeared to be a deliberate attempt to cripple the military's current leadership (S. A. Cook 2014).

Another early sign of authoritarianism was in the arrests of journalists and harassment of people who criticized the regime or exposed irregularities and corruption. In 2012, the Journalists Union of Turkey reported that ninety-four Turkish journalists languished in the country's jails and prisons, and more than half of them were of the Kurdish minority. This made Turkey the country with the highest number of imprisoned journalists, even more than totalitarian states like Iran and China (Filkins 2012). More journalists were arrested in July 2013, following mass protests in Istanbul's Gezi Park. RPP leader Kemal Kılıçdaroğlu claimed in a press conference that 64 journalists had been tried and imprisoned, another 123 were facing trial, and 59 had been removed from their posts, mainly after reporting about the Gezi protests (Aras 2013). In October 2015, the editor in chief of the popular daily newspaper *Zaman* was arrested for insulting Erdoğan,[22] and in March 2016 the government took over the paper (Timur and Arango 2016). Another tactic was to financially ruin the regime's critics. This approach was exercised in the exorbitant $2.5 billion fine levied against the Doğan Yayin media group for alleged tax evasion after it exposed corruption in the regime (Arsu and Tavernise 2009).

The government also took repressive measures against social media outlets in the wake of a corruption scandal that broke in December 2013, when the police launched investigations of more than four dozen high-ranking government officials. Measures included shutting down access to Twitter and YouTube and restricting access to Facebook to prevent the distribution of recorded discussions and video clips about the corruption allegations. In April 2014, the constitutional court overruled these measures as violating basic civil rights like privacy and freedom of speech. In response, the state prosecutor accused Twitter of evading tax payments (Yeginsu and Arango 2014). In addition, in September 2014 the GNA approved legislation allowing the government to block internet sites for a period of four hours without prior authorization by the courts (*The Economist* 2014b).

In another controversial measure aimed at impeding the corruption investigation, Erdoğan fired thousands of police officers and arrested dozens more. As justification for the purge, he claimed that the individuals involved were followers of his former ally and now archenemy, preacher Fethullah Gülen, whom Erdoğan accused of orchestrating the corruption scandal and seeking to infiltrate state institutions in an effort to unseat the government (S. A. Cook 2014; *Daily Sabah* 2014a, 2014b). Meanwhile, new appointments to the police—and to other public sector positions, such as teachers—were designed to favor government loyalists, with interview processes including questions engineered to weed out those who did not support the government (Ayan 2014). Similarly, critics argue that the Supreme Council of Judges and Prosecutors, Turkey's top judicial disciplinary body, was packed with Erdoğan loyalists (*Hurriyet Daily News* 2014).

The AKP's growing authoritarianism generated courageous attempts by civil society associations—religious and secular alike—to confront the government. A wave of demonstrations against the regime began in METU's Ankara campus in December 2012 and climaxed in the Gezi Park protests in Istanbul in summer 2013 (Gürcan and Peker 2015). Importantly, the protesters came from various backgrounds and ways of life, including pious

Muslims who wished to defend pluralistic democracy against the regime's emerging hegemonic tendencies. Among others, the Anti-Capitalist Muslims—a left-wing Islamic activist group—was instrumental in the protests, despite sharing the same faith as the ruling AKP (Erdeniz 2016). In this respect, one observer argues that the Gezi events surpassed the old secular–religious divide and represented a new threshold for democracy in Turkish society (Göle 2013). Regardless, these protests were repressed by the regime in a fashion similar to that previously employed by the Kemalists (Dağı 2015). The police responded with clearly disproportionate violence against the protesters in "a brutal denial of the right to peaceful assembly" that resulted in several deaths and hundreds of injured and detained civilians (Amnesty International 2013).

The regime's assault on democratic principles in Turkey was accompanied by growing religion-based intervention in social policy at the expense of individual preferences and lifestyles. In 2013, the GNA rushed through a set of regulations that prohibited retail sales of alcoholic drinks after 10 p.m., banned alcohol advertising, and proscribed the opening of new bars and shops selling alcohol within 100 meters of schools and mosques (Letsch 2013). To critics, Erdoğan recommended replacing alcohol with *ayran*, a Turkish yogurt drink (Tremblay 2013). Erdoğan also launched an attack on gender equality, arguing in November 2014 that "women are not equal to men" (BBC News 2014). In a more recent series of controversial statements, the president branded women who refrain from having children for the sake of their careers as "incomplete," and added that no Muslim family "should consider birth control or family planning" (BBC News 2016).

The four years after Erdoğan's election as president of Turkey—from 2014 to late 2018—represent the most worrying downturn in Turkish democratic performance. Until 2007, the Turkish president was above politics and had mostly ceremonial duties; the management of government was in the hands of the prime minister. The 2007 constitutional amendment that introduced the direct vote for president modified only how the president was to be selected; it did not amend the rights and duties associated with the office or the division of power between branches of government. However, when Erdoğan occupied the presidency in August 2014, he interpreted the direct popular vote as granting the president unprecedented political jurisprudence. After his election as president, the AKP selected Ahmet Davutoğlu as the party's chairman and prime minister (*The Economist* 2014a). Davutoğlu, a professor of politics and former minister of Foreign Affairs, was known as an Erdoğan loyalist who lacked independent political backing in the ranks of the AKP and was expected to act as Erdoğan's mouthpiece (Arango 2014). The hierarchy between Erdoğan and Davutoğlu was clear and enabled the former to consolidate his rule as the unrivaled ruler of Turkey (Yeşilada 2016). The consolidation of power almost solely in the hands of one person, Erdoğan, without the previous containing influence of the armed forces on politics, resulted in a breakdown of checks and balances in the political regime.

Erdoğan's authoritarian tendencies were further abetted by Turkey's increasingly disordered domestic and regional environment, including the influx of more than 2.5 million refugees from Syria and Iraq into Turkish territory; terrorist attacks by militant Islamists in the heart of Istanbul and Ankara; and resumed PKK attacks against military and civilian targets across the country (Gunter 2015; Dal 2017). The incumbent regime interpreted these challenges as threats against national security that necessitated a strong and intolerant state—an understanding that had a further crippling effect on democracy. A US State Department report on human rights in Turkey describes how security considerations affect the November 2015 parliamentary elections in Turkey. According to the executive summary of the report, "official observers . . . noted that a 'challenging security environment' and attacks on party officials and campaign staffers in some cases 'hindered contestants' ability to campaign freely' and expressed concern that media restrictions during the campaign period 'reduced voters' access to a plurality of views and information' " (Bureau of Democracy, Human Rights and Labor 2016).

In May 2016, after expressing concerns over Erdoğan's intentions to establish a full-fledged presidential system, Davutoğlu was forced to resign as prime minister, leaving the entire political arena in Erdoğan's hands. Davutoğlu was replaced with Binali Yildirim, another yes-man who was incapable of checking Erdoğan's single-rule political ambitions. As one pundit concluded, "Davutoğlu's resignation may well be remembered as the moment when Turkish democracy finally perished" (Filkins 2016).

The failed military coup on July 15, 2016, accelerated the retreat from democracy even further. The coup attempt was initiated by high-ranking officers alleged to be followers of Gülen, whose movement was labeled a terrorist organization by Erdoğan's government (the movement is referred to by the government as Fethullahçı Terör Örgütü [FETÖ], or the Fethullah Terrorist Organization) (Yavuz and Koç 2016). The coup was conducted poorly and was quelled within several hours by military and police units that remained loyal to Erdoğan. Nonetheless, it provided Erdoğan with the ultimate excuse to crack down on every form of political and ideological dissent. Under a state of emergency enacted in the wake of the coup,[23] the government instituted wide-ranging restrictions on civil and political rights (Bağlayan 2017). The regime also took the opportunity to detain more than 113,000 people, of whom more than 47,000, including judges, state prosecutors, and military and police personnel of all ranks, are still imprisoned as of this writing (Vonberg, Said-Moorhouse, and Fox 2017). In addition, almost 100,000 government employees lost their jobs without due process. The regime called Turkish academics from around the world back to Turkey, suspended all rectors and deans in public universities, and arrested journalists and bloggers who expressed any form of criticism or opposition to the regime (Human Rights Watch 2017).

On December 10, 2016, after eradicating all forms of civil and political challenge, the regime put forward a package of eighteen constitutional amendments that concentrated unprecedented powers in the hands of the president while weakening the capacity of the judicial and legislative branches to check the power of the executive branch (Peker 2016; Ekim and Kirişci 2017). The amendments were passed by the GNA in January 2017 and then put to a referendum in April 2017, where they passed by a narrow margin of 51.4 percent in favor. International monitors from the Organization for Security and Co-operation in Europe and the Council of Europe criticized the conduct of the referendum, emphasizing that "under the state of emergency, essential fundamental freedoms were curtailed" and that "the legal framework remained inadequate for a genuinely democratic referendum" (BBC 2017). This development may have marked the consolidation of Erdoğan's authoritarian rule (Kadercan 2017; Koplow 2017)—and Turkey's full retreat to the hegemonic style of Atatürk almost a century before.

What Role for Religion in Turkey's Democratic Downturn?

The foregoing discussion suggests that the political history of Turkey in the twenty-first century is characterized by the emergence of two simultaneous trends. One is the increased presence of religious actors and rhetoric in Turkey's public and political sphere, manifested most clearly in the hegemonic status achieved by the Islamic AKP and Erdoğan in Turkish politics. The other is a major democratic downturn in Turkey's political system, the erosion of state institutions and checks and balances, the repression of political opposition and free media, and mass violations of civil rights and freedoms. The simultaneity of these trends may lead one to infer that the increased presence of religion in the public and political spheres is responsible for the erosion of democratic performance here. But that inference does not rest on solid foundations. There is no causal arrow between the empowerment of religious actors in Turkey and the country's democratic decline. Rather, the latter is an outcome of the winner-take-all political culture put in place during the formative years of the state by the Kemalists and currently imitated by the incumbent regime. It is not an outcome of religion's increased penetration into the public and political spheres (Dağı 2015; A. Rubin 2016, 2017).

Several lines of evidence support this proposition. First, despite the AKP's long incumbency, the party has refrained from introducing deep changes in the constitutional role of religion in the state. The proreligion legislation introduced mainly makes relatively minor conservative gestures, such as legalizing Islamic head coverings in public spaces and marginal restrictions on the consumption of alcohol in the public sphere. The regulation making Imam Hatip graduates equal in status to graduates from the public education system was arguably the most important proreligious reform. Moreover, while the restrictions on alcohol consumption and occasional offensive rhetoric against women stem from the AKP's religious foundations, the laws relating to head coverings and religious schools are in fact corrections to the cultural discrimination against religious populations in Turkey imposed under Kemalism and do not disadvantage the rest of the population (Kortweg and Yurdakul 2014; Gür 2016). Meanwhile, the AKP regime refrained from introducing changes that would increase the presence of religion in crucial areas of Turkish law, such as personal status law. The government did not modify the monopolistic civil marriage system, despite the fact that more than 85 percent of Turks who marry conduct private religious ceremonies in addition to the required civil marriage (Golan-Nadir 2016). Most strikingly, despite their power, the AKP and its leader did not exploit the 2017 referendum to introduce a constitutional change in the role of Islam in the state. All eighteen amendments that were approved in April 2017 dealt with institutional changes, remaining silent on the role of religion or the official constitutional status of secularism. The same attitude has been apparent in political campaigns in recent years and in public speeches made by the AKP's leadership.

Furthermore, when looking at Turkey's political and public landscapes, religious agency has presented some of the most serious challenges to Erdoğan's authoritarian tendencies. Most notable here is the abrupt end of the partnership between the Gülen movement and the AKP, which was instrumental in bringing the latter to power in 2002 and 2007 (Turam 2007). The Gülen movement had established itself as an important player in Turkey's civil and public life, with the most widely circulated newspaper (*Zaman*), the Hizmet educational system, various welfare services, and millions of followers. Gülen and his intellectual sympathizers heralded the democratization of Turkey and particularly its ability to merge an Islamic value system with a democratic system of rule (Yavuz 1999; Gülen 2001; Bilici 2006; Gözaydın 2009). The present dispute between the AKP and the Gülen movement is an intrareligious power struggle and has little to do with the secular–religious divide.

More recently, the religious Saadet Partisi, the current incarnation of the Milli Görüş (the AKP's mother movement), voiced its opposition to the AKP's presidential reform as concentrating too much power in the hands of the president without sufficient checks and balances (Basaran 2017). Intellectuals and politicians who were staunch defenders of religious pluralization and democratization in Turkey, and instrumental in the AKP's empowerment, have expressed criticism against the AKP's ruling style and in turn have been harassed by the party. Fatma Bostan Ünsal, one of the AKP's founders and a former deputy in the GNA, was purged from the party ranks after criticizing the AKP's lack of interest in promoting the headscarf issue and for her sympathetic approach to the Kurdish minority. Following the failed 2016 coup, her academic position was revoked, her passport was taken, and she was accused of supporting PKK terrorism and FETÖ. Longtime pro-AKP scholar and columnist İhsan Dağı was also accused of being a FETÖ supporter after he criticized the party's illiberal conduct (Dağı 2015), and his assets were confiscated (Öğret 2016). Dağı was acquitted from all charges in 2018. Another figure to suffer for criticizing the government was Ali Bulaç, a leading Islamic scholar, intellectual, and public figure and one of the intellectual fathers of Islamic politics in Turkey (Karasipahi 2009; Guida 2010). Bulaç was arrested immediately after the July 2016 coup and accused of connections with FETÖ. In June 2018, he was sentenced to eight years in prison. Another founder of the party, Abdüllatif Şener, who served as its deputy prime minister until he left the party in 2007 and who now leads a group of former AKP officials who oppose the government, noted that "the AKP is no longer a humble party. It cannot hear any criticism" (Farooq 2017).

Conclusion

The AKP's current authoritarian ruling style is not an outcome of its Islamic identification. Rather, it is influenced by a hegemonic political culture introduced by Atatürk during the formative years of the state that was continued by the Kemalist alliance that ruled the country for decades and is practiced today by the incumbent power in Turkish politics. The AKP uses every measure to consolidate its hegemonic position, at the expense of human rights, democratic principles, a pluralistic discourse, and a vibrant religious and secular civil society. That this is more a quest for power than religious conduct is manifested clearly by the AKP's relatively minimal measures to change the official identity of the state and its harassment and repression of leading religious figures who were once part and parcel of the movement, who were later pushed aside because of their insistence on a minimum pluralistic and democratic threshold in Turkey.

The evolving situation with regard to policies toward religion and the country's democratic performance also reinforces three elements of this book's analytical perspective. First, the early years of AKP in power demonstrate that deviation from secular models of democracy do not necessarily mean the deterioration of the democratic system. On the contrary, the AKP's rise to power was characterized by a more democratic and pluralistic regime in Turkey. Second, this period reflects the dynamic nature of the interaction between religion and state and its effect on democratic performance. Finally, Turkey's democratic downturn exposes the enormous influence of norms and practices of political culture that were set in the formative years of the state, in this case, hegemonic tendencies and illiberal worldviews on political reality a century later.

Chapter 6

Zionism and Religion before Independence

The interaction between religion and the state in Israel evolved in a very different way from the strictly imposed secularism that characterized Turkish politics. The Zionist movement, and later the state of Israel, deviated from the secularist prescription that was offered to and often imposed on postcolonial societies by Western powers. Instead, Israel chose to formally recognize the Jewish religion in the polity. This was done in multiple domains, including incorporating explicitly religious actors in the political system, officially recognizing symbolic religious content by the state, establishing state-backed religious institutions, and allocating significant resources to maintaining religious causes. As suggested in chapter 2, the roots of this course of action should be sought in the interaction between the Jewish religion and Zionism during the prestate period, first in the Diaspora and later in the Jewish community in Palestine.

The social, structural, cultural, and demographic attributes of the Jewish nation during the emergence of the Zionist movement stimulated the integration of religion into the ideology and institutions of the movement, then into the political framework of the Yishuv (the Jewish community in Palestine), and eventually into the legal and institutional configuration of the new country. Three factors were of particular importance. First, the Jewish religion lacked political authority, both in Palestine and in the Diaspora, and thus did not threaten the authority of the emerging secular Zionist leadership. Second, despite its secular convictions, the Zionist elite acknowledged the inseparable fusion between the religious component of Jewish identity and its other ingredients (national, linguistic, cultural, and ethnic). Third, the Jewish faith served as a common source of identity and the most effective recruitment tool for Jews from different states of origin, languages, and value systems who otherwise had little in common.

These underlying factors, and the ability of the Zionist leadership to acknowledge their political significance to the success of the Zionist project, dictated how the leadership would treat the Jewish religion. They also shaped the nature of the interaction between the Zionist leadership and religious factions in the Jewish nation and set the foundations for their later integration into state affairs following the establishment of the state.

The "Jewish Problem" and the Emergence of the Zionist Movement

The modern phase of Jewish nationalism began in Europe in the nineteenth century with the emergence of the Zionist movement. The Jewish collective identity, however, is one of the most ancient ethnonational identities, with origins tracing back thousands of years. Historians and students of nationalism regard the Jewish nation as an archetype of modern nationalism and the Bible as the founding textbook of European nationalism (Hastings 1997; Ben-Israel 2000; A. D. Smith 2000).

The history of Judaism is too long and detailed to cover adequately here, but it is evident that throughout it the Jewish people steadfastly retained a link with the land of Israel, either physical or spiritual or both, depending on historical circumstances. According to Jewish doctrine, the connection with the land of Israel dates back to God's covenant with Abraham, the first of the three Jewish patriarchs, who settled in the land with his wife Sarah and nephew Lot. Three generations later, famine in the land forced the Israelites to emigrate to Egypt.[1] As detailed in the book of Exodus, the Jews escaped from Egypt after 400 years of slavery and, following two generations of nomadic existence in the Sinai Desert, conquered the land of Israel from its Canaanite inhabitants. This resulted in six centuries of Jewish political independence in the land, whose high point, according to the Bible, was the prosperous united kingdom of David and Solomon.

Following Solomon's reign, the polity split into the two kingdoms of Israel in the north and Judah in the south.[2] The kingdom of Israel was conquered by the Assyrians in 722 BCE and its people exiled. In 586 BCE, the kingdom of Judah met the same fate at the hands of the Babylonians. For the next few hundred years—barring brief moments of Jewish independence during the Maccabean Revolt (160s BCE) and the Hasmonean kingdom (110–63 BCE)—the land was ruled by one foreign empire after another: the Babylonians, then the Persians, then the Seleucids, and then

Rome. An ill-advised effort to throw off Roman rule ended with the second exile of Jews from the land in 70 CE, this time by Roman Emperor Titus.[3]

From that point on, for nearly two millennia the center of Jewish existence was in the Diaspora. Jews spread throughout the world and commonly suffered discrimination and persecution in both Christian and Muslim lands (though significantly less in the latter). Yet throughout this long history there remained a small minority of Jews in the land of Israel, especially in the cities of Hebron, Safed, Tiberias, and Jerusalem, who identified themselves in purely religious terms and stayed there to work the holy land (Reich 2005).

The relationship between the Jewish religion and the Zionist movement is complex. On the one hand, the Jewish religion and the Jewish people are intricately linked—historically, culturally, and spiritually—with the land of Israel. The land is therefore a source of both religious and national identification. Ahad Ha'am (Asher Ginsberg), a prominent Zionist thinker, captured this fusion between the Jews' religious identity and their national longing when he wrote: "Judaism is fundamentally national, and all the efforts of the 'Reformers' to separate the Jewish religion from its national element have had no result except to ruin both the nationalism and the religion. Clearly, then, if you want to build and not to destroy, you must teach religion on the basis of nationalism, with which it is inseparably intertwined" (in Hertzberg 1969, 262).

On the other hand, the modern and revolutionary nature of Zionism put it in continuous conflict with the religious-based traditional elements among the Jewish nation. The main source of disagreement between the two camps seemed to be the proactive ideology of Zionism, which stood in obvious contradiction to the passive waiting for messianic redemption that had characterized traditional Judaism. This mode of passive waiting is the reason that throughout its existence in the Diaspora the Jewish people maintained their spiritual longing for Zion (one of the biblical names for Jerusalem) but took no active measures to bring about their national aspirations (A. Rubinstein 1984). Indeed, even today some streams in Jewish orthodoxy perceive any proactive behavior to promote or sustain a Jewish polity in the ancient land of Israel as an act of heresy and violation of God's will (Salmon 1990, 314; Ravitzky 1993; Vital 1998).

Zionism emerged as a solution to two kinds of "Jewish problem," persecution in Eastern Europe and emancipation and greater integration in Western Europe, both of which were outcomes of growing nationalistic sentiments in these lands (Avineri 1998). In Eastern Europe—Romania,

Ukraine, Poland, tsarist Russia, and the Baltic states—ethnic nationalism was accompanied by rampant anti-Semitism, discrimination, and pogroms against local Jewish communities, which were implicitly encouraged by the local governments. Unbearable living conditions stimulated Eastern European Jews to find refuge in other places. While many fled to the New World, mainly the United States, others endeavored to find a permanent political solution that would provide a physical safe haven for the Jewish people (Shapira 1995; Reich 2005, 14–15).

At the same time, Western European Jews enjoyed an unprecedented level of integration in the broader society that presented them with new dilemmas. In those nations, until the eighteenth century, segregation within their countries of residence helped Jews preserve their distinct culture. Later, emancipation policies allowed the Jews to work in public service, occupy new professions, and enter the public education system. These measures elevated their living conditions but also generated threats of cultural assimilation. Participation in public higher education came at the expense of religious education. Employment in the public sector often required violating the Sabbath. Likewise, socializing with non-Jewish friends in eating places required giving up *kashrut* (Jewish dietary laws). The other "Jewish problem" was therefore how to ensure that the distinctive Jewish culture did not disappear as a consequence of their integration into the larger society (Avineri 1981; Reinharz 2000).

Paradoxically, even as the Jews began to confront this new threat to their religion and culture, the old problem of anti-Semitism took on new forms. Legal and material assimilation could not overcome the problem of the Jews' distinct identity. Growing national sentiments in Western and Eastern Europe created an old–new problem of inclusiveness for the Jews. Although former social categorization in European societies was based on religion and thus excluded Jews for not being Christians, the new social categorization was based on national heritage and ancestral roots and still excluded the Jews. Jews in Western Europe faced the threat of losing their culture and heritage without even enjoying the full benefits of assimilation.

The dual problem facing European Jews in the nineteenth century thus was a catalyst for the emergence of a new national movement with two main objectives. The first was pragmatic and directed at physical preservation—the need for a place of refuge from persecution. The second was more fervent and directed at cultural preservation—the realization of Jewish national aspirations by forming a self-governing Jewish society. Zionist ideas began spreading in the second half of the nineteenth century with two major publications, Moses Hess's *Rome and Jerusalem* (1862) and Leon Pinsker's *Auto-Emancipation* (1882). These books discussed the "Jewish problem" explicitly, and asserted that Jews would never be fully integrated in their countries of residence and thus should seek to reestablish an autonomous Jewish polity.

The novel ideas expressed in these books hastened the formation of Hibbat Zion (Love of Zion), a proto-Zionist organization of pioneers with a traditional religious orientation, almost exclusively from Eastern Europe (Romania, Galicia, and Poland), who immigrated to Palestine in the 1870s and 1880s to settle and cultivate the land of Israel. The motivation of Hibbat Zion members was primarily religious, and their leadership consisted mainly of religious figures such as Rabbis Yehiel M. Pines, Zvi Hirsch Kalischer, Judah Alkalai, Samuel Moheliver, and Isaac Jacob Reines. These pioneers sought to build in the land of Israel a religiously observant community, and they concerned themselves with religious themes such as not cultivating the land during the Jewish sabbatical year (the Shemitah), protesting the establishment of secular schools in Jaffa, and seeking to force the observance of religious rituals among secular pioneers (e.g., the B'nei Moshe, a movement headed by Ahad Ha'am, and the Biluim, who settled in Gedera). Rabbis Pines and Moheliver even demanded that pioneers who cultivated the land during the sabbatical year be expelled from Palestine because they violated a religious commandment and contaminated the sanctity of the holy land (Salmon 1990, 20, 112–39).

There is a clear distinction between the first proto-Zionist wave of immigration under Hibbat Zion and later Zionist waves, which is rooted in their orientation toward modernity. Proto-Zionism was traditional and religious, whereas the movement that emerged in the 1890s was fervently modernist (Reinharz 1993, 60–61; Vital 1998, 207). In this respect, the inauguration of the Zionist Organization (later renamed the World Zionist Organization, WZO) and the convention of the First Zionist Congress in Basel in 1897 signified an ideological and structural shift in Jewish nationalism.[4] In contrast to the proto-Zionists, whose migration to Palestine reflected a deep sense of religious obligation, the emerging leadership of political Zionism—Theodor Herzl, Max Nordau, Leon Pinsker, Moses Hess, and Moses Lilienblum—were mostly Western European liberal-secular Jews, who defined Jewishness in ethnic-national terms rather than religious-spiritual terms.[5] All were products of emancipation and the Enlightenment, and they saw the Jewish traditions, ceremonies, and special attachment to the land of Israel as ingredients of an ethnic Jewish identity. Correspondingly, they wanted the construction in Palestine of a free, pluralist, and secular society, with no clerical influence in social or political matters. The best manifestation of this vision appears in Herzl's classic publications, *Judenstaat* (The Jewish State) in 1896 and *Altneuland* (Old New Land) in 1902. In *Judenstaat*, Herzl articulates a liberal secular vision according to which, in the state of the Jews, rabbis will be restricted to their synagogues and military officers to their barracks. Similar liberal expressions can be found in the published works of Max Nordau, Herzl's aide (Baldwin 1980; Mosse 1992).

Religion and Zionism: The Formative Years

The Zionist movement developed a convoluted relationship with the religious component of Judaism and with religious factions in the Jewish world from a very early stage. This complexity was embedded in the conflicting motives of the movement. On one hand, the Zionist leadership endeavored to establish secular and liberal values as an ideological platform for the future Jewish polity. On the other hand, the movement needed the broadest possible support among the scattered Jewish populace. Hence, the WZO tried to avoid factionalism and it did its best to recruit groups with diverse outlooks, including religious ones. These contradictory motives led the Zionist leadership to seek a modus vivendi with religion rather than exclude it altogether (Almog, Reinharz, and Shapira 1998).

The formation of an institutionalized Zionist movement divided the religious segment of the Jewish world, with some supporting the movement and others boycotting it as heretical. The leadership of Hibbat Zion joined the WZO and in 1902 formed within it a religious-Zionist faction called Mizrahi (from *Merkaz Ruhani*, spiritual center), which promoted the establishment of a vibrant observant community in Palestine. Conversely, ultraorthodox Haredi communities, especially in Germany, Galicia, and Hungary, opposed the establishment of the WZO and rejected its modern secular outlook (Salmon 1990).

The WZO soon became an arena of heated debates between secular and religious delegates. The two fiercest disputes in the first decade of the twentieth century were over the irreplaceability of the land of Israel as the Jewish national home and the cultural duties of the movement. Both issues were closely bound with religion and set the foundations for secular–religious divisions in the Jewish world before independence and in Israeli politics after independence. These debates highlighted the religious attachment of the Jewish people to the land of Israel and consolidated the pivotal role of the biblical territory in Zionist ideology.

With regard to the territorial question, there existed a fundamental disagreement between two camps.[6] One camp—the territorialists—sought an immediate and pragmatic solution to the misery of European Jews, especially after another wave of bloody pogroms in Russia and Ukraine in 1903 and the mass expulsion of Jews from Romania. Ottoman opposition to mass immigration of Jews to Palestine (Mandel 1974) compelled this camp to advocate alternative territorial options for a Jewish polity. Over the years, the movement considered several possible destinations, including Argentina, Cyprus, Mesopotamia (the Syria–Iraq border), El-Arish (Egypt), and East Africa. The other camp emphasized the inseparable attachment of Jews to the ancient land of their ancestors and insisted that Palestine was the only viable territorial solution. Some of the movement's leaders, including Herzl, supported the alternative solutions, especially the so-called Uganda option—some 5,000 square miles in an isolated area of what is now Kenya, suggested as a possible homeland for the Jewish people by British Colonial Secretary Joseph Chamberlain. The Uganda option was put to a vote at the Sixth Zionist Congress (1903), where its main opponents were the Russian delegation and parts of Hibbat Zion (Goldstein 1986). Despite being supported by a majority of delegates, it caused such division in the ranks of the movement that it was never pursued. Instead, the movement initiated a second wave of immigration (*aliyah*, ascent) to Palestine in 1904, emphasizing the Zionist conviction that a Jewish polity must be reestablished in the biblical land of Israel. Eventually, the territorialist camp faded away, and a firm commitment to a Jewish home in the land of Israel became the dominant worldview in Jewish circles (Almog 1996).

The second dispute concerned the authority of the Zionist institutions to direct cultural and educational projects among Jewish populations within and outside the land of Israel. Mizrahi's philosophy held that Judaism and Zionism are mutually interdependent—Zionism could not survive without linking it to the Jewish religion; likewise, Orthodox Judaism could remain relevant only if it dealt with the full range of contemporary issues confronting the Jewish nation (Reinharz 1993). These ideas, however, were overshadowed by the movement's dominant vision of a liberal secular Jewish polity. During the first decade of the twentieth century, Mizrahi's main goal was restricting the activities of the Zionist movement to political Zionism and keep it out of cultural and educational domains. In contrast, the dominant Russian branch insisted that the movement should spread its ideas via educational programs throughout the world's Jewish communities and take the lead in training and educating the pioneers in Palestine. After a decade during which Mizrahi was able to postpone a decision on culture, the Tenth Zionist Congress (1911) tried to steer midway between respecting different communities' religious and cultural autonomy and establishing the authority of the Zionist movement over cultural indoctrination. While approving the authority of the Zionist Congress's executive committee to lead cultural activities, this authority was confined to Palestine and the Orient; the European communities would retain autonomy in cultural matters. Also, to appease the religious factions, Article 2 of the decision included a caveat: "The Tenth Zionist Congress declares its intention that nothing which is contrary to the Jewish religion should be undertaken by any institutions for cultural activity created by the Zionist organizations" (in Reinharz 1993, 68).

In the wake of this resolution, the religious bloc in the WZO split into two rival factions. One faction, headed by Mizrahi's leadership, decided reluctantly to accept the resolution, remain in the WZO, and continue to influence the Zionist movement from within. The other faction saw the resolution as a resounding defeat, and as the beginning of a Kulturkampf between Judaism and Zionism. That camp withdrew from the Zionist movement and joined with ultraorthodox groups who had opposed Zionism from the outset to form a global anti-Zionist organization—Agudat Israel (Union of Israel) (Bacon 1999). The result was that the role of religious actors within the Zionist movement declined significantly, leaving decision making entirely in the hands of the secular leadership.

The Emergence of a Jewish Political Platform

The Zionist movement mobilized five waves of aliyah to the land of Israel between the early 1880s and the beginning of World War II.[7] Those who came in the first three waves (1882–1903, 1904–1914, and 1919–1923), while often fleeing anti-Semitism and persecution, came to Palestine mainly for idealistic reasons. Their compatriots who primarily sought security and a better life largely fled elsewhere, many to the United States. By the fourth and fifth waves, immigrants were arriving for economic and security reasons as well (Shapiro 1984, 20–23). Most leaders of the Yishuv were members of the Zionist movement and arrived in Palestine in the second wave of aliyah from Eastern Europe. In contrast with the founders of political Zionism, who came from Western Europe with a liberal, bourgeois worldview, the

Eastern European leaders of the second wave supported Marxist-socialistic ideas. Also in contrast with the founders of Zionism, who concentrated their activities in the Diaspora, the Yishuv leadership emerged from within the Jewish community in Palestine and enjoyed high levels of legitimacy among the domestic population (A. Rubin 2009, 269). This group included people who later occupied the highest positions in Israeli politics (including David Ben-Gurion, Israel's first prime minister), as well as influential intellectual and cultural figures such as publisher Berl Katzenelson, author Yosef Chaim Brenner, Labor Zionist thinker Aharon David Gordon, and Israel's national poet, Chaim Nahman Bialik. The ascendance of Yishuv leaders to political power signified a shift of weight from the Diaspora to Palestine and an ideological conversion from a liberal to a socialist worldview.

Until the 1920s, the liberal ideology was dominant among the Zionist leadership. This stream was headed by Chaim Weizmann, a British Jew and reputed scientist who served as the chairman of the WZO and later as the first president of Israel. The main power bases of the liberal stream were the Zionist institutions in the Diaspora and the influence wielded by their leaders in European politics. Weizmann's crucial influence on the 1917 issuance of the Balfour Declaration, which acknowledged the right of the Jewish people to a national home in Palestine, was of particular importance, as was British recognition of the WZO as the formal representative of the Jews in pre–British Mandate Palestine in 1920. Another important success was the agreement between various factions in the Zionist movement of a broadly accepted constitution for the newly formed Jewish Agency (an offshoot of the WZO), which became the basis for Israel's relatively inclusive political system (Migdal 1988). In this case and others, Weizmann invested a great deal of effort in finding common ground for collaboration among Jewish groups and factions and preventing one stream from dominating the others.

By the 1930s, Labor Zionists had increased their weight in the WZO and acquired a dominant position in the Jewish Agency. In 1935, Ben-Gurion became chairman of the agency's executive committee, which was recognized by the British authorities as the official representative of the Yishuv. As noted already, in contrast to earlier Zionists, the Labor Zionist leadership emerged in Palestine and enjoyed the support of the local Jewish community. They managed the daily life of the Yishuv through an executive Vaad Leumi (National Council) on behalf of the Asefat HaNivharim (Convention of Delegates), which served as an elected parliament. The broader political institution of the Yishuv, from which the governing bodies were elected, was known as Knesset Israel; its membership was voluntary and extended to all

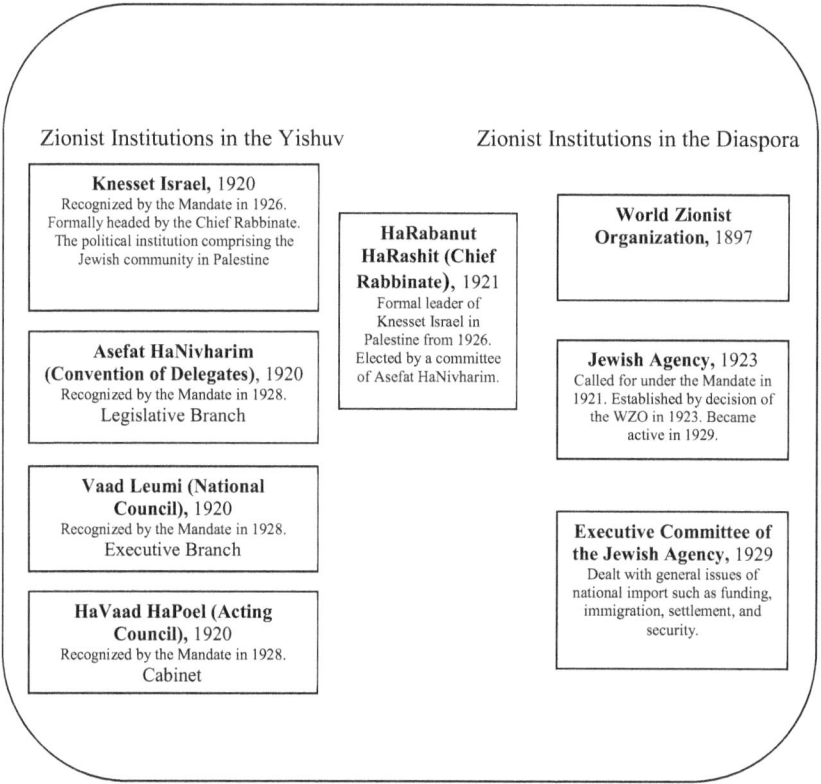

Figure 6.1. The structure of prestate Zionist institutions, with their year of establishement.

adult Jews living in Palestine. Figure 6.1 illustrates the structure of pre-state Zionist political institutions in the diaspora and the Yishuv.

With time, Labor Zionism consolidated its dominance in the Yishuv by soliciting and exploiting increasingly autonomous authority from the British government. Labor Zionism extended its authority to new areas such as housing, employment, health, and education and enjoyed an unparalleled degree of independence compared with other local governments under British rule (Migdal 1988, 157). It established local labor associations, including in 1919 Ahdut HaAvoda (Union of Labor)—from which later emerged Mapai (Mifleget Poalei Eretz Yisrael, Land of Israel Workers Party), which ruled Israel for three consecutive decades—and in 1920 Histadrut HaOvdim HaKlalit (General Federation of Laborers), which remains the dominant labor union in Israel today.

Labor Zionism exploited its control over material resources and offered various social services to the working class, ranging from absorption of new immigrants to an independent proletariat educational stream. This expansion to social realms was imitated by other political factions in the Yishuv, including Mizrahi and Agudat Israel. Each stream formed a political party, established complementary social institutions, and provided civil services in exchange for political support. The peaceful competition and intermingling among the different political factions facilitated a vibrant civil society in the Yishuv that mediated between the political system, the British authorities, and the Jewish population. The characteristics of this social and political environment—an active civil society, lack of sovereignty and coercive capabilities, and impressive and extensive performance of political parties—enhanced the absorption of democratic values and became the cornerstone of the Israeli political system after independence (Horowitz and Lissak 1973; A. Rubin 2009).

Religious Structures and Authority

As argued in chapter 1, the status and centrality of religion in the old political order has an effect on the ability and willingness of the national movement to integrate religion into the emerging order. The Israeli case supports this proposition nicely. Specifically, the lack of a central authority and clear hierarchy in Jewish doctrine and the absence of established religious institutions in Israel prior to 1948 enabled the leadership of the Zionist movement to integrate religion into the political structure without fearing the latter's potential to seriously challenge the legitimacy and authority of the secular Zionist establishment (M. Friedman 1984).

The structural features of Judaism stem from religious doctrine but were also significantly shaped by historical circumstances. Doctrinally, Judaism is similar to Islam in that it lacks a clear hierarchy like that found in Catholicism. All rabbis (religious scholars) are equal in authority and the ability to interpret or apply *halachot* (abiding regulations under Jewish law) for their communities, within the bounds of Jewish legal tradition. The pluralistic nature of the Jewish leadership structure was accompanied by the absence of an independent Jewish polity for more than two millennia. Jewish communities in the Diaspora were subject to non-Jewish local governments that regulated the profane, while the rabbis regulated the cultural and religious dimensions of Jewish life. During the nineteenth and early twentieth centuries, Jewish communities in much of Eastern Europe were organized in Hasidic courts, sometimes with as many as 100,000 followers. Each Hasidic court was named after its religious leader or the latter's place of origin. Among the leading courts are the Lubavitch-Chabad, Ruzhin, Belz, Ger, Satmar, and Sadigura. The courts competed with each other over followers, prestige, and influence, and over time experienced significant changes in structure and the distribution of power as a result of generational shifts, personal feuds, or internal splits. This reality has led to competing customs, recurrent power struggles, and an inability to reach a consensus on basic issues of relevance to the Jewish people.

The Hasidic courts were divided on the issue of Eretz Yisrael (Land of Israel), with those in Romania, Russia, and Poland tending to view immigration to Palestine with sympathy, and those in Galicia and Hungary vociferously opposing any proactive action to reestablish a Jewish polity in the land (Salmon 2006, 194–206). This was coupled with power struggles in the Old Yishuv (the pre-Zionist Orthodox population in Palestine) and an intricate relationship between the Old Yishuv and Diaspora Haredi leaders that made it impossible to organize a unified ultraorthodox front vis-à-vis the Zionist movement. Furthermore, the two main religious political factions, the pro-Zionist Mizrahi and the anti-Zionist Agudat Israel, were far from unitary and suffered multiple splits and internal power struggles.

At the same time, the Jewish religious establishment in Palestine lacked institutional capacity and real political power. The formal Jewish representative to the government during Ottoman rule, the Hakham Bashi, served as chief rabbi in Istanbul, as speaker of the Jewish millet (autonomous religious community), and as mediator between the authorities and the Jewish community. This position was made official in 1835 and was maintained until the disintegration of the empire in 1920. The Ottoman administration also appointed local Hakham Bashis to represent and oversee Jewish communities in the provinces of the empire, and in 1841 a Hakham Bashi was appointed in Jerusalem. The position combined secular and religious duties but was mainly ceremonial and lacked substantial political authority (Levi 1993, 38–56).

In 1920, the British Empire was appointed by the League of Nations to administer a protectorate in Palestine (the precursor to the Mandate), and the British authorities adopted the religious-based millet system of social categorization. Accordingly, the Chief Rabbinate (CR), established in 1921, was the first Jewish institution to be recognized by the British administration. It took until 1928 before the British administration recognized the other, secular institutions of Knesset Israel—the Asefat HaNivharim and Vaad Leumi. The CR included two chief rabbis, one Ashkenazi (representing Jews of European origin) and the other Sephardi (representing Asian and North African Jews). The Sephardi chief rabbi replaced the Ottoman position of Hakham Bashi. It is also known as Ha-Rishon le-Zion (First of Zion). The two rabbis headed a rabbinic council whose members were elected by a special committee of Asefat HaNivharim. Election procedures for the CR have changed several times since then, but the structure of the institution was transferred as is to the state of Israel and remains intact today.

The foundation of the CR as an institution of Knesset Israel was originally advanced by Mizrahi, which sought to establish a supreme religious authority for the Yishuv (Don-Yehiya 1984, 161). The first Ashkenazi chief rabbi was Avraham Yitzchak HaCohen Kook (Rav Kook; 1865–1935), an extremely charismatic figure with original and distinct theological views, whose writings serve as the ideological cornerstone of religious Zionism to this day (Aran 2013). The aspirations of Mizrahi and Kook regarding the role of the CR in the life of the nation were very high. Kook endeavored to consolidate the CR as a guiding spiritual authority for the Jewish people (M. Friedman 1972, 120). However, the CR confronted myriad limitations—lack of real authority, insufficient administrative capabilities, and limited resources at its disposal—which hampered its ability to exercise a significant political role in the Yishuv. In addition, the Yishuv's population was mainly hostile toward religious involvement in public life and tried to minimize the role and authority of the CR in Knesset Israel. Finally, the CR's authority in issues of marriage and divorce only extended to those who chose to participate in Knesset Israel.

From 1920, the Yishuv was de facto managed by the secular organs of Knesset Israel and the Executive Committee of the Jewish Agency (ECJA). This arrangement was made formal in 1928, after the British authorities recognized Knesset Israel as an autonomous Jewish community. Soon thereafter, the community's leadership was asked to submit a preliminary draft of a communal constitution specifying what authorities would be granted to each institution in the Yishuv. This draft did not mention the CR even once, a clue to the leadership's low esteem of this institution. Although the religious-based principles of the millet system obliged the British to officially recognize the CR as the leading institution of the Yishuv (M. Friedman 1972, 123), the latter's legal authority was restricted to matters of personal status and the official position carried little more than ceremonial value (Eliash 1985, 34).

According to Friedman, writing in the early 1970s, the CR of prestate Israel and through the first decades of the state was confronted by an ongoing existential dilemma. On the one hand, the CR desired to be widely acknowledged by the secular majority as a spiritual authority. However, the CR also tended to isolate itself from this public, fearing that intermingling with secular people and ideas could subject it to negative influence. At the same time, the ultraorthodox populace and its leadership posed a serious challenge to the CR's authority. Most notably, increased Jewish migration to Palestine in the wake of the Holocaust brought a collection of highly reputed religious scholars with more religious authority than the chief rabbis. Consequently, the ultraorthodox population did not follow the decisions of the CR and the CR itself was aware of its relative religious inferiority, and therefore it largely refrained from issuing rulings on sensitive religious themes. Finally, power struggles within the ultraorthodox world, and the reluctance of its leaders to take part in an official organ of the secular state, led many leading rabbis to refuse to sit in the Rabbinic Council. These factors reduced the relevance of the CR as an institution for substantial parts of the Jewish population in Mandatory Palestine, and later in the state of Israel (M. Friedman 1972).[8]

The ultraorthodox establishment further eroded the CR's authority by founding a competing institution—the Moetzes Gedolei HaTorah (MGH, Council of Torah Sages). The MGH is an informal religious institution that enjoys great clout among the ultraorthodox population because of its members' spiritual and theological authority. In contrast to the CR, this institution is isolated from the secular public and its members are not subject to elections. Membership in the MGH is offered to new members by incumbents in the council. There was (and still is) a qualitative difference between the MGH and the CR in terms of authority. The CR was an official organ in the institutional matrix of the Yishuv and thus was restricted from involving itself in political issues. The political leadership of Mizrahi set its own limits to the authority and involvement of the CR in political matters (Schwartz 1999, 48–52). Conversely, the MGH has never been restricted by any other group or institution, and for its adherents it has the final word in earthly political matters and spiritual ones (Don-Yehiya 1984).

To conclude this point, three factors—the disintegrated structure of the religious camp during the prestate era; the absence of hierarchy and a central clerical authority within Judaism; and the limited functions granted to the CR, the sole officially recognized religious institution in the Yishuv—left the religious establishment politically weak in the first third of the 1900s.

This establishment was thus prevented from offering real unified political competition for the secular leadership of the Zionist movement.

Prestate Arrangements: The "Status Quo Agreement"

The final period prior to Israeli independence was characterized by intense and dynamic interaction between the secular establishment and the religious factions, creating the circumstances that led to official recognition of the Jewish religion in the state after independence. In particular, the need to form broad coalitions within the Yishuv and vis-à-vis international pressures motivated the secular establishment and the religious factions to reach a compromise regarding the role of religion in the institutional structure of the new state.

The 1930s and 1940s confronted the Yishuv with intensifying challenges, ranging from security to absorption of masses of Jewish refugees from Europe. During that time, Mizrahi served as a minor partner in the Jewish representative institutions. It "followed the footsteps of secular Zionism and endeavored to find positive aspects to it, but did not attempt to guide the Zionist enterprise in a particular direction" (Harkabi 1988, 146). In 1922 a splinter group from Mizrahi with a socialist orientation formed a new pro-Zionist religious faction, HaPoel HaMizrahi (Mizrahi Workers), which soon outnumbered Mizrahi and became the largest religious-Zionist political faction in the Yishuv. The partially similar political worldviews of HaPoel HaMizrahi and Mapai facilitated political and institutional collaboration between the parties (Salmon 1990, 340–50).[9]

Agudat Israel's situation was more complicated. On the one hand the party refused to take an active role in a secular regime or promote the establishment of a secular Jewish polity, a standpoint that led it to boycott elections in the Yishuv and its institutions until 1947 (with the exception of the first election to Asefat HaNivharim in 1920). On the other hand, the ultraorthodox establishment was badly affected by events in Europe between the world wars and even more by the Holocaust, and it could not stay blind to the grave situation of European Jews and the prospect of saving Jews by creating an independent Jewish state. The ultraorthodox establishment needed to overcome the loss of important religious scholars following the complete extermination of some Jewish communities by the Nazi regime. Since immigration certificates, funding for absorption, and other civil activities were under Labor Zionist control, the only way to achieve these goals was by cooperating with the institutions of the Yishuv. To complicate the situation further, the warming relationship between Agudat Israel and the Yishuv generated disputes in the ultraorthodox population. In 1935 a group of radical ultraorthodox adherents separated from Agudat Israel and formed a militant group, Neturei Karta (an Aramaic term meaning guardians of the city), which opposed any collaboration with the secular establishment and was involved in recurrent violent clashes with the secular public over religious issues (M. Friedman 1984, 69–70).

During these years Mizrahi (and HaPoel HaMizrahi) played a key mediating role between the Zionist leadership, the CR, and Agudat Israel. Mizrahi leaders mediated an important agreement on public funding for religious services in 1936, arranged immigration certificates for ultraorthodox Holocaust survivors, and embraced the relationship between the CR and Agudat Israel. Working inside the institutional framework of the Yishuv as a bridge between the secular and ultraorthodox establishments positioned Mizrahi at a strategic political intersection. Every comprehensive agreement in the Yishuv era was coordinated by this party. The result was the establishment of a political alliance between Mizrahi and Mapai, known as HaBrit HaHistorit (Historic Alliance), which lasted from 1935 to 1977, during which time it was the strongest axis in Israeli politics (Sandler 1996).

The secular establishment understood the importance of unifying the Jewish community in Palestine in preparation for future challenges. It was willing to go a long way in meeting the demands of the ultraorthodox. Partnership with the ultraorthodox population was also important on the diplomatic level. In 1937 the British Peel Commission on Palestine recommended partition of the land between Arabs and Jews as a first step toward an independent Jewish entity in Palestine. Even before the commission published its recommendation, the ultraorthodox leadership initiated a number of diplomatic countermeasures aimed at preventing the partition plan, including meeting with high-ranking British officials (M. Friedman 1999, 451). This behavior alerted the Zionist establishment that ultraorthodox opposition might put the whole Zionist project at risk. Specifically, the Zionist leadership feared that Agudat Israel would use its contacts and influence abroad and in Palestine to prevent the establishment of a Jewish state, and they concluded that the best way to prevent this danger was to compromise with this group.

However, not only pragmatic motivations guided the Zionist attempts to seek common ground with Agudat Israel. The Yishuv leadership acknowledged the centrality of religion in the collective national identity and therefore presumed that some Haredi requirements should be accommodated in a future Jewish state (Zameret 2002, 192–203). Things like declaring Shabbat the official day of rest and regulating marriage and divorce according to Jewish law were accepted by many secular Jews, including dominant figures in Mapai. This ideological worldview was especially advocated by Ben-Gurion, who said on several occasions that he would have promoted these arrangements regardless of religious participation in politics, because "this is the right thing to do" (Eilam 2000, 73–74).

The pressing need to find a solution to the situation of Jewish survivors in Europe, a majority of whom were ultraorthodox, further warmed the relationship between Agudat Israel and the Zionist establishment. In the 1940s, Agudat Israel changed its position regarding the establishment of a Jewish state from complete hostility to implicit toleration (M. Friedman 1999, 453). Unable to find a solution to the dilemma of how to cooperate with the Zionists while opposing a secular state, the Agudat Israel leadership first avoided a clear policy on the issue, but the emerging circumstances soon compelled it to take sides.

In 1946 the British returned the Mandate on Palestine to the United Nations. In response, the UN appointed the United Nations Special Committee on Palestine (UNSCOP)—a committee of eleven countries charged with providing recommendations for a permanent political solution in Palestine. UNSCOP came up with two alternatives—a two-state solution or one federative binational state. Shortly before the arrival of the UNSCOP representatives to Palestine in June 1947, the ECJA and Agudat Israel engaged in discussions to secure Agudat Israel's support for the two-state solution. In return, Agudat Israel demanded guarantees from the ECJA that various religious principles would be respected in the new state. Four particular issues were raised: (1) a religious monopoly in matters of marital status; (2) observance of kashrut in public facilities; (3) the sanctity of the Shabbat; and (4) an autonomous religious education system.

On June 19, 1947, the ECJA sent a letter to Agudat Israel in which it agreed to comply with the Orthodox demands. The letter, which was signed by Ben-Gurion, Rabbi Yehuda Leib (Fishman) Maimon of Mizrahi, and Yitzhak Gruenbaum of the General Zionists (the main nonsocialist Zionist faction), reflected broad agreement within the Zionist establishment and is often referred to as the Status Quo Letter (or Document). The nuanced language of the letter, particularly its effort to balance democratic values, religious demands, state sovereignty, and international pressures, is very telling.

As the Chairman of the Executive has informed you, neither the Executive management of the Agency nor any other institution in the Yishuv are authorized to determine in advance the Constitution of the future Jewish State. The establishment of the State requires the approval of the UN and it will not be given unless freedom of conscience is guaranteed to every citizen, and it is made clear that there is no intention to establish a theocracy. In the Jewish State there will also be non-Jewish citizens, Christians and Muslims, and it is obvious that the State will have to secure complete equality for all citizens and avoid coercion or discrimination on religious issues or others.

We were glad to hear that you accept that no institution is authorized to determine the constitution of the State in advance and that the State will be free on certain issues to decide on its regime in accordance with its citizens' preferences.

Notwithstanding, the Executive appreciates your demands, and knows that these things concern not only the members of Agudat Israel alone, but many others in the Jewish nation who care for the Jewish religion. . . .

The Agency's Executive Council has authorized the undersigned to respond to your demands as follows:

A. **Saturday**. It is obvious that the legal day of rest in the Jewish State will be Saturday, without violating the right of people of other religions to choose their days of rest.

B. **Kashrut**. All measures will be taken to guarantee that in every public kitchen serving Jews, the food served will be kosher.

C. **Marital issues**. All members of the Executive acknowledge the seriousness of the problem, and all measures will be taken by the Agency's organs to satisfy the concern of the guardians of religion and avoid the division of Beit Israel [the people of Israel].

D. **Education**. Full autonomy will be guaranteed to every educational stream, and there will be no violation by the authorities of religious recognition and religious conscience

of any community in Israel. The state will decide on a minimum mandatory curriculum, Hebrew language, history, the
sciences, etc., and will supervise the fulfillment of it, without
restricting complete religious freedom and the authority of
every educational stream to manage its educational system
as it sees fit.[10]

The Status Quo Letter prescribed the role of the Jewish religion in the
future Jewish polity and was institutionalized following the foundation of
the state. This document is a masterpiece of balance between accommodating religious needs and securing pluralism, granting preferred status to
the Jewish religion while guaranteeing the rights of non-Jews, and showing
sensitivity to the collective demands of one segment of the population
without compromising the sovereignty of the people and the primacy of
democracy. More than its content, however, the document reflects the
national movement's cognizance of the centrality of religion in the life of
the nation and its willingness to deviate from the secularist prescription
and officially integrate religion into the political order (an acknowledgment
that was absent in the Turkish case). The ability of the Zionist leadership
to offer such a far-reaching compromise depended largely on the unique
historical, structural, and ideological circumstances of the Jewish nation in
the decades that preceded the formation of the state. As in the Turkish case,
these prestate arrangements created resilient path-dependent institutional
arrangements that have shaped the nature of the state–religion relationship
up to today and have proved very hard to transform.

Scholars and politicians are divided about the relative weight of the
Status Quo Letter in shaping policy in matters of religion and state.[11] Nevertheless, there is unquestionably significant value in the fact that the Zionist
leadership issued a formal document acknowledging the special role of the
Jewish religion in the future state and declaring its intention to integrate
religious content and religious actors into the political system. It is also evident that the letter achieved its goal. It appeased Agudat Israel and enabled
its integration in the contemporary institutions of the Yishuv. Agudat Israel
refrained from testifying to UNSCOP against the two-state solution and the
idea of an independent Jewish state, and they participated in preparing the
Yishuv for the War of Independence and statehood. Even more, its becoming
part of the political establishment smoothed secular–religious cooperation
and facilitated ultraorthodox acceptance of otherwise unthinkable political
outcomes, like a declaration of independence with wording that contained

no reference to God or the Jewish religion. Although this created a minor political crisis immediately prior to the actual declaration on May 14, 1948, the secular leaders quickly appeased the religious factions by agreeing to add the expression "Tzur Yisrael" (Rock of Israel), an implied reference to God. The lenient approach of the religious factions in this matter is all the more surprising given that only a year earlier the ultraorthodox leadership would not accept less than a Torah-based constitution in exchange for its support for a Jewish state.

Conclusion

This chapter explored the multifaceted relationship between the Zionist movement and religious factions in the Jewish world during the prestate period. Based on the theoretical perspective of this work, I demonstrated how political, cultural, historical, and demographic circumstances shaped the way the Zionist leadership treated religious content and actors in the national movement. Although the Zionist movement was revolutionary in offering a modern ethnic-based collective identity, a combination of political pragmatism and ideological considerations compelled it to seek the integration of religious content and religious actors into emerging national institutions. Zionist leaders understood the importance of religion as a marker of collective identity and as an effective instrument for mass recruitment. They also acknowledged that Jewish history, identity, and belief are all fused together in an inseparable connection and that this had to be reflected in some way in a Jewish polity for purposes of political legitimacy and of creating an authentic and commonly shared collective identity.

The Zionist leadership made sincere efforts to maintain a positive relationship with the religious factions in the Jewish world and paid a significant political price to integrate them into the national project. This effort succeeded fully, with Mizrahi remaining an important faction in the Zionist institutions throughout the prestate era and following the establishment of the state. Likewise, the Status Quo Letter guaranteed Agudat Israel's support for the national project immediately prior to the foundation of the state. As the next chapter demonstrates, the mutual recognition and collaboration between the national movement and the religious factions benefited all parties and shaped the formation of state institutions and the evolution of the state–religion relationship after the foundation of the state in significant, largely positive ways.

Chapter 7

An Era of Constructive Collaboration, 1948–1967

This chapter explores the religion–state relationship in Israel between Israel's proclamation of statehood in 1948 and the Six-Day War of 1967. Unlike Turkey in the early republican period, after independence the state of Israel recognized religion in the public and political spheres in ways that created particular patterns of interaction between religious groups and the state— patterns that largely held steady until the far-reaching events of 1967 set old expectations adrift. For the most part, this period is characterized by ongoing participation of religious parties in government coalitions, along with recurrent clashes over religious issues between these parties and the secular leadership. Both sides were compelled to accept compromises. Nonetheless, the overall outcome of this interaction in terms of democratic performance was positive in that it facilitated a stable political system and a pluralistic arena of negotiation over religious matters.[1] In addition, the establishment of official religious institutions such as the rabbinical courts, the Chief Rabbinate (CR), and the Ministry of Religions gave religious actors a strong incentive to collaborate with the state in return for allocation of economic resources and other forms of patronage and cooptation.[2] These arrangements fulfilled two goals. They were a marker of official collective identification with Judaism and a major source of employment, funding, and bureaucratic potency for the religious populace.

The bulk of this chapter outlines this sometimes uneasy but largely fruitful collaboration between the state and religious actors. The last section deals with a different sort of relationship, one that developed between the state and a small group of religious Jews who favored radical interpretations of their religion and elected to isolate themselves from the state. Aggregate data on the political behavior of religious groups during this period reveals striking differences between the collaborative behavior of a majority in the religious public and a radical anti-Zionist minority, HaEdah HaHaredit,[3] which refused to engage with the secular system and actively defied the rules of the political game to the extent of engaging in violence and other uncivil forms of expression. This difference nicely illustrates that the Jewish religion, like any other, contains fundamentalist ingredients, and unlimited integration of religious elements that might have satisfied the most radical religious segments would have meant a serious undermining of democratic principles and infringing the rights of other publics in the state.

State Recognition of Religion

The state of Israel was founded in the territory of Mandatory Palestine on May 14, 1948, in the midst of a civil war that erupted between Jews and Palestinians following UN Resolution 181 (November 29, 1947), which ordered the partition of Mandatory Palestine into two independent nation-states, one Arab and one Jewish (Morris 2009). Since 1948, Israel's democracy has remained unbroken, with no gaps or undemocratic interventions in the political system. In fact, Israeli democracy has been preserved despite a succession of serious challenges through the country's short history, including recurrent violent conflicts with neighboring states, economic recessions, and an early wave of mass immigration that changed the young state's demography and social fabric and tested its capacity for rapid absorption. Given these extraordinary circumstances, the relative success of Israeli democracy—even considering its qualified nature and substantial shortcomings, primarily the long-term occupation of Palestinian territory after 1967 and often discriminatory policies toward its Arab citizens (Peled 1992; Smooha 2002; A. Rubin 2018)—demands explanation.

Studies often emphasize the strong social cohesion and collectivist ethos of the Jewish majority in Israeli society in the early years of independence as a primary reason for the political stability. However, given the great diversity of Israel's Jewish society—newcomers and longtime residents; city dwellers and inhabitants of rural settlements; secular, traditional, and Orthodox; educated and uneducated; rich and poor; of varied origins—a high level of social cohesion was far from assured. Some explanations for the endurance of Israel's democracy rely on the country's ongoing external and internal security concerns and the continuing appeal of the Zionist ethos and its founding leaders (Shapiro 1984; Ezrahi 1998; Barzilai 1999); still others cite the collective trauma of the Holocaust (Segev 1991; Yablonka 2001; Zertal 2002; Burg 2007). I argue that although these arguments have some validity, it is impossible to understand the social solidarity among Jews in Israel, which has been instrumental to its democratic stability, without considering the impact of state policies on religion and the evolving interaction between the state and its religious publics.

Israel was established as a democratic state that guaranteed equal civil and political rights and freedoms, including the freedom of religion, to all its inhabitants. Israel's declaration of independence declares that the state "will foster the development of the country for the benefit of all its inhabitants; it will be based on freedom, justice and peace as envisaged by the prophets of Israel; it will ensure complete equality of social and political rights to all its inhabitants irrespective of religion, race or sex; it will guarantee freedom of religion, conscience, language, education and culture; it will safeguard the Holy Places of all religions; and it will be faithful to the principles of the Charter of the United Nations."[4] Although the declaration guarantees unqualified freedom of religion in the newly established state, it says nothing about a formal role for or recognition of the Jewish religion. It does refer to "Medina Yehudit" (a Jewish state), but the core of the term "Jewishness" remains vague and open to interpretation, especially about the relative weight of religious versus ethnic elements. Other than that, the wording expresses a standard liberal approach toward religion and is far from reflecting the true complexity of the state–religion relationship in Israel and the multifaceted recognition of religion in the state.

As I argued in chapter 1, Israel's independence was a critical juncture around which the state shaped its treatment toward religion. Following the proclamation of independence, the government of the new state chose to deviate from the common secularist prescription, expanded existing arrangements with religious groups, and adjusted the role of religion to fit a sovereign reality. The mainstream leadership of Mapai, the Labor Zionist party, acknowledged the spiritual value of religion for the masses, its central weight in the Jewish national identity, and the political benefits likely to arise from alliances with the religious factions (Zameret 2002). The latter were, from their perspective, committed to Jewish state-building, but in return they required broad recognition of Jewish religion as a guiding force in the state. The outcome of this mutual dependence was the state adoption of existing Yishuv–religion arrangements in addition to new forms of religious recognition.

Notably, the decision to grant the Jewish religion official status and authority was not shared by the entire political leadership. The secular Zionist camp was divided on the issue of religious integration, and its executive leadership confronted substantial pockets of resistance on this matter. Three groups were especially opposed to official recognition of religion in Israel. The first group comprised strictly secularist leaders with key positions in Mapai; these included Pinhas Lavon, Golda Meir, Bebe Idelson, Ami Assaf, and, to a lesser extent, Moshe Sharett (David Ben-Gurion's second-in-command). Not surprisingly, Idelson and Meir, the two most vocal opponents of religious accommodation, were women who opposed the gender inequality inherent in traditional Judaism, especially the idea of granting religious courts monopolistic authority over marital issues (Zameret 2002, 178–88). A second type of opposition came from the socialist Mapam (United Workers Party), which, in keeping with socialist dogma, opposed any accommodation of religion (Tzur 2002). A third group included members of Zionist circles in the United States, who believed Israel should emulate the US model of separation between church and state.[5]

In spite of the opposition, following independence the political leadership of Israel took a series of measures that recognized the role of the Jewish religion in the structure and institutions of the new state.[6] This recognition extended into the symbolic, political, institutional, and economic domains.

Symbolic recognition. From its inception, the state of Israel adopted various state symbols with religious meanings. The Israeli flag, with its two blue stripes on a white background, is designed to resemble a tallit (prayer shawl); in the center is the Star of David, a traditional Jewish symbol. The formal emblem of the state features a menorah, the seven-branched candelabrum used in the temple.[7] Official holidays in the state of Israel follow the Jewish calendar, and the weekly day of rest runs from Friday night through Saturday night—that is, the Jewish Sabbath or Shabbat.[8] The Hebrew date, following the lunar-based Jewish calendar, appears on every state document in addition to the Gregorian date,[9] and only kosher food may be served in public facilities.

Integration of symbolic Jewish content was not coincidental. Following independence, Mapai transformed its attitude toward the Jewish religion from confrontation to selective reinterpretation of religious content in accordance with a newly designed narrative of Jewish national identity. Instead of trying to shake off or minimize the religious component of Jewish identity, the secular leadership exploited religious symbols and historical events but loaded them with modern national meanings. They thereby facilitated the construction of a new civil religion (Liebman and Don-Yehiya 1983).

Political inclusion. In contrast with many contemporary democracies, Israeli law permits religious groups to operate in national and local politics and participate in government. And religious parties do participate in politics. With rare, short-lived exceptions—such as the period between 1958 and 1960 when the National Religious Party (Mafdal) left the government after the "Who is a Jew?" crisis, or the final stages of the second Rabin government in 1994–1995 (see chapter 9)—religious parties have participated regularly in Israeli governments. Indeed, as Zevulun Orlev, former Mafdal chair, once noted, Israel's parliamentary system is so fractured that no government can be established without the participation of religious parties.[10]

Political recognition extends well beyond formal politics to include various interactions behind the scenes. Secular politicians are well aware of which figures play key roles in determining their parties' political line on any given issue. Hence, meetings between the incumbent prime minister, cabinet ministers, and leading rabbis aimed at resolving political conflicts are common. Ben-Gurion himself initiated this practice, holding occasional meetings with leading rabbis on issues of concern for the new state. Several of these issues involved conscription to the Israel Defense Forces (IDF), which under the Defense Service Act of 1949 applied to all citizens and permanent residents aged eighteen and over (Arab citizens of Israel were exempted, along with a few other minor categories). In May 1950, Ben-Gurion met with the heads of major yeshivot (colleges of religious education) to discuss the exemption of yeshiva students from military service;[11] in September 1952 he met with Rabbi Avraham Karlitz (known in Hebrew as the Hazon Ish) in an attempt to reach a compromise over the conscription of religious women.[12] This pattern, of a head-covered secular prime minister paying a visit to influential rabbis before substantive political decisions are made, has persisted in recent decades among leaders from both sides of the political spectrum.

Institutional inclusion. From its inception, the state of Israel established a series of authoritative institutions that operate under the aegis of Halakha (Jewish law). The Ministry of Religions (now the Ministry of Religious Services) was established in the first government; it deals mainly (but not exclusively) with the provision of ritual services to observant Jews. The CR became a formal state institution charged with supervising kashrut regulations, appointing *dayanim* (religious judges) and municipal rabbis, and consulting the state and the public about questions of religious concern; the two chief rabbis serve in rotation as president of the Supreme Rabbinical Court.[13] The rabbinical courts were established in 1953. They were entrusted with monopolistic authority over marriage and divorce for Jewish citizens, including coercive powers to enforce their decisions, such as confiscation of property and detention in prison for people who are deemed to have refused a rabbinically sanctioned divorce.[14] Finally, with respect to education, Zionist and non-Zionist religious groups run their own state-funded education systems.[15] Each provides all levels of education, from elementary school to yeshiva, and has considerable autonomy to decide on curriculum.[16]

Some additional areas of state recognition became relevant only after independence. For instance, the state had to design new policies regarding military service for Orthodox citizens, the role of religion in the IDF,[17] and military operations and training during Shabbat.[18] Likewise, there was no precedent on which to draw in regulating essential services such as hospitals, electricity, transportation, and policing on Shabbat, as well as nonessential services such as entertainment. Often, state policies on these questions were shaped by contemporary political circumstances and compromises, rather than clear doctrinal or ideological principles (Eilam 2000).

Economic recognition. The state not only recognizes Jewish religious institutions but also provides them with considerable funds to operate and grow. Funding and sectarian benefits such as housing, stipends, and specific subsidies come from various state offices, including the National Insurance Institute and the ministries dealing with education, interior affairs, housing, welfare, religious affairs, and finance. Specific channels for allocating funds for religious purposes depend on contemporary coalition agreements.

Importantly, while some religious recognition was initiated by the state, other types of recognition required political struggle. Examples of sectarian recognition that were (or are) the object of political maneuvering include allocating resources for religious services such as synagogues and *mikvaot* (ritual baths); exempting religious men and women from military service; constructing specific housing projects for religious communities; closing public transportation networks on Shabbat and Jewish holidays; and increasing the autonomy of and funding to religious education systems. Examples of theocratic recognition include stricter public observance of Shabbat and kashrut; a religious monopoly over marriage, divorce, and burials; continuing state disregard of the non-Orthodox (Reform and Conservative) streams in Judaism; and Orthodox control over the definition of *Mihu Yehudi* ("Who is a Jew?")

Religious Responses to State Recognition

Despite some public frustration with religious recognition, it was precisely the integration of religious content and groups into state affairs that mitigated tensions between the secular state and its observant Jewish populations, motivated the religious camp to identify with the state, and brought all parties to resolve their disagreements through legal political channels. Indeed, the multifaceted recognition of religion placed religious actors in a delicate and challenging situation which I have elsewhere called "bifurcated loyalty" (A. Rubin 2014). On the one hand, religious citizens found it difficult to accept a secular Jewish state that was not run according to Halakha, even though Halakha by itself is inadequate for managing a sovereign state, and Jewish tradition offers few ways of resolving the permanent tension between halakhic injunctions and democratic decision making. On the other hand, an independent Jewish state was perceived to be a substantial accomplishment after many generations in exile. Jewish independence was hard to explain without considering it, even among the mainstream ultraorthodox, as an act of divine intervention (M. Friedman 1999; Ravitzky 2005). While each religious camp attributed distinct meanings and theological importance to the events that led to the creation of the state, eventually the majority of Israel's religious population came to recognize and participate in it.

The religious population in the state can be divided into three distinct camps: (1) Zionist, (2) non-Zionist, and (3) anti-Zionist. I first introduce these camps and then discuss the character of their interactions with the state during this period.

Zionists. In 1948 the Zionist camp included the Mizrahi and HaPoel HaMizrahi parties, which joined together in 1956 to create the Miflaga Datit Leumit, or Mafdal (the National Religious Party). These parties cooperated with the state in all realms, from participation in coalition governments to serving in the military to being part of the national education system (under separate and autonomous supervision). Collaboration with the secular state accompanied a modern worldview and an ongoing effort to reconcile daily life with religious observance.

The Zionist religious elite included political figures such as Rabbi Yehuda Leib (Fishman) Maimon, Rabbi Meir Bar-Ilan, Zerach Warhaftig, Yosef Burg, and Rabbi Moshe Shapira, along with the leadership of the religious kibbutz movement (HaKibbutz HaDati), which combines Labor Zionist values with a religious way of life. Until 1967 this elite saw itself as a minor partner in fulfilling of the Zionist project and did not challenge the secular leadership in profane matters. For this reason, Mapai favored collaboration with Mafdal over more militant religious parties. Indeed, in Mapai's view, "the NRP was a vehicle for mobilizing support among religious voters for a Mapai-dominated government" (Sandler 1996, 137). Rabbi Yuval Sharlo (Cherlow) argues that continuous attempts to reconcile the religious and statist-modern poles led this group to a pragmatic and tolerant approach, but also to religious mediocrity and selective observance of *mitzvot* (religious acts) (Sharlo 2007, 336). Conversely, Conforti emphasizes that during the 1950s and 1960s this camp was far more diverse, pluralistic, and open to different interpretations of the complex relationships between state, religion, and nation than it is currently.[19]

Non-Zionists. This camp includes Agudat Israel (Union of Israel) and the smaller Poalei Agudat Israel (Workers of the Union of Israel), or Pagi. As mentioned in chapter 6, Agudat Israel was established in 1912 as an institutionalized opponent of Zionism. Starting in the late 1930s, however, the organization tightened its connections with secular Zionism and abandoned its anti-Zionist fervor before the foundation of the state. This attitudinal change can be partly explained as the result of its achievements in the arena of religious recognition, which are reflected in the Status Quo Letter of 1947 (described in chapter 6), and partly because of Agudat Israel's acknowledgment of the unique circumstances in the wake of the Holocaust that necessitated its support for the establishment of a Jewish state. This new approach was headed by the influential Ger Hasidim, a Hasidic court that emigrated from Europe in the 1930s and 1940s and became the biggest Hasidic court in Israel. The small Pagi party was generally more cooperative toward the state but on religious issues subordinated itself to a considerable extent to Agudat Israel's rabbinic policy-making body, the Moetzet Gedolei HaTorah (MGH). Pagi's need to maneuver between these two opposing poles resulted in occasional zigzagging between opposition and coalition.

Anti-Zionists. This was by far the smallest group within the religious camp in 1948, but at the same time the one most resistant to the state. Its most extreme faction included the small Neturei Karta group of militants, who seceded from Agudat Israel in 1935 when the latter became more sympathetic toward the Zionist movement. Neturei Karta were and remain fierce opponents of any Zionist initiative, particularly the establishment of an independent Jewish state, which they perceive as blasphemy. Its members restrict their use of Hebrew to study and prayer, refuse to carry Israeli identity cards, and abstain from active involvement in state institutions

(Beit-Hallahmi 1992). In 1948 the group was based in the Mea Shearim quarter of Jerusalem and led by the militant Rabbi Amram Blau.

More numerous anti-Zionists factions today include various Haredi communities, especially the Satmar Hasidic court, whose leader, the late Rabbi Yoelish (Joel) Teitelbaum was known as the most important anti-Zionist intellectual thinker of his time (Z. J. Kaplan 2004). The Satmar court is one of the biggest in the world, with centers in both the United States and Israel. In Israel the Satmar reside mainly in Jerusalem and the city of Bnei Brak. Other anti-Zionist groups include followers of the Soloveitchik family of Brisk (Brest-Litovsk, in what is now Belarus), and the Hazon Ish group, led by the Kanievsky family of rabbis (M. Friedman 1975, 94).

I now describe the political behavior of these groups and the character of their interaction with the state.

The Zionist and non-Zionist religious factions accepted the idea of a Jewish state, although they differed on their interpretation of its meaning. The Zionists interpreted this development in divine terms as *reshit tzmihat geulatenu* (the beginning of redemption). This theological line of thinking translated into a deep commitment to serve the state in all realms. Also important for this camp, the lack of doctrinal capacity to offer comprehensive halakhic guidance for running a modern sovereign state (Eilam 2000, 30–44; Ravitzky 2005) was a compelling reason to accept compromises on the status of religious norms in different realms of public and individual life.

Conversely, the non-Zionist factions downplayed the theological importance of the establishment of the state. According to their reasoning, the establishment by Jews of a secular political entity, based on ethnic affiliation and modern nationalism but not run in accordance with halakhic norms, could not bring redemption to the Jewish people. But they recognized that the vision of a truly halakhic state simply was not feasible in a reality of a secular majority inspired by Zionist ideas. Therefore, Agudat Israel treated the state as similar to other non-Jewish regimes and interacted with it on the basis of their interests and needs.

At first, these very differing approaches about the sacred meaning of the state did not stand in the way of uniting the two factions into one political bloc, the United Religious Front (URF, Hazit Datit Leumit), which included all four religious parties—the right-wing Zionist Mizrahi; left-wing Zionist HaPoel HaMizrahi; right-wing non-Zionist Agudat Israel; and left-wing non-Zionist Pagi. These four parties ran a joint campaign in the first national elections in January 1949. The URF won 14 percent of the vote,

which translated to 16 out of 120 seats in the Knesset, and joined the first
Mapai-dominated government with three cabinet ministers. The religious
parties remained a united faction only until 1952, after which the Haredi
parties left the government and divorced from the URF due to disagreements
with the Zionist factions and Mapai about conscription of ultraorthodox
women. Agudat Israel continued to participate in national and municipal
elections and recognized the legitimacy of the state, but it did not join the
executive branch again until after 1977. The smaller Pagi stayed in opposition
between 1952 and 1960 and then resumed its membership in government.

The religious political unity thus lasted only four years. Nevertheless,
it was an important milestone in the relationship between the state and
its religious populaces and provided the state with an invaluable stamp of
legitimation by most of the rabbinic establishment, which was needed for
domestic cohesion as well as for international legitimacy.[20]

As shown in figure 7.1, during Israel's first two decades, the religious
parties participated continuously in parliamentarian politics, winning from
a low of 15 out of a total of 120 Knesset seats in 1951 (11.9 percent) to
a high of 18 seats in 1959 (13.8 percent) and 1961 (14.6 percent). Also
noteworthy, the Zionist religious parties gradually strengthened their political
support from ten to twelve seats, and the non-Zionist camp remained steady
with an average of six seats. Mafdal's electoral expansion can be explained
by its successful penetration of state institutions and effective collaboration
with the secular establishment, which translated into patronage in return for
votes (Sandler 1996, 137). It can also be explained by the massive flow of
immigrants from Middle Eastern countries shortly after the establishment
of the state. These immigrants held traditional values and thus found the
religious-Zionist parties to be a more suitable political home.

From 1952 to 1967, Mafdal was a constant partner in the governing
coalition, with the exception of two years between 1958 and 1960. Indeed,
Ben-Gurion preferred working with religious parties in the government to
compromising with the rival left-wing Mapam party, the extreme right-wing
revisionist Herut party, or the left-wing communist Maki party. He found
it strategically convenient to make certain concessions on religious issues
in return for the religious parties' passive support in secular matters such
as security, diplomacy, and the economy (Sandler 1996; Shapiro 1998).

The participation of religious parties in politics created a set of
arrangements with long-term effects on Israel's political and legal systems.
One significant success for the religious parties was the ongoing deferral
of efforts to approve a constitution. Despite initial intentions to approve a

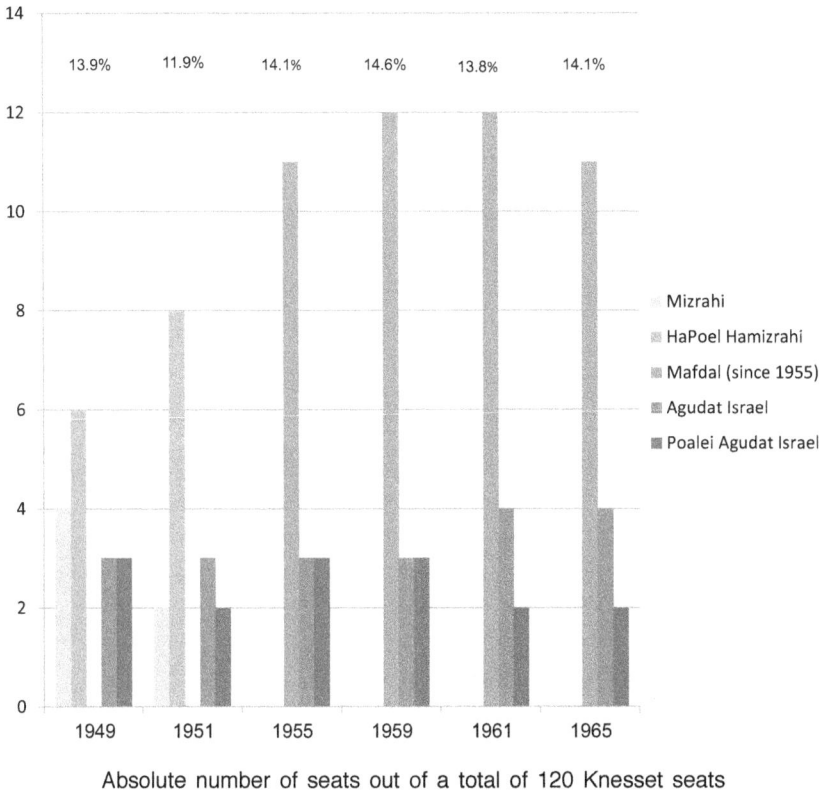

Figure 7.1. Distribution of seats among religious parties in the Knesset and total vote percentage for religious parties, 1948–1967. *Source:* The Knesset, www.knesset.gov.il.

constitution immediately after independence, debates about the nature of this constitution, especially regarding protections for religion on one hand and liberal human rights on the other, generated disputes between religious and secular factions. The religious parties demanded that Judaism enjoy constitutional protection in the state.[21] In contrast, suggested drafts for a constitution emphasized liberal rights and freedoms and did not give religion preferential constitutional status.[22] In the end, the interdependence of both sides channeled them toward a compromise. The religious parties gave up their demand for constitutional protection of religion,[23] but prevented any other constitution from moving forward (Lerner 2011). Seven decades after independence, Israel still lacks an official constitution, and even though the

Knesset has approved a series of basic laws that protect fundamental civil rights, their legal status is not entirely determined and they are far from providing a full constitutional framework for the state.[24] On the other hand, this compromise eased the tension between the factions and enabled their joint participation in government.

As described already, the religious camp achieved a number of significant victories in various realms of law, including laws relating to personal status, the rights and obligations of citizens, and the place of religion in the public sphere. But as with the religious camp's obstructionist attitude toward a constitution, these victories also came at a cost to government's smooth operation. Whether with respect to matters perceived as salient to the Jewish-religious character of the state or sectarian benefits to religious groups, the religious parties did not hesitate to act assertively, skillfully applying all the political tools at their disposal—to the point of instigating political crises so as to force or threaten new elections. As can be seen in table 7.1, religion–state issues during this period precipitated some thirty political crises over less than two decades and caused the dissolution of several coalition governments. At the same time, secular issues were given only secondary consideration by the religious parties and generated minor political crises in only two cases (in 1949 and 1967).

Interestingly, in striking contrast to the case in more recent decades, until 1967 the sanctity of the land of Israel was not given high priority in the agenda of the religious parties. A review of *Yediot Ahronot*, then Israel's largest daily paper, yields no record of significant public comments by religious politicians on territorial issues or on the sanctity of the land in this period, despite difficult territorial concessions by the Israeli government (e.g., giving up its claim to sovereignty over all of Jerusalem as part of the armistice with Jordan in 1949, or the withdrawal from the Sinai Peninsula after the Sinai War of 1956). This is because the religious parties understood their primary responsibility in Israeli politics as protecting the status of religion in the state in general and advancing the distinct interests of different sectarian populations in particular. They regarded territorial matters as secular issues and thus something on which they preferred not to take a political line.

To return to table 7.1, it should be noted that the religious delegates in government were not successful on every issue. Although some religious demands were fully met, others were rejected. The important point is that in most cases, an agreement was reached either by compromise or following a clear political victory of either the secular or the religious camp. Only in four cases did bargaining fail and result in the dissolution of government

Table 7.2. Crises involving religious parties in the Israeli government, 1948–1967

	Year	Issue	Actions by Religious Parties	Political Outcome
1.	1948	Authority of rabbinic courts	Religious minister resigns	Compromise
2.	1948	Soldiers punished for observing Shabbat	Religious minister resigns	Demand accepted; punishment cancelled
3.	1949	Import of non-kosher meat	Boycott of government	Unspecified
4.	1949	Riots in Jerusalem over Shabbat observance	Threats to resign	Unspecified
5.	1949	Revisions to the tax code (secular issue)	Boycott of government	Compromise
6.	1949	Mandatory education	Threats to resign	Unspecified
7.	1950	Education of immigrants	Threats to resign	Compromise
8.	1950	Various (religious services, import of non-kosher meat, religion in the IDF; status of CR and Shabbat)	Religious minister resigns	Compromise
9.	1950	Import of non-kosher meat	Religious parties leave coalition	Govt. falls, new govt. appointed
10.	1951	Education of immigrants; Women's Equal Rights Act	Religious parties leave coalition	Govt. falls; elections
11.	1951	Import of non-kosher meat	Popular protests	Demand rejected
12.	1952	Religious education; recruitment of religious women to the IDF	Popular protests, Haredi ministers resign	No formal change in policy; no enforcement
13.	1953	Religious education	Threats to resign	Demand accepted

continued on next page

Table 7.2. Continued.

	Year	Issue	Actions by Religious Parties	Political Outcome
14.	1953	Raising and sale of pork	Public protests, threats to resign, proposed legislation	Demand rejected
15.	1953	Religious education	Boycott of government	Demand accepted
16.	1953	Recruitment of religious women to the IDF	Threats to vote against government	Compromise
17.	1954	Recruitment of religious women, *dayanim* (religious judges); oath of loyalty to state	Boycott of government	Compromise
18.	1956	Exhibition on Shabbat	Threats to vote against govt., popular protests	Compromise
19.	1957	Breach of coalition agreement on religious education and Shabbat	Threats to resign, meetings with PM	Demand accepted
20.	1958	Operation of mixed-sex swimming pool on Shabbat	Popular protests	Demand rejected
21.	1958–1960	"Who is a Jew?"	Religious parties leave coalition	Religious parties in opposition, demand accepted
22.	1958	Autopsies; violation of graves	Protests, demands to revise legislation	Unspecified
23.	1959–1962	Elections to the Chief Rabbinate	Threats to resign, demand to postpone elections	Elections postponed; eventual compromise
24.	1960	PM gives secular interpretation to religious text	Threat to vote against govt.	PM publishes public clarification
25.	1961	Coalition negotiations	New demands raised	Negotiations fail; new elections

26.	1961	Soccer game on Shabbat	Demands to sanction the soccer association	Demand rejected
27.	1961	PM visits a Buddhist shrine in Burma	Religious ministers boycott PM reception	Unspecified
28.	1962	Public television broadcast	Threat to vote against govt.	Compromise
29.	1963	Various (Shabbat, education, Chief Rabbinate)	Threats to resign	Compromise
30.	1964	Kosher food on board Israeli vessels	Threats to resign	Compromise
31.	1965–1966	Shabbat legislation; operation of port on Shabbat; military service; elections	Threats, negotiations	Compromise
32.	1967	Increases to public-sector salaries (secular issue)	Threats to resign	Compromise

Source: Yediot Ahronot daily newspaper, January 1948–June 1967

or new elections (numbers 9, 10, 21, and 25 in the table). Naturally, the more important an issue was perceived by the religious parties, the harder they pushed their position. The most contentious issues in this respect were the crisis over the education of Jewish immigrants in 1951, and the "Who is a Jew?" controversy of 1958–1960. The former concerned the huge influx of immigrants, mainly from the Middle East and North Africa, flowing into the country in the wake of the 1948 Arab-Israeli war, whose children provided a vast pool of potential supporters ripe for indoctrination. In contrast to the official policy, which allowed parents to decide what type of educational stream their children would attend (religious, agricultural, secular, etc.), the children of immigrants housed (as most of these newcomers were) in large absorption camps were forced to receive a secular education, even though many were observant Jews. This generated initiatives to offer religious education in the camps. Attempts by the Ministry of Education to shut down these initiatives sparked crisis in the coalition and threats by Mafdal to dissolve the government and trigger new elections, compelling Prime Minister Ben-Gurion to nominate a commission of inquiry. The Frumkin Commission recommended that religious students receive a religious education in the camps, ending the political crisis.

The "Who is a Jew?" crisis concerned how the new state would define "Jewish" for the purpose of obtaining automatic Israeli citizenship. Under Orthodox practice, to be considered Jewish one must be able to trace one's Jewish ancestry through the maternal line or have converted to Judaism under Orthodox auspices. Having a Jewish father but non-Jewish mother, or having converted through the Conservative or Reform movements, did not make a person Jewish according to the Orthodox interpretation of Halakha. What was to be done with potential immigrants who failed to meet this Orthodox standard? The question was of particular importance to the religious parties because the definition by which individuals are considered part of the nation defines the boundaries of the nation. Losing Orthodox control over this definition would have undermined the power of the Orthodox establishment in the state and opened the way for Conservative, Reform, or secular groups to participate in shaping the character of the nation. The issue generated a two-year crisis and the only phase during which no religious party participated in government. Eventually Mafdal enforced its political will and regained control over the registration of Jewish identity in 1961 (Eilam 2000; Don-Yehiya 2002).

The few major crises notwithstanding, the most significant point about the interaction between the secular establishment and the religious parties is that the whole process—the debates, struggles, compromises, victories, and defeats—took place in the political arena via lawful and peaceful forms of action. Giving the religious sector space in the political arena to defend and promote its worldview and interests made other forms of political behavior unnecessary. Furthermore, participation of religious actors in politics challenged the primacy of religious doctrines and subjected them to rational political calculations. Although the rabbinic establishment took an uncompromising line over religious issues, the religious political leadership demonstrated political wit and often preferred compromises that guaranteed significant religious achievements to a totalistic standpoint that might have threatened them.

Two examples illustrate this point. The first is a debate that took place in 1951 between political leaders, the chief rabbis, and Agudat Israel's MGH regarding the appropriate response to the proposed Hours of Work and Rest Act. This act guaranteed Shabbat as the weekly day of rest, but emphasized its social rather than religious value. In addition, the proposed act allowed the secular state authority to issue work permits for Shabbat on an as-needed basis. Asher Cohen's (2002) account of this debate highlights the difference between the militant standpoint of Chief Rabbi Herzog and the MGH against the pragmatic standpoint of Mafdal legislators. Whereas the former vehemently opposed the bill, the latter argued that this was the best possible outcome under the circumstances, given that it would guarantee legal protection of Shabbat. The legislators' approach also reflected the tension between religious doctrine and political wisdom—while the law could not be supported on halakhic terms, it made no political sense to withdraw from government at that point. Hence, although all religious parties harshly criticized the new law, none left the government following its approval.

The second example relates to the debate over conscription of Orthodox women to military service. In 1953, following a long political crisis and recurrent popular protests on this issue, the Hazon Ish (Rabbi Avraham Karlitz)—the most important religious authority of his time—ordered religious Knesset members Shapira and Warhaftig to vote against a proposed bill that authorized the conscription. Despite this explicit order, the two members supported the law.[25] This example illustrates how religious politicians perceived themselves not so much as the political branch of the rabbinic establishment but more as authentic representatives of the religious population, with at least partial autonomy to represent their constituents' preferences in the best possible way.

Finally, various forms of religious activity in civil society aided the process of religious interaction with the state. The religious parties, especially

Mafdal, had established diverse civic associations that promoted religious ideas in society, and that provided the religious political leadership with solid popular support. These included the religious kibbutz movement,[26] the Bnei Akiva and Ezra youth groups, various women's clubs, and yeshivot of all sorts. These associations were occasionally involved in popular protests on religious issues, but there is no evidence that these actions involved violence or challenged the legitimacy and sovereignty of the state.

Civil society associations also served as platforms for grassroots activity at the mass level and linked the political elite with the religious masses. Subsequently, the culture of tolerance diffused to the general religious population and made it more pluralistic and open to different ways of life. The results of a survey conducted among religious teenagers in 1964 found that a clear majority subscribed to democratic values: 95 percent of the respondents supported mixed-sex education, and two thirds thought that a religious government should fund secular education and permit transportation on Shabbat.[27] These results support the supposition that exposure to democratic values through participation in the system made participants more receptive to diverging opinions and worldviews.

Also important, religious institutions provided jobs for thousands of religious people. The biggest employer in this regard was the Ministry of Education, which employed thousands of religious teachers (Schiffer 1999). Economic dependency created complicity and loyalty, and being part of the national education system necessitated a shared core curriculum in secular and religious-Zionist schools, which partially lessened the knowledge and value disparities between the two populations. Other significant sources of funding and co-optation included the Ministry of Religions, the municipal rabbinates, the municipal religious councils, and the religious courts. The addition of religious institutions to the public sector implied certain duties and limitations, which helped restrict militant or antistate expressions among religious people, required them to maintain constructive relationships with society at large, and ensured their cooperation with other state institutions. The result was a broad de facto legitimation of the state among religious institutions, which boosted popular religious support for the state.

Among the religious institutions, the CR was instrumental in establishing constructive exchanges between the religious and secular camps until 1967. The first Ashkenazi chief rabbi, Isaac Herzog, enjoyed leadership qualities and religious prestige that made him successful in uniting modern Orthodox and Haredi groups under his authority. Rabbi Herzog perceived the establishment of the state as an act of divine intervention, advocated a prostatist attitude, and, whenever possible, considered the special needs of the state when religious issues arose. His rabbinical decisions included permission to introduce general conscription on the eve of independence, which fell on Shabbat;[28] permission to manufacture ice on Shabbat;[29] a lenient approach to kashrut approval for imported meat and the conscription of Orthodox women;[30] and conditional approval of autopsies for medical studies and research.[31] At the same time, the CR did not automatically subordinate religious principles to the perceived needs of the state. Examples include the CR's decision to force the relocation of the new government campus in Jerusalem when human remains were discovered interred on the land;[32] its decision to abstain from a ceremony commemorating Israel's first president because it took place on the Gregorian date of death;[33] its opposition to the Hours of Work and Rest Act 1951 and the Women's Equal Rights Act 1951; its opposition to the nomination of Rabbi Ya'akov Moshe Toledano, of Mizrahi, as minister of Religions;[34] and its insistence on preserving the monopolistic authority of the CR over kashrut certification and the nomination of dayanim.[35]

Being part of the state structure and a firm and independent voice on religious issues positioned the CR as an essential mediating link between the religious establishment and the state and assisted in mitigating tensions between the two sides. To be sure, the CR was subject to intrigues and power struggles among the different religious factions.[36] However, in 1966 the CR consolidated its status as the sole official rabbinate following an agreement between Mafdal and Agudat Israel, according to which Agudat Israel would henceforth have representatives in the CR.[37] This agreement ended forty years of competition between the two factions and concentrated both Zionists and non-Zionists under the institutional umbrella of the CR, thus amplifying the power and legitimacy of this institution among the general religious public and vis-à-vis the state.

In conclusion, it is evident that state recognition of religion brought a sheer majority among the religious population, including its political and rabbinic elites, to accept the rules of the political game set by the secular leadership and to participate in democratic politics as a means of realizing their collective goals. The participation of religious groups in the democratic game also exposed them to the benefits of political power and made them more committed to the results of the political process. Succinctly put, state recognition invited religious groups to become part of civil society, motivated them to channel their collective demands into participation in politics, and consequently promoted pluralist democracy in Israel.

In the final section of this chapter, I discuss the relationship that evolved between the state and its religious anti-Zionist minority.

Ultraorthodox Anti-Zionism and the State: Isolation and Extremism

Long before the establishment of the state, two fundamentalist ultraorthodox groups—HaEdah HaHaredit and its most militant splinter group, Neturei Karta—opposed the warming relationship between Agudat Israel and the Zionist establishment and positioned themselves as the true defenders of the Jewish religion against the threat of secular nationalism. Following the establishment of the state, figures from both groups took various actions to undermine its legitimacy. These included meeting with foreign figures, including representatives of the Vatican, which at the time did not recognize Israel and sought to make Jerusalem an international city;[38] applications to Jordan to take up residence in Jordanian-controlled areas of Jerusalem;[39] refusal to pay state and municipal taxes;[40] and boycotts of national and municipal elections.[41] In addition, Neturei Karta instigated violent protests and riots over matters like the observance of Shabbat, kashrut, and autopsies. Although these issues were also of concern to the religious parties in the state, the parties used legitimate political techniques from within the state matrix to persuade the secular establishment to satisfy their demands, whereas the anti-Zionists made use of violence and intimidation to terrorize ordinary civilians and the police.

Table 7.2 logs the most serious violent incidents initiated by anti-Zionist factions. Standing out are an attempt by a radical anti-Zionist underground to set the Knesset on fire (1951), death threats against the speaker of the Knesset Yosef Sprinzak and Agudat Israel minister Yitzhak-Meir Levin (1950, 1951), arson attacks against nonkosher abattoirs and butcher shops (1953), and recurrent assaults against Christian priests, who were accused of missionary activities. In addition, throughout the period fundamentalist anti-Zionists initiated riots and other forms of mass violence in protest against violations of Shabbat, autopsies, and the sale of nonkosher meat. These protests lasted many weeks, sometimes stretching to months, and included roadblocks, stone throwing, vandalism of public and private property, and clashes with the police (1954, 1957, 1958, 1963, 1967). Other, rarer activities included threats and violence against mixed-sex activities outside the Haredi camp and assaults against secular and religious individuals who did not follow an ultraorthodox way of life.

Table 7.2. Press reports of illegal behavior by religious anti-Zionist groups, 1948–1967

	Date of Report	Activity and Outcomes
1.	June 5, 1949	Riots, attacks on police over perceived desecration of Shabbat.
2.	Aug. 5, 1949	Meetings with Vatican representatives and officials of foreign governments.
3.	Aug. 14, 1949	Application for residence in Jordanian-controlled East Jerusalem.
4.	Oct. 11, 1949	Declaration by Neturei Karta that its members would boycott elections and would not pay taxes.
5.	Oct. 12, 1949	Stones thrown at secular passersby. Several protesters arrested.
6.	Apr. 16, 1950	Construction of roadblocks and violent clashes with police over desecration of Shabbat.
7.	June 26, 1950	Death threats to Agudat Israel minister.
8.	May 15, 1951	Attempt to burn down the Knesset. Underground group, Kanaei Brit HaShabbat uncovered. Weapons found.
9.	June 5, 1951	Death threats to Speaker of the Knesset.
10.	Apr. 20, 1952	Riots over desecration of Shabbat. Calls to defend Shabbat at the price of imprisonment. Several arrests.
11.	Mar. 17, 1953	Two butcher shops selling pork set on fire.
12.	May 15, 1953	Death threats to owners of pork-selling butcher shops and restaurant in Jerusalem.
	June 11, 1953	Riots over desecration of Shabbat. Vehicles vandalized.
13.	Dec. 16, 1953	Riots over conscription of yeshiva students to the IDF. Many wounded and arrested.
14.	Jan. 25, 1954	Teenager assaulted and badly injured for smoking on Shabbat.
15.	June 15, 1954	Mass assault by Haredim on a youngster returning by car from a medical examination during Shabbat.
16.	1954–1955	Riots over desecration of Shabbat. Clashes between Haredim, secular citizens, and police. Many arrested or wounded.
17.	Oct. 10, 1954	Neturei Karta leader Amram Blau accused of violating public order during riots over desecration of Shabbat.
18.	Dec. 27, 1954	Violent interruption of mixed-sex religious-nationalist activity.

continued on next page

Table 7.2. Continued.

	Date of Report	Activity and Outcomes
19.	1954–1955	Recurrent violence and stone-throwing against a women's club in Jerusalem.
20.	Jan. 16, 1955	Application for residence in Jordanian-controlled East Jerusalem.
21.	June 19, 1995	Haredi man assaulted in synagogue over allegations that he might vote in national elections.
22.	June 20, 1955	Violent clashes between Satmar and Belz Hassidim over the latter's participation in elections.
23.	Aug. 5, 1956	Police remove Neturei Karta roadblocks.
24.	Sept. 1, 1956	Haredi man killed during riots over Shabbat desecration in Jerusalem.
25.	July 7, 1957	Riots over Shabbat desecration in Netanya, including roadblocks.
26.	Sept. 7, 1957	Riots over Shabbat desecration in Tel Aviv.
27.	June 1, 1958	Riots over mixed-sex swimming pool operating on Shabbat. Dozens arrested and wounded. Organized buses bring Haredi protesters from around the country.
28.	Aug. 3, 1958	Riots, stone-throwing at police following presidential amnesty to Rabbi Blau and followers.
29.	Nov. 1, 1959	Violent clashes between Agudat Israel and Neturei Karta followers on participation in elections.
30.	Aug. 5, 1960	Rabbi Blau and follower arrested after sabotaging ads for new movie on Queen of Sheba.
31.	Jan. 8, 1961	Riots against Haredi Rabbi Yekusiel Yehudah Halberstam, head of the Klausenburg Hassidic court, following his decision to allow the teaching of modern Hebrew at his yeshiva. Several Neturei Karta members wounded.
32.	July 16, 1961	Violent riots against public transportation on Shabbat. Buses and bus stations vandalized.
33.	Oct. 12, 1961	Riots against a non-kosher butcher shop require police intervention.
34.	Mar. 12, 1962	Police plan to send body of Haredi man for autopsy generates violent riots. Over 30 arrested and/or wounded.
35.	Apr. 7, 1962	Protests against non-kosher butcher shop in the city of Herzliya. Many arrests.

36.	Jan. 4, 1963	Riots against Christian missionary activity in Jerusalem. Seven Haredim arrested.
37.	June 2, 1963	Riots in Bnei Brak against autopsies
38.	July–Dec. 1963	Recurrent violent protests against transportation on Shabbat. Dozens wounded and arrested; vehicles sabotaged; police, tourists, and civilians stoned; Ministry of Education damaged.
39.	Oct. 13 1963	Christian priests assaulted and stoned by Haredi youth.
40.	June 21, 1964	Signs for Reform synagogues vandalized by underground religious group. Threatening letters left.
41.	Aug. 19, 1965	Riots against sect of Messianic Jews. Sect members assaulted; their leader flees.
42.	Jan. 9, 1966	Riots in Ashdod against operation of port on Shabbat.
43.	Jan. 16,1966	Stones thrown at members of a youth group affiliated with the Labor Zionists, Bnei Brak branch.
44.	Apr. 17, 1966	Riots over Shabbat desecration. Many arrested and wounded.
45.	July 25, 1966	Woman attacked in Jerusalem and her home vandalized over allegations of immodesty.
46.	Feb.–Jun 1967	Mass protests and riots against autopsies. Dozens wounded and arrested.

Source: Yediot Ahronot daily newspaper January 1948 – June 1967.

These acts not only violated the law but also exacerbated tension and hostility between anti-Zionists, state authorities, and the secular public. Occasionally the state and society reacted to anti-Zionist provocations with force. These clashes were costly. They claimed the life of one person and caused hundreds of injuries among Haredim and policemen; hundreds of people were arrested; and public and private property was damaged.

The activities of the anti-Zionist zealots were directed not only against the state and secular society but also against religious groups that acknowledged the state or maintained some form of collaboration with its institutions (M. Friedman 1975). For instance, the zealots attacked rabbis who acknowledged the state or approved of teaching modern Hebrew. In several cases, anti-Zionist and non-Zionist Hasidic courts clashed over various matters, especially participation in elections.

Anti-Zionist activities engendered complex responses by religious Zionist and non-Zionist groups. The religious parties and the chief rabbis could not dismiss the actions of the zealots out of hand, given that their primary intention was to defend a halakhic way of life. Hence, they backed these groups in the Knesset and in government and prevented state sanctions against them following provocative events.[42] At the same time, religious leaders were not afraid to use institutional and religious sanctions against those engaged in anti-Zionist activity. For instance, in 1953 and 1954, Agudat Israel and Chief Rabbi Herzog publicly criticized Neturei Karta's interactions with foreign bodies aimed at delegitimizing the state in the international arena;[43] in 1958 Sephardi Chief Rabbi Yitzhak Nissim and former Mizrahi leader Rabbi Fishman-Maimon called on the religious communities to boycott the Satmar Hasidic court in response to the latter's anti-Zionist agitation.[44]

In sum, anti-Zionist activity against the state was the exception rather than the rule. Nevertheless, it had a negative impact on the relationship between the religious populace, state authorities, and society as a whole. In failing to respect state laws, alternative interpretations of Halakha, or the preferences of the general public, anti-Zionist activity deepened the secular–religious divide, caused rifts between different religious groups, and generated anger and mistrust among secular members of society. Fortunately, this activity was restricted to a very small minority within the state.

Conclusion

The account of the state–religion relationship in Israel between 1948 and 1967 reveals a multifaceted integration of the Jewish religion and religious groups in the political and public spheres of the new state. The state of Israel used religious symbols, encouraged participation of religious parties and individuals in all branches of government, accommodated the special needs of observant Jews in public facilities, and established formal state institutions that operated in accordance with Jewish law. The religious camp also benefited from preserving a Jewish character in the public sphere, such as observance of Shabbat and Jewish law in matters of personal status.

Notwithstanding the problems that such deep integration introduced—particularly the far-reaching compromises imposed on the secular majority, who were compelled to accept some violation of their liberal rights—the integration of religion proved to be a stabilizing and legitimating force in Israeli politics. A majority of the religious population embraced the legitimacy of the state, participated in its institutions, and operated to advance their worldview and special interests almost exclusively within the confines of the law. Although the role of religion in the state remained a contentious issue throughout the period, disagreements were resolved almost exclusively in the political realm. The small ultraorthodox anti-Zionist minority that chose not to collaborate with the state was a source of social instability and extreme behavior, but it did not succeed in persuading the whole religious population to follow its lead and shatter ties with the state. The striking disparity between the behavior of the majority that accepted the state and the minority that opposed it illustrates the mitigating effect of religious inclusion and its effect on religious behavior.

Indeed, religious integration undoubtedly had a positive impact on Israel's political stability. Throughout the period, with all its challenges, Israel's democratic regime remained unbroken. The policy of integration provided strong incentives to religious parties to participate in society and in politics without infringing the rights of other collectivities. Although some compromises were required by the secular majority, these were mild compared with the positive effects of integrating religion in the state. In contrast, had Israel marginalized religious groups from the public sphere (as did Turkey following the establishment of the republic), a large proportion of the religious population might have taken a militant line and engaged in violent and extreme behavior, thereby destabilizing the political system.

Finally, this account also serves as an important reminder that democracy should be regarded not as an ideal type of political governance but as a realm in which balanced and mutually beneficial compromises are required. In this respect, religious integration in Israel between 1948 and 1967 succeeded in providing political stability, a pluralist realm of debate, and broad respect for democratic rules.

Chapter 8

A Period of Transition, 1960s–1980s

In the previous chapter, we saw how the foundations of religious integration in Israel following independence shaped the subsequent interaction between religion and the state and Israel's democratic performance. Indeed, official recognition of religion in Israel proved successful. Religion was given a significant role in public and political life, and in return, religious groups collaborated with the institutions of the state, espoused legal and peaceful channels of political expression, and embraced the principles and values of democratic rule. The subsequent period, covered in this chapter, reveals the dynamic element in the religion–state relationship and its susceptibility to social, political, and economic changes. The two decades from the mid-1960s to mid-1980s illustrate the importance of understanding the state–religion relationship as a dynamic phenomenon influenced by external and domestic developments, including demographic changes, political realignments and new electoral designs, war and peace, economic conditions, and modernization. As will be shown here, all of these can modify state policies toward religion, as well as alter the political agenda and behavior of religious groups vis-à-vis the state and society.

During the 1960s and 1970s, the Israeli political system experienced significant changes, including two major wars and a reshuffling of political power, which resulted in three consecutive developments in the state–religion interaction. The first development was the radicalization of parts of the religious-Zionist sector. The Six-Day War victory brought to a peak an ideational shift in segments of this population by amplifying the sanctity of Eretz Yisrael (Land of Israel) while undermining other values, such as the rule of law, Judaism's humanistic tradition, and the sanctity and legitimate authority of the Jewish state. The result was the foundation of the settle-ment enterprise in the Occupied Territories and, more generally, a shift in the political behavior and goals of this group, from institutionalized politics with a focus on religious and educational issues to extraparliamentarian mobilization with an emphasis on security and territorial expansion.

The second development was the increased involvement and leverage of the Haredi parties in Israeli democracy. The electoral victory of the right-wing Likud party in the 1977 elections transformed the political system in Israel from a hegemonic one-party structure to a bipolar political stalemate between the right and left blocs, which worked against the stability of the system and endowed the Haredi parties with disproportionate political leverage. On the other side, the motivation of the Haredi establishment to maintain the community's structure as a "society of scholars" required considerable state benefits, especially for educational facilities, continued exemption from military service, and subsidies in housing and other social services. These needs pushed the Haredi sector out of its longtime opposition to increased involvement in government.

The third development involved the emergence of a Mizrahi Haredi[1] politics in the form of the Shas party. Starting in the early 1980s, Shas's entry to the political scene attracted electoral support from both Haredi and non-Haredi populations. Besides increasing the weight of religious parties in the Knesset overall (see figures 8.1 and 8.2), Shas was able to take control of important cabinet ministries, which it used to provide benefits to its electorate through a state-funded network of clientelism.

Figure 8.3 presents a genealogy of religious parties in Israel. In gen-eral, this period is characterized by a recurrent process of splintering and merging among religious factions. Nevertheless, the general picture shows three main clusters of religious sectors in Israel since 1967, two of which remained active from earlier decades—the religious-Zionist camp with its representative political party Mafdal[2] (since 2009 HaBayit HaYehudi) and various splinter groups, and the non-Zionist Haredi Agudat Israel and other nonparticipating anti-Zionist Haredi factions. The third camp, represented by Shas, reflected the growing power of the Mizrahi ultraorthodox population in Israeli society. Offshoot religious associations and parties such as Tami, Meimad, Morasha, Tkuma, and Degel HaTorah emerged as well but left a relatively minor mark on the role of religion in the state or the dynamics of the state–religion relationship.

This chapter demonstrates the dynamic nature of the state–religion relationship as it took place in Israel in the explored period. The chapter introduces these new developments and shows how they influenced the

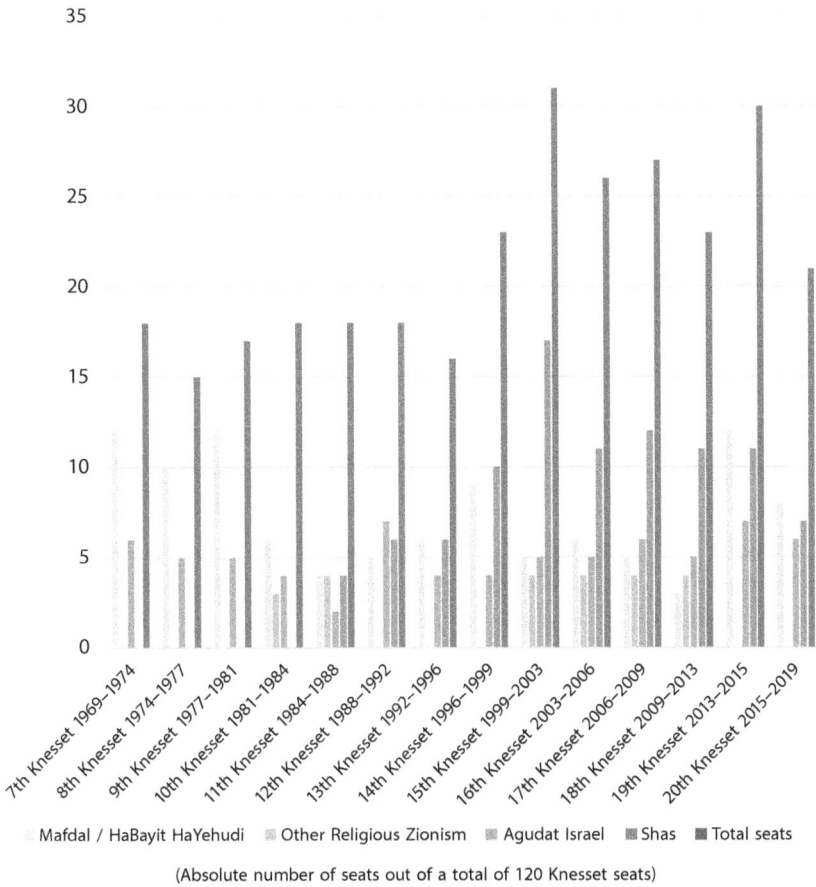

Figure 8.1. Religious seats in the Knesset, 1969–2019. *Source:* The Knesset, www.
knesset.gov.il.

emergence of new forms of state–religion engagement. The next chapter
explores the political and social consequences of these developments and
the capacity of Israeli democracy to contain them.

The Radicalization of Religious Zionism

The religious-Zionist camp has arguably experienced the most fundamental
transformation after 1967 compared with any other group in Israeli society.
From a trusted partner of the secular establishment, it became a recurrent

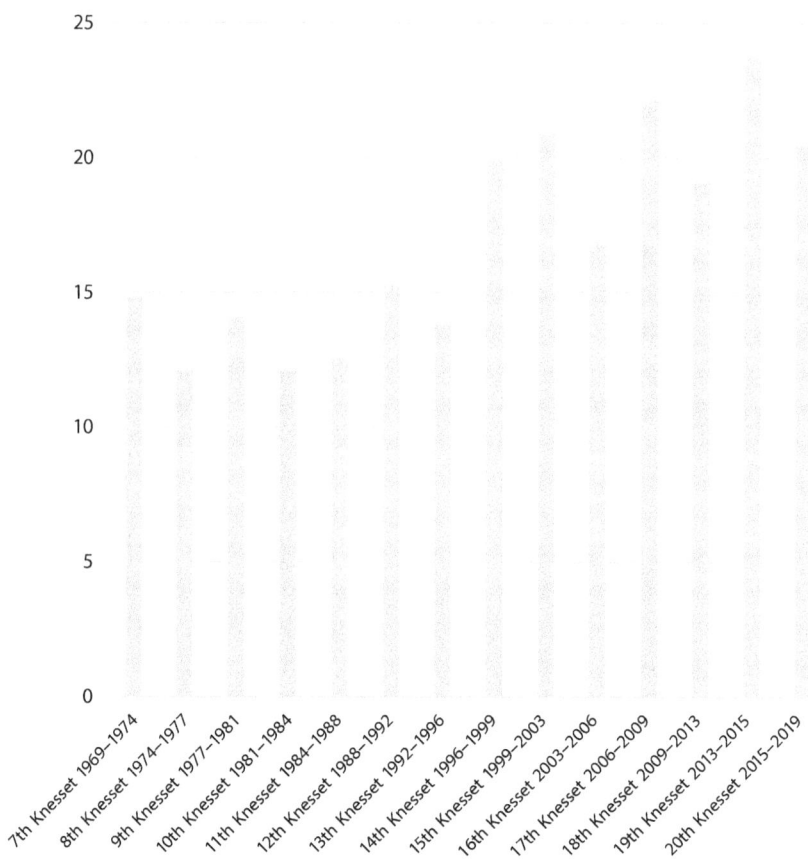

Figure 8.2. Electoral support (percentage) for religious parties in the Knesset, 1969–2019. *Source:* The Knesset, www.knesset.gov.il.

challenger of government policies. From an emphasis on spiritual and sacred issues and protecting the Jewishness of the public sphere, it moved to concentrate on protecting the sanctity of greater Eretz Yisrael. During that time, significant elements of the religious-Zionist population shifted their political agenda and behavior from parliamentarian activity, adherence to democratic procedures, and collaboration with the secular state to extraparliamentarian, often illegal activity through nonstate associations and social mobilization.

This transformation emerged from a convergence between social in-group trends and Israel's changing political situation in the Middle East. During the 1960s, the religious-Zionist camp confronted a profound crisis

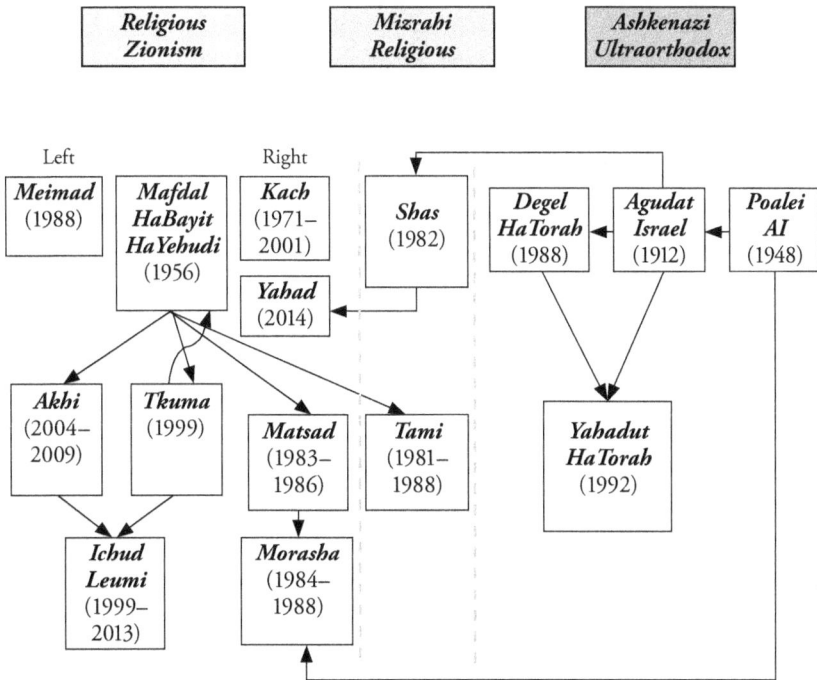

Figure 8.3. Genealogy of religious parties in Israel.

of identity that generated growing criticism by the young generation against the old leadership (Aran 2013, 73–87). The efforts of religious Zionists to participate in Israel's modern secular society while preserving their Orthodox way of life resulted in selective observance of mitzvot (religious rules) and silent approval of Mapai's secular leadership as the country's political elite. This was coupled with difficulties associated with living in mixed (secular-religious) urban populations and growing secular-modern trends such as consumerism and materialism that diffused into the religious-Zionist population. Also, religious education under the aegis of the state education system suffered from "religious mediocrity"[3]—namely, insufficient Torah studies and a low level of knowledge and observance among teachers in the system (M. Friedman 1982; Sharlo 2007, 336).

These trends empowered certain religious-Zionist institutions and weakened others. In the educational realm, new religious schools—*yeshivot tichoniyot* (high-school yeshivas) for boys and *ulpana* schools for girls, both often with a boarding component—were founded in an effort to restore

religious knowledge, observance, and dedication among the younger generation. These soon became more than educational institutions. They facilitated
strong social and intellectual networks among their students in which political
ideas were developed and challenged and social ties emerged (M. Friedman
1982; Sandler 1996; Newman 2005).

Equally important was the ascendance of Yeshivat Merkaz HaRav
Kook (Rav Kook Yeshiva Center) to prominent status among religious
Zionists.[4] The yeshiva was established in 1923 by Rabbi Avraham Yitzhak
HaCohen Kook (Rav Kook), the first Ashkenazi chief rabbi of Mandatory
Palestine until his death in 1935. Between 1935 and the mid-1950s, the
yeshiva had been a relatively small and insignificant institution of higher
religious learning compared with the leading Haredi yeshivas. In 1952, Rav
Kook's son, Rabbi Zvi Yehuda Kook (also known as Rav Kook) became the
head of the yeshiva. He adopted his father's theological worldview, which
perceived the secular Zionist movement and the creation of the state of
Israel as integral components in a redemption process. The Israel Defense
Forces (IDF) and the pioneers were, according to Rav Kook (both father
and son), manifestations of holiness whose deeds hastened the coming of
the messiah (Don-Yehiya 1987).

In addition, Rav Avraham Yitzhak Kook emphasized the religious
centrality of the land of Israel and the "holy trinity" of the Jewish Torah,
the Jewish nation, and the Jewish land—Torat Yisrael le-Am Yisrael be-Eretz
Yisrael (Torah of Israel for the people of Israel in the land of Israel). This
philosophy stood in sharp contrast to the Haredi theological perspective,
which opposed Zionist proactivity and downplayed the religious value of
a secular Jewish state. At the same time, Rav Kook's teachings departed
from the mainstream religious-Zionist worldview in some ways. Although
the traditional Mizrahi movement based its worldview on two legs,[5] Torah
V'Avoda (loosely translatable as religious study and working the land of
Israel, or, more bluntly, the earthly and the divine[6]), for Rav Kook every
part of reality was a manifestation of divinity. In this respect, Rav Kook's
school is closer to Haredi perspectives than to the Mizrahi movement (Kehat
2002; Sharlo 2007, 337–39).[7]

Despite similarities in the doctrines of Rav Kook, father and son, the
two differ in some important ways. The son leaned toward vanguard political
activity, putting greater emphasis on the sanctity of the land of Israel, and
drew a clear outline of the redemption process, whereas the father was more
ambiguous about the sequence and shape of redemption and was influenced
by dialectical Hegelian and Marxist ideas. These differences, along with the

fact that Rabbi Zvi Yehuda Kook provided his intellectual input after the establishment of the state, made his teachings a powerful ideological basis for political activity (Don-Yehiya 1987; 225–28).

Indeed, the ideological crisis that struck the religious-Zionist population during the 1960s led to a remarkable elevation in the status and influence of the Merkaz HaRav, which became a leading center of religious-Zionist learning. The authority and appeal of Rabbi Zvi Yehuda Kook and other charismatic rabbinic figures, such as Avraham Shapira, Shaul Israeli, Moshe Zvi Nerya, and Chaim Druckman, attracted many religious-Zionist younger people, who sought a new religious perspective.[8] The Merkaz HaRav offered its enthusiastic students new theological horizons, original interpretations of current events, and a strong emphasis on national redemption. Between 1960 and 1964, the Merkaz HaRav doubled the number of its annual graduates from 100 to 200. Then in 1964, a group of enthusiastic religious-Zionist youngsters with the name Gahelet, a word meaning "ember" and an acronym for Gar'in Halutzi Lomdei Torah (Cadre of Torah Learning Pioneers), joined Merkaz HaRav and subjected themselves to the leadership of Rav Zvi Yehuda Kook. From that point on, the religious perspective of Merkaz HaRav diffused into the entire religious-Zionist educational stream. Its graduates became teachers and heads of yeshivas throughout the country and indoctrinated young students in the religious division of the public education system. In the early 1960s Rabbi Zvi Yehuda showed no interest in earthly political matters and even publicly prohibited his students' participation in elections,[9] but by the middle of the decade he had pivoted in the opposite direction, toward active involvement in national politics. Eventually, this became central to his teachings.

Around the same time, the younger generation in Mafdal was rebelling against the party's old guard, challenging the latter's political pragmatism and submission to Mapai. In 1963 a young group headed by Zevulun Hammer established the Mafdal Young Faction (Tz'irei HaMafdal). The Young Faction criticized the old leadership's overemphasis on religious themes and apologetic standing vis-à-vis secular Zionism and advocated a more comprehensive agenda, one that would provide an alternative vision to that of the secular parties in profane matters such as the economy, security, and foreign policy. The theological sophistication of the Merkaz HaRav in combination with the political enthusiasm of the Young Faction resulted in a significant shift in the religious-Zionist agenda and in its relationship with the state, the secular establishment, and the rest of Israeli society. This process only needed an external stimulation, which came in 1967.

On the eve of Israel's nineteenth Independence Day in May 1967, Rabbi Zvi Yehuda delivered a famous sermon, "Mizmor HaYud-Tet shel Medinat Yisrael" (the Nineteenth Psalm of the State of Israel), in which he mourned Israel's lack of sovereignty over the biblical heartland of Eretz Yisrael:

> Nineteen years ago, on that famous night, upon the acceptance of the positive decision of the United Nations on the foundation of the State of Israel, when the entire nation flooded the streets to celebrate its joy, I could not go out and join the celebrations. I sat alone and silent because I felt a heavy burden. During those first hours I could not accept God's awful message which appears in the prophecy in *Tre-Asar* (the Twelve Prophets)—*My land shall be divided*. Where is our Hebron—have we forgotten it?! And where is our Shechem (Nablus)—have we forgotten it?! And where is our Jericho—have we forgotten it?! And where is our Transjordan?! Where is every piece of land, each and every part of God's land? Is it in our right to give up even a millimeter of it? *Khalila V'Has V'Shalom*! (God forbid!) (translation mine)[10]

Three weeks later, on June 5, 1967, Israel initiated a successful preemptive attack against neighboring Arab countries, gained military superiority on all three fronts, and took control of large swaths of territory—the West Bank and eastern Jerusalem from Jordan, the Gaza Strip and Sinai Peninsula from Egypt, and parts of the Golan Heights from Syria. The military outcome of the Six-Day War, especially the occupation of Jerusalem, was not influenced by religious motives but by security considerations (Oren 2003). Nevertheless, the liberation of the holy places mentioned in Rabbi Kook's prophetic sermon consolidated the rabbi's leadership and spiritual status. No less important, it reinforced a perception of congruence between the interests and actions of the state during the war and the divine plan of redemption. Indeed, the enormous consequences of the 1967 military victory made it the most significant turning point in the history of modern Israel. The occupation/liberation of the holy places denoted the beginning of a deep transformation in Israeli society,[11] with new dilemmas about how to manage these places and their Arab inhabitants, the manner by which they altered the status of Israel in the Middle East, and the theological meaning of the Jewish state, while triggering messianic radicalization among parts of the religious-Zionist public (A. Rubinstein 1984; Hertzberg 1986; Sprinzak 1998; Oren 2003; Segev 2005; Aran 2013).

Following the 1967 military victory, religious-Zionist attitudes became more messianic and land-oriented. The occupation of historic Jewish territories was perceived by Rabbi Kook's followers as a deliberate act of God, the beginning of messianic redemption, and a manifestation of the nonseparable triangle of the Jewish people, the Torah, and the Land of Israel (Tirosh 1974). Notably, Jewish sovereignty is missing from this triangle, which means that the link between the people and the land does not inherently depend on the existence of a Jewish state. Rather, in this view, the state is merely an instrument of redemption and justifiable only as long as it serves redemption through the liberation of the land. Conversely, in situations where the state departs from the path of redemption (i.e., gives up sacred territory), it loses its sacral value and its rulings can be ignored. This theological perspective divided the religious-Zionist population between two opposing poles—redemption and sovereignty (D. Rubinstein 1982; Newman 1986; Don-Yehiya 1987; Taub 2007; Aran 2013).

One of the most contentious arenas since 1967 has been control over the Temple Mount, Judaism's holiest site, known to Muslims as Haram al-Sharif. Following the war, the Israeli government gave primacy to diplomatic and security considerations over Jewish spiritual longing. To minimize international pressure and Muslim rage, Jews were denied the right to pray on the mount itself. To accommodate Jewish prayer at the mount, the government constructed a large plaza outside it, adjacent to the Western Wall—one of the retaining walls built to create the mount as part of Herod the Great's expansion of the Second Temple at the dawn of the first millennium. Yet some rabbinic figures, particularly IDF chief rabbi Rav Shlomo Goren, perceived this compromise as humiliating: why, they asked, should Jews have to restrict themselves to praying outside what had been the temple complex when the site of the temple itself was liberated and under Jewish rule? These tensions stimulated later attempts to reestablish Jewish sovereignty in the holy place (Shragai 1995, 28–38; Inbari 2007, 2012) (more on this in chapter 9).

In light of the messianic tendencies now filtering through the Merkaz HaRav, the terminology of its followers shifted from civic-nationalistic to religious-messianic. Most important, this camp abandoned use of the country's official name, Medinat Yisrael (State of Israel), and instead made frequent use of the biblical term Eretz Yisrael (Land of Israel) (Bartal 2001). The holiness of the land was linked to God's promise to give the land as an inheritance to the Jewish people, even though some parts of the Occupied Territories, such as the Golan Heights and the Gaza Strip, were not part of biblical Eretz Yisrael. Furthermore, the redemption project was interpreted by some messianic rabbis as reflecting a superior moral standard, even if at times this standard violated basic moral values and legal norms, for instance, by sanctioning violence against Palestinian inhabitants in the Occupied Territories and systematic infringement of state laws. In time, the occupation of the land became superior to any other mitzvah and narrowed the entire corpus of Jewish morals to one debatable obligation (Lustick 1987; U. Tal 1987; Aran 2013).

Of all the movement's activities, the settlement enterprise carried the gravest political consequences. Immediately following the 1967 war, religious-Zionist teams under the leadership of Rav Kook's students Hanan Porat and Moshe Levinger began to establish communities on occupied plots of land in Gush Etzyon,[12] Hebron,[13] and the Old City of Jerusalem.[14] Between the end of the Six-Day War in 1967 and the Yom Kippur War in 1973, eighteen settlements were established, and that number increased significantly after 1977. The early settlements were erected with the implicit support of the government. Several Mapai leaders, including Ministers Yigal Alon and Israel Galilee, perceived these new settlement projects as a natural continuation of the Zionist ideology, while failing to grasp either the theological motivation behind them or the far-reaching ramifications they entailed. Others, like Pinchas Sapir and Prime Minister Levi Eshkol, were more reluctant about settlement initiatives but could not resist the passion and energy of the young settlers (Gazit 1999; Zertal and Eldar 2004, 25–28). David Ben-Gurion was the only person who recognized the dangers inherent in such a policy. He warned Mapai's leadership that Israel should not deepen its hold in the Occupied Territories and, indeed, should seek to return the territories in exchange for peace with the Arab world at the earliest possible opportunity. But he failed to convince his former disciples, who now held political power (Hertzberg 2003, x–xi).

The settlements were also backed by the security apparatus and the courts. The IDF's higher command supported Israeli control over the mountainous slopes of the West Bank because of the increased margin of security this provided (Gazit 1999). Although this had nothing to do with the redemptionist vision of the settlers, it conferred an important stamp of legitimacy on the project. Furthermore, until 1979 the IDF's security rationale was respected by the High Court of Justice, despite the court's growing doubts about the legality of settling on private Palestinian lands (Negbi 1981).[15] This interinstitutional support for the settlement enterprise convinced the settlers that there was no contradiction between state sovereigny and the promotion of redemption. On the contrary, it made them believe that in constructing settlements, they were in fact implementing the will of the government, which could not publicly support them because of diplomatic considerations. Their interpretation of the admittedly ambiguous signals from the state was far from the truth, but it facilitated what Ehud Sprinzak called politico-cultural illegalism—a basic disrespect for state laws and institutions and a worldview that justifies illegal actions deemed to accord with divine imperatives (Sprinzak 1986, 121)—and an intensification of the settlement enterprise.

Mafdal, the political platform of religious Zionism, was also deeply influenced by the evolving trends. Moderate party leaders like Yosef Burg, Moshe Unna, and Moshe Shapira were confronted by the Young Faction with a demand to dissolve Mafdal's historical alliance with Mapai. In January 1968, Unna and Shapira still supported negotiations on the future of the Occupied Territories,[16] but this time there was no consensus around the old guard's pragmatist approach. The outcome of the war crystallized the political agenda of the Young Faction, with the territorial integrity of Eretz Yisrael at its core (Don-Yehiya 1987, 23; Newman 2005, 203–4), and they increased their attacks on the old leadership. In May 1968 the Young Faction announced the foundation of a political faction—Gush Le-Shinui HaTnua (Bloc for Change in the Movement)—within Mafdal.[17] Both developments signaled the outbreak of rebellion and generational shift within the religious-Zionist party.

The 1973 Yom Kippur War accelerated changes in the political structure of the settler movement and increased its militancy. On October 6, 1973, Israel was caught by surprise by the Egyptian and Syrian armies. Over three weeks of fighting, Israel succeeded in blocking the combined attack and gained a military advantage on both fronts, but the cost was extremely high. Israel lost almost a third of its armored and aerial forces, with more than 2,600 soldiers killed and more than 7,200 injured. The results of the Yom Kippur War contrasted painfully with the glorious victory of 1967 and shook the trust of Israeli society in the supremacy of the IDF and the capabilities of Mapai's political leadership (I. Tal 1996, 184–91). Adding to the feeling of despair, in 1974 the Palestine Liberation Organization (PLO) gained considerable international recognition, and international criticism against the state of Israel and the Zionist project became louder and more explicit. The most important reflections of this double-edged trend were UN General Assembly Resolution 3237, which approved a PLO observer delegation to the UN (accepted November 22, 1974) and Resolution 3379, which equated Zionism with racism (accepted November 10, 1975).

These events increased tension among the settlers, the state, and the rest of Israeli society. Although the state apparatus and most of the Israeli public interpreted the events of 1973 as a lesson in humility and the limitations of military power, Rav Kook's followers perceived the traumatic near-defeat—called *sibuchim* (complications) by Rabbi Kook—as a direct consequence of Israel's failure to carry through God's plan of redemption. In their understanding, the only way to prevent future malfunctions down the road of redemption was to commit more forcefully to settling the land. Toward this end, in 1974 a group of Rav Kook's followers established Gush Emunim (Bloc of the Faithful).

Gush Emunim was originally established as a faction within Mafdal. But party politics require intraparty as well as interparty compromises, obedience to state laws and the rules of the political game, which would have weakened Gush Emunim's ability to accomplish its religious goals. Indeed, "to participate in politics on these terms, challengers implicitly or explicitly accept major restrictions on claims and forms of action" (McAdam, Tarrow, and Tilly 1997, 165). Hence, the bloc separated from Mafdal and was loosely reestablished as a social movement. The new movement maintained open channels with the political establishment, but it freed itself from the chains of institutionalized politics.

Soon thereafter, Gush Emunim entered into direct confrontation with the incumbent Rabin-led Mapai government (1974–1977), which refused to tolerate activities that contradicted the policies of the elected government. The bloc's first settlement initiative was Keshet in the Golan Heights in 1974, but in 1975 Gush Emunim launched a large-scale settlement campaign throughout the Occupied Territories that aimed to create a reality of a dense Jewish population in the territories that would hinder any future attempt to bargain the land for peace. The Rabin government accepted the foundation of scattered settlements with strategic value, especially along the Jordan Valley, but it opposed Jewish residence in close proximity to densely populated Arab areas. It thus resisted recurrent attempts by Gush Emunim's Elon Moreh Group to settle in different locations in Samaria (the northern West Bank) despite the settlers' motivation and persistence (Hertzberg 1986, 90; Gazit 1999, 233). Between 1974 and 1976, only six new settlements were established, the total number of settlers in the West Bank did not exceed 3,200,[18] and the whole settlement project remained relatively insignificant.

The government objection to the settlements led Mafdal, now with more militant leadership, to end its historical alliance with Mapai. The arrival on Israeli soil of three F-16 jet fighters, part of a shipment of US arms aid, after the start of the Sabbath on December 10, 1976, furnished Mafdal with the excuse they needed to cut ties. After Mafdal's ministers deliberately abstained from a no-confidence vote brought over the Sabbath breach by Agudat Israel, Rabin dissolved his government and called for new elections in May 1977. These elections were to mark the beginning of a new era in the relationship between the state and the religious-Zionist camp.

Increased Haredi Involvement in Politics

The second development, increased involvement of the Haredi parties in Israeli democracy, took place after the 1977 general elections, in which Mapai lost its longtime political hegemony to the Likud party. Mapai's collapse was the culmination of a gradual multidimensional decline whose causes included the trauma of the Yom Kippur War, a dire economic situation, the mediocre performance by Rabin's government, maltreatment of specific segments in society (especially lower socioeconomic strata of Mizrahi descent), and visible friction among Mapai's leaders. Likud's chairman, Menachem Begin, needed both Mafdal (twelve seats in the Knesset) and Agudat Israel (four seats) to build a right-wing coalition,[19] and was therefore willing to offer significant concessions to build a political alliance with those factions. In contrast to Mafdal, which had served regularly in Mapai's coalitions, the Haredi Agudat Israel joined the government after more than twenty-five years in opposition. Their return to the government increased Haredi involvement in Israeli politics, deepened the mutual interconnectedness between the political system and this previously remote sector, and exposed the Israeli democratic system to Haredi sectarian demands.

The Haredi population in Israel has traditionally been relatively small but fast-growing. In 1948 it numbered approximately 35,000 people altogether. By the late 1970s, it had reached 140,000, making the Haredim 3.5 percent of Israel's total population of 3.8 million (Cahaner, Yozgof-Aurbach, and Sofer 2012). The Haredi sector includes militant anti-Zionist ultraortho- dox and mainstream non-Zionist ultraorthodox factions (Neuberger 2006, 179–95).[20] Until the formation of Shas in 1982, the Ashkenazi Agudat Israel was the main Haredi party, usually running in a united front with the small Poalei Agudat Israel party. Despite various internal personal and ideological disputes, until 1977 the mainstream Haredi population largely remained politically united under the platform of Agudat Israel.

The rapid enlargement of the Haredi population created social and economic incentives for Agudat Israel to increase its share of state resources by exploiting its political leverage. The goal of the Haredi leadership was to enable the community to maintain its social structure as a "society of scholars," in which adult men could devote their days to religious study rather than profane occupations. As Rabbi Yaacov Ariel, the chief rabbi of the city of Ramat Gan, told me: "The greatest mitzvah in Judaism is Torah studies . . . Jewish education means Torah studies, every day and all day long. This is the Jewish heritage."[21] One might also observe that only by maintaining their existing social structure could the Haredi leadership sustain rabbinical control over the population and prevent defection to secular life. Maintaining this structure, in turn, was contingent on the community's ability to provide its young members with material benefits on a par with those found in the surrounding secular world (M. Friedman 1991). However, the capability of a society largely isolated from the labor market to produce goods comparable to those of a largely employed society is very limited. The rapid demographic growth of the Haredi population made it almost impossible to fund its autonomous educational system from internal communal resources.[22] Finally, maintaining an isolated society of scholars mandates mass exemption of yeshiva students from military service and minimum daily interaction with the surrounding secular populace. Hence, the Haredi leadership had strong internal reasons to throw itself into the political game.

Equally important, the political atmosphere after 1977 became more fertile to Haredi participation. As noted, Begin needed Haredi collaboration to form his coalition, and he was willing to go a long way to ensure their participation in government. As part of the negotiations, Begin's government agreed to remove limits on the exemption of male Haredi students and Haredi women from military conscription. This decision reversed the Mapai policy that had driven Agudat Israel out of the government in the early 1950s (see chapter 7). In addition, Begin approved allocations of significant resources from several ministries, including the Ministries of Housing, Education, and Welfare, directly to Haredi institutions and specific social needs. Likud's ascent to power meant also a genuine change in attitudes toward the needs and worldviews of the Haredi population. As Friedman asserts: "Begin was a prime minister whom the Haredim could appreciate. He spoke their language, rather than that of the native-born Israelis and the Zionist left. . . . For the first time, Haredim felt at home in the corridors of government, and not like stepchildren or total strangers" (M. Friedman 1994, 190).

Finally, the aftermath of the 1973 war facilitated Haredi participation in government. The devastating outcome of the war convinced the ultraorthodox leadership that the Israeli population were primed to realize the fallacy of the Zionist project and the superiority of a religious way of life. They therefore regarded it as an opportune time to join the government and take advantage of state infrastructures to guide Israeli society closer to religion and away from the secular Zionist ideology (Liebman 1995).

Agudat Israel's official anti-Zionist stance prevented it from occupying full ministerial positions. Instead, its delegates accepted deputy ministerial positions and chairmanships of parliamentary committees. Over the years Agudat Israel (and later its successor party, United Torah Judaism [Yahadut HaTorah]) demanded that its representatives hold the chairmanship of the Knesset's monetary committee, which approves the national budget and can secure allocations of funding for sectarian ultraorthodox needs. With their control over funding ensured, from 1977 onward Haredi parties became regular partners in government, siding alternately with different ideological camps. Their growing electoral weight and new political behavior created a fundamental shift in Israel's distribution of political power, giving the Haredim unprecedented political leverage that would influence Israeli politics in a profound way.

Shas and the Birth of Mizrahi Haredi Politics

The third influential development took place in the early 1980s with the formation of a Sephardic Haredi political party Hitahdut HaSepharadim HaOlamit Shomrei Torah (Global Union of Torah-Observant Sephardic Jews)—a name that was eventually shortened to Shomrei Sepharad, or Shas. The emergence of Shas and its ascendance to power in Israeli politics have been the subject of extensive research (Yuchtman-Yaar and Hermann 2000; Peled 2001; Fisher 2004; Deshen 2006; Lehmann and Siebzehner 2006; Lupo 2006; Ravitzky 2006).[23] Shas is a relatively recent phenomenon in Israeli politics, especially compared with most other political platforms, whose formation predated statehood. Between 1948 and the early 1980s, the Sephardi religious population in Israel did not have its own educational or political institutions. Less observant Israelis of Mizrahi backgrounds sent their children to religious-Zionist schools and voted Mafdal, while the more observant among them sent their children to Ashkenazi yeshivas and gave their votes to Agudat Israel. Despite the distinct theological and cultural foundations of Sephardic Judaism, to which Middle Eastern and North African Jews traditionally adhered, Israelis of Mizrahi origin adopted an Ashkenazi (primarily Lithuanian) theological worldview and habits, a process that Jacob Lupo describes as the emergence of a Sephardi-Lithuanian ultraorthodoxy (Lupo 2006).

Shas was established by a charismatic scholar, the former Sephardi Chief Rabbi Ovadia Yosef (Aloush and Elituv 2004; Lau 2005; Picard 2007; Leon 2015). Rav Elazar Menachem Shach, leader of the Lithuanian faction in Agudat Israel, gave his blessing to the formation of a Sephardi ultraorthodox party in a sector that was then dominated by Ashkenazi rabbis and practiced considerable discrimination against Sephardi rabbis and yeshiva students. Rav Shach's approval and support derived from a mixture of moral considerations and sober political calculus. He wanted to eliminate anti-Sephardi sentiment in the Haredi world, but at the same time expected the new Sephardic faction to remain under his umbrella and expand the political weight of the Lithuanian faction vis-à-vis the dominant Hasidic courts.[24]

Shas was founded in 1982 and participated in municipal elections in Jerusalem in 1983. In its first participation in national elections in 1984, it won four seats in the Knesset. Soon thereafter, Rav Ovadia Yosef broke free from Rav Shach's patronage and consolidated his own religious authority, supported by a rabbinical council called the Moetzet Hakhmei HaTorah. Although the council imitated Agudat Israel's Moetzet Gedolei HaTorah,[25] Shas's council has had less independent rabbinical weight, as it was largely dominated by Rabbi Yosef until his death in 2013.

From the moment of its formation, Shas has challenged the distribution of power in Israeli politics and confronted the hegemonic status of Ashkenazi culture in Israeli society. It has done this by using original strategies of popular recruitment and engagement with the state, distinct from those practiced by the Ashkenazi Haredi parties. First, while Mafdal and United Torah Judaism recruit their electorate from well-defined segments in society—the modern Orthodox and ultraorthodox, respectively—Shas aims to represent a mixture of populations, appealing to the Haredi, traditional,[26] and secular sectors, particularly people from the periphery and lower socioeconomic strata. The common thread among all these sectors is their Sephardi/Mizrahi origins. Shas's electorate is thought to have a Mizrahi Haredi nucleus of 25–40 percent, with another 20–25 percent drawn from the Mizrahi religious-Zionist population and 40–50 percent from the traditional and secular Mizrahi population. Although the true number of Mizrahi Haredi voters is difficult to pin down, the size of that nucleus is thought to be fairly constant, whereas the size of the other two groups is contingent on strategies of recruitment and contemporary political configurations. As a result, Shas's performance in general elections fluctuates much more than that of the other religious parties (Bick 2001, 58–59; Neuberger 2006, 193–94).

Shas's electoral strategy relies heavily on recruiting voters at a young age, through its platforms on issues such as welfare and education. In this, Shas resembles religious parties in the Muslim world, such as the Muslim Brotherhood in Egypt and the Welfare Party and AKP in Turkey (as well as militant groups such as Hizballah in Lebanon and Hamas in the Palestinian Authority), more than it does other religious parties in Israel (Jaber 1997; Shah and Toft 2006; Turam 2007; Ashour 2009).

Shas's diverse electorate has provoked scholarly debate regarding the relative dominance of religious, ethnic, and socioeconomic components in the party's agenda and source of appeal. Peled (2001) argues that Shas is predominantly a socioeconomic phenomenon that uses an integrative religious-social agenda to appeal to Israelis of Sephardi and Mizrahi descent, many of whom feel marginalized in Israeli society. According to this approach, Shas filled a vacuum created by the Israeli regime in the 1980s, an era of economic liberalization and massive privatization that eroded the Israeli welfare state, and it uses its political platform to meet its electorate's material needs through sectarian representation (Gutwein 2007). Ravitzky (2006) emphasizes the religious and spiritual elements of Shas's worldview and the theological leadership and charisma of its founder and longtime leader, Rabbi Ovadia Yosef. Sarfati (2014), on the other hand, emphasizes the social movement element of Shas, namely, its capacity to frame its demands and grievances and the party's ability to mobilize its mass electorate.

The present work contends that despite the party's direct involvement in secular socioeconomic issues, understanding it only as a class cleavage phenomenon or as a social movement is inaccurate. The entire party leadership is Haredi and adheres to Rabbi Yosef's leadership, Shas's educational platform is entirely religious, the core of its electoral support comes from the Mizrahi Haredi sector, and religious rhetoric is dominant in its public messages. Thus, Shas should be understood as centered on an amalgam of religious and ethnic renewal. The party's core line is theological, and its economic policies and sectarian rhetoric help recruit broader audiences (Lehmann and Siebzehner 2006, 2008; A. Rubin 2015).

Since its inception in the early 1980s, Shas has developed a distinct strategy of interaction with the state that has endowed it with considerable sectarian benefits but also exposed it to serious social criticism within the Israeli public. Unlike the Ashkenazi ultraorthodox, Shas sought full participation in Israeli politics, including taking ministerial positions in government. This policy has facilitated the allocation of considerable resources to Shas's educational platform Maayan HaChinuch HaTorani (Spring of Torah Education) and social services platform El HaMa'ayan (To the Spring), and its occupation of a central role in religious–state issues through the ministries under its responsibility. The party has traditionally demanded control of the Ministry of the Interior, which controls conversion, immigration, and municipal affairs, and the Ministry of Religious Services, which supervises and allocates resources to religious services. Other ministries occupied by the party in the past include those responsible for health, welfare, and housing, facilitating the distribution of state resources to the Shas electorate (Cohen and Susser 2003, 119–26). The party's strategy of wide-ranging engagement with the secular state and its emphasis on educational infrastructure as a source of indoctrination are additional points of resemblance with the Islamic parties of Turkey (Tepe 2008; Sarfati 2014).

Conclusion

The religion–state relationship in Israel underwent a deep and comprehensive transformation between the 1960s and 1980s, one that demonstrates the dynamic element of the state–religion relationship. This chapter articulated the three most significant developments in this period, which include the radicalization of religious Zionism, increased involvement of Haredi parties in politics, and the formation of the Mizrahi Haredi Shas party.

It is difficult to weigh the relative influence of complex social, economic, theological, and international factors on the relationship between the state and religious publics. Nevertheless, it is clear that the outcome of the Six-Day War stimulated the rise of a messianic theological worldview in Israel and shifted the religious-Zionist public from political moderation with a focus on religious issues to territorial expansionism. At the same time, the sectarian interests of the Haredi community (e.g., maintaining its social structure as a "society of scholars"), combined with the political turnover from Mapai to the Likud, motivated the Haredi leadership to increase its engagement with the state. Finally, Shas is a multifaceted phenomenon, combining a strong religious element with ethnic and class-based grievances in an era of privatization. Yet its electoral success and its willingness to participate fully in the political system have increased the weight of Haredi preferences in Israeli politics, shifting institutionalized political power from religious Zionism to the Haredi parties and exposing Israeli politics to excessive religious demands. The next chapter explores the impact of these developments on the state–religion interaction and on the current state of democracy in Israel.

Chapter 9

Mounting Challenges, Successful Containment, 1980s-2017

The current chapter accounts for the most recent tendencies in the state–religion relationship in Israel. It covers a period of almost four decades, between the early 1980s and 2017, and explores how Israeli democracy was influenced by previous changes in the relationship between the state and religious actors. In particular, this period allows us to look at what happens when religious groups, left unrestrained, seek to impose a proreligious agenda at the expense of democratic norms and practices. Israel's experience shows that the ability of religious actors to impose their agenda depends partly on the state's response to these challenges and partly on the background and initial structure of the state–religion relationship.

The past few decades in Israel exemplify that inclusive state policies are better able than noninclusive policies to protect the fundamentals of a democratic regime against challenging religious behavior. At the same time, this period also reveals that religious actors, like representatives of other collective identities, should be accommodated in the democratic state only as long as they embrace core democratic principles. When the costs of integration—democratic erosion and violation of the rights of other publics in society—begin to outweigh its benefits, the democratic state must respond by limiting religious initiatives to the bounds of democracy. In this regard, Israel's recent record is mixed and can be divided roughly into two periods, before and after Benjamin Netanyahu's election as prime minister in 2009.

Until the first decade of the twenty-first century, the state of Israel was relatively effective in containing challenges from militant religious-Zionist factions. True, the state faced mounting attacks on its sovereignty and legitimacy—attacks that reached a zenith with the assassination of Prime Minister Yitzhak Rabin in 1995 and recurrent violations of state restrictions on settling in occupied Palestinian territories. Nonetheless, in the 1980s and 1990s most of the religious-Zionist public continued to respect state laws. During that time, the state (which was ruled alternately by left- and right-wing coalitions) signed and executed peace agreements with Egypt (1979), Jordan (1994), and even the Palestinians (1990s), all without facing significant illegal or violent reactions and without interruption to the democratic regime. The last decade, however, has seen a deeper penetration of the religious-Zionist sector into state structures and the political system (Haklai 2007), including in the ranks of the ruling Likud party, which may seriously undermine the state's capacity to execute policies that run against this sector's agenda in the future.

As for the Haredi sector, the political stalemate after 1977 and Shas's entrance to politics boosted the Haredim's access to sectarian benefits from the state, often at the expense of the rest of society. Notwithstanding the opportunistic and abusive nature of Haredi political activity, however, this sector has operated within the confines of the democratic regime. This reality can be partially explained by the Haredi parties' dependence on the democratic regime to achieve their goals, but it can also be attributed to the inclusive nature of Israeli democracy, which reinforced the identification of religious populations with the Jewish state and motivated them to work in the system rather than challenge its foundations. To be sure, Haredi political activity may have negatively affected important democratic principles, but it has not threatened the sustainability of the democratic regime. Also interesting, the added weight of Haredi parties in government has not expanded the public role of religion in Israel. That is, the increased presence of religious actors in government did not lead to increased enforcement of religious content on Israeli society. Instead, sectarian interests came to the fore. Theocratic demands related to religious principles such as the public observance of Shabbat or kashrut, which in earlier decades had dissolved governments and forced new elections, became less significant.

Also important, the political stalemate that emerged in the late 1970s reduced the ability of the legislative and executive branches to contain excessive religious demands. This paralysis left control over religious challenges in the hands of the judicial branch, and primarily the High Court of Justice (HCJ), which ruled against religious claims that violated the principles of democracy and exceeded the upper limit of bounded integration. Nonetheless, the judiciary did take on and accomplish the task that fell to it. As such, these two parts of the equation—the initial democratic inclusion of religion, and then the state's relative efficacy (mainly by the judiciary) in checking undemocratic behavior when it arose—prevented political instabil-ity, alleviated serious challenges to Israeli democracy, and facilitated a more constructive outcome than in Turkey.

Religious Zionism's Interactions with the State

Recurrent Confrontations, Successful Containment, 1977–1992

The Likud government that took power in 1977 facilitated the implemen-tation of religious Zionism's territorial ambitions. Under Menachem Begin, the religious parties sensed that Israeli society had arrived at a consensus around their agenda. Begin often used terminology employed by observant Jews as part of their day-to-day speech, such as *baruch HaShem* (blessed be the Lord) or *b'ezrat HaShem* (with the help of the Lord), and he adopted the religious term Eretz Yisrael, the Land of Israel, instead of the mod-ern secular term Medinat Yisrael, the state of Israel (M. Friedman 1994, 190). Immediately following his election, Begin visited the Elon Moreh group's Kadum settlement in the West Bank and announced that "we will have many more Elon Morehs." On another occasion he corrected a TV reporter: "What occupied territories? These are liberated territories" (Shafat 1995, 298). According to Gazit: "The message was clear—the Likud holds a very different opinion regarding the establishment of new settlements in Samaria. The Mapai Settlement policy has come to an end" (Gazit 1999, 241; translation mine).

Begin's rhetoric was matched by decisive actions. Likud governments recognized seventy-seven new settlements in the West Bank between 1977 and 1984,[1] with the total number of settlers multiplying by eleven, from 3,200 settlers in 1976 to 36,900 in 1984 (see fig. 9.1).[2] Another eighteen settlements in the Sinai Peninsula and twelve in the Gaza Strip added sev-eral thousand more settlers. The settler movement also benefited from the active support and patronage of Ariel Sharon, Begin's minister of Agriculture (1977–1981) and Defense (1981–1983), who advanced settlement initiatives throughout the Occupied Territories and was commonly referred to by the settlers as the patron or father of the settlement movement (Shafat 1995, 311–12).

Equally important, Begin complied with Mafdal's demand that it take charge of the Ministry of Education, thus giving a religious party unprecedented control over the public education system, the most important

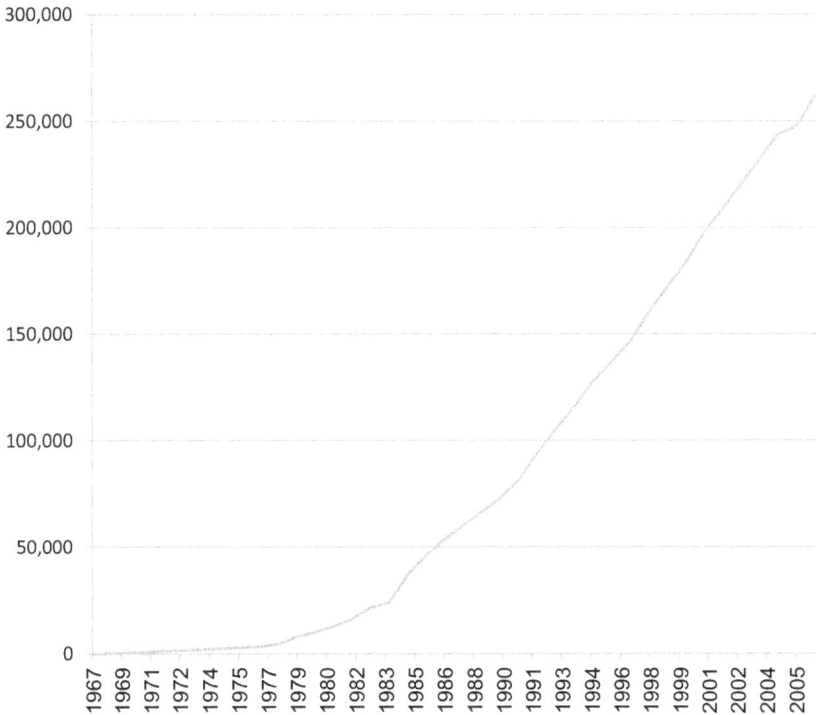

Figure 9.1. Number of settlers in the West Bank by year.

indoctrination system in modern states. Controlling the Ministry of Education became a standard demand of Mafdal in later coalition negotiations with Likud.[3]

Begin and the settlers advocated perpetual Israeli hold over the Occupied Territories, although they used very different rationales. Begin was motivated by an Eastern European type of romantic nationalism complemented by realistic security considerations, whereas the settlers sought the occupation of the land as a herald and sign of redemption (Taub 2007; Aran 2013). As long as the policies of the government and the objectives of the settler movement converged, no tensions arose between them, and the latter were able to carry forward their political intentions without considerable opposition or constraints. Nevertheless, the insoluble conflict between political sovereignty and messianic redemption remained intact, and it surfaced before long. It came to the fore within a year after the inauguration of the Begin government following two separate yet related events—the Camp David Accords and the Elon Moreh court decision. The former event revealed the differing perspectives and considerations of the government and the settler movement in regard to the status of occupied land. The latter signaled the beginning of a protracted dispute between the judiciary and the settler movement and highlighted the HCJ's important role in containing unlawful activity by the settlers.

The Camp David Accords, two documents signed by Israel, Egypt, and the United States on September 17, 1978, marked a high point in the first peace process between Israel and an Arab state. The first agreement adopted the principle of land for peace as an outline for Egyptian–Israeli reconciliation. Based on it, Israel agreed in March 1979 to dismantle military bases and civil settlements in the Sinai Peninsula and return the peninsula to Egypt in exchange for peace and normalization between the countries. The second agreement acknowledged the idea of Palestinian self-rule in the West Bank and Gaza.

The settlers perceived the accords as threatening the redemption project, and their signing constituted a critical juncture in the relationship between the settler movement and the state. The Begin government, despite its right-wing tendencies, gave primacy to security and diplomatic goals, whereas the settlers were fixated on their messianic dream and would not compromise it for profane considerations. Indeed, "on that day when Menachem Begin signed the famous accords with Egypt, he gave a kiss of death to the unity of the right" (Sprinzak 1989, 172).[4]

The second event, a year later, was an HCJ ruling that ordered the dismantling of Elon Moreh, a Gush Emunim settlement built on land that Israeli government had confiscated from private Palestinian owners in the West Bank. The decision, on October 22, 1979, had high resonance. It was the first occasion the HCJ rejected the Israel Defense Forces (IDF)'s arguments about the strategic value of a settlement and chose to defend Palestinian property rights, thereby subjecting Israel's military rule in the Occupied Territories to Israeli and international laws.[5]

The ruling shook the settler movement in two respects. First, the decision to prioritize state sovereignty, human rights, and the rule of law over settling the land positioned the HCJ as hostile to the settlement movement and spawned a long-lasting dispute between the Israeli judiciary and the settlers. In the words of religious-Zionist leaders, "the HCJ is the institution that most threatens the partnership between the religious population and the State of Israel,"[6] and "the HCJ is not fulfilling its responsibility to preserve

Israel as a Jewish democratic state."[7] Second, to the settlers' disappointment, instead of taking legal and institutional actions to bypass the court's decision, the Begin government adhered to it and ordered the dismantling of the settlement. This policy sent a clear signal that government support for the settlement project was not without limits and the project would be subjected to state sovereignty and the rule of law (Negbi 1981, 69–74; Gazit 1999, 239–44).

The combined impact of the Camp David Accords and the Elon Moreh decision shattered the euphoria of Gush Emunim and pushed it to more militant behavior in the political, institutional, and social realms. In politics, Gush Emunim sought to promote its agenda in government by lobbying and pressing its patrons and representatives in the cabinet, namely, Ariel Sharon and the Mafdal ministers. The secretariat of Gush Emunim initiated numerous meetings with cabinet ministers, aiming to convince them of the strategic value of the settlements (Shafat 1995, 338–39). The impact of these efforts was debatable. Although they managed to recruit sympathy and even support for new outposts, these efforts did not change Begin's mind about the Elon Moreh case, keep Sharon from executing the evacuation of Sinai in 1981 in his capacity as minister of Defense, or reverse Mafdal's decision to remain in government following the Camp David Accords.

Gush Emunim also tried to increase its political representation in the Knesset by dividing its religious-Zionist electoral support, under the belief that distributing votes among several parties would benefit the political leverage of the movement (Pedahzur 2000, 102). Three new religious-Zionist political platforms were established in the 1980s:[8] Techiya (1981–1992), a mixed secular-religious party with an ultra-right-wing worldview;[9] Matsad, which later became Morasha (1983–1988), a hawkish offspring of Mafdal;[10] and Kach (1971–1988), the most extremist religious political faction in Israeli politics.[11] These political gambles did not fare well. Splitting the religious-Zionist vote among several parties resulted in an overall decline in parliamentarian weight. Figure 8.1 demonstrated Mafdal's sharp electoral decline from twelve seats in 1977 to six in 1981 and just four in 1984. The twelve-seat record of 1977 was achieved only once since then, in the 2013 national elections. The most important religious party in Israeli politics during the first three decades of Israeli statehood gave up its place to the Haredi parties and was relegated to a relatively insignificant political position until 2013.

Furthermore, the party's constant slide to the right end of the political spectrum resulted in losing the electoral support of traditional Jews, who sought to be represented by more moderate parties. Thus they turned their support in the 1980s to Tami (a moderate Mizrahi offshoot of Mafdal),[12] Shas, and Likud. Importantly, Mafdal's decline until the 2010s was closely related to the party's failure to take a clear stand on important civic and religion–state issues.[13] While advocating for a greater Israel, Mafdal was silent on other issues, religious and profane alike, such as conversion, Shmita (the biblically mandated sabbatical year), conscription of yeshiva students, civic marriage, and the economic crisis of the 1980s, which led its traditional electorate to seek new political platforms (Cohen and Susser 2003, 126–37).

For its part, the state blocked extreme manifestations of religious messianic behavior and showed the democratic regime's limit of tolerance for deviations from bounded integration. This is manifested by the case of Kach. After winning one seat in the Knesset in 1984, the Kach party was disqualified by the Central Elections Committee from running in the 1988 elections because of its overt racist and antidemocratic agenda (Margui and Simonnot 1987), which contradicted Article 7A in Israel's Basic Law: The Knesset. Kach's debarment in 1988 and its classification as a terror organization in 1994 sent a clear message about the limits of religious integration and the right of the democratic state to defend itself against religious extremism (Pedahzur and Ranstorp 2001).

Institutionally, the settlers recognized that an effective political campaign would require a functioning institutional platform to coordinate its actions. Hence Gush Emunim's leadership established the Yesha Council (Moetzet Yesha), an institutional body composed of heads of local and regional councils in the West Bank and Gaza, with a separate organizational arm (Amana), which was responsible for coordinating and managing new settlement initiatives. Along with the Yesha Council and Amana, the settlers established a third institution, the Moetzet Rabbanei Yesha (Council of West Bank and Gaza Rabbis), an informal council of religious-Zionist rabbis who provided the political leadership with guidance on Jewish law and a religious stamp of legitimacy. This rabbinical council included Chief Rabbis Mordechai Eliyahu and Avraham Shapira and other disciples of Rabbi Zvi Yehuda Kook. Although the Council of Rabbis had (and continues to have) no formal role in the decision-making process of the political leadership, no substantial decision was taken (until the establishment of HaBayit HaYehudi in 2013) without rabbinic approval. The transfer of power from the political leadership to the rabbis restricted the ability of elected politicians to represent the religious-Zionist camp vis-à-vis the state and further curtailed the effectiveness of party politics (Cohen and Harel 2004; Bick 2007; Sharlo 2007).

In keeping with these political and institutional changes, the settler movement modified its mode of social mobilization and the character of its engagement with the state. The circumstances after 1979 presented the settler movement with tremendous challenges. Not only did the movement fail to prevent the state from signing international agreements and retreating from occupied land, they had to accept that a majority of Israelis supported the peace initiative with Egypt. Surveys in 1980 found that approximately 75 percent of Israel's Jewish population trusted Egyptian intentions and believed that peace with Egypt would improve the country's security.[14] As one Gush Emunim leader confessed: "We realized that we could not mobilize them [the Israeli public] to join popular protest activities against government policy. The religious-Zionist public remained lonely in its fight against the retreat from Sinai and opening the door to the establishment of a Palestinian state, which was agreed upon in Camp David" (Shafat 1995, 356–57; translation mine).

The distress of the settler movement sparked a wave of violence against state authorities and Palestinians in the Occupied Territories. This violence—rationalized by settler leaders as following the ethos of the prestate undergrounds—enjoyed encouragement from rabbinical authorities and reflected a deeply entrenched belief that exceptional circumstances justify exceptional measures (Gal-or 1986). In particular, the settlers clashed with state authorities during the withdrawal from Sinai. Their motivation in so doing was twofold. First, they believed that resolute action might convince God to change the fate of the Sinai settlements. Second, more pragmatically, the settlers hoped that by making the evacuation extremely costly, they could deter the state from executing similar policies in the future (Aran 1985). The withdrawal fast turned into a bitter struggle between two determined opponents: "If serious bloodshed did not take place, everything else did. Fierce struggles between soldiers and desperate settlers were conducted. . . . The Israeli public witnessed the longest and most intense period of civil disobedience and organized extralegalism in the history of the state" (Sprinzak 1989, 177).

The radicalizing rhetoric of the movement facilitated the emergence of extreme cells with more concrete goals. In 1979 the Israeli police arrested Yoel Lerner, a disciple of Rabbi Kahane and the leader of an underground group that planned to destroy the Islamic holy places on the Temple Mount (the al-Aqsa Mosque and the Dome of the Rock), in the hope that the subsequent catastrophe might lead to the foundation in Israel of a halakhic (i.e., theocratic) state.[15] Despite no documents to support his claim,

Lerner insisted that Rabbi Zvi Yehuda Kook had given his personal blessing to these plans (Shragai 1995, 85–90). After serving two years in prison, Lerner formed another underground group that again plotted to blow up the Dome of the Rock. The group was discovered and Lerner was arrested again (Shragai 1995, 91–95).[16]

While Yoel Lerner's groups were easily discovered by the authorities, the Jewish Underground, founded in 1980, presented a more serious threat. Like Lerner, the group sought to hasten the process of redemption by blowing up the Dome of the Rock. The Jewish Underground prepared a detailed plan, which included stealing explosives and other weapons from the IDF, frequent drills, and careful collection of relevant intelligence. The founders of this organization were all Gush Emunim members and former combat officers in the IDF. Yehuda Etzyon was a member of Gush Emunim's secretariat, Menachem Livni a lieutenant colonel in the IDF, and Yeshua Ben-Shoshan a rabbi and favored student of Rabbi Zvi Yehuda. The Underground presented its plan to explode the Dome of the Rock to dozens of rabbis, including Zvi Yehuda Kook, Moshe Levinger, Moshe Segal, Shlomo Aviner, Eliezer Waldman, Tzvi Tau, and Dov Lior. Although most of the rabbis were reluctant to approve the plan and some failed to condemn it, a minority actively supported it—and none found it necessary to report either the plan or the Underground to the authorities (Aran 1985; Gal-or 1986; Shragai 1995, 109). The plan was not put into action for various reasons, but until its exposure in 1984, the group was involved in a number of deadly attacks on Palestinian targets. These included assassination attempts against the Palestinian mayors of Nablus and Ramallah in June 1980, which left the mayors severely wounded, and a fatal attack on the Islamic College in Hebron in July 1983, which left three students dead. The Underground came into the hands of the security services on April 26, 1984, just hours before it planned to blow up five Palestinian buses in East Jerusalem.

Settler activists used violence to target Israeli citizens with opposing political views. In February 1983, an extremist named Yonah Abrushmi threw a hand grenade into a crowd of protesting peace activists, killing a young teacher, Emile Greenzweig, and wounding several others (Sprinzak 1995, 88). Although this was an exceptional case in its outcome, it was unexceptional in intent. Settlers engaged in frequent harassment of peace activists, along with daily violence against Palestinians in the Occupied Territories and clashes with IDF troops (Jones 1999; Zertal and Eldar 2004).

Nonetheless, to the settlers' dismay, all the new strategies of engagement with the state—legal and illegal, social and political—failed to turn the tide of events their way. State policies like the retreat from Sinai and the dismantling of Elon Moreh were carried out as planned. Extremist schemes were exposed and contained. The Madrid Conference—a regional forum cosponsored by the United States and the Soviet Union—was held in October 1991, paving the way for multilateral and bilateral negotiations that led to the Oslo Accords (1993–1995) and Israel-Jordan peace treaty (1994). Most important, extremism did not win the support of the general public. On the contrary, following a decade of radicalization, in the 1992 general election the Israeli public voted for moderate parties, facilitated the establishment of a left-wing government under Yitzhak Rabin, and drove the settlers further away from their objectives.

Mounting Attacks, 1992–2009

The post-1992 period intensified earlier trends but did not change the grand picture of the state–religion dynamic in Israel. During this time, successive Israeli governments (both left and right) accepted the principle of land for peace and the two-state solution as the main platform for peace negotiations and promoted a peace process with the Palestinians, including transferring occupied lands to Palestinian responsibility. This policy deepened the rift between the state and the settler movement and generated unprecedented responses, including direct attacks on Israel's democratic legitimacy. Yet Israeli democracy proved its strength, and even the most explosive events—the Hebron massacre in 1994, Rabin's assassination in 1995, and the fallout from the disengagement from Gaza in 2005—failed to destabilize the political system or undermine its democratic foundations.

Rabin's government accelerated the Israel–Palestinian peace process and in 1993 agreed on a Declaration of Principles with the Palestinians, which officially launched the Oslo Accords process. The declaration was signed in September 1993 on the White House lawn. Radical responses came almost immediately. On February 25, 1994, Dr. Baruch Goldstein, a physician and Kahane disciple, massacred 29 praying Palestinians and wounded 125 more in the Tomb of the Patriarchs in Hebron. Goldstein's actions were planned carefully and were meant to halt the implementation of the Oslo Accords. However, after a short setback the process resumed with implementation of the second phase in 1995 (Sprinzak 1995, 101–3).

Rabin's government accelerated the Israel–Palestinian peace process and The most radical attack on the Israeli regime was the assassination of Prime Minister Yitzhak Rabin. The settlers launched an aggressive campaign against the Rabin government, including personal incitement against Rabin and minister of Foreign Affairs Shimon Peres. The extent of the agitation was reflected in pictures shown on protest signs in the months before Rabin's assassination. In some of these pictures, Rabin's face is edited onto photos of Hitler and Yasser Arafat, bitter enemies of the Jewish nation. In another, Rabin's face is adorned with a sniper target, and the words *HaBoged* and its English translation, "The Traitor," written above and below. These images portrayed Rabin as a threat to the nation who should be treated in accordance. At the same time, militant religious-Zionist rabbis defined Rabin as a *moser*, meaning a person who hands over Jews or Jewish property to foreign authorities, and a *rodef*, a person who threatens another's life—both categories of individuals whom one is halakhically permitted to kill. This interpretation gave a religious stamp of legitimacy to those who felt Rabin had to be stopped by any means necessary. Importantly, such incitement was not confined to the outermost fringes of the settler movement: "[This] was not an isolated expression of a few extremist individuals who came to the conclusion that the two Halakhic concepts of *moser* and *rodef* had to be invoked. It was, instead, a reflection of intense scholarly discussion conducted in many extremist Yeshivas and religious circles" (Sprinzak 1999, 255).

The combined effect of political incitement and halakhic legitimation motivated religious-Zionist law student Yigal Amir to assassinate Rabin on November 4, 1995 (Peri 2001; S. Peleg 2002). When asked in court about his motives, Amir admitted that he acted according to *din rodef*—the halakhic law permitting the killing of a rodef—and that his actions were meant to prevent further territorial concessions to the Palestinians (Aran and Hassner 2013, 360).

Amir and Goldstein conducted the most profound attacks on Israeli democracy in the name of religious imperatives. But there were many other acts of religious-Zionist opposition to the Oslo Accords process. These included mass civil disobedience, interference with the public order, and violent clashes with state authorities. Much of this activity was coordinated by ad hoc associations, a trend that signified a decline in the authority of the Yesha Council as the representative institution of the settlers. A case of such an opposition organization was Zu Artzenu! (This Is Our Land!), headed by Benny Elon and Moshe Feiglin (who later became members of the Knesset). At the height of the Oslo Accords process, the movement mobilized its supporters to stage mass protests and roadblocks. The volume of activity declined after Rabin's assassination but resumed in 2003 before the disengagement from Gaza. Other protest organizations with a religious-Zionist orientation included Women in Green, Gamla Shall Not Fall Again,

Professors for a Strong Israel, Chai Vekayam (Living and Everlasting), and Matteh Maamatz (Staff of Strength) (Haklai 2003, 798). Yet again, these contentious activities did not undermine the government's capacity or will to advance the peace process. To the contrary, Netanyahu's right-wing government (1996–1999) continued the implementation of the Oslo Accords process by signing the Hebron (1997) and Wye (1998) agreements and transferring large territories in the West Bank to Palestinian rule.

A similar dynamic characterized the settlers' engagement with the state around the disengagement from Gaza during the second Sharon government (2003–2006).[17] The core of the plan was a unilateral civil and military withdrawal from the Gaza Strip and four isolated settlements on the northwestern edge of the West Bank (northern Samaria).[18] Sharon initially failed to muster support for the plan in a referendum of Likud voters, but he submitted a revised version of the plan to the Knesset, which approved it on October 24, 2004. The right regarded Sharon's political conduct as undemocratic and demanded a national referendum on the plan (Don-Yehiya 2005). On several occasions, including March 28, 2005, the Knesset rebuffed attempts to force a national referendum on the issue, although by that time it was clear that the plan had the support of at least 70 percent of the Israeli population.[19] The disengagement took place in August 2005. It required some 10,000 police officers and soldiers to evacuate more than 7,000 settlers from the Gaza Strip.

The disengagement from Gaza exposed serious disagreements in the religious-Zionist sector about its relationship with the state and the broader society and about the limits of political protest (Billig 2005; Inbari 2007a, 2009; Tabory and Sasson 2007).[20] For one thing, the disengagement instigated profound debates among rabbinic authorities. Some leading rabbis, such as Shlomo Aviner, Zvi Tau, Yoel Bin-Nun, and Yehuda Amital, embraced democratic principles and the rule of law. They emphasized the religious value of the state and the obligation (civil and religious) to obey an elected government (Dina Demalchuta Dina, "the law of the land is the law").[21] Conversely, militant rabbis like Yitzhak Ginsburg, Dov Lior, Shalom Dov Wolpa, and Eliezer Melamed called on Israeli soldiers to disobey orders to evacuate Jewish settlements and even to defect from evacuating units.[22] Two former chief rabbis and incumbent heads of Merkaz HaRav Yeshiva, Avraham Shapira and Mordechai Eliyahu, likewise called on all Jews to resist the eviction of Jews from their homes in every possible way, including disobedience.[23]

At the mass level, the Yesha Council mobilized a popular campaign to intensify public pressure on decision makers to cancel the disengagement. The campaign included billboards and banners bearing slogans in support of the settlers, orange flags and ribbons,[24] mass protests, and other mostly legal means of expression. Other efforts included lobbying members of the Knesset and government, popular demonstrations, public conferences, and appeals to the HCJ.[25] Illegal activities before and during the evacuation included roadblocks, interference with the IDF's preparations for the evacuation, and violent protests in which demonstrators clashed with soldiers tasked with executing the plan.[26] The disengagement also generated sporadic violent responses by small extremist groups, like the Eliran Golan underground,[27] and individuals, like Eden Nathan Zada and Asher Vizgen,[28] who targeted and killed both Palestinian residents of the Occupied Territories and Arab Israeli citizens. However, there was no evidence of links between these individual acts and the religious-Zionist rabbinic or political establishment. All in all, only a small fraction of the protesters engaged in illegal behavior, and the whole process was accomplished in an orderly manner. Also important, there was a relatively negligible number of cases of disobedience among IDF soldiers,[29] and there were Jewish residents of Gaza who participated peacefully in the eviction of their settlements and families. In short, we can conclude that the majority of the religious-Zionist population, including the evacuated settlers, subjected themselves to the decisions of the democratic regime and refrained from extreme responses, despite profound disagreement with government policies.

Following the disengagement, religious-Zionist rabbis, intellectuals, politicians, and members of the lay public engaged in a critical debate about the profound consequences of the evacuation from Gaza. In particular, they endeavored to redefine the relationship of this camp with the secular state. The public parts of this process exposed a broad spectrum of contemporary political ideas and corresponding behavior in religious-Zionist circles. On one side, a small group of hard-liners argued that the settler sector should divorce itself from the rest of Israeli society and collaborate with the Haredi sector in the formation of a theocratic state in Israel.[30] Most rabbis, however, chose to reemphasize religious Zionism's commitment to the state and the need to reconnect with the rest of Israeli society.

One of the manifestations of the hard-line faction that persists today is the phenomenon of aggressive young zealots known as the Hilltop Youth. The Hilltop Youth are small bands of teenagers and young adults who reject the Gush Emunim leadership and seek to bring about a theocratic state through violence and other forms of extreme behavior against both Palestinians and representatives of Israeli institutions in the Occupied Territories. One of their signatures is the so-called Tag Mechir (Price Tag) attacks, which include sabotaging private property, mosques, and churches; violent clashes with Palestinian residents; and in one notorious case, the murder of three members of a Palestinian family by arson in the village of Duma in July 2015 (S. Friedman 2015; Eiran and Krause 2018; Krause and Eiran 2018).[31] Extremists from radical settlements like Yitzhar and Har Bracha, which are associated with the Hilltop Youth, clash regularly with IDF forces, using tactics like verbal abuse (e.g., calling soldiers Nazis), puncturing tires, and throwing stones (Kershner 2008; Harel 2014; Eiran and Krause 2018).

In another sign of radicalization, the eviction of settlers from a number of unauthorized outposts in the West Bank after 2005 did not resemble the relatively peaceful disengagement from Gaza. A case in point is Amona, a single unauthorized outpost of thirty families in the West Bank. During the evacuation in February 2006, clashes between security forces and protesters resulted in hundreds of wounded settlers and policemen and dozens of arrests (Weiss 2006).[32] Likewise, the eviction of settlers from a single house in Hebron in December 2008 (known by supporters as the House of Peace and by the media as the House of Contention) required many troops and led to tens of wounded settlers and several arrests (McCarthy 2008).

However, as indicated already, despite the emergence of these poststatist approaches, a large majority of the religious-Zionist population continued to identify with—and remained loyal to—the state of Israel (Moses 2009). Despite the visibility of the more radical elements in religious Zionism, their demographic weight is relatively small. During the period of the disengagement, the number of people engaged in continuous active protest reached only about 20,000, out of a religious-Zionist population of approximately 800,000. Also, there was and remains a profound difference in behavior and opinion between religious-Zionist settlers in the Occupied Territories (about a quarter of the religious-Zionist population) and religious Zionists who live in the recognized boundaries of Israel. Notwithstanding all their efforts, by the end of the first decade of the twenty-first century, the more radical elements in religious Zionism had failed to mobilize a critical mass of followers to fulfill their redemptionist agenda, substantially influence the course of events, or alter the democratic regime in Israel.

Returning to Politics, Penetrating the State, 2009–2017

From 2009 to 2017, there has been a considerable change in religious Zionism's mode of engagement with the state, which may have far-reaching consequences for the relationship between them and for Israel's democratic performance. For its part, religious Zionism rediscovered the primacy of the political realm and invested considerable effort in strengthening its leverage in institutionalized politics, partly by shoring up its own party, HaBayit HaYehudi, and by building an effective pressure group within the ranks of the ruling Likud party. Likewise, religious Zionism identified the state apparatus as a primary target for penetration,[33] occupying key positions in the IDF and security forces, the education and legal systems, and public service more generally. At the same time, following its failure to prevent the disengagement from Gaza, religious Zionists sought to broaden their ties with wider society and enlarge their potential electorate beyond their limited sector. Meanwhile, Netanyahu identified the strategic value of religious Zionists (and, more generally, of the religious sector in Israel) for his rule and has made considerable concessions to keep them happy. The convergence of these trends—religious Zionism's return to institutionalized politics, its penetration of the state, and its pursuit of broader coalitions—accounts for a sizable contemporary shift in the relationship between the religious-Zionist sector and the Israeli state and society. I briefly cover these trends.

The return to institutionalized politics. As described already, after 1977 religious Zionism relegated institutionalized politics to secondary importance and invested most of its efforts in extraparliamentarian actions. The internal debate between creating facts on the ground and winning hearts was determined in favor of the former. But the failure to prevent the disengagement from Gaza in 2005 was a blow to this approach. It underscored the relative isolation of the settlers from the rest of Israeli society and their vulnerability to political decisions taken over their heads, even by right-wing politicians like Sharon (Roth 2013; Rubin 2014). The primary lesson from the trauma of eviction was that institutionalized politics is a crucial arena that deserves more attention.

In the lead-up to the 2009 elections, there had been a failed attempt to unite all factions in the sector into one political platform. In 2013, Mafdal and the ultrahawkish Tkuma party joined forces, ran in a united front as HaBayit HaYehudi (Jewish Home), and won twelve seats in the Knesset, the sector's record political representation since 1977. Indeed, "the 2013 elections represent[ed] a true landmark for the settlers" (Perliger and Zaidise 2015, 195), one that signified fresh forms of political behavior and a new strategy of engagement with the state. The main message of the party's effective 2013 election campaign was "stop apologizing." Naftali Bennett, chairman of the party since 2013, introduced new and ambitious terminology for religious Zionism in politics. Bennett argued that his mission was to put his hands on the "political wheel" and keep an eye on other elites, on the left and the right, because only this could prevent further surprises in the political realm. He also claimed that the party was leading a movement for comprehensive change among elites in all realms, including culture, the law, the media, and the academy, and should aspire to eventually lead the national camp in Israel.[34]

In 2015, the party suffered a relative electoral setback, winning only eight seats in the Knesset, following an effective cannibalistic electoral strategy by Netanyahu that shifted voters in the bloc from HaBayit HaYehudi to Likud (Navot, Rubin, and Ghanem 2017). Despite shrinking in size, though, the party secured two key cabinet positions, with responsibility for the two most important public indoctrination systems—education and the law. Bennett became minister of Education and his second-in-command, Ayelet Shaked, became minister of Justice. Both advanced far-reaching reforms in their ministries. Most important, Bennett ordered the rewriting of the public system's high school civics textbook to express more nationalistic and religious standpoints (Gravé-Lazi 2016); appointed ideological allies to the Council on Higher Education (Skop 2016); and initiated the imposition of a new ethical code for faculty in public universities (Skop 2017). Shaked promoted some debatable laws, including the Basic Law: Israel the Nation State of the Jewish People, which prioritizes the Jewish element of the state over its democratic elements (Lis 2017). She also nominated conservative judges to the Supreme Court (*The Economist* 2017) and passed laws aimed at curtailing the influence of associations that acknowledge the Palestinian Nakba (the Palestinian catastrophe of 1948) and associations that receive funding from foreign countries (Beaumont 2016; Tepperman 2016). In addition, the party's ministers are active in debates over profane issues such as constitutional reforms, the economy, security, and foreign policy, and they enjoy broad coverage in the domestic and international media.

Another political strategy of the settler movement was to join the ranks of Likud in large numbers and seek to influence it from within. Between 2010 and 2012, 30 percent of new Likud members came from the settler movement, endowing the settlers with disproportionate power in the institutions of Likud, while not obliging them to vote for the party in general elections. In 2012 the settlers encompassed more than 9 percent of Likud members (11,391 out of 125,696 registered members) while making up only 4.1 percent of the party's voters (Levinson 2012). This is manifested in the significant discrepancy between the religiosity of Likud's voters and members.

While two-thirds of Likud voters (66 percent) are secular, the weight of secular party members is less than half (48 percent). This disproportionate power, based on what some call a Trojan horse strategy, makes the settlers the most influential pressure group in Likud (Kenig, Philippov, and Rahat 2013, 20) and has increased their capacity to shape the political line of the party's members of Knesset.

State penetration. Religious Zionists realized that in a democracy, political power obtained through the electoral process is always under threat, given the likelihood of fluctuations in voter preferences and coalition politics. They thus targeted the state apparatus as a primary arena for penetration and control. Religious Zionists used several methods to increase their representation in key public-sector offices and positions. For example, they saw that the ministries under religious-Zionist control could serve as critical facilitators for religious-Zionist recruitment into state institutions (as in Bennett's appointment of ideological allies to the Council on Higher Education, or Shaked's similar nominations to the Supreme Court). Another source of recruitment at the highest echelons of public service is the office of the prime minister. Acknowledging the political importance of this sector, Netanyahu surrounded himself with religious Zionists, including former Chief of Staff Nathan Eshel, Head of Communications Yoaz Hendel, former Shabak (Israel's internal security service) head Yoram Cohen, former National Security Advisor Yaakov Amidror, Mossad head Yossi Cohen, Police Chief Commissioner Roni Alsheich, and others.

Perhaps the most dramatic penetration of the religious-Zionist sector into the state has taken place in the ranks of the IDF. In recent years, a growing number of religious-Zionist officers have been rising up the ladder and now hold key field and staff positions in the IDF. This development relates closely to what Yagil Levy calls "the theocratization of the Israeli military" (Levy 2014). The growing role of religion in the IDF manifests itself in the proliferation of rabbis in deployed units, growing gender-based exclusion, and changes in the IDF's ethical principles (Levy 2016). The most contentious public debate over religion in the military relates to the bifurcated loyalty of religious soldiers and officers when military orders contradict rabbinical positions (A. Rubin 2014).

State penetration has increased the settlers' capacity to impose their theological agenda. The power of the settlers in the state apparatus deters the political level from executing state policies with regard to Jewish settlements in the Occupied Territories (Haklai 2009; Pedahzur and McCarthy 2015), extends privileges to the settlers at the expense of Palestinian West Bank residents and lessens the prospects for future reconciliation between Israel and the Palestinians. The issue of illegal outposts illustrates this reality. A special report produced by the Ministry of Justice in 2005 at the request of then-Prime Minister Ariel Sharon determined that 105 outposts in the Occupied Territories were illegal and should be dismantled (Sasson 2005, 21). Nevertheless, as of this writing, more than a decade later, there still exist ninety-seven illegal outposts throughout the West Bank. Moreover, the total number of settlers increased during the past decade by almost 50 percent, from 261,600 in 2006 to 385,900 by the end of 2015 (PeaceNow 2017).

Expansion of the electoral base. After 2009, HaBayit HaYehudi realized that its sectarian self-segregation, the dominance of the territorial issue, and the primacy of rabbinical authority over political leadership limited the party's electoral potential. Subsequently, the party put efforts into opening its ranks to other, more diverse audiences. One of the first steps in this direction was the election of Naftali Bennett to lead the party. Bennett represents a different profile than the settlers' average leadership. He lives in Ra'anana, a bourgeois suburb of Tel Aviv, and before entering politics he founded a successful high-tech company. Likewise, Ayelet Shaked is a computer engineer, a wealthy secular woman from Tel Aviv. This pair served for several years as aides to Netanyahu and entered politics with a broader vision of the state and society than the relatively narrower perspective of the settlers. As chair of the party, Bennett constantly tries to recruit secular and moderate figures who will appeal to people outside the religious-Zionist camp. His political messages cover different domains of government, from the economy to military operations to foreign policy (Roth 2013). As a result, under his leadership the party significantly increased its representation in the Knesset (twelve seats in 2013 and eight in 2015) over previous decades.

These new forms of engagement provide religious Zionists with new paths to political influence, and their impact is already apparent in state policies. Most significant, the party publicly opposes the two-state solution, which has been the sole platform for negotiations on a future peace with the Palestinians since 1967. Instead, it supports annexation of large parts of the West Bank to Israel, while providing the Palestinians with limited political autonomy on part of the land.[35] Although this policy has generated considerable international criticism and further isolated Israel, it has gained momentum in Israeli society, especially among right-wing politicians.[36] The party compelled the Likud government to pass a law that allows retroactive expropriation of private Palestinian land in the Occupied Territories (Kaplan

Sommer 2017). Party members stated outright that this was a first step toward Israeli annexation of large territories in the West Bank (Sharon 2016).

The party is also behind growing nationalistic and xenophobic sentiment against Palestinian citizens of Israel. Arab Israelis face accusations of being a fifth column and are often treated as second-class citizens (Ghanem 2016; A. Rubin 2018). Under HaBayit HaYehudi's leadership, the Knesset passed a controversial bill that allow the impeachment of elected MKs for acts against the state (BBC 2016). In addition, the party pushed for a government decision to outlaw the Northern Branch of the Islamic movement in Israel (L. Rubin 2015) and supported new policies that destabilize the explosive situation on the Temple Mount/Haram al-Sharif (Hasson 2017). Taken together, these policies work against substantive elements of Israeli democracy.

To conclude, between 1977 and the first decade of the twenty-first century, parts of the religious-Zionist sector adopted messianic ideology and behavior, which gave primacy to control over sacred territory at the expense of other religion–state issues. Over time, Israeli society and the settlement movement grew apart. Although parts of the settler movement radicalized and confronted the regime with mounting pressures, including extreme violence, the state was largely successful in containing these activities. Instead of recruiting public support, radical behavior only deepened the isolation of the settler movement in the social and political realms and prevented it from realizing its goals. The state was able to execute its policies in the Occupied Territories despite fierce opposition, and the democratic regime remained relatively immune.

The disengagement from Gaza in 2005 drove a profound change in religious Zionism's mode of engagement with the state. Since that time, the sector has reemphasized institutionalized politics, penetrated the state, and appealed to new audiences, while lessening its use of illegal and extra-parliamentarian activity. These new strategies of engagement have increased religious Zionism's political leverage in ways that seem to have already started to undermine democratic principles. However, it is still too early to evaluate the impact and sustainability of this trend.

The Haredim and the State, 1980s–2000s

Significant changes also characterized the interaction between the state and the non-Zionist Haredi population. As argued in chapter 8, new political constellations since 1977, especially following the establishment of Shas in the early 1980s, led to increased Haredi involvement in Israeli politics and subjected the democratic regime to unprecedented Haredi sectarian and theocratic demands, with some becoming highly explosive political issues.

The ultraorthodox establishment conceives political parties as an unwanted necessity, in that they are the only platform able to secure the special interests of the sector. As former Ashkenazi Chief Rabbi Yona Metzger noted: "[The word] *miflaga* [party] comes from the root *pilug* [division, partition]. *Pilug* is a negative thing. Nevertheless, it is the only way to prevent the democratic regime from infringing the rights of certain sectors. For its part, the majority needs to protect the rights of the religious minority."[37] Such language from an official religious authority is significant. On the one hand, Rav Metzger admits the potentially negative consequences of sectarian representation and the hostility it could generate among other groups in society. On the other hand, he underscores the capacity of political leverage to secure individual and collective rights in a democratic regime, thereby implicitly acknowledging the value of democracy. Regarding the latter point, even though ultraorthodox Israelis do not endow democracy with intrinsic value, they have learned how to exploit it for their own purposes. As one yeshiva scholar told me: "As far as the Haredi public is concerned, democracy stands in complete contradiction to Daat Torah [the word of Torah], which means that the elders and sages should determine public issues. . . . Nevertheless the Haredi population decided to join the democratic system in a partial and conditional way. . . . There are economic interests but the main reason was to save our Jewish brothers from *shmad* [assimilation]."[38] Of course, the problem arising from this instrumentalist view of democracy is that those subscribing to it apply it selectively and only when democratic procedures and restraints on the power of the secular majority align with their interests. In contrast, when democratic values contradict their interests, they dismiss it in ways that deepen the already existing secular–religious cleavage. The post-1977 interaction between the state and the ultraorthodox sector exposes the problems that can arise where significant political leverage is accompanied by selective adherence to democratic values.

Ultraorthodox parties have become a crucial actor in Israeli politics in recent decades. Between the 1980s and 2009, the Haredi parties filled a vacuum left by religious Zionists in Israeli politics and became the dominant religious power in government. As figure 8.1 revealed, the flip side of Mafdal's sharp electoral decline after 1977 was the impressive electoral growth of the Haredi parties. In 1977 Mafdal and the Haredi parties had twelve and five seats in the Knesset, respectively, and in 2006 this picture had turned upside down, with only four seats to Mafdal and an astounding eighteen for Haredi representatives. In the twentieth Knesset (2015–2019), religious-Zionists held eight seats and Haredi parties occupied thirteen (seven by Shas and six by United Torah Judaism).

The turning point in the political status of the ultraorthodox parties came with the transformation of the Israeli political system from one-party dominance to a left-right bipolar structure, with Mapai and later Avoda (Labor) leading the left bloc and Likud leading the right bloc.[39] Unlike Mafdal, whose religious-Zionist nationalistic agenda confined it to participating only in right-wing coalitions, the ultraorthodox parties demonstrated more flexibility on profane issues—specifically the peace process and foreign policy (Yuchtman-Yaar and Hermann 2000; Leon 2015)—as long as their sectarian material benefits were secured.[40] This approach made the Haredi parties potential partners in every political configuration. It is important to note, however, that the Haredim prefer right-wing governments, which are often more sympathetic to specific ultraorthodox values and material needs. A majority of the Haredi electorate, particularly Shas voters, hold hawkish worldviews and perceive partnership in right-wing governments as more natural (Leon 2015).

Since 1977, at least one (and usually both) ultraorthodox parties have served in government. Agudat Israel (later United Torah Judaism) participated in coalitions in 1977–1992, 1996–2006, 2009–2013, and from 2015 to the present. Shas participated in all governments from its establishment until 2003, including the Rabin (1992–1995) and Ehud Barak (1999–2001) governments, though it left the first in 1994 following the signing of the Oslo Accords and the second before Barak convened with Arafat at Camp David in 2000. On the other hand, Shas remained in opposition during Sharon's second government (2003–2006) because of Sharon's alignment with the secularist Shinui and during Netanyahu's third government (2013–2015), which included the secularist party Yesh Atid (Rubin, Navot, and Ghanem 2014).

The willingness of ultraorthodox parties to serve in governments of both blocs and their lenient position on secular issues endowed them with outsized control over the balance of power in Israeli politics. The result is that from 1977 onward, it became difficult to construct a stable coalition without Haredi participation.[41] In turn, the blocs showed themselves willing to offer far-reaching concessions to the Haredi parties, including allocating significant material resources and selective exemption from civic duties in return for Haredi political support.

The Haredi parties skillfully exploited the deadlock in Israeli politics. Haredi blackmailing hit its highest point between 1984 and 1992, a time of political stalemate that gave rise to two national unity governments. Each bloc sought to overcome this stalemate by building a narrow coalition with ultraorthodox support. In 1990, Shimon Peres tried to construct a narrow Labor-led government to replace the Likud-led unity government with the active assistance of the Haredi parties. In a political maneuver that became known as the dirty trick, Peres succeeded in constructing the foundation of such a government, but disagreements among the leaders of the three main ultraorthodox factions (Elazar Shach of Degel HaTorah,[42] Ovadia Yosef of Shas, and Menachem Mendel Schneerson of Agudat Israel) foiled the attempt.

The dirty trick highlighted the mainstream parties' overreliance on Haredi support and generated initiatives to contain the Haredi challenge with institutional reforms (Diamond and Sprinzak 1993; Diskin and Diskin 1995; Hazan 1997; Brichta 1998). In 1990, the Knesset approved two bills that were meant to strengthen governance and restrain future Haredi coercion. The first instituted direct elections to the prime ministry, modifying the Israeli political system from a full parliamentary system to a semi-presidential one.[43] The idea was to increase the prime minister's political leverage and popular legitimacy and thereby limit small parties' ability to condition participation in government on outrageous demands (Diskin and Diskin 1995). The second bill tightened regulation on allocation of public funding to registered associations and subjected it to principles of transparency and equality (De Hertoch 1999).[44]

Both bills failed to achieve their goals. The direct election reform, which took effect between the 1996 and 2001 elections, only fragmented Israeli politics further. It enabled a strategic vote for the prime minister and a separate vote for parties that represented the individual's preferences more closely. This reduced voters' incentive to vote for the big parties. The combined electoral weight of Likud and Labor fell from seventy-six seats in the 1992 elections to sixty-six in 1996 and only forty-five in 1999, whereas Shas's representation rose from six seats to ten and then seventeen in the same years. In addition, the reform suffered from two significant structural shortcomings that erased the advantage of having a directly elected prime minister for coalition building: namely, it kept a low 1.5 percent electoral threshold and it made the formation of a government conditional on a majority vote of confidence (61 out of 120 MKs). Overall, the Knesset became weaker while individual lawmakers became stronger (Hazan 1997, 344; Ottolenghi 2001), and the ultraorthodox factions retained their power in politics. This reform was reversed in 2003 after three rounds of elections, but its fragmenting impact has remained.

The new regulation on governmental funding also failed to achieve its goal. This was especially true in the case of the ultraorthodox parties. Unregulated funding for ambiguous purposes continued to flow to ultraorthodox destinations, particularly from the ministries of Education and Religions. Between 1992 and 1998, the allocation of state resources for religious purposes almost doubled, from 2.14 to 4.04 billion Israeli shekels, and the number of funded associations expanded from 3,000 to almost 5,000 (Lupo 2004, 36).

The continued deficiencies in the electoral and regulatory realms only improved the appetite and capacity of the Haredi parties to pursue selective material benefits and sectarian exemption from otherwise universal civic duties.[45] Selective material benefits include allocating disproportionate resources to all levels of education, from kindergarten upward; construction of designated neighborhoods (in cities like Petah Tikva, Beit Shemesh, and Jerusalem) and even cities (Kiryat Sefer, Modiin Ilit, and Elad) for ultraorthodox populations; and tax exemptions and subsidies for families contingent on the number of their children. Exemptions from civic duties include the release of yeshiva students and women from military or civil service and the exemption of Haredi educational institutions from state supervision and core curricular content (Schiffer 1999). To this one should add a sophisticated system of clientelism and patronage that includes numerous appointments in ministries controlled by Haredi parties and in rabbinic courts, municipal religious councils, and burial societies, all of which provide a living to thousands of ultraorthodox people.

To non-Haredi Israelis, arguably the most frustrating realms of preferential treatment for the ultraorthodox population are education and military service. Education is sensitive for two reasons. First, the secular education system has suffered constant budget cuts in recent decades while more money has been allocated to ultraorthodox schools. Second, subsidized ultraorthodox educational institutions eschew core curricular requirements, like English language, civics, general history, and postelementary math that provide essential skills for citizenship and productive participation in the labor market.

The Haredi parties rank the autonomy and funding of their educational institutions quite high on the political agenda. Because of their political influence, it has become customary political practice to assign a deputy minister from one of the Haredi parties to supervise the Haredi educational stream in the Ministry of Education and secure Haredi budgets and curricular autonomy (Weissblau 2012). In contrast to public schools, which receive funding only from the Ministry of Education through local municipalities, Haredi schools receive additional funding from sources like the Ministry of Religions, the Jewish Agency, and municipal authorities (Schiffer 1999). These enhanced budgets for Haredi education facilitate a higher teacher/ student ratio, smaller class sizes, and more hours per student compared with the public system. Given this discrepancy, many non-ultraorthodox parents, especially from lower socioeconomic strata, send their children to Haredi institutions. As a result, growth in the proportion of Haredi students over recent years has significantly exceeded the Haredi growth rate. The weight of Haredi institutions in Jewish elementary schools nationwide increased from 7.6 percent in 1990 to 11.4 percent in 1995 and 19.4 percent in 2005 (Schiffer 1999, 9; Weissblau 2005, 2). The Israel Central Bureau of Statistics predicts that the Haredi sector will account for half of all additional first-grade pupils (4,852 out of 9,694) joining the education system between 2016 and 2021 (2016, 4).

The other issue is Haredi exemption from service in the IDF. Military service is mandatory in Israel and provides an entry card to full participation in Israeli society. Thus, it is not surprising that many in the broader society often perceive universal exemption of ultraorthodox men from conscription as parasitism (Kook, Harris, and Doron 1998, 3; Sasson, Tabory, and Selinger-Abutbul 2010). The roots of Haredi exemption from military service go back to the early 1950s, when Prime Minister David Ben-Gurion exempted 400 religious scholars from service to make up for the loss of Jewish knowledge during the Holocaust. Thereafter the number of exemptions rose gradually to 1,200 a year, until Begin gave the Haredim sweeping exemption in return for their participation in his Likud-led coalition in 1977. The exemption was executed through regulation by the minister of Defense until the HCJ decided in 1999 that the scale of the exemption required legislation by the Knesset.[46] More recently, the Knesset has tried to resolve the issue by enacting legislation to reduce the exemptions. The most notable attempts were the Tal Law arrangements, which remained intact for a decade (2002–2012) (Bick 2010), and a 2014 law enforcing mandatory conscription of yeshiva students. The latter lasted a year, until the new coalition of 2015, which included the Haredi parties, reversed it again (Navot, Rubin, and Ghanem 2017).

The frustrations of ordinary citizens aside, the influence of Haredi political power in Israel should be examined not in isolation but in light of its effect on the performance of Israeli democracy. In most circumstances, Haredi political parties have exhibited sharp political skills and secured benefits and exemptions without violating the basic principles of the democratic system. Of course, as former Minister of Education Yael Tamir argues, the participation of the Haredi parties does not signify their acceptance of its fundamental values. Rather, they participate in democracy only because this is the best way to achieve their current goals (Tamir 1998, 88). Given their small weight as a proportion of Israeli society (about 8 percent in 2017), this challenge will not materialize in the near future. Moreover, social trends beyond the scope of this study (modernization; growing entanglement with secular society; the emergence of feminist ideas and the integration of Haredi women in the secular labor market; and increased exposure to the mass media, especially the internet) could transform the social and ideational characteristics of this group in ways that are difficult to predict and make it more receptive to democratic ideas (K. Kaplan 2007; Kaplan and Stadler 2009).

Recent countermeasures taken by the Israeli state and society against the Haredi population's opportunistic behavior demonstrate that the secular–Haredi political cleavage can be contained in the institutions of the democratic system. One arena of containment is the Knesset. The recent performance of two secularist parties, Shinui (Change) and Yesh Atid (There Is a Future), demonstrates this point nicely. Shinui was active from the 1960s and gained significant political power under the leadership of Yosef "Tommy" Lapid between 1999 and 2006. The party advanced an extreme anti-Haredi agenda, part of a bid to present a counterbalance to these parties. It won six seats in the 1999 elections and fifteen seats in the 2003 elections, a meteoric rise that reflected a popular aspiration to fight Haredi abuses of Israeli democracy. Shinui's parliamentarian weight motivated Prime Minister Sharon to invite the party to join his 2003 coalition, leaving longtime partner Shas in opposition. In coalition, Shinui fought against Haredi favoritism. It pushed to eliminate the Ministry of Religions, cut child subsidies, and control the allocation of public resources to Haredi associations. Personal disputes and the lack of an agenda on other issues hastened Shinui's electoral disappearance in 2006 and restored the pivotal role of the Haredim in Israeli politics. Nevertheless, the party's performance while in power demonstrated the capacity of an efficient political organization to counterbalance the interests of the Haredi parties in the democratic system (Shelef 2010).

Tommy Lapid's son, Yair Lapid, heads Yesh Atid, Shinui's successor. The party first ran in national elections in 2013, won nineteen seats, and became senior partner in Netanyahu's coalition, including heading the Ministry of Finance, while leaving the Haredi parties in opposition. Like its predecessor, Yesh Atid advanced prosecular reforms, including mandatory conscription of yeshiva students to the IDF and shrinking subsidies for Haredi activities. After two years, in 2015, Netanyahu dissolved his government and announced new elections. This time he left Yesh Atid, now with eleven seats, outside the government and took the Haredi parties in. The current government reversed most of Yesh Atid's reforms (Navot, Rubin, and Ghanem 2017).

The other area of democratic containment of Haredi demands is the court system. The political stalemate during the 1980s and 1990s limited the capacity of the executive and legislative branches to deal with Haredi abuses of the democratic process and left this arena of confrontation to the HCJ. Consequentially, from the late 1980s the HCJ became the main barrier against excessive Haredi claims.[47] Some highlights: in 1988 the court ruled that municipal religious councils could not exclude women as members on the basis of their gender.[48] In 1993 it approved the importation of pork meat to Israel based on the principle of freedom of occupation.[49] In 1994 the court subjected the rabbinical courts to its decisions,[50] sanctioned the representation of non-Orthodox Jewish streams in municipal religious councils,[51] and acknowledged the right of women to pray at the Western Wall.[52] In 1998–1999 the court produced some of its most important resolutions on religion–state issues. During those years it ruled the exemption of yeshiva students from military service unconstitutional,[53] canceled the allocation of state funding to Haredi youth groups that did not meet the eligibility criteria of the Ministry of Education,[54] and overturned a decision by the minister of Transportation to close a central traffic route in Jerusalem on Shabbat.[55] Another wave of important decisions took place in 2004–2006, during which time the HCJ suspended municipal legislation in Beit Shemesh that prohibited the sale of pork;[56] declared subsidies to Haredi schools that did not teach the core curriculum to be unlawful;[57] recognized non-Orthodox Jewish conversions conducted abroad;[58] and authorized a gay pride parade in Jerusalem despite fierce Haredi opposition.[59]

The HCJ's role in preventing some serious religious abuses in the democratic system led the ultraorthodox to perceive the court as an emblem and instrument of a secularist agenda.[60] Results from the Israeli Democracy Index, an annual public opinion survey, are enlightening. In general, during the first decade of the twenty-first century, the secular–religious cleavage in Israel was viewed as deep and broad, with some three-quarters of respondents (76 percent in 2003 and 74 percent in 2006) stating that the relationship between the religious and secular sectors was either not good or not good at all (Arian, Atmor, and Hadar 2006, 39). Most respondents viewed the HCJ as an active player in the secular–religious dispute. However, a large discrepancy is apparent between secular and religious perceptions of the court's activist stance. In 2005, 71 percent of respondents who identified as Orthodox (modern Orthodox and ultraorthodox) but only 29 percent of those who identified as secular thought the HCJ intervened too much in government decisions, while only 10 percent of Orthodox and 50 percent of secular respondents did not agree with this statement. At the same time, a significant part of the public perceived the judiciary as the branch of government most protective of Israeli democracy, with almost 50 percent of the respondents agreeing with this statement; the legislative and executive branches were considered most protective of democracy by only 13 percent and 15 percent of respondents, respectively (Arian, Atmor, and Hadar, 2006, 38). Further, in 2009 the court emerged as the second most trusted state institution with 68 percent (the IDF came out first with 79 percent), whereas the Knesset was trusted by only 33 percent and political parties by a low 22 percent (Arian, Philippov, and Knafelman 2009, 59). These results reflect a broad vote of confidence in how the court handles political issues, including the highly contentious religious–secular divide—at least among the non-Haredi population.

Finally, the replacement of religious-Zionist parties by ultraorthodox ones in government resulted in a somewhat perplexing phenomenon. The transfer of political salience from Mafdal to the Haredi parties led to erosion in the public role of religion. Haredi parties did not dissolve coalitions over religious issues, even though violations of the status quo became a matter of routine. Israeli society turned Shabbat into a shopping day, kosher regulations became less effective, and more Israeli couples now marry in secular or alternative ceremonies or choose to be buried outside the auspices of the state rabbinate (Ben Porat and Feniger 2009; Ben Porat 2013). Themes that before 1967 led to governments breaking up have become practically nonissues in contemporary Israeli politics. This trend is in keeping with the theological worldviews of Haredim and religious Zionists. The latter endow the state with sacred status. Hence, until 1977 they concentrated on theocratic demands and took an assertive stance against attempts to secularize the public sphere. In contrast, the Haredi establishment does not credit the state of Israel with sacred value. They concentrate on sectarian demands and show little interest in the religiosity of the public sphere (Neuberger 1994; Kook, Harris, and Doron 1998). As such, ultraorthodox parties have taken good care of their publics but have not made significant efforts to secure the role of religion in the state.

Conclusion

The period covered in this chapter deals with challenges to democracy that can arise from changes in religious actors' engagement with the state and the greater capacity of inclusive democratic regimes to contain them (compared with militantly prosecular regimes). Since 1977, Israel has confronted mounting challenges by its religious publics. Extreme religious-Zionist factions—notably followers of Merkaz HaRav and the settler movement—advanced a territorially oriented agenda and attempted to stop the state from executing its policies in the Occupied Territories. Nevertheless, until recently the state proved able to contain these challenges. On one hand, recognition of religion preserved the allegiance of most of the religious-Zionist public and intercepted the intentions of radicals to block the execution of state policies or damage the democratic regime. On the other hand, while tolerating religious-led activities that fell within the bounds of democratic integration, the government and the courts responded assertively to violations of these bounds. Since 2009, the religious-Zionist sector has changed its mode of engagement with the state. Religious Zionists returned to institutionalized politics, penetrated the state, and reduced their social movement activities. Although it is too soon to offer a full evaluation, this new strategy seems to restrain the state's capacity to contain religious violations of democratic principles.

As for the Haredi factions, increased involvement in institutionalized politics, combined with a political stalemate between the left and right, gave them outsized influence over Israeli politics and enabled them to put forward excessive sectarian demands. As much as these demands deepened the cleavage between the secular and religious sectors, they have all been exercised within the bounds of the democratic system. In the main, they have not violated the basic principles of democracy, and when they sought to do so, they were checked by either a militant secularist party or an independent and activist judiciary. The initial recognition of the Jewish religion and the inclusive foundations of the state–religion relationship enabled the state to effectively contain and isolate excessive demands for religious integration while maintaining democratic stability.

Chapter 10

Religion, State, and Democracy

Conclusions and Lessons for Emergent Arab Regimes

Contemporary global trends, including democratic expansion, the decline of the liberal order, and the resurgence of religion in many parts of the world, call for careful reassessment of the role of religion in democratic societies. This is especially true given the simultaneous transitions to democracy and rise of religion in societies with distinct historical and cultural features that have taken various paths toward modernity. Cultural and historical diversity broadens the role of religion as a political tool and as an ingredient of identity in ways that extend well beyond the conceptual boundaries of Western thinking and practice. We must question whether Western experiences and values should continue to dominate debates over defining proper integration of religion in democratizing countries with diverse backgrounds.

This chapter has two goals. First, I summarize how the findings of this study highlight the relative advantages of the analytical framework of analysis offered at the beginning in explaining the religion–state relationship and its impact on democratic performance, and I offer broad theoretical insights for scholarship in comparative politics, religion and state, and democratic theory. Second, I appraise the relevance of the study to the role of religion in democratizing Arab regimes in the post–Arab Spring Middle East.

Let us consider first the main findings on the Turkish and Israeli cases and their contribution to scholarship. Later I assess the relevance of this study to contemporary Middle Eastern societies.

What Have We Learned from the Turkish and Israeli Cases?

With respect to the prescribed role of religion in modern democratic states, there is an undeniable gap between the narrow yet still broadly accepted notion of secularization—at least as a normative prescription for the role of religion in democratic politics—and the remarkable diversity among societies that seek to democratize while preserving a significant public role for religion. The European experience—with a steady decline in the role of religion as an organizing principle of society, and an evolving separation between the spiritual and political domains—was unique. Overwhelming European dominance in global affairs until the first half of the twentieth century led to the imposition of distinct European values on the rest of the world regarding the appropriate public role of religion. In many cases, this imposition brought political friction, extreme behavior, and violent repression, and it worked against the formation of a well-functioning democratic governance.

The most important contribution of this work is the demonstration that religious integration in democratic or democratizing regimes is not necessarily antithetical to sustainable democracy. Put baldly, democracy does not have to be strictly secular to perform well. Indeed, where recognition of religious content and actors coincides with popular preferences, as in Israel, religious recognition by the state will aid rather than hamper democratic performance. In contrast, where the regime insists on an approach toward religion that is not in keeping with popular preferences, as in Turkey, democratic performance may suffer. Finally, as these cases reveal, democratic performance depends on the ability of the state to block or contain excessive religious demands that clash with democratic principles. Taken together, these observations suggest that recognition and accommodation of religion should reflect a balance between two desirable goods: one, responding to the needs and preferences of the religious population, and two, adherence to the fundamental values of democracy, including the rights of nonreligious publics and members of minority religions, within the state. I define this balance as a bounded range of religious integration, or *bounded integration*. As the empirical inquiry reveals, a constructive integration of religion in politics takes place when the role of religion is circumscribed within a range with lower and upper bounds. Conversely, forcing religion below the lower bound or allowing it to surpass the upper bound is likely to produce negative consequences for democracy. I elaborate more on the findings and their theoretical meaning.

The Weaknesses of Existing Religion–State Theories

The Lakatosian methodology of scientific programs (Lakatos 1978) holds that the first step in the development of a new explanatory framework or mechanism is falsifying existing explanations for the researched phenomenon. My structured comparison of Israel and Turkey accomplishes this task. Most notably, it exposes the inability of separation models to account for the dynamic dialogue between the state and religious actors in Turkey and Israel and to explain changes in this relationship over time. It also shows that the secularization thesis generates a false prediction with respect to Israel and Turkey. Turkey, a state that followed the Western secularist prescription, ended up less democratic and also less secularist than Israel, a state that challenged the secularist prescription.

As my empirical inquiry demonstrates, the Turkish state adhered to the Western secularist prescription by bundling modernization with secularization and took assertive measures to marginalize the Islamic faith from the public and political spheres. Against what theories of separation would predict, this policy proved futile in two respects. First, it failed to achieve secularization at the societal level—that is, eliminating the attribute of religion as an ingredient of identity and powerful mobilizing tool in politics. Today, despite almost a century of efforts to marginalize religion, Islam in Turkey has only grown stronger, and the Islamist AKP has consolidated its hegemonic status in Turkish politics. As of 2019, the AKP controls the presidency, the government, the security apparatus, and the legislative branch, and popular identification with Islam seems more robust than ever. Equally important, the Turkish secularizing project has failed to instill democratic governance in the country. In fact, the opposite happened. Imposed secularization from above, in disregard of popular preferences, necessitated recurrent military interventions in politics and regular violations of the civil rights and liberties of religious (and other) people. Finally, the prediction of the secularization thesis falls short in explaining various dramatic changes in the interaction between the state and Islamic actors in Turkey. For instance, it cannot account for the moderating effect of religious parties' participation in politics in the 1970s on the behavior of religious actors. It cannot explain the empowerment of religion in urban centers following rapid modernization in the 1970s and 1980s, which, according to the premises of the secularization thesis, should have brought about the decline of religion in society and in politics.

The secularization thesis equally fails to account for the dynamic reality of the state–religion relationship in the Israeli case. Israel represents a unique example of a postcolonial state that deviated from the common prescription regarding the appropriate role of religion in state affairs. Despite this deviation—indeed, probably because of it—Israel succeeded in maintaining a steady democratic regime from its foundation in 1948. Moreover, state acknowledgment of religious content and actors in Israeli politics brought about not an increase in religiosity but decreasing levels of religious observance among the Jewish population. Finally, the secularization thesis cannot explain the profound changes in the nature of the state–religion interaction in Israel following the Six-Day War in 1967, from constructive collaboration to self-exclusion, extreme forms of behavior, and disrespect for the preferences of other publics.

Other theories of religion and state cannot explain the state–religion relationship in Israel and Turkey. In particular, the inclusion-moderation thesis is right in emphasizing that under certain circumstances, inclusion may bring about religious moderation in politics. However, it does not draw a clear conceptual upper limit of religious integration beyond which the costs of integration surpass its benefits. Thus, it can hardly justify state restrictions of dangerous religious manifestations in politics, like extreme right-wing religious-Zionist movements (e.g., Kach, Zu Artzenu!), whose agenda undermines democratic principles. Similarly, it cannot explain why a decade of AKP integration into Turkish politics has resulted in a debasement of democracy.

The twin tolerations theory is also only partially adequate. Although it is right in advocating substantial autonomy for religious institutions and perceiving mutual respect between them and secular state institutions as a recipe for democracy, two shortcomings make it insufficient as an analytical prism for the state–religion relationship. First, while accepting religious activity in the public and civic spheres, the twin tolerations approach prohibits direct religious influence in the political arena. It cannot account for the overall moderating effect of religious parties' participation in institutionalized politics in Israel and Turkey in the 1970s. In addition, the twin tolerations theory is static in that it does not provide an explanation or mechanism for realignments in the state–religion relationship over time, something that has happened in both cases throughout the explored period.

Finally, while Fox's (2015) competition approach provides a largely accurate description of the relationship between religious actors and the state, as an ongoing arena of bargaining and mutual pressure, it does not provide an essential conceptual link between the nature of this interaction and the democratic character of the regime.

The Advantages of a Bounded Integration Perspective

Based on the empirical findings and in light of the incapacity of existing theories to offer a plausible explanation for the complex state–religion relationship in Turkey and Israel, this book advocates bounded integration as an alternative explanatory mechanism for the state–religion interaction. Its departure point is an inquiry into the deep historical origins of the role assigned to religion in the national project. In divergence from other studies, this work submits that it is impossible to gain a deep understanding of the religion–state relationship by simply examining the role of religion in a state from its formation. Such a method is likely to miss fundamental factors and processes that are highly relevant to the observed outcome (Kitschelt 2003; A. Rubin 2009). Instead, it suggests that the ideological role assigned to religion following a proclamation of independence is itself contingent on structural and ideational variables that predate independence by decades, sometimes longer. The empirical findings from Israel and Turkey reinforce this assertion. In Turkey, the emergence of the Young Turk movement and the subsequent Kemalist revolution were merely the final phases in a long effort to remove Islam from its central place in the Ottoman Empire, which began with the reforms of the Ottoman Sultan Selim III at the end of the eighteenth century. Likewise, the decision of newly formed Israel to grant the Jewish religion official status cannot be isolated from debates and power struggles between secular and religious factions from the birth of the Zionist movement in mid-nineteenth century Europe and later in Mandatory Palestine.

The theoretical proposition that follows is that the capacity of the political elite to shape the character of the political order at the critical juncture of independence is not free from constraints. Rather, competing narratives and structural and ideational parameters define and shape the spectrum of alternatives open for consideration by the elite about the role of religion in the state (Kaufman 2001; Kubik 2003). In Turkey, the institutional and cultural centrality of Islam in the Ottoman Empire and the need to disentangle the country from the burden of its relationships with its former Islamic non-Turkish colonies made it almost necessary for the Kemalists to eliminate the Islamic religion and preempt it from seriously challenging the Westernizing project of the emerging regime. In contrast, the tight bond between the religious and national identity ingredients of Judaism, coupled with the mobilizing capacity of religion in portions of the Jewish population, restricted the ability and willingness of the secular Zionist elite to exclude religious content from the national project.

A third component is the need to assign considerable import to developments around the emergence of statehood. As the inquiry into the case studies reveal, the moment of transition from national movement to sovereign state is critical in that it consolidates patterns of state–religion interaction with far-reaching ramifications. This is because institutional and legal designs establish formulas of religious recognition, which create resilient path dependency. In Turkey, constitutional restrictions on religion continue to deny any role to religion in the state even though Islam has been the most entrenched identity in Turkish politics for more than two decades. Likewise, despite serious decline in the legitimacy and social relevance of the chief rabbinate in Israel, this institution has retained its initial form for seven decades.

A fourth lesson from the cases relates to the attention we should give to the dynamic aspect of the religion–state interaction, namely, to temporal changes in its nature. Exclusion of religious actors may generate frustration and alienation and lead to extreme forms of behavior by the marginalized public, as was the case in Turkey in the 1920s and 1930s. On the other hand, when religious groups and values are granted a legitimate space in civil society, contingent on their adherence to basic principles of democracy, the political outcome becomes more inclusive and consequently more supportive of democratic governance. Such was the case in Israel between 1948 and 1967. The broad recognition of religious content and actors led an over-whelming majority among the Jewish religious population to legitimate the state and advance their political interests mainly through state institutions. Furthermore, the cases reinforce the assumption that the relationship between the state and religion is not necessarily a zero-sum game in which the state and religious actors are in unceasing conflict. Under certain circumstances, the outcome of the interaction may benefit both sides. To illustrate this, the decision of the Kemalist state to tolerate a religiously based party in 1971 and the latter's participation in government during the 1970s resulted in substantial material benefits for the Islamic population. In turn, the religious segment of the population was less involved in extreme violent activity against the regime compared with left-wing and right-wing factions. Conversely, at other times the interaction can work against both sides. For example, the advocacy of a militant agenda by the settler movement in Israel after 1967 was responsible for a decline in its institutionalized political representation and subsequently to diminished influence on government policies, while exposing the Israeli state and society to extreme, undemocratic, and some-times violent types of behavior.

This leads me to the most fundamental inference of this work: that the impact of religious integration on democratic governance is neither deterministic nor linear. Instead, it changes in response to various exogenous and endogenous events and processes initiated by the religious populations, by their surrounding environment, or by state organs. The radicalization of religious-Zionism after 1967 is a relevant example. An exogenous event with enormous theological meaning and profane consequences, coupled with internal currents in the religious-Zionist public and indecisive state policies, seriously distorted the formerly constructive interaction between religious-Zionism and the state. An illustration of an opposite trend, from clash to potential collaboration, is found in the ideological and terminological modifications that happened in Turkey following the shift of religious representation from the Welfare Party to the early days of the AKP, especially until 2007. This point is crucial because it repudiates the deterministic perception according to which the tension between religious content and democratic governance is inherent and unchangeable.

Nor do the findings support a simple linear understanding of the relationship between religious integration and support for democracy. While granting some public role to religion within the bounds of basic democratic principles may support the democratic regime, unlimited or excessive integration may prove inimical to democratic performance. Under such circumstances, the comparative advantages of democratic regimes—tolerance, respect for civil rights, limits on the use of governmental power, and acceptance of cultural diversity—become their weakness. Unchecked submission to religious demands may motivate religious groups to violate democratic principles and disregard the basic rights of other collectivities to advance their values and preferences freely in the public and political spheres. Such a process took place after the Welfare Party came to power in Turkey in the 1990s and currently under Recep Tayyip Erdoğan's power-hungry authoritarian tendencies. Similarly, Haredi abuse of political power for sectarian benefits has led to various political and institutional counteractions. Although previous attempts to contain religious abuses of democracy were relatively successful, Benjamin Netanyahu's most recent government (2015–2019) has submitted to religious demands in ways that discriminate against the secular and non-Jewish publics.

All this suggests that a bounded range of religious recognition by the state is likely to produce the most constructive outcome for democratic performance. There is one simple criterion for the bounds—respect for basic democratic principles. Remaining above the lower bound requires a minimum level of state recognition of religious content and actors. Remaining below the upper bound requires state intervention in cases where religious groups repudiate democratic principles and the equal rights of other publics. Of course, this range should respect popular preferences, be sensitive to contextual diversity, and adjust over time in response to demographic, cultural, and social trends. Any attempt to design a parsimonious one-size-fits-all framework while disregarding popular preferences, contextual diversity, and contemporary circumstances risks falling into the same deterministic and oversimplistic outlook as existing theories.

Understanding the nature of the state–religion interaction as a bounded integration within democratic limits, with constructive and destructive zones, offers an innovative and policy-relevant perspective and facilitates ongoing dialogue regarding the optimal formula for religious recognition. The empirical parts of this book show that in a state where a significant religious population sought recognition and the right to express its worldview and advance its preferences in the public and political spheres, attempts to impose a Western-type secular model of democracy only impeded the transition to and stabilization of democracy (Turkey). Imposing a secularist agenda from above, especially just after the emergence of the new regime, alienated large segments of the population who could not freely advocate their worldview within civil society and politics. Alternatively, a state that granted some role to religious actors and content in politics within the bounds of basic democratic conditions (Israel) strengthened its base of support and cooperation with the religious segments and consequently facilitated better democratic performance.

From a policy perspective, the state should seek to strengthen civil society by incorporating more societal groups into the public sphere, including religious ones. Furthermore, it can accomplish this by recognizing religious actors and religious content in various official realms of the state. Broader political inclusion of religion in the state facilitates a more pluralistic public discourse, requires less repression from above to control ideological dissent, and should result in a freer, stronger, and more stable democratic regime. Conversely, strict implementation of secularism requires repression of any political affiliation with religion, risks alienating large segments of the population, and is likely to result in poorer democratic performance.

Integrating religion into politics ought not be unconstrained. Just as strict secularism risks impairing democratic performance, so does the absence of restraints that would prevent a dominant religion from occupying too much power in politics and exploiting it at the expense of other groups in society. Both situations undermine the extent of civil society as the "setting of settings" (Walzer 1992), impede the free exchange of ideas, and are likely to erode democratic performance. Hence the notion of bounded integration.

Keeping religion within these boundaries holds the best prospects for developing a constructive relationship between the state and religion and promoting democratic performance. Both below and above these boundaries—too little or too much integration—the interaction between religious actors and the state may develop in destructive and mutually harmful paths. The goal of the state regarding the role of religion (indeed, with regard to every group or worldview in society) is to maintain stable relationships among the state, religious groups, and society as a whole and promote mutual acceptance among these actors by confining religious activity and its public role within the above-mentioned boundaries.

Finally, the empirical investigation makes clear that there is no preordained correlation between modernization, societal secularization, the nature of the state–religion relationship, and successful democratic governance. In fact, the findings demonstrate that an upsurge of religion in politics can be an outcome of modernization trends. This is because material modernization improves the ability of religious groups to use advanced technologies and the mass media, which facilitate effective penetration to potential electorates. In Turkey, the empowerment of the religious Welfare Party and AKP from the early 1980s involved using modern tools of recruitment such as mass public sermons and religious media outlets. Shas's ascendance to power in Israel reflects a similar pattern. The framework offered in this book enables its application to cases that represent different departure points and paces of development. Israel was a relatively modern society at the time of independence, and afterward it continued to modernize in a gradual way. In contrast, the starting point of the Turkish Republic in terms of modernization was relatively low, but the country experienced phases of dramatic progress in the twentieth century, especially under the Menderes government in the 1950s, the Özal government in the 1980s, and most recently under Erdoğan. Changing levels of modernization undoubtedly influenced the social status of religion and the interaction between religious actors and the state in these cases. Nevertheless, we should be cautious in seeking to stipulate a specific correlation between modernization, religious integration, and democratization. In Israel, modernization produced lower overall levels of observance (Ben Porat 2013) and the ascendance of the Haredi parties. In contrast, the state–religion relationship in Turkey in the 1970s was more constructive than during the 1990s, despite the rapid modernizing progress the country experienced in the 1980s.

Additional Theoretical Implications

Typically, the process of researching and writing raises additional questions that cannot receive adequate treatment in a single study. Some of these questions can serve as departure points for further research.

The first point relates to the probably negative consequences of granting a dominant religion preferable official status for two groups in society—women and members of nondominant religions (Künkler, Lerner, and Shankar 2016). The concerns about women stem from the fact that most religions are traditional social systems that favor men in various domains. Secular democratic states are committed to gender equality in their legal and institutional frameworks. Things get more complicated where specific religious content becomes part of the official institutional matrix of the state. For example, under what condition should the democratic state allow the operation of religious courts that rely on discriminatory principles? The intricate relationship between gender equality and the official integration of religious content in democratic societies generated normative scholarship, mainly with regard to women's rights in illiberal groups. Feminist scholar Susan Okin (2002) emphasized that the state should ensure that women are treated fairly and equally within illiberal (including religious) communities, because their right of exit from their group is rarely a viable option. But her prescription does not apply in cases where illiberal and discriminatory policies are backed by the state. As Jobani and Perez convincingly argue, even liberal supporters of the dominant culture view (like Weiler, Miller, or Joppke) may encounter real difficulties in justifying state recognition of religion that discriminates between citizens on gender grounds (Jobani and Perez 2014, 2017).

Protecting the equality of members of minority groups in the state also raises considerable challenges for nonseparation models of religion and state. Here, too, there exists a lively normative debate between those who support the privatization approach and oppose any official promotion of religious content in the public sphere (like Nusbaum, Barry, and Dworkin) and those who are willing to accept culturally differential treatment of religion(s) as an ingredient of national culture (like Miller, Joppke, Tamir, and others). This debate highlights a relatively overlooked tension between liberalism and pluralism in democratic systems and liberal thinking. Although liberals tend to view liberalism and pluralism as complementary elements, in the real world the promotion of one of them may contradict the other. In the United States and in France, constitutional principles reflect liberalist principles like freedom and gender equality. But the promotion of liberal principles limit the extent to which pluralism can be exercised. Examples include the ban on the burka in France's public sphere or the inability to teach religious contents in public schools in the United States. In both countries, political parties cannot form around religious principles. In contrast, pluralist principles may support a more inclusive public dialogue, in which more groups and worldviews compete for political power, but this may come at the expense of liberal rights, like freedom from religion, gender equality, and so on. Every democratic society that manages diverse identities, especially religious ones, should pay attention to this tension and attempt to strike a healthy balance between the two principles.

Although it is impossible to delve adequately into the debates about minority religions and women's rights in the context of religion and state, these debates inform the current work and may be informed by it in two important respects. First, whereas this work presents an empirical macro-analysis of the effect of religious recognition on democratic trends, the normative considerations raised in the literature require a more refined design of the bounded integration, in a way that will ensure that liberal principles are not violated. On the other hand, the normative argumentation will benefit from empirical insights about the impact of different policies in the real world. Both aspects should be subject to future research.

The second point relates to the relationship between inputs from the international arena and the religion–state relationship in the domestic arena. Although this book does not affirm a categorical relationship between international trends and the state–religion relationship, findings from the case studies imply that such an influence—what Peter Gourevitch (1978) calls the second image reversed—does exist. In Turkey, the decision of the Kemalist government in 1946 to open the political arena to competitive elections, which facilitated the empowerment of religion in politics, was highly dependent on the context of the Cold War, particularly the aspiration of the Turkish elite to align with the West and resist communist influence. Similarly, the decision of the Turkish military to intervene in politics in 1980 depended on the outcome of the Iranian Revolution and the anxiety it provoked among the Kemalist elite. In Israel, the relationship between religious-Zionism and the Jewish state changed in response to the country's wars (1967, 1973, etc.) and developments in the relationship with the Palestinians, such as violent clashes and peace agreements. This observable trend still requires further research and theorization.

Another point relates to generalizability. While this study employs religious identity, its analytical framework may be applicable (with necessary contextual adjustments) to studying interactions between the state and other collective identities (linguistic, national, ethnic, or racial) and the effect of these interactions on democratic performance. The building blocks of this approach—particularly its dynamic perspective, generic definition of democracy, understanding of the public sphere as an arena of vibrant cultural exchange, and view of the constructive zone of interaction as a bounded range—make it an efficient descriptive, prescriptive, and predictive tool of analysis for interaction between various collective identities and the state.

It is also of value to identify circumstances in which this perspective and the notion of bounded integration are less usable. To begin, it is more applicable to young democracies or countries that are in the midst of transition to democratic governance. Of course, nondemocratic regimes may also accommodate religion in the political order for various reasons, mostly related to legitimacy and stability. This was the case in Egypt under Anwar Sadat (Hinnebusch 1981; Ashour 2009) and Chile under Augusto Pinochet (Behrman 1974; Fleet and Smith 1997). Nevertheless, the ability of nondemocratic regimes to arbitrarily change their attitude toward religion whenever such a change fits their interests makes the lessons of this study less applicable to such regimes. Likewise, the framework offered here may be less relevant to consolidated Western democracies, where a high level of democratic governance guarantees a minimum level of respect for collective and individual cultural preferences in the public and political spheres. In addition, a high degree of constitutional liberalism (Zakaria 1997) and consolidated institutional structures ensure that religious integration in Western democracies remains within the bounded range and that the boundaries of this range are subject to little fluctuation, thus making the dynamic approach less profound.

A third point of applicability relates to the overlap between identity regimes and demographic realities. Bounded integration is most efficient as a tool of analysis for majority identities. In Israel and Turkey, a clear overlap between religious and national identities for a majority of the population facilitates a high degree of fusion between these identities. In both cases explored here, it is conceivable that religion serves a core component of national identity (Rustow 1970; Juergensmeyer 1995). Similar cases include Egypt, with a large Sunni majority and a 10 percent Coptic minority, or Indonesia, with a large Muslim majority and a Chinese minority. It follows that where it is impossible to fuse a specific identity (religious or otherwise) into the national character, the proposed mechanism has limited applicability. For instance, the degree to which the Jewish religion can be integrated into an Israeli nationality and Israel's public character are fundamentally different from the possible degree to which an Arab or Islamic identity can be integrated into the Israeli national character. The mechanism is also restricted in societies where there is no dominant majority group. Lebanon is a good example of such a case, with a population divided between at least five distinct groups: Sunni Muslims, Shiite Muslims, Maronite Christians, Druze, and Palestinian refugees (mostly Sunni by religion). Such a division makes it almost impossible to construct a joint national identity around a certain religion or ethnicity (Salloukh 2009). Although some recognition of religious or ethnic identity in Lebanese nationality is an option, the character of such integration is likely to be fundamentally different from cases where a fusion between national and religious ingredients is possible.

This point also reflects the varying capacity of a certain identity to act as a societal bond in different contexts and demographic realities. In places where a certain collective identity (e.g., religion) is shared by different communities (e.g., linguistic or national) coalescing around the common identity is more likely to promote social cohesion and aid democratic performance. Such is the case of Islam in Turkey, which is shared by both ethnic collectives—the Kurdish minority and the Turkish majority. It is thus not surprising that the Kurdish population found it easier to collaborate with the Islamic AKP during the first decade of the twenty-first century than with the Kemalist regime in the preceding decades. In contrast, where there is an overlapping cultural cleavages among collectives in the state, the ability to promote a certain aspect of identity as a cultural common ground in the polity is less likely. This is the case in Israel, where the Jewish majority and Arab minority do not share any aspect of collective identity (linguistic, religious, national, ethnic).

Finally, two interesting findings deserve further empirical inquiry and theoretical foundation. The first is the impact of the specific state organ that takes the front stage against religious attempts to trespass beyond the upper bound. In Turkey, the military took this role. It protected the fundamentals of the Kemalist project and repeatedly used coercive capabilities to prevent further religious empowerment. The results of military intervention, however, were counterproductive for both democracy and institutional stability. In Israel the judicial branch took this responsibility. Although the goal of the two institutions was essentially the same—blocking religious abuses of democracy—in Israel the liberal camp aligned with the court, and in Turkey it aligned with religious groups in opposition to the military. This disparity supports Migdal's assertion that the state is by no means a unitary actor, and that an adequate analysis of state policies requires breaking it down into its various organs (Migdal 2001). The methods and means used by different state organs to achieve the same goals could produce distinct political results. It follows that it is insufficient merely to identify the intentions of the state vis-à-vis certain identity groups in society.

The second point relates to the link between formal integration of religion in the state and levels of social secularization. Here the cases demonstrate a puzzling trend. The Israeli state integrated Jewish religion in the public sphere and, at the same time, the Jewish population became less observant. In contrast, Turkey tried to secularize society by rooting out religion from public life, but this attempt resulted in higher levels of popular observance and identification with religion. Although these observable trends might be purely accidental, another alternative merits further inquiry. It may be that by integrating the religious element into the public sphere, the state (Israel) becomes a "public guarantor of religion" and frees the individual or groups in society from the obligation to preserve religion at the societal level. Conversely, when the state (Turkey) rejects all religious identity, it "transfers" the duty to preserve religious identity onto society. Of course, this preliminary idea requires more elaboration and articulation of a plausible theoretical explanation that integrates assertions from studies in political psychology and identity politics. Nevertheless, proceeding on this path could shed light on the mechanisms behind increased religiosity and secularization in modern societies.

Religion–State Interaction and Democratic Governance: Lessons for Emergent Arab Regimes

When I embarked on this project about a decade ago, the Middle East was the most solidly authoritarian region on Earth. That began to change in December 2010, when the turmoil called the Arab Spring ignited a series of profound upheavals around the Middle East and North Africa (MENA). As of this writing, the regional disorder has produced a relatively modest harvest, with the toppling of rulers in Tunisia, Egypt, Yemen, and Libya, and has brought long-lasting democratic momentum to only one state, Tunisia (Stepan 2012; Filali-Ansary 2016). After tentative openings to democracy, other countries, such as Egypt, Libya, Morocco, and Jordan, quickly slid back into authoritarianism. In all other MENA countries, from Algeria to Saudi Arabia, the system retained its authoritarian structure (Brownlee, Masoud, and Reynolds 2015; Hinnebusch 2015b).

The future of the region's polities is still largely uncertain. This is because factors behind contemporary political events are complex and hard to comprehend without considering a plethora of structural, cultural, and socioeconomic factors. These include elite configurations, natural resource wealth, allocation regimes, and demographic composition (structural factors); the tribal way of life and hereditary mechanisms (cultural factors); and education and unemployment, human rights violations, international pressures, and the logic of the rentier state (socioeconomic factors) (Gause 2011; Gerges 2014b; Brownlee, Masoud, and Reynolds 2015; Hinnebusch 2015a; Sassoon 2016; Abulof 2017; Haas and Lesch 2017).

One factor that has stood out in the midst of the political changes is the dramatically growing presence of the Islamic religion in diverse forms throughout the region. In places like Egypt, Tunisia, and Morocco, longtime religious social movements formed political parties that sought institutionalized political power through electoral procedures (Rosefsky-Wickham 2013; Masoud 2014; Yildirim 2016; Filali-Ansary 2016). Elsewhere, especially in the region's monarchies, Islamists strengthened their alliances with the ruling dynasty, boosting the legitimacy of the king in return for an expanded role in politics (Frisch 2011; Köprülü 2017). In a few countries, especially Syria and Libya, Islamist militants chose to arm themselves and fight violently against the incumbent rulers (Pierret 2013; Gerges 2014a; Cronin 2015).

Even if major democratic advances in MENA countries do not seem likely in the near future (Masoud 2015), the political events of the Arab Spring are important for the state-religion-democracy triangle in at least two respects. First, recent events signify movement away from a four-decades-long political equilibrium during which the region was not only the most authoritarian but also the most stable. The current political volatility may lead to further changes, including democratization trends, which will make deliberation about the role of religion highly pertinent. Second, recent democratic openings in places like Tunisia, Egypt, Morocco, Libya, Yemen, and Jordan, even if short-lived and limited, provide precious insights about the centrality of religion in Arab politics and highlight possible scenarios for the state treatment of religion and its effect on democratization.

Early in the Arab Spring, Arabs throughout the region embraced the Turkish religion–state model as a desired archetype for their emerging regimes. Shibley Telhami, who has been conducting polls in Arab countries for a decade, noted in 2013 that "Turkey is increasingly seen as a desirable political model across the Arab world" (Telhami 2013, 155). Significantly, in 2011 Turkey ranked first, with 44 percent, as the type of regime Arabs would like to have for their countries, followed by France with only 10 percent. When compared in 2012 only with other Islamic regimes, Turkey ranked first again, this time with 54 percent (Telhami 2013, 155–56). Commentators and scholars also praised the Turkish model as the most viable option open to Arab societies. Leading intellectual Tariq Ramadan (2011) titled one of his publications "Democratic Turkey Is the Template for Egypt's Muslim Brothers." Turkish thinkers Alper Dede (2011) and Mustafa Akyol (2011) argued that the Turkish model can and should serve as an exemplar for emerging Arab regimes. A 2011 report by the Carnegie Endowment claimed that the Turkish experience should be a source of inspiration to Arab societies (Ülgen 2011).

The lessons of the current study, however, question the adequacy of the Turkish religion–state model and recommend against its imitation in Middle Eastern societies that seek to develop functioning democratic systems. Despite the seeming appeal of the Turkish model, it is inadequate for Middle Eastern societies for several reasons. To being, Islam plays a significant social and political role in the Middle East and is a core ingredient of individual and collective identity. Polls show that the peoples of the Middle East value their religious identity more than their local (e.g., Egyptian, Yemeni) or pan-Arab national identities (Telhami 2013, 28–33). Telhami also found that Arabs not only identify with religion but also want to base their political systems on principles from Islamic doctrine, namely, to integrate religious content in the polity. Indeed, "Almost all agreed that Sharia should be the basis of the constitution" (Telhami 2013, 157). Furthermore, the first wave of democratic elections demonstrated that Arab populations want to see Islamic actors actively engaged in national politics. The first to mark this trend was the Tunisian Al-Nahda Party, which won over 40 percent of the vote in the first Tunisian national elections in October 2011. A month later in Morocco, the Islamist Justice and Development Party won 30 percent of the vote in national elections, and King Mohammed VI appointed the party's chairman as prime minister. In Egypt, the Freedom and Justice Party, the political branch of the Muslim Brotherhood, won approximately 47 percent of the vote in the 2011 national elections, and the militant Salafi faction Al-Nour (The Light) won roughly 25 percent. In June 2012, Mohamed Morsi won presidential elections and became the first Islamist president of Egypt. The bounded integration perspective suggests that the lower bound of integration should respect popular preferences and allow the recognition of religious actors and content in the polity. The Turkish model, however, prohibits any type of official recognition of religious content or actors.

Equally important, Arab (and, more generally, Muslim) societies reject the concept of secularism as a Western product that is foreign to Islamic culture (Fish 2011, 242–49). For many inhabitants of the region, local authoritarian elites embraced Western principles, including secularism, long after the end of the colonial era, at the expense of authentic popular sovereignty. Indeed, the most ambitious modernization projects in the region, including the Syrian and Iraqi Ba'athist regimes, the Iranian Pahlavi regime, the Tunisian and Algerian regimes, and the Nasserite regime in Egypt, all enforced secularism and repressed religious movements. In contrast, the moment of popular uprisings in Middle Eastern societies represented a shift toward authentic self-determination (Abulof 2015). As inquiry into the Turkish case reveals, the Turkish marginalization of religion in the early years adopted a Western rather than a local outlook. The Kemalist elite artificially imported the idea of top-down secularization from the Western experience and imposed it without regard for the preferences of the Turkish people.

Finally, the current treatment of religious actors in places like Egypt, Syria, and Algeria resembles how the Kemalist regime treated religious actors in Turkey. In Egypt, the military intervened in civil politics and removed an elected Islamist president from his position in July 2013, after one year in office. The incoming regime outlawed the Muslim Brotherhood, declared it a terrorist organization, confiscated its property, shot hundreds of its members who protested the coup, and arrested its leadership. However, the lessons from the Turkish case suggest that pushing a broad spectrum of religious activities, especially elected politicians, outside the legal realm does not help democratic performance. In fact, the Turkish state's marginalization of religious content and actors worked to the detriment of democracy, political stability, and respect for human and civil rights. Although present circumstances in Turkish politics are more inclusive toward religious affiliation in the public sphere, they cannot obscure that implementing strict secularism came at a very high price, including a long undemocratic period, recurrent interference of unelected actors in politics, and mass violations of human rights. The Turkish model also facilitated the entrenchment of hegemonic tendencies in Turkish politics, which accounts for the country's recent democratic downturn (A. Rubin 2016).

Given the inherent problems in the Turkish model and the fact that its outcomes were largely negative to Turkey's democratic development, Middle

Eastern societies in which Islam constitutes a substantial element must look elsewhere to borrow—or independently develop—a state–religion model that captures the preferences of these nations' populations. Only such a model will enable sustainable democratic transitions.

As Middle Eastern societies seek to borrow or to design a religion–state interaction that supports democracy, several aspects of the bounded integration perspective may hold relevance and deserve close attention. First, all those involved in the design of the new regime should be cognizant of the centrality of Islam in the life of individual Arabs, as well as in the collective identity of Arab societies and in their public and political life. The convergence of religious affiliation and domestic nationalism in contemporary Middle Eastern societies can give rise to a new form of collective national identity, one centered on religious nationalism. Instead of rejecting this trend, Middle Eastern elites should embrace it, officially acknowledge the Islamic religion in the institutional matrix of the state, and make it a unifying and restraining rather than exclusionary and radical social and political force. Religion can thereby become a common denominator around which a national identity and stable democratic polity can coalesce. Such a policy respects the lower bound of religious integration and is likely to produce a more constructive interaction between religious actors, the state apparatus, and broader society.

Second, according the bounded integration perspective, Middle Eastern societies should adopt a dynamic, nondeterministic understanding of the relationship between the state and religious actors. Put simply, the attitudes and behavior of religious actors toward the state and democracy react to real-life circumstances and change over time. Although the state should defend itself against radical and violent behavior from religious actors (thereby preventing violations of the upper bound), the state should embrace the participation of religious factions in the public and political spheres to the extent that these factions abandon militancy and embrace behavioral and ideological deradicalization and moderation.

This latter point requires a note about democracy as an open-ended process characterized by institutional uncertainty (Przeworski 1986). Religious actors embrace democratic principles with the expectation that they will be able to realize their political worldview via the ballot box. Close inspection of religious factions in the Arab world reveals that many of them deradicalized and moderated in recent years, with former jihadists renouncing the use of violence as a legitimate political strategy and accepting pluralism and democratic procedures, before and more so after the Arab Spring

(El-Ghobashy 2005; Leiken and Brooke 2007; Ashour 2009; Ghanem and Mustafa 2011; Cesari 2014; Yildirim 2016). As long as integrative policies persist, the Islamic factions are likely to play by the rules of the game and concentrate their political efforts in electoral and parliamentarian channels. On the other hand, state-led exclusion or marginalization of religious actors may push them outside the legal institutionalized arena and reradicalize them in response. This is even truer in cases where religious factions were included in the process of democratic transition and then were forcefully pushed out of it. Pre–Arab Spring examples of such reradicalization in response to state repression include the Islamic Salvation Front in Algeria in 1991–1992 and Hamas in the Palestinian Authority in 2006–2007. In these cases, denying the right of Islamist parties to participate in the political process resulted in bloody civil wars. In Egypt, a similar process took place in 2013 with the ousting of the Muslim Brotherhood from political office.

In contrast, when religious parties receive fair and inclusive treatment in politics, the outcome may be supportive of democracy. The case of Tunisia is very telling in this regard. The Islamist Al-Nahda party won the first postrevolutionary elections in 2011, but after a full term in office lost the subsequent elections because of poor performance in several policy areas. Al-Nahda embraced the voters' verdict, handed governmental powers to its political rivals, and initiated a comprehensive reform in the party, including separating its activities as a political party from its activities as a social movement (Filali-Ansary 2016; Stepan 2016).

Third, the cases explored in this book reveal that religious recognition, like secularism, is a multifaceted principle. The state can implement it in various ways at different times, to accommodate various contexts and popular preferences. One important distinction is between religious content and religious actors. Granting jurisprudence to Sharia courts on certain issues, funding religious education, or recognizing Islam as an official state religion in the constitution is likely to generate different dynamics with religious populations than allowing religious actors to form political parties and compete in elections. Likewise, religious recognition can take place in various domains, from funding religious services (economic integration) to establishing state-run religious institutions (institutional integration) to allowing religion-based participation in government (political integration) to granting official status to Islamic symbols (symbolic integration). Various combinations of these domains enable many fine-tuned configurations of religious recognition that could be tailored to fit particular Middle Eastern societies.

Fourth, the Middle East is divided broadly between two systems of governance—republics and monarchies. Republics have proved more vulnerable to popular protest and regime change than have monarchies. In fact, all monarchies survived the Arab Spring. Several studies have tried to account for the impressive resilience of monarchic regimes in the Middle East. Some have emphasized hereditary mechanisms, whereas others have concentrated on resource wealth, rentier practices, and tribal and dynastic mechanisms (Frisch 2011; Menaldo 2012; Yom and Gause 2012; Bank, Richter, and Sunik 2015; Abulof 2017). An important element of resilience in these regimes relates to the legitimacy claims made by their rulers. Unlike republics, which base their legitimacy on popular sovereignty and thus are secular, monarchies base their legitimacy on religious ancestry (Morocco, Jordan) or on a pact between a royal family and the religious establishment (Saudi Arabia). This difference may allude to different roles for religion in democratization processes and democratic rule. In other words, the democratization of monarchies can take place under monarchic rule while maintaining religion-based legitimacy mechanisms (Morocco, Kuwait, Jordan). By contrast, in republics, power transition between religious and secular factions is necessary to achieve a minimum level of religious recognition in the regime (Tunisia, Egypt).

Finally, despite regional excitement with the Turkish model, the findings of this book suggest, somewhat ironically, that Israel, an illegitimate political entity in the eyes of many in the region, may serve as an intriguing and relevant religious–state model for emergent Arab regimes. Interestingly, despite deep hostility to the state of the Israel, Muslim thinkers have long perceived Zionism as a relevant political role model for their societies. Leading religious scholars from all around the Middle East, such as Yusuf al-Qaradawi, Muhammad Jalal Kishk, Abd al-Nasser Tawfiq al-Attar, Faisal al-Mawlawi, and Rashid al Ghannushi, heralded the Zionist fusion between religion and nation. For them, Israel's endurance and military superiority stems from the political reliance of the state on religious ideology and identity. Thus, some of them called for imitation of Zionism in the treatment of Islam in Arab political regimes (Shavit and Winter 2016, 67–79). There is rare evidence, however, that this standpoint, with overt reference to Israel, has found its way to political discourses in Arab countries following the Arab Spring.

Israel, the only long-lasting democratic political system in the Middle East, deviated from the standard prescription of the secularization thesis, integrated religious actors and content into its system of governance, and bequeathed the Jewish religion significant official status in the country's institutional, political, and symbolic realms. This integration generated a complex and dynamic interaction in which ongoing partnership of religious parties in government coalitions coexists with recurrent political crises over religious issues. Still, the overall outcome of this contentious interaction has been supportive of democratic governance. Both sides have been compelled to accept uneasy compromises that facilitated a stable political system and the development of a pluralistic arena of negotiation, at least in regard to the Jewish faith.

Even with vicissitudes in the religion–state relationship over time, the Israeli state has succeeded in maintaining religious recognition within a constructive range of integration that has mitigated tensions between the secular state and its religious populations, motivated religious sectors to identify with the state, and compelled parties (except for marginal extremist factions) to resolve their disagreements through legal institutionalized channels. The failure of radical movements to recruit popular support is linked directly to state policies on religion. While recognizing religious content and enabling religious actors' participation in society and in politics (thereby respecting the lower bound of religious integration), the state by no means gave carte blanche to nondemocratic religious activities. On the contrary, the Israeli state tolerated religious activities only as long as they were in line with basic democratic principles. Conversely, when religious militancy interrupted democratic principles in ways that violated the rights of other groups or challenged the authority and legitimacy of the state, the state acted decisively to contain such actions (thereby enforcing the upper bound of religious integration).

Of course, Middle Eastern states and societies are different from each other, and none are similar to Israel. Each is unique in its history, resources, demographic distribution, and regime type. Therefore, borrowing from the Israeli experience should be cautious and selective. Yet learning from the long and relatively successful Israeli experience with the state–religion relationship could support democratic transitions and political stability in the region.

Notes

Introduction

1. According to accepted indices, such as Freedom House or the Polity IV Project. Israel's democratic regime has not been interrupted since its establishment in 1948. Turkey had a nondemocratic regime between 1923 and 1950, and since then has been governed mostly democratically until recently, except for four occasions when the military took control of the political system for short periods (1960, 1971, 1980–1982, and a soft coup in 1997). Turkey experienced another military intervention in politics (known as the e-coup or midnight coup) in 2007 and a failed coup in the summer of 2016. After the failed coup, the current president, Recep Tayyip Erdoğan, consolidated his grip on state power at the expense of civil rights and liberal freedoms, which eroded Turkey's democratic performance. In addition, particularly in the 1980s, the military is considered to have exercised an important veto over civilian policies. The limited democratic nature of Turkey is discussed in more detail in chapters 4 and 5.

2. For an excellent summary of the debates and streams of research related to Jewish identity and its different components (ethnic, national, religious, etc.), see E. Cohen (2010).

Chapter 1

1. There are numerous studies on the modernization theory. For excellent recent accounts, see Przeworski and Limongi (1997) and Inglehart and Welzel (2005). For a thorough yet debated investigation of the connections between modernization and secularization, see Norris and Inglehart (2004).

2. Notably, Habermas's notion of a postsecular era assumes that at one point, there was a secular era, with secularism as the common norm. This assumption is highly debated among social scientists and historians.

3. The Seymour Martin Lipset Lecture on Democracy in the World is sponsored by the National Endowment for Democracy and has been presented every year since 2004. Lipset was a scholar of democracy and, as it happens, one of the founding fathers of modernization theory.

4. Most scholars date the emergence of the state as a primary political order back to the 1648 Peace of Westphalia.

5. The 1970s produced intensive Marxist scholarship on the state. Yet for most Marxists, the state is not an autonomous political player. Rather, it serves the reproduction of wealth distribution (Jessop 1977).

6. With regard to goals, there is wide disagreement on the distributive goals of democracy, in both material (economic) and nonmaterial (cultural) respects. Some argue that democracy is a vehicle for alleviating high levels of socioeconomic inequality, and thus should regulate the market (Petras and Vieux 1994; Oxhorn and Ducatenzeiler 1998), while others posit that democracy should be detached from the market as much as possible. Likewise, scholars disagree over the role of the state in promoting cultural content, with standpoints ranging from liberal neutrality to dominant culture to multiculturalism and systems of governance ranging from autonomy to consociationalism to majority rule. Difficulties arise with regard to the source of authority as well. Although democracy implies popular sovereignty, scholars with an elitist perspective argue that inherent deficiencies in democracy deprive the masses from having significant input into state policies, despite democratic procedures. Based on this perspective, it has been argued that the United States is not a democracy but an oligarchic regime (Winters and Page 2009). Likewise, Przeworski (2016) called into question popular sovereignty in the contemporary United States, where half the population refrains from participating in elections, capital controls the media, and the party system has long been stagnant.

7. A more recent conception of democracy, liberal democracy, largely overlaps with Dahl's definition but elaborates more explicitly on the substantive elements of democracy, such as the rule of law, equality, and protection of civil and minority rights (Diamond 1996, 23–24).

8. Secularism is also absent as a precondition for democratic governance in other definitions of democracy, like those of Lijphart (1999), Linz and Stepan (1996), Huber, Rueschemeyer, and Stephens (1993), and Diamond (1996).

9. Of course, in many cases theocratic demands may be materially beneficial to the sector. For example, the expansion of dietary regulations, religious services, or religious educational programs may provide sources of income for many religious individuals.

10. This Protestant exception is in line with the most well-known study of Max Weber—*The Protestant Ethic and the Spirit of Capitalism* (1905), in which Weber argues that the separation of the political and spiritual spheres is typical to Protestantism, as oppose to other religions, and is a key determinant of its accommodation with democracy.

11. In some religions, this code is more complete and detailed than in others and regulates every aspect of life, including diet, personal status, prayers, and social obligations. The extent to which a religious code is detailed determines whether a religion is based primarily on belief or on practice. In the case of the monotheistic religions, Islam and Judaism are practice religions, and Christianity is a belief religion.

12. This discussion of this proposition builds in part on Rubin (2013).

Chapter 2

1. Notably, Kemal was religiously observant and highly committed to Islamic principles. He was known to remark that "our only real constitution is the Sheriat [Sharia]." He also stated that "the Ottoman state is based on religious principles, and if these principles are violated the political existence of the state will be in danger" (in Davison 1968, 86). In some of his late works, Kemal attempted to reconcile Montesquieu's *Spirit of the Laws* (among the most important intellectual foundations of Western-liberal political thought) with the principles of Sharia (Lewis 1983, 115). As I will elaborate, the Young Ottomans' attempt to promote constitutional and liberal ideas while preserving the primacy of Islam carried inherent tensions and exposed this ideology to serious critique.

2. For many Islamists, Abdülhamid II's reign is considered a golden age of religion in the empire. Thus, it is not surprising that during recent national elections in Turkey, supporters of religiously oriented parties hung pictures of Abdülhamid II next to pictures of President Recep Tayyip Erdoğan.

3. The CUP was the main opposition group during Abdülhamid II's regime, but it was not the only one. For an elaborate discussion of other movements that opposed the sultan between 1875 and 1908, with particular focus on the Freemasons, see Hanioğlu (1989).

4. For a detailed comparison between the French and Turkish revolutions, see Mardin (1971).

5. The most well-known large-scale violence against a non-Muslim community in the empire was the Armenian massacre in 1915–1916, but there were many others.

6. Senior ulema did not support the revolt and later denounced it overtly, but lower-ranking ulema, religious students, and the sheikhs of the Sufi dervish orders were dismayed by the constitutional regime and sought its replacement by the old order (Ahmad 1968; Farhi 1971; Zürcher 2005, 120–23).

7. Brackets here in the original.

8. See, for example, Lewis (1983, 261–62), for a discussion of an article from 1904 by Yusuf Akçura, a Tatar Turkic intellectual, elaborating on the failure of both Ottomanism and Islamism. See also Uzer (2016, 56–63).

9. Unlike other (pan-)Turkist thinkers, Gökalp tried to incorporate Islamic identity as a core element of his nationalistic understanding (Zürcher 2005, 158–59).

10. In some works, these associations are referred to as "societies for the defense of rights."

11. It is beyond the scope of this chapter to discuss Atatürk's biography at length. For an excellent discussion of Atatürk, see Mango (2008).

12. *Cumhuriyet*, January 16, 1923.

Chapter 3

1. It should be noted that such wholesale social engineering was by no means unique to Republican Turkey. Western examples include the French Jacobin movement, the Russian Leninist movement, and Bismarck's rule in Germany.

2. Ibrahim Kalin, interview by the author, May 11, 2009. Kalin was formerly director of the Foundation for Political, Economic and Social Research. In 2014, Kalin was appointed as Erdoğan's press secretary, and since 2018 he serves as spokesperson and special adviser to the President.

3. Attila Yayla, interview by the author, May 12, 2009. Yayla is the founder and head of the Association for Liberal Thinking.

4. Although these principles were formally integrated into the Turkish constitution only in 1937, they served as the political compass of the Kemalist party (the Republican People's Party) from the foundation of the Turkish Republic on October 29, 1923.

5. Yayla interview by the author. Yayla is known as the father of liberalism in Turkey. He was sentenced to prison in 2006 after criticizing Kemalism and the cult around Atatürk.

6. *Cumhuriyet*, February 25, 1925.

7. *Cumhuriyet*, November 30, 1925.

8. *Cumhuriyet*, December 26, 1925.

9. *Cumhuriyet*, March 8, 1929.

10. *Cumhuriyet*, April 7, 1929.

11. *Cumhuriyet*, November 27, 1934.

12. *Cumhuriyet Encyclopedia*, entry for January 6, 1924.

13. *Cumhuriyet*, November 12, 1929 and September 23, 1930.

14. *Cumhuriyet*, October 17, 1930.

15. *Cumhuriyet Encyclopedia*, entry for November 20, 1925.

16. *Cumhuriyet Encyclopedia*, entry for November 22, 1925.

17. *Cumhuriyet Encyclopedia*, entry for November 25, 1925.

18. The independence tribunals had initially been established during the war of independence, but were mainly shut down in 1921. Two of these courts were reinstated under the Law for the Maintenance of Order.

19. Restrictions on freedom of expression in the media continued even after the government shut down the free media in 1925. For instance, in 1929 the state closed several newspapers in Sivas and Bursa because they expressed opposition to

the language reforms (*Cumhuriyet*, January 7, 1929). This was yet another demonstration of state actions against civil society activity designed to prevent the resistance to the imposed reforms.

20. These included the Mutki Uprising, Second Ararat Operation, and Bicar Tenkil Operation in 1927; the Asi Resul Uprising and Tendürük Operation in 1929; and the Savur Tenkil Operation, Oramar Uprising, Third Ararat Operation, and Pülümür Operation in 1930. Also in 1930 was the massacre of approximately 15,000 Kurds during an uprising in the Zilan Valley, in the province of Ararat.

21. The Menemen Incident is perceived by most Turkish historiographers as an act of religious reaction to Kemalist secular policies. For a critical review of this trend, see Brocket (2006).

22. *Cumhuriyet*, January 3 and 30, 1931.

23. *Cumhuriyet*, March 8 and 11, 1931.

24. *Cumhuriyet* January 21, January 31, and February 4, 1932.

25. *Cumhuriyet* reported incidents that included the arrest of people in Bursa (February 6, 8, and 12, 1933), Biga (February 16, 1933), Corum (March 31, 1933), and Amasya (May 29, 1933).

26. These came in the form of manifestos by the Ministry of Internal Affairs; *Cumhuriyet*, November 27, 1934.

27. *Cumhuriyet*, September 5, 1945.

28. *Cumhuriyet* January 8, 1946.

29. In some respects, the terms of opening the political arena resembled the practice of pacting as a means of departing from authoritarian rule, which was common among Latin American and southern European countries (O'Donnell and Schmitter 1986).

30. *Cumhuriyet*, January 28, 1947.

31. *Cumhuriyet*, February 8, 1947.

32. *Cumhuriyet*, July 3, 1947.

33. *Cumhuriyet*, November 8,1947.

34. *Milliyet*, February 18, 1948.

35. *Milliyet*, May 21, 1948, and January 16, 1949. The Imam Hatip schools were established in 1924, when the medreses were abolished, to train government-approved imams. However, these schools were closed in 1933 (Sarfati 2014).

36. *Milliyet*, June 5, 1949.

37. Milliyet, February 18, 1950.

38. Alparslan Isikli, interview by the author, May 13, 2009. Isikli is a board member of the Atatürkist Thought Association.

Chapter 4

1. *Milliyet*, June 17, 1950.

2. *Milliyet*, October 4, 1950.

3. *Milliyet*, September 30, 1950.

4. *Milliyet*, May 13, 1951.

5. *Milliyet*, May 15, 1951.

6. *Milliyet* alone reports more than twenty cases of raids on these orders and arrests of their followers between 1952 and 1959. Given the harsh restrictions on the press during the second half of the 1950s, the real number was probably much higher.

7. See, for example, speeches by Menderes (*Milliyet*, January 17 and February 8, 1953) and Bayar (*Milliyet*, July 8, 1953 and June 9, 1957) in support of secularism.

8. *Milliyet*, July 21, 1953. Issues arising from mixing politics and religion were ongoing throughout this period. For instance, in 1957, DP deputies proposed a bill to pardon an imam who had been jailed for criticizing the RPP's antireligious stance and propagandizing in favor of the DP. The bill was opposed by the RPP, and its leader, former president Inönü, accused the DP of manipulating religion for political gain. Facing such pressures, the Grand National Assembly was forced to reject the proposed bill and the imam remained in jail. *Milliyet*, June 8–11, 1957.

9. *Milliyet*, January 28, 1954.

10. *Milliyet*, December 25, 1959.

11. *Milliyet*, December 31, 1959.

12. *Milliyet*, January 9, 1960.

13. This practice was tolerated by the government until 1954. *Milliyet* has one report of a special operation by the police against people who violated the hat and clothing laws (May 18, 1954).

14. *Milliyet* reports on a single incident in Izmir (December 30, 1953).

15. *Milliyet*, December 12, 1954.

16. Two cases are reported in *Milliyet* (February 24, 1951, and June 26, 1952). Reed mentions "a number of statues" but does not provide a precise figure (Reed 1954, 274).

17. The Kemalist elite were assisted here by what can loosely be called Kemalist civil society—for example, secular urban-based student associations and women's associations that pressed the government to remain loyal to the principles of the Kemalist revolution.

18. The DP leadership was later tried by a special court on a small island in the Marmara Sea in what is known as the Yassıada Trials. Many DP leaders were sentenced to long terms of imprisonment, and the top leadership, including Menderes and Bayar, were sentenced to death. Bayar's sentence was commuted to life imprisonment, and he was eventually released in 1964 due to his advanced age. Menderes and two others (Foreign Minister Fatin Rüştü Zorlu and Hasan Polatkan) were executed.

19. *Milliyet*, July 26 and August 17, 1960.

20. *Milliyet*, December 3, 1960.

21. 1961 Turkish Constitution, Article 2. The full English translation of the 1961 constitution can be found at http://www.anayasa.gen.tr/1961constitution-text.pdf.

22. *Milliyet*, August 26, 1963.

23. *Milliyet*, March 4, 1964.

24. *Milliyet*, February 13, 1966.

25. *Milliyet*, May 10, 1968.

26. *Milliyet*, January 29, 1966.

27. *Milliyet*, February 7, 1966.

28. *Milliyet*, June 10, 1966, July 11, 1966, and March 10, 1967.

29. *Milliyet*, June 12, 1966.

30. *Milliyet*, September 7, 1966.

31. *Milliyet*, September 22, 1966.

32. *Milliyet*, April 16–30, 1968.

33. *Milliyet*, April 16, 1972.

34. *Milliyet*, October 22, 1977.

35. These parties are the National Order Party, 1970–1971; National Salvation Party, 1972–1980; Welfare Party, 1983–1998; Virtue Party, 1998–2001; and Felicity Party, 2001–present. I use the phrase "religious parties" even though legal restrictions meant these parties could not present themselves as religious. Instead, they used terms such as "conservative" and "traditional"—ambiguous phrasing whose main purpose was to obscure their religious core.

36. This was roughly the content of subsequent religious parties until the founding of the AKP in 2001 (Yilmaz 2005; Atacan 2006; Dağı 2008a, 100–116, 2008b; Tepe 2008).

37. *Milliyet*, February 17, 1974.

38. *Milliyet*, April 2, 1974, and February 21, 1976.

39. *Milliyet*, May 24, 1974.

40. *Milliyet*, May 4, 1974.

41. *Milliyet*, April 11, 1976.

42. *Milliyet*, June 25, 1974.

43. *Milliyet*, August 26, 1976. The government authorized a bill to allocate 82 million Turkish lira for the construction of new mosques.

44. On one occasion, Erbakan stated that "this society will be moral only with imams and hatips. People should lead their children to take education in Imam Hatip schools and afterwards they can become engineers or architects" (*Milliyet*, June 15, 1975). In an even more provocative statement just before the 1977 elections, Erbakan promised an enthusiastic crowd that "we will turn all schools into Imam Hatip schools after June 5th," the scheduled election date (*Milliyet*, May 23, 1977).

45. *Milliyet*, October 1, 1975, and February 22, 1978.

46. In December 1976, President Fahri Korutürk vetoed a bill that would have allowed graduates of Imam Hatip schools to enter military schools (*Milliyet*, December 26, 1976). Similarly, the president appealed to the constitutional court to annul a legal amendment that would have dropped the charges against Erbakan (*Milliyet*, March 30, 1978).

47. For example, an inquiry committee of the Senate found the former deputy chairman of the Diyanet guilty of supporting Nurculuk members (*Milliyet*, February 25, 1975), and the general editor of a daily newspaper was sentenced to thirteen months in prison for antisecular propaganda (*Milliyet*, October 8, 1977).

48. *Milliyet*, December 30, 1970.

49. The MHP remains the main right-wing platform in Turkey today.

50. *Milliyet*, May 22, 1971.

51. The Alevi are a heterodox Shia minority sect. As a minority religious group, the Alevis have always been in favor of Kemalist secularism as a defense against the formation of a Sunni theocracy that might infringe on their rights. They have traditionally opposed the allocation of state resources to religious education and supported left-wing political platforms.

52. *Milliyet*, December 24–27, 1978.

53. *Milliyet*, February 2, 1979.

54. *Milliyet*, September 7, 1980.

55. The 1982 constitution of the Republic of Turkey passed on October 18, 1982. An English translation of the document can be found at https://global.tbmm.gov.tr/docs/constitution_en.pdf.

56. Alparslan İsikli, interview by the author, May 13, 2009.

57. In October 1981 an Organisation of the Islamic Conference (now the Organisation of Islamic Cooperation) international development summit took place in Istanbul (*Milliyet*, October 24, 1981).

58. *Milliyet*, March 8, 1982.

59. *Milliyet*, May 22, 1982. In 1984, President Kenan Evren, another former chief of staff, participated in an Islamic conference in Morocco.

60. *Milliyet*, November 13, 1990.

61. The coalition was nicknamed the Refahyol because it was formed by the WP (Refah Partisi) and the Doğru yol Partisi.

62. *Milliyet*, June 4, 1986, December 3, 1986, March 19, 1987, January 14, 1989, March 12, 1990, July 26, 1990, October 6, 1993, February 12, 1994, and December 14, 1994.

63. The initial decision to allow headscarves in universities was made in May 1984. Over the next five years, this issue was debated in various state institutions in Turkey, including the GNA, the constitutional court, the presidency, and the Council of Higher Education, until the decision of the constitutional court to keep the ban on headscarves in place in March 1989.

64. *Milliyet*, January 17, 1987.

65. *Milliyet*, March 21, 1988.

66. *Milliyet*, January 9, 1995. A similar violation of Taksim Square by the AKP sparked the Gezi protests in summer 2013.

67. *Milliyet*, February 24, 1994.

68. *Milliyet*, March 27, 1996.

69. *Milliyet*, December 23, 1985, and June 19, 1986.

70. *Milliyet*, July 17, 1986.

71. *Milliyet*, March 1, 1995.

72. See the Committee to Protect Journalists website, entry on Ugur Mumcu, https://cpj.org/killed/1993/ugur-mumcu.php.

73. *Milliyet*, September 7, 1986, and March 1, 1992.

74. *Milliyet*, June 8, 1995.

75. *Milliyet*, July 3, 1993.

76. *Milliyet*, March 13, 1995.

77. *Milliyet*, July 14, 1996.

78. *Milliyet*, July 15, 1996.

79. *Milliyet*, August 20, 1996.

80. *Milliyet*, August 24, 1996.

81. *Milliyet*, September 21, 1996.

82. *Milliyet*, January 20, 1997.

83. *Milliyet*, February 3, 1997.

Chapter 5

1. Retrieved on August 8, 2017, from http://www.ysk.gov.tr.

2. More information about this think tank can be found on its official website, http://www.liberal.org.tr/engindex.php.

3. The organization's official website is at https://www.facebook.com/gencsivillerpage/. I interviewed leading activists of the YC, SETA, and BKP for this research.

4. See http://www.setav.org.

5. See http://www.baskentkadin.org/.

6. Attila Yayla, interview by the author, May 12, 2009.

7. *Milliyet*, February 1, 2004.

8. Faruk Ünsal, interview by the author, May 14, 2009.

9. In December 2009, the Kemalist-controlled constitutional court banned the Kurdish Democratic Society Party, sparking riots in the heavily Kurdish southeastern part of Turkey.

10. Burhan Kayatürk, interview by the author, May 15, 2009. Kayatürk is an AKP representative in the GNA from Ankara.

11. Ünsal interview.

12. From a speech given by Erdoğan at the American Enterprise Institute, January 29, 2004 (in Yavuz 2006).

13. Personal conversation with Hakan Yavuz, APSA Annual Conference, Boston, August 2008.

14. Ibrahim Kalin, interview by the author, May 16, 2009.

15. *Milliyet*, March 25, April 7, April 9, and April 15, 2007. Other big marches took place in Marmaris, Çannakale, and Adana.

16. There were many illustrations of this phenomenon. For instance, in January 2004, the commander of the First Army (one of the Turkish army's four field armies), General Hurşit Tolon, made a speech claiming that members of the AKP government sought to reestablish Sharia law (*Milliyet*, January 18, 2004). Likewise, Şener Eruygur, head of the Turkish gendarmerie, argued in August 2004 that the democratic regime was giving cover to malicious people to pursue activities against the republic (*Milliyet*, August 27, 2004). Similar political statements were made by Chiefs of Staff Yaşar Büyükanıt and İlker Basbuğ (*Milliyet*, April 21, 2005, and September 26, 2006, respectively).

17. It is noteworthy that in later court testimony, General Buyukanit argued that the midnight memo was not a coup, only an attempt to protect the constitutional order and the well-being of the Turkish Armed Forces. "Turkey's former chief of staff rejects 'coup attempt' in e-memorandum testimony," *Hurriyet Daily News*, December 15, 2015. Retrieved from http://www.hurriyetdailynews.com/turkeys-former-chief-of-staff-rejects-coup-attempt-in-e-memorandum-testimony-92560.

18. Nezir Akyeşilmen, interview by the author, May 14, 2009.

19. The Economist Democracy Index, https://infographics.economist.com/2017/DemocracyIndex/.

20. See https://freedomhouse.org/country/turkey/freedom-world/2017.

21. Ergenekon was alleged to be a clandestine secularist organization with ties to the military. From 2008 through 2011, more than 500 people, including journalists and opposition lawmakers as well as military officers, were arrested and charged with plotting against the government. In April 2016, all convictions in the case were annulled by the country's highest appeals court. Operation Sledgehammer was an alleged military coup plan, publicized in 2010 but supposedly dating back to 2003, that involved bombing mosques in Istanbul to cause chaos and justify a military takeover. Several hundred military officers, active and retired, were imprisoned. All were acquitted following a retrial in March 2015, when evidence submitted in the case was shown to have been forged.

22. As mentioned, in 2008 the GNA passed a constitutional amendment establishing elections to the presidency by direct popular vote, enabling Erdoğan's election as president in 2014.

23. The state of emergency was initially called for a period of three months, but was repeatedly extended until lifted in July 2018.

Chapter 6

1. The terms "Jew," "Jewish," and "Judaism" are anachronistic when applied to the early biblical era. The early books of the Hebrew Bible typically use terms like "Hebrews" or "Israelites" for the people who later became known as Jews. The words "Jew" and "Jewish" derive from a later period, when the Israelite polity comprised the separate kingdoms of Israel and Judah.

2. Archaeologists and biblical scholars are divided over the extent to which Israelite society and culture up through the supposed united kingdom actually resembled the picture painted in the Bible and whether purported historical events and personages—including David and Solomon—really existed. However, there is ample archaeological evidence, including extrabiblical textual sources, for the existence of the divided kingdoms of Israel and Judah and for at least some of the people and events mentioned in the relevant biblical texts.

3. What put the final nail in the coffin of an independent Jewish polity in first-century Israel was the failure of the messianic Bar Kokhba revolt of 132–135 CE. Following the Roman victory over that revolt, Jews were forbidden from entering Jerusalem, which was renamed Aelia Capitolina. The province of Judea (whose name derived from the former kingdom of Judah) was renamed Syria Palaestina—giving rise to the name Palestine.

4. The WZO and the annual Zionist Congress became the main institutions of the Zionist movement.

5. Leon Pinsker was in fact instrumental in founding Hibbat Zion, despite his secular outlook.

6. A third camp, outside the Zionist movement, promoted an ideology known as Jewish autonomism. The autonomists opposed the idea of an independent Jewish polity, in Palestine or elsewhere, and sought the establishment of autonomous self-regulated communities for Jews in their countries of residence. This ideology gradually disappeared as mainstream Zionism became more firmly established.

7. Even though Hibbat Zion preceded the formation of the Zionist institutions, it is commonly regarded as the first wave of Zionist immigration to the land of Israel.

8. Much of Friedman's analysis of the CR remains true today.

9. Mizrahi and HaPoel HaMizrahi have always participated together in coalitions and shared (with slight differences) the same agenda. In 1956 the two groups reunited and became the Mafdal (Miflaga Datit Leumit, or National Religious Party). In what follows I refer to both as Mizrahi.

10. Hebrew version from the Zionist archive; translation mine. Document S25/1446, http://www.zionistarchives.org.il/AttheCZA/Pages/%D7%9E%D7%A1%D7%9E%D7%9A-%D7%94%D7%A1%D7%98%D7%98%D7%95%D7%A1-%D7%A7%D7%95%D7%95.aspx.

11. Some argue that the letter was the outcome of a long bargaining process between the secular Zionist establishment and the leadership of Agudat Israel and reflected their ultimate understandings of the role the Jewish religion should play in the future state. According to this approach, the Status Quo Letter is a founding document that represents a turning point in the state–religion relationship. In contrast, others contend that the letter was not at all central or innovative and did little more than restate the arrangements that were already in effect in the Yishuv. Under this approach, long-term political circumstances before and after Israel's proclamation of independence shaped the nature of the state–religion relationship far more than this single agreement (Vasserman 2002).

Chapter 7

1. It is noteworthy that not all cleavages in Israeli society enjoyed the same pluralistic and tolerant approach. The most problematic was government treatment of the Arab population in Israel, which on grounds of security was governed by a military administration between 1948 and 1966.

2. In 1981, the Ministry of Religions was renamed the Ministry of Religious Affairs. In 2004 it was dissolved, then reestablished four years later as the Ministry of Religious Services. These events are discussed in later chapters.

3. The term HaEdah HaHaredit means "the Community of the God-Fearing" (Haredi literally means "trembling [before God]"). It is sometimes referred to in English as the Orthodox Council of Jerusalem. HaEdah HaHaredit is to be distinguished from the Haredim, or ultraorthodox, more generally. Not all Haredim were (or are) anti-Zionist.

4. The Declaration of the Establishment of the State of Israel, *Official Gazette* no. 1; 5 Iyar 5708, May 14, 1948, 1. The legal status of Israel's declaration of independence has long been debated among legal scholars, judges, and lawmakers in Israel. Although it is commonly accepted that the declaration is legally inferior to regular legislation, it has been acknowledged by the High Court of Justice (HCJ) as a founding document and a source of legal interpretation. See, for instance, HCJ 450/70, *Rogozynski vs. The State of Israel*, ILR 26, 135; HCJ 958/87, *Poraz vs. the Mayor of Tel-Aviv-Yaffo*, ILR 42:2, 309.

5. American Jews, under the leadership of the charismatic Reform rabbi Abba Hillel Silver, exerted considerable influence over Zionist politics because of its size, disproportionate influence on US domestic politics, and financial support to the new state. A few months before Israel declared independence, Silver announced to representatives of the Jewish Agency that the new state would exercise complete separation of religion and state. This statement generated harsh responses from the religious parties in the Yishuv and forced Ben-Gurion to respond that no such

decision about the future role of religion in Israel had yet been made (*HaTtzofe*, December 8, 1947).

6. Some scholars label the relationship that evolved between religion and the state in Israel as a specific form of Arend Lijphart's consociational democracy (Don-Yehiya 1999; Cohen and Susser 2003). Although similarities do exist, there are at least three critical differences between Lijphart's consociational model and the situation in Israel. The first difference relates to the supposition that consociational arrangements are more likely to endure in demographically and culturally stable societies. This supposition stands in contradiction to the dynamic character of Israeli society and the evolving nature of the state–religion relationship in Israel, an issue that I discuss in more detail in chapter 8. The second difference relates to the impact of consociational arrangements on the whole society. Lijphart emphasizes the creation of autonomous spaces for distinct cultural subgroups in which they can safeguard their culture, education, language, and so on, and at the same time maintain minimum connections with other subcultures (Lijphart 1969, 220–21). The religious populace in Israel does enjoy considerable autonomy in different realms. However, it is also characterized by another dimension that does not get much echo in Lijphart's theory—namely, it does not limit its political demands to the protection of its own culture and interests. Rather, the religious community in Israel seeks to impose its worldview on all Jewish Israelis, including the secular majority. This paternalistic approach is rooted in the rabbinic principle *kol Yisrael arevim ze la-ze* (the Jewish people are mutually responsible for one other), which motivates the religious minority in Israel to impose a Jewish character on the whole public sphere. Finally, consociational arrangements in Israel are partial and regulate only certain societal cleavages. While the religious cleavage is definitely regulated by arrangements with consociational elements, other cleavages, primarily the Arab–Jewish one, are not treated in the same accommodative manner. In this they deviate from Lijphart's "grand coalition" or "cartel of elites" scheme (Lijphart 1969).

7. The flag of the state of Israel was announced by the Temporary State Council on October 28, 1948. The emblem, which also features an olive branch (a symbol of peace) on each side of the menorah, was announced by the Temporary State Council on February 10, 1949.

8. This was legislated immediately after the declaration of independence in Article 18A of the Order on Governance and Legal Procedures Act 1948.

9. Adding the Hebrew date was regulated by secondary legislation until approved by the Knesset in the Use of the Hebrew Date Act 1998.

10. Zevulun Orlev, HaBayit HaYehudi–Mafdal (Jewish Home–NRP), a successor party to Mafdal, lecture given at a panel on education, religion, and politics in Israel, Bar Ilan University, Israel, January 29, 2009.

11. *Yediot Ahronot*, January 3, 1950.

12. *Yediot Ahronot*, September 24, 1952.

13. The current authorities of the CR are specified in the Chief Rabbinate Act 1980, which revised and replaced previous laws on this matter.

14. Rabbinical Courts Jurisdiction Act (Marriage and Divorce) 1953, and Rabbinical Courts Act (Enforcement of Divorce Judgments) 1995. It should be noted that there is no civil marriage in Israel. Under the Ottoman-era millet system, which was retained in Israel, marriage and divorce in general fall under the jurisdiction of the religious community to which the couple belongs, whether Jewish, Christian, Muslim, or Druze. Civil marriages entered into abroad are recognized by the state.

15. See State Education Act 1953, Articles 1, 13–16.

16. For a full description of religious education in Israel, including its curricular autonomy and associated problems, see Maoz (2006).

17. The IDF has its own chief rabbi, who participates in meetings of the Rabbinic Council. In addition, every IDF unit is served by a rabbi and kashrut supervisor.

18. For example, in September 1948 two observant soldiers were sent to military prison after refusing to cook for their squad on Shabbat. The punishment was withdrawn following a political crisis and criticism by religious ministers. *Yediot Ahronot*, September 9, 1948.

19. Yitzchak Conforti, interview by the author, August 10, 2008. Conforti is professor of Jewish studies at Bar-Ilan University.

20. Political collaboration between Zionist and non-Zionist Haredi parties with such differing theological perspectives is far from obvious and certainly inconceivable in Israeli politics today. Rabbi Yaacov Ariel, interview by the author, November 20, 2008. Ariel is chief rabbi of Ramat Gan and a leading religious-nationalist rabbinic figure.

21. *Yediot Ahronot*, January 21 and 28, 1949.

22. *Yediot Ahronot*, August 31, 1948.

23. *Yediot Ahronot*, February 3, 1949.

24. Two basic laws passed in 1992—the Basic Law on Human Dignity and Liberty and Basic Law on Freedom of Occupation—have been interpreted by the High Court of Justice as having constitutional supralegal status. I elaborate on this in chapter 9.

25. *Yediot Ahronot*, August 20, 1953.

26. For a detailed account of the intellectual foundations of HaKibbutz HaDati and its relationships with the rest of Israeli society generally and the Orthodox population specifically, see Fishman (1983).

27. *Yediot Ahronot*, December 3, 1964.

28. *Yediot Ahronot*, May 14, 1948.

29. *Yediot Ahronot*, July 19, 1951.

30. *Yediot Ahronot*, March 1, 1954, and April 8, 1954.

31. *Yediot Ahronot*, November 22, 1951.

32. *Yediot Ahronot,* July 1, 1953.

33. *Yediot Ahronot,* October 12, 1958.

34. *Yediot Ahronot,* November 17, 1958.

35. *Yediot Ahronot,* June 19, 1959.

36. Elections to the Rabbinic Council were often loaded with emotion and were a source of tension between the different factions. During this period, Mafdal exerted particular influence over the CR, which was justifiably accused by the Haredi establishment of not representing the whole religious population in an equal manner. In 1958 Haredi rabbis abstained from the inauguration ceremony for the new CR building in protest against their underrepresentation in the institution (*Yediot Ahronot,* May 7, 1958), and in 1963 they announced their intention to found a Haredi rabbinate that would compete with the CR.

37. *Yediot Ahronot,* June 16, 1966.

38. *Yediot Ahronot,* August 5, 1949.

39. *Yediot Ahronot,* August 14, 1949.

40. *Yediot Ahronot,* October 11, 1949.

41. *Yediot Ahronot,* November 14, 1949.

42. *Yediot Ahronot,* March 22, 1950, and February 22, 1955.

43. *Yediot Ahronot,* July 30, 1953.

44. *Yediot Ahronot,* June 23, 1958.

Chapter 8

1. The word "Mizrahi" here refers to Jews of Middle Eastern and North African origin. Mizrahi Jews tend to follow Sephardi religious customs and practices, and the two words are often treated as synonyms. Technically, Sephardi Jews are those who trace their origins to the Iberian Peninsula, whereas Mizrahi Jews are largely descended from ancient Jewish communities of the Middle East. The Mizrahi population group should be distinguished from the religious-Zionist faction (and later party) called Mizrahi, which is actually an abbreviation for Merkaz Ruhani, "Spiritual Center." In this chapter, "Mizrahi" refers to the population group except where noted.

2. As noted earlier, Mafdal was created by a merger of Mizrahi and Hapoel HaMizrahi in 1956.

3. Rabbi Yuval Sharlo, interview by the author, October 19, 2008.

4. Historical data on the Merkaz HaRav Kook in this section are taken from the yeshiva's website at http://www.mercazharav.org.il/?pg=11 (accessed July 20, 2017).

5. Here I refer to the religious-Zionist faction described in chapter 7.

6. The expression Torah v'Avoda is actually a pun. In the Bible, the word "avoda" means religious worship, while in modern Hebrew it means work. Thus, the phrase implies that working the land of Israel is a religious act.

7. This is why Kook's followers are commonly referred to as Hardal (Haredi Leumi, the Zionist ultraorthodox).

8. Rabbi Zvi Yehuda's charisma and coherent teaching were undoubtedly appealing. Other rabbis had reservations about his uncompromising and intolerant theological style. For instance, Rabbi Yehuda Amital, an important teacher and educator in the religious-Zionist camp, criticized Rabbi Zvi Yehuda's monopolistic control over Gush Emunim, which led to Rabbi Amital's separation from the movement (Reichner 2008).

9. *Yediot Ahronot*, February 11, 1963.

10. The Hebrew version can be found at http://www.mercazharav.org.il/?pg=11.

11. Terminology with regard to the West Bank is politically sensitive in Israeli and Jewish politics, as it is largely dependent on one's political worldview. People holding a rightist agenda, including many religious believers, see in the results of the Six-Day War a territorial liberation of the ancient Jewish polities of Judea and Samaria. Those holding a leftist worldview emphasize the legal status of this land as an occupied territory according to international law and call it the West Bank.

12. *Yediot Ahronot*, September 26, 1967.

13. *Yediot Ahronot*, April 17, 1968.

14. *Yediot Ahronot*, May 27, 1968.

15. HCJ 302/72, *Sheikh Suleiman Abu Hilu and Others vs. The Government of Israel*, ILR 27(2), 169; HCJ 834/78, *Salame vs. the Minister of Defense*, ILR 33(1), 471; HCJ 606/78, 610/78, *Suleiman Taufik vs. the Minister of Defense*, ILR 33(2), 113; HCJ 258/79 *Hussein Ibrahim Amira vs. the Minister of Defense*, ILR 34(1), 90.

16. *Yediot Ahronot*, January 3, 1968.

17. *Yediot Ahronot*, February 5, 1968, and June 5, 1968.

18. Settlement list and number of settlers by year from Peace Now website settlement list webpage (https://peacenow.org.il/en/settlements-watch/israeli-settlements-at-the-west-bank-the-list) and population data webpage (https://peacenow.org.il/en/settlements-watch/settlements-data/population). The most important settlement founded during this period was Ofra, which is still considered an intellectual and political hub of the settlement movement.

19. A few months later a new liberal party, the Democratic Movement for Change (known by its Hebrew acronym, Dash), joined the coalition, expanding it to seventy-six members of the Knesset.

20. A detailed account of the anti-Zionist factions, the emergence of Agudat Israel in response to Zionist developments, and the party's participation in Israeli politics during the early decades of the state can be found in chapters 6 and 7.

21. Rabbi Yaacov Ariel, interview by the author, December 4, 2008.

22. The Haredi population continues to grow at accelerated speed. For more on the impact of this phenomenon in contemporary Israel, see chapter 9.

23. A comprehensive account of the historical, cultural, theological, and social foundations of Shas and the various ways it challenges the political and

public spheres in Israel are beyond the scope of this research. Interested readers are referred to the relevant literature.

24. As described in chapter 6, the mainstream ultraorthodox camp was (and remains) divided between Hasidic courts and Lithuanian yeshivas. The Lithuanian ideology is more strictly anti-Zionist, whereas the Hasidic courts, especially the Chabad and Gur sects, have more sympathy for the state.

25. Both terms are properly translated as Council of Torah Sages. In the former case, a more literal translation is "Great Torah Sages," and in the latter it is "Wise Torah Sages."

26. The term "traditional" in the context of Jewish religiosity in Israel, refers to individuals who observe elements of Jewish law and practice, particularly in the home, without being fully Orthodox.

Chapter 9

1. State of Israel, General Bureau of Statistics, in Zertal and Eldar (2004, 570–73).

2. See https://peacenow.org.il/en/settlements-watch/settlements-data/population.

3. Naftali Bennet, chairman of HaBayit HaYehudi (the successor party to Mafdal), became minister of Education in the coalition established after the 2015 elections.

4. For a differing perspective on Begin's intention to annex the West Bank and his unreserved commitment to Eretz Yisrael, see Rynhold and Waxman (2008).

5. HCJ 390/79, *Dwikat and Others vs. The Government of the State of Israel*, ILR 24(1), 1. Two pieces of evidence convinced the court that security considerations were minor in the settlement establishment. First, the appellants provided testimony by a retired general that contradicted the IDF's claims of a security rationale for preserving the settlement. Second, the settlers attested in court that divine obligation was the real motive behind construction of the settlement (rather than security considerations).

6. Rabbi Yuval Sharlo, interview by the author, October 19, 2008.

7. Rabbi Yaacov Ariel, interview by the author, December 4, 2008.

8. In 1988 two more right-wing parties, Tzomet (Intersection) and Moledet (Motherland), participated in national elections for the first time, each gaining a portion of their vote from the religious-Zionist camp. These parties are not discussed in the current work because they were both predominantly secular and were headed by two charismatic secular figures: former General Rehavam Zeevi (Moledet), who was assassinated by Palestinian militants while serving as a cabinet minister in 2001; and former Chief of Staff Rafael Eitan (Tzomet). For a full discussion of the parties of the radical right in Israel, religious and secular, see Pedahzur (2000).

9. The party was established in response to the Camp David Accords and the government decision to retreat from Sinai, and it headed the protest movement against the evacuation. Its leadership included secular leaders such as Yuval Neeman and Geula Cohen and notable religious Zionists, including Rabbi Eliezer Waldman, Hanan Porat, Benni Katsover, and Gershon Shafat. The party reached its peak electoral success in 1984, winning five seats in the Knesset. It was dissolved after failing to win seats in the 1992 elections.

10. Morasha members left the mother party in reaction to the latter's moderate response and decision to remain in government following the Israeli retreat from Sinai. The party participated in the 1984 elections and won two seats, and it rejoined Mafdal in 1986.

11. Kach was established in 1971 but came to the fore only after the Camp David Accords. Its founder and leader was the fanatic Rabbi Meir Kahane, a Jewish immigrant from the United States whose followers engaged in brutal harassment of Palestinian residents, recurrent acts of violence, and hooliganism (Sprinzak 1991). The radicalization of the right following the retreat from Sinai carried Kahane into the Knesset, but in 1988 the party was disqualified because of its racist and antidemocratic positions (Pedahzur 2000, 104; for more on this, see later in this chapter). Kahane was killed in New York in 1990 by an Arab assassin. The party splintered after his death. One branch persisted as an illegal association under his son, Binyamin Zeev Kahane, until the latter's death in a terror attack in 2000. The other branch is still active on the fringes of the Israeli extreme right. For good coverage of Kach and Meir Kahane, see Sprinzak (1991) and Margui and Simonnot (1987).

12. Tami won three seats in the 1981 elections and one seat in 1984. Although Tami was more moderate than Mafdal, the split was not rooted in disagreements about the settlement movement but was derived from a cleavage within Mafdal between Ashkenazi and Mizrahi sects.

13. Rabbi Michael Melchior, interview by the author, July 21, 2008. Melchior represented a relatively small left-leaning sector in religious Zionism. While in the Knesset (in a union between Meimad and Labor), he condemned religious Zionism's obsession with territorial issues.

14. Source: Israel Democracy Institute (IDI) at https://www.idi.org.il/articles/8609.

15. Lerner's group was known as Gal, a Hebrew word meaning "wave" and an acronym for Geulah Le-Yisrael (Redemption for Israel).

16. The second underground was a youth group known as the Brit Hashmonaim, named after the family that led the Maccabean revolt against the Hellenists (and Jewish Hellenizers) around 160 BCE. For a 1998 interview with Yoel Lerner, see Juergensmeyer (2003, 46–50). In the interview Lerner praises Rabin's assassin, advocates a halakhic state, and reiterates his commitment to rebuilding the Jewish Temple on the Temple Mount.

17. Scholars disagree over Sharon's primary incentive to initiate the disengagement. Some emphasize his involvement in corruption investigations, while others see a deep ideological shift in Likud's leadership as a whole and Sharon in particular (A. Shavit 2005; Rynhold and Waxman 2008).

18. A complete version of Sharon's Disengagement Plan can be found on the Knesset website, https://www.knesset.gov.il/process/docs/DisengageSharon_eng_revised.htm.

19. A survey on May 13, 2004, found that 71 percent of the Israeli public supported the evacuation from Gaza, while 24 percent opposed it. *Yediot Ahronot*, May 14, 2004.

20. Rabbi Yoel Bin-Nun, interview by the author, July 15, 2008.

21. *Yediot Ahronot*, April 12, 2005. Rabbi Yoel Bin-Nun interview.

22. *Yediot Ahronot*, April 3, 2005.

23. *Maariv*, April 7, 2005.

24. Orange, from the flag of the Gaza Coast Regional Council, was adopted as the color of opposition to the disengagement; blue, evoking the flag of Israel, symbolized support for the plan.

25. HCJ 1661/05, *Municipal Council Hof Azza and others vs. Prime Minister Ariel Sharon and others* (not published).

26. *Yediot Ahronot*, April 20–23, 2005.

27. On March 4, 2004, the police uncovered a contemporary version of the Jewish Underground in Haifa. This organization, headed by Eliran Golan, was responsible for planting explosives in mosques and under vehicles belonging to Arab members of the Knesset. *Ynet*, March 4, 5, and 11, 2004. Golan committed suicide while in detention in December 2005.

28. Eden Nathan Zada was a religious soldier; on August 4, 2005, he opened fire in a bus in the Israeli Arab city of Shfaram, killing four passengers and wounding nine others. He was lynched to death by the raging crowd. Investigations revealed that he was a resident of the Tapuach settlement and a member of the Kach movement. He had told his relatives he was going to impede the execution of the disengagement from Gaza—exactly the same line of thinking that had guided Dr. Baruch Goldstein a decade earlier; *Ynet*, August 4, 2005. Two weeks later, on August 17, 2005, in the midst of the disengagement, Asher Vizgen, of the settlement Shvut Rachel, shot dead four Palestinian workers at a factory in Shiloh. Vizgen said during his trial that his actions were intended to stop the withdrawal from Gaza. He was sentenced to four lifetimes in prison, and a year later he committed suicide in jail.

29. The chief of the joint staff reported in testimony before the Knesset that sixty-three soldiers disobeyed orders during the evacuation. According to the military prosecutor, there were a total of 163 cases of disobedience related to the disengagement. Data taken from a report to the Knesset on disobedience to military orders, January 19, 2010 (Unger 2010).

30. *Haaretz*, November 12, 2005, and November 18, 2008; *Yediot Ahronot*, November 27, 2005.

31. For the arson attack, see Israel Ministry of Foreign Affairs, "Arson Terror Attack at Duma," July 31, 2015, http://mfa.gov.il/MFA/PressRoom/2015/Pages/Arson-terror-attack-in-Duma-31-Jul-2015.aspx.

32. While some permanent structures in Amona were demolished, settler families persisted in returning to the outpost, leading to eleven more years of clashes over the site in the courts, within government, and on the ground. The last families were evicted from Amona in February 2017.

33. I have borrowed the concept of "state penetration" from Haklai (2007).

34. Naftali Bennett, opening remarks at a conference to mark a decade since the disengagement from Gaza, Jerusalem, July, 13 2015, https://www.youtube.com/watch?v=VxItHtauzsc.

35. Under the Oslo Accords, the West Bank was divided into three administrative divisions. Areas A and B are inhabited solely by Palestinians and governed by the Palestinian Authority (Area A) or jointly by the Palestinian Authority and Israel (Area B). Area C, about 63 percent of the West Bank, includes all the Israeli settlements and numerous Palestinian towns and villages and is under Israeli civil and military control.

36. Naftali Bennett, interview with Jake Tapper, CNN, December 28, 2016, https://www.cnn.com/videos/world/2016/12/28/settlements-bennett-tapper-interview.cnn.

37. Yona Metzger, interview by the author, April 20, 2009; translation mine. A similar attitude was expressed by Rabbi Yaacov Ariel, chief rabbi of the municipality of Ramat Gan, in an interview with me on December 4, 2008. Interestingly, Metzger and Ariel competed in 2003 for the Ashkenazi chief rabbi position. While the religious-Zionist camp supported Rav Ariel, the ultraorthodox leader Rav Elyashiv supported Metzger's candidacy, who was ultimately given the position. This is another indication of the declining political power of religious-Zionism and increasing political power of ultraorthodoxy.

38. Anonymous yeshiva student, interview by the author, November 19, 2008; translation mine.

39. This system remained intact until 2005, when Sharon and Peres broke from their old parties and founded the centrist Kadima (Forward) party.

40. In the early 1990s Rav Ovadia Yosef issued a ruling that true peace allows the transfer of parts of Eretz Yisrael to foreign hands. This made Shas a convenient partner in the Rabin government.

41. Zevulun Orlev, lecture at Bar-Ilan University, January 27, 2009.

42. Degel HaTorah and Agudat Israel were the two component parties of United Torah Judaism.

43. Basic Law: The Government (approved in 1992).

44. Article 3A, Foundations of the Budget Act 1985 (amendment approved in 1992).

45. The Arab population in Israel is also exempted from some civic duties, primarily military service, but for different reasons.

46. HCJ 3267/97, *Amnon Rubinstein vs. the Minister of Defense*, ILR 52(5), 481.

47. The HCJ became active on other politically loaded issues in Israeli politics as well, including the rights of non-Jewish citizens and Palestinian residents of the occupied territories, gender equality, rights of prisoners and detainees, and corruption, among others.

48. HCJ 153/87, *Lea Shakdiel vs. The Minister of Religions*, ILR 42(2), 221.

49. HCJ 3872/93, *Mitrael vs. The Prime Minister*, ILR 47(5), 485.

50. HCJ 1000/92, *Hanna Bavli vs The Supreme Rabbinic Court*, ILR 48(2), 221.

51. HCJ 955/89, *Hoffman vs. The Municipality of Jerusalem*, ILR 48(1), 678.

52. HCJ 257/89, *Hoffman vs. the Supervisor of the Western Wall*, 48(2), 265.

53. HCJ 3267/97, *Amnon Rubinstein vs. the Minister of Defense*, ILR 52(5), 481.

54. HCJ 8569/96, *Ha'Noar Ha'oved Ve'Ha'lomed vs. The Minister of Education*, ILR 52(1), 597.

55. HCJ 5016/96, *Horev vs. The Minister of Transportation*, ILR 51(4), 1.

56. HCJ 953/01, *Solodkin vs. The Municipality of Beit Shemesh*, ILR 58(5), 595.

57. HCJ 10296/02, *The Teachers Union vs. the Ministers of Finance and Education*, ILR 59(3), 224.

58. HCJ 2597/99, *Rodriguez vs. The Minister of Interior*, ILR 58(5), 412.

59. HCJ 8988/06, *Meshi Zahav vs. The Commander of the Jerusalem* (unpublished, given December 27, 2006). In addition, during those years the HCJ, in its role as Israel's supreme court, took a hard line against Haredi leaders, mainly from Shas, who were accused of corruption. The most celebrated case in this regard was against former Shas head Rav Arie Deri, who was sentenced to three years in prison for bribery. See CA (criminal appeal) 3575/99, *Arie Deri vs. The State of Israel*, ILR 54(2), 721.

60. Ultraorthodox protest against the court reached its zenith on February 14, 1999, when a quarter of a million Haredim demonstrated at the court's premises in Jerusalem. For a critical analysis of the implications of this protest on Israeli democracy see Gordon (1999).

Bibliography

Abou El Fadl, Khaled. 2001. "The Place of Tolerance in Islam." *Boston Review of Books* 26 (6): 34–46.

Abulof, Uriel. 2014. "The Roles of Religion in National Legitimation: Judaism and Zionism's Elusive Quest for Legitimacy." *Journal for the Scientific Study of Religion* 53 (3): 515–33.

———. 2015. " 'The People Want(s) to Bring Down the Regime': (Positive) Nationalism as the Arab Spring's Revolution." *Nations and Nationalism* 21 (4): 658–80.

———. 2017. " 'Can't Buy Me Legitimacy': The Elusive Stability of Mideast Rentier Regimes." *Journal of International Relations and Development* 20 (1): 55–79.

Abutbul-Selinger, Guy. 2017. "Shas and the Resignification of the Intersection between Ethnicity and Religion." *Journal of Ethnic and Migration Studies* 43 (9): 1617–34.

Acemoglu, Daron, and James A. Robinson. 2005. *Economic Origins of Dictatorship and Democracy.* New York: Cambridge University Press.

Ahmad, Feroz. 1968. "The Young Turk Revolution." *Journal of Contemporary History* 3 (3): 19–36.

———. 1981. "Military Intervention and the Crisis in Turkey." *MERIP Reports* 93: 5–24.

———. 1988. "Islamic Reassertion in Turkey." *Third World Quarterly* 10 (2): 750–769.

———. 1991a. "Politics and Islam in Modern Turkey." *Middle Eastern Studies* 27 (1): 3–21.

———. 1991b. "The Progressive Republican Party, 1924–1925." In *Political Parties and Democracy in Turkey*, edited by Metin Heper and Jacob Landua, 65–82. London: I.B. Tauris.

———. 1993. *The Making of Modern Turkey.* New York: Routledge.

Akin, Erkan, and Ömer Karasapan. 1988. "The 'Turkish-Islamic Synthesis.' " *Middle East Report* 153: 18.

Aksakal, Mustafa. 2008. *The Ottoman Road to War in 1914: The Ottoman Empire and the First World War.* Cambridge: Cambridge University Press.

Akşin, Sina. 2007. *Turkey from Empire to Revolutionary Republic: The Emergence of the Turkish Nation from 1789 to Present*. New York: New York University Press.

Akyol, Mustafa. 2011. *Islam without Extremists: A Muslim Case for Liberty*. New York: Norton.

Almog, Shmuel. 1996. "People and Land in Modern Jewish Nationalism." In *Essential Papers on Zionism*, edited by Yehuda Reinharz and Anita Shapira, 46–62. New York: New York University Press.

Almog, Shmuel, Jehuda Reinharz, and Anita Shapira, eds. 1998. *Zionism and Religion*. Hanover: University Press of New England.

Almond, Gabriel, Scott Appleby, and Emmanuel Sivan. 2003. *Strong Religion: The Rise of Fundamentalisms around the World*. Chicago: University of Chicago Press.

Almond, Gabriel, and Bingham D. Powell. 1966. *Comparartive Politics: A Developmental Approach*. Boston: Little, Brown.

Almond, Gabriel A., and Sidney Verba. 1963. *The Civic Culture: Political Attitudes and Democracy in Five Nations*. Princeton, NJ: Princeton University Press.

Aloush, Zvi, and Yossi Elituv. 2004. *Rabbi Ovadia Yosseph*. Or Yehuda: Kinneret, Zmore Bitan Dvir.

Amnesty International. 2013. *Turkey: Gezi Park Protests: Brutal Denial of the Right to Peaceful Assembly in Turkey*. Amnesty International Report. https://www.amnesty.org/en/documents/EUR44/022/2013/en/.

Anderson, Benedict. 1991. *Imagined Communities: Reflections on the Origin and Spread of Nationalism*. London: Verso.

Anderson, John. 2004. "Does God Matter, and If So Whose God? Religion and Democratization." *Democratization* 11 (4): 192–217.

Aran, Gideon. 1985. *The Land of Israel between Religion and Politics: The Movement to Stop the Retreat in Sinai and its Lessons*. Jerusalem: Jerusalem Institute for the Study of Israel.

———. 2013. *Kookism: The Roots of Gush Emunim, Jewish Settlers' Sub-Culture, Zionist Theology, Contemporary Messianism*. Jerusalem: Carmel.

Aran, Gideon, and Ron Hassner. 2013. "Religious Violence in Judaism: Past and Present." *Terrorism and Political Violence* 25 (3): 355–405.

Arango, Tim. 2014. "Turkish Leader, Using Conflicts, Cements Power." *New York Times*, October 31. http://www.nytimes.com/2014/11/01/world/europe/erdogan-uses-conflict-to-consolidate-power.html.

Aras, Nisan Su. 2013. "64 Journalists under Arrest, Turkish Main Opposition Announces." *Hurriyet Daily News*, July 23. http://www.hurriyetdailynews.com/64-journalists-under-arrest-turkish-main-opposition-announces.aspx.

Arian, Asher, Nir Atmor, and Yael Hadar. 2006. *Auditing Israeli Democracy 2006: Changes in the Israeli Party System*. Jerusalem: Israeli Democracy Institute.

Arian, Asher, Michael Philippov, and Anna Knafelman. 2009. *Auditing Israeli Democracy 2009*. Jerusalem: Israeli Democracy Institute.

Armstrong, John A. 2000. "Nations before Nationalism." In *Nationalism: Critical Concepts in Political Science*, vol. 1, edited by John Hutchinson and Anthony D. Smith, 216–43. London: Routledge.

Armstrong, Karen. 2014. *Fields of Blood: Religion and the History of Violence*. New York: Alfred Knopf.

Arsu, Sebnem, and Sabrina Tavernise. 2009. "Turkish Media Group Is Fined $2.5 Billion." *New York Times*, September 9. http://www.nytimes.com/2009/09/10/world/europe/10istanbul.html.

Ashour, Omar. 2009. *The De-Radicalization of Jihadists: Transforming Armed Islamist Movements*. New York: Routledge.

Atacan, Fulya. 2006. "Explaining Religious Politics at the Crossroad: AKP-SP." In *Religion and Politics in Turkey*, edited by Ali Çarkoğlu and Barry Rubin, 45–57. London: Routledge.

Avineri, Shlomo. 1981. *The Making of Modern Zionism*. New York: Basic Books.

———. 1998. "Zionism and the Jewish Religious Tradition: The Dialectics of Redemption and Secularization." In *Zionism and Religion*, edited by Shmuel Almog, Jehuda Reinhartz, and Anita Shapira, 1–9. Hanover: University Press of New England.

Ayan, Arslan. 2014. "Politicized Interviews for Public Sector Employment on the Rise." *Today's Zaman*, November 5. http://www.todayszaman.com/newsDetail. action;jsessionid=nqrh9FEqNFiuTdc68gCMQfAi?newsId=363640&columnist Id=0.

Ayata, Sencer. 1996. "Patronage, Party, and State: The Politicization of Islam in Turkey." *Middle East Journal* 50 (1): 40–56.

Aydin, Aysegul, and Cem Emrence. 2015. *Zones of Rebellion: Kurdish Insurgents and the Turkish State*. Ithaca, NY: Cornell University Press.

Bacon, Gershon. 1999. "Imitation and Rejection: Agudat Israel and the Zionist Movement (1912–1939)." In *Zionism and the Return to History—A Reevaluation*, edited by S. N. Eisenstadt and Moshe Lissak, 438–46. Jerusalem: Yad Yitzhak Ben-Zvi.

Bader, Veit. 2010. *Secularism or Democracy? Associational Governance of Religious Diversity*. Amsterdam: Amsterdam University Press.

Bağlayan, Başak. 2017. "The Turkish State of Emergency under Turkish Constitutional Law and International Human Rights Law." *American Society of International Laws Insights* 21 (1). https://www.asil.org/insights/volume/21/issue/1/turkish-state-emergency-under-turkish-constitutional-law-and.

Baldwin, P. M. 1980. "Liberalism, Nationalism, and Degeneration: The Case of Max Nordau." *Central European History* 13: 99–120.

Bank, André, Thomas Richter, and Anna Sunik. 2015. "Long-Term Monarchical Survival in the Middle East: A Configurational Comparison, 1945–2012." *Democratization, 2015* 22 (1): 179–200.

Baran, Zeyno. 2010. *Torn Country: Turkey between Secularism and Islamism*. Palo Alto, CA: Hoover Institution Press.

Bartal, Israel. 2001. "One Language Two Dialects, Secular Nationalism and Religious Nationalism during the First Century." In *A State on the Making*, edited by Anita Shapira, 230–48. Jerusalem: Zalman Shazar Center for Jewish History.

Barzilai, Gad. 1999. "War, Democracy, and Internal Conflict: Israel in a Comparative Perspective." *Comparative Politics* 31 (3): 317–36.

Bar Zohar, Michael. 1987. *Ben-Gurion*. Tel Aviv: Zmora-Bitan.

Basaran, Ezgi. 2017. "Why Erdogan's Turkish Victory May Rally His Opponents." BBC, April 18. http://www.bbc.com/news/world-europe-39622440.

BBC. 2016. "Israeli Parliament Passes Controversial Impeachment Law." BBC, July 20. http://www.bbc.com/news/world-middle-east-36845688.

———. 2017. "Turkey Referendum: Erdogan Dismisses Criticism by Monitors." BBC, April 18. http://www.bbc.com/news/world-europe-39622335.

BBC News. 2014. "Turkey President Erdogan: Women Are Not Equal to Men." BBC, November 24. http://www.bbc.com/news/world-europe-30183711.

———. 2016. "Turkey's Erdogan Says Women Who Reject Motherhood 'Incomplete.'" BBC, June 5. http://www.bbc.com/news/world-europe-36456878.

Beaumont, Peter. 2016. "Israel Passes Law to Force NGOs to Reveal Foreign Funding." *Guardian*, July 12. https://www.theguardian.com/world/2016/jul/12/israel-passes-law-to-force-ngos-to-reveal-foreign-funding.

Behrman, Lucy. 1974. "Catholic Priests and Mass Politics in Chile." In *Religion and Political Modernization*, edited by Donald E. Smith, 183–201. New Haven, CT: Yale University Press.

Beit-Hallahmi, Benjamin. 1992. "Israel's Ultra-Orthodox: A Jewish Ghetto within the Zionist State." *Middle East Report* 179: 22–28.

Bell, Daniel A. 2006. *Beyond Liberal Democracy: Political Thinking for an East Asian Context*. Princeton, NJ: Princeton University Press.

Bellin, Eva. 2004. "The Robustness of Authoritarianism in the Middle East: Exceptionalism in Comparative Perspective." *Comparative Politics* 36 (2): 139–57.

Ben-Israel, Hedva. 2000. "Reflections on Zionist History." In *The Age of Zionism*, edited by Anita Shapira, Jehuda Reinharz, and Jay Harris, 19–36. Jerusalem: Zalman Shazar Center for Jewish History.

Ben Porat, Guy. 2013. *Between State and Synagogue: The Secularization of Contemporary Israel*. New York: Cambridge University Press.

Ben Porat, Guy, and Yariv Feniger. 2009. "Live and Let Buy? Consumerism, Secularization and Liberalism." *Comparative Politics* 41 (3): 293–313.

Berger, Peter. 1967. *The Sacred Canopy: Elements of a Sociological Theory of Religion*. New York: Open Road.

———. 1974. "Some Second Thoughts on Substantive versus Functional Definitions of Religion." *Journal for the Scientific Study of Religion* 13 (2): 125–33.

———. 1999. "The Desecularization of the World: A Global Overview." In *The Desecularization of the World: Resurgent Religion and World Politics*, edited by Peter Berger, 1–18. Grand Rapids, MI: Eerdmans.

Berkes, Niyazi. 1954. "Ziya Gökalp: His Contribution to Turkish Nationalism." *Middle East Journal* 8 (4): 375–89.

———. 1964. *The Development of Secularism in Turkey*. Montreal: McGill University Press.

Bick, Etta. 2001. "The Shas Phenomenon and Religious Parties in the 1999 Elections." *Israel Affairs* 7 (2–3): 55–100.

———. 2007. "A Clash of Authority: Lay Leaders and Rabbis in the National Religious Party." *Israel Affairs* 13 (2): 401–17.

———. 2010. "The Tal Law: A Missed Opportunity for 'Bridging Social Capital' in Israel." *Journal of Church and State* 52 (2): 298–322.

Bilici, Mucahit. 2006. "The Fethullah Gülen Movement and Its Politics of Representation in Turkey." *Muslim World* 96 (1): 1–20.

Billig, Miriam. 2005. *Settlers' Perspectives on the Disengagement from Gaza*. Jerusalem: Floersheimer Institute for Policy Studies.

Bouchard, Gérard, and Charles Taylor. 2008. *Building the Future: A Time for Reconciliation*. Consultation Commission, Gouvernement du Québec. https://www.mce.gouv.qc.ca/publications/CCPARDC/rapport-final-integral-en.pdf.

Brichta, Avraham. 1998. "The New Premier-Parliamentary System in Israel." *Annals of the American Academy of Political and Social Science* 555: 180–92.

Brockett, Gavin. 2006. "Revisiting the Turkish Revolution, 1923–1938: Secular Reform and Religious 'Reaction.'" *History Compass* 4 (6): 1060–72.

Brownlee, Jason, Tarek Masoud, and Andrew Reynolds. 2015. *The Arab Spring: Pathways of Repression and Reform*. Oxford: Oxford University Press.

Brubaker, Rogers. 2012. "Religion and Nationalism: Four Approaches." *Nations and Nationalism* 18 (1): 2–20.

Bruce, Steve. 2011. *Secularization: In Defence of an Unfashionable Theory*. Oxford: Oxford University Press.

Bülent, Ceyhan, and Fatih Vural. 2009. "Intellectuals Condemn Military Memorandum on Second Anniversary." *Today's Zaman*, April 27.

Bunzl, John. 2004. "Introduction: In God's Name?" In *Islam, Judaism, and the Political Role of Religions in the Middle East*, edited by John Bunzl, 1–16. Gainesville: University Press of Florida.

Bureau of Democracy, Human Rights and Labor. 2016. *Turkey 2015 Human Rights Report*. Country Reports on Human Rights Practices for 2015, Bureau of Democracy, Human Rights and Labor, US Department of State. https://2009-2017.state.gov/documents/organization/253121.pdf.

Burg, Avraham. 2007. *Victory over Hitler*. Tel Aviv: Miskal.

Cahaner, Lee, Nikolay Yozgof-Aurbach, and Arnon Sofer. 2012. *The Haredim in Israel: Space, Society, Community*. Haifa: Chaikin Chair of Geostrategy, University of Haifa.

Calhoun, Craig, Mark Juergensmeyer, and Jonathan VanAntwerpen, eds. 2011. *Rethinking Secularism*. New York: Oxford University Press.

Capoccia, Giovanni, and Daniel R. Kelemen. 2007. "The Study of Critical Junctures: Theory, Narrative, and Counterfactuals in Historical Institutionalism." *World Politics* 59 (3): 341–69.

Carothers, Thomas. 1997. "Think Again: Democracy." *Foreign Policy* 107: 11–18.

Casanova, José. 1994. *Public Religions in the Modern World*. Chicago: Chicago University Press.

———. 2001. "Civil Society and Religion: Retrospective Reflections on Catholicism and Prospective Reflections on Islam." *Social Research* 68 (4): 1041–80.

———. 2006. "Rethinking Secularization: A Global Comparative Perspective." *Hedgehog Review* (Spring and Summer): 7–22.

Central Intelligence Agency. 2017. *The World Fact Book*. https://www.cia.gov/library/publications/the-world-factbook/geos/is.html.

Cesari, Jocelyne. 2014. *The Awakening of Muslim Democracy: Religion, Modernity, and the State*. New York: Cambridge University Press.

Çetinsaya, Gökhan. 1999. "Rethinking Nationalism and Islam: Some Preliminary Notes on the Roots of 'Turkish-Islamic Synthesis' in Modern Turkish Political Thought." *Muslim World* 89 (3–4): 352–76.

Chaves, Mark. 1994. "Secularization as Declining Religious Authority." *Social Forces* 72 (3): 749–74.

Cizre, Umit. 2008. "Ideology Context and Interest: The Turkish Military." In *The Cambridge History of Turkey: Turkey in the Modern World*, vol. 4, edited by Reşat Kasaba, 301–32. New York: Cambridge University Press.

Cizre-Sakallioğlu, Umit. 1996. "Parameters and Strategies of Islam State Interaction in Republican Turkey." *International Journal of Middle East Studies* 28 (2): 231–51.

Cizre-Sakallioglu, Ümit, and Menderes Çinar. 2003. "Turkey 2002: Kemalism, Islamism, and Politics in the Light of the 28 February Process." *South Atlantic Quarterly* 102 (2/3): 309–32.

Cleary, Edward. 1985. *Crisis and Change: The Church in Latin America Today*. New York: Orbis Books.

Cohen, Asher. 2002. "Halacha and State, Daat Torah and Politics: Linkages between the Religious and Political Leadership in the Religious Parties." In *On Both Sides of the Bridge: Religion and State in the Early Years of Israel*, edited by Mordechai Bar-On and Zvi Zameret, 435–51. Jerusalem: Yad Yitzhak Ben-Zvi.

Cohen, Asher, and Israel Harel. 2004. *Religious Zionism: The Era of Changes*. Jerusalem: Bialik Institute.

Cohen, Asher, and Bernard Susser. 2003. *From Accommodation to Escalation: The Secular Religious Divide at the Outset of the 21st Century*. Tel Aviv: Shoken.

Cohen, Erik. 2010. "Jewish Identity Research: A State of the Art." *International Journal of Jewish Education Research* 1: 7–48.

Collier, David, and Steven Levitsky. 1997. "Democracy with Adjectives: Conceptual Innovation in Comparative Research." *World Politics* 49 (3): 430–51.

Cook, Guillermo, ed. 1994. *New Face of the Church in Latin America.* New York: Orbis Books.

Cook, Steven A. 2014. "Turkey's Democratic Mirage." *Foreign Affairs*, January 8. http://www.foreignaffairs.com/articles/140640/steven-a-cook/turkeys-democratic-mirage.

Cronin, Audrey Kurth. 2015. "ISIS Is Not a Terrorist Group: Why Counterterrorism Won't Stop the Latest Jihadist Threat." *Foreign Affairs*, March/April. https://www.foreignaffairs.com/articles/middle-east/2015-02-18/isis-not-terrorist-group.

Cumming-Bruce, Nick, and Steven Erlanger. 2009. "Swiss Ban Building of Minarets on Mosques." *New York Times*, November 29. https://www.nytimes.com/2009/11/30/world/europe/30swiss.html.

Daği, Ihsan. 2006. "The Justice and Development Party: Identity, Politics, and Human Rights Discourse in the Search for Security and Legitimacy." In *The Emergence of a New Turkey: Democracy and the AK Party*, edited by Hakan M. Yavuz, 88–106. Salt Lake City: University of Utah Press.

———. 2008a. *Turkey: Between Democracy and Militarism: Post Kemalist Perspectives.* Ankara: Orion.

———. 2008b. "Turkey's AKP in Power." *Journal of Democracy* 19 (3): 25–30.

———. 2015. *What Went Wrong in Turkey? From Muslim Democracy to Illiberal Democracy.* Ankara: Pheonix.

Dahl, Robert. 1971. *Polyarchy: Participation and Opposition.* New Haven, CT: Yale University Press.

———. 2005. *Who Governs?: Democracy and Power in an American City.* New Haven, CT: Yale University Press.

Daily Sabah. 2014a. "17 Gulen-Linked Police Officers Detained Due to Illegal Wiretapping." *Daily Sabah*, November 8. http://www.dailysabah.com/investigations/2014/11/08/new-parallel-structure-operations.

———. 2014b. "Seven Gulen-linked Police Officers Arrested over Illegal Wiretapping." *Daily Sabah*, November 6. http://www.dailysabah.com/nation/2014/11/06/seven-gulenlinked-police-officers-arrested-over-illegal-wiretapping.

Dal, Emel Parlar. 2017. "Impact of the Transnationalization of the Syrian Civil War on Turkey: Conflict Spillover Cases of ISIS and PYD-YPG/PKK." *Cambridge Review of International Affairs* 29 (4): 1396–420. doi: 10.1080/09557571.2016.1256948.

Davie, Grace. 1990. "Believing without Belonging: Is This the Future of Religion in Britain?" *Social Compass* 37 (4): 455–69.

———. 2006. "Religion in Europe in the 21st Century: The Factors to Take into Account." *European Journal of Sociology* 47 (2): 271–96.

———. 2013. *The Sociology of Religion: A Critical Agenda*, 2nd ed. London: Sage.

Davison, Roderic H. 1968. *Turkey.* Upper Saddle River, NJ: Prentice Hall.

Dede, Alper Y. 2011. "The Arab Uprisings: Debating the Turkish Model." *Insight Turkey* 13 (2): 23–32.

De Hertoch, Amnon. 1999. *Inequality in State Support to Public Institutions*. Jerusalem: Floersheimer Institute.

Demiralp, Seda. 2012. "White Turks, Black Turks? Faultlines beyond Islamism versus Secularism." *Third World Quarterly* 33 (3): 511–24.

Deshen, Shlomo. 2006. "The Rise of the Haredi-Mizrahim Movement." In *Israel and Modernity*, edited by Uri Cohen, Eliezer Ben Rafael, Avi Bareli, and Ephraim Yaar, 313–36. Jerusalem: Yad Yizhak Ben-Zvi.

Deutsch, Karl. 1961. "Social Mobilization and Political Development." *American Political Science Review* 55 (3): 493–514.

———. 1980. *Politics and Government: How People Decide Their Fate*. Boston: Houghton Mifflin.

Diamond, Larry. 1996. "Is the Third Wave Over?" *Journal of Democracy* 7 (3): 20–37.

———. 2010. "Why Are There No Arab Democracies?" *Journal of Democracy* 21 (1): 93–104.

Diamond, Larry, and Ehud Sprinzak. 1993. "Directions for Reform." In *Israeli Democracy under Stress*, edited by Larry Diamond and Ehud Sprinzak, 361–74. Boulder, CO: Lynne Rienner.

Diskin, Hanna, and Abraham Diskin. 1995. "The Politics of Electoral Reform in Israel." *International Political Science Review* 16 (1): 31–45.

Don-Yehiya, Eliezer. 1984. "Religious Leaders in the Political Arena: The Case of Israel." *Middle Eastern Studies* 20 (2): 154–71.

———. 1987. "Jewish Messianism, Religious Zionism and Israeli Politics: The Impact and Origins of Gush Emunim." *Middle Eastern Studies* 23 (2): 215–34.

———. 1999. *Religion and Political Accomodation in Israel*. Jerusalem: Floersheimer Institute for Policy Studies.

———. 2002. "Religion, National Identity, and Politics: The Crisis over 'Who Is a Jew,' 1958." In *On Both Sides of the Bridge: Religion and State in the Early Years of Israel*, edited by Mordechai Bar-On and Zvi Zameret, 88–143. Jerusalem: Yad Yitzhak Ben-Zvi.

———. 2005. "Democracy and Halakha in Political Decisions: Trends in Religious Zionism in the Face of the Disengagement Plan." *Akdamot* 16: 11–22.

Easton, David. 1965. *A Framework for Political Analysis*. Englewood Cliffs, NJ: Prentice Hall.

The Economist. 2014a. "Davutoglu's Moment: Turkey's New President, Recep Tayyip Erdogan, Picks a Loyal Prime Minister." *The Economist*, August 30. http://www.economist.com/news/europe/21614191-turkeys-new-president-recep-tayyip-erdogan-picks-loyal-prime-minister-davutoglu."

———. 2014b. "Secularists at Bay: Recep Tayyip Erdogan Seems Bent on Strengthening the Influence of Islam." *The Economist*, September 13. http://www.economist.com/news/europe/21616998-recep-tayyip-erdogan-seems-bent-strengthening-influence-islam-secularists-bay?zi.

———. 2017. "Israel's Justice Minister Imposes Four New Supreme Court Justices." *The Economist*, Febraury 24. https://www.economist.com/news/middle-east-and-africa/21717721-more-conservative-court-will-be-result-israels-justice-minister-imposes.

Eilam, Yigal. 2000. *Judaism as a Status Quo: The Who Is a Jew Controversy in 1958 and Some Remarks on Secular-Religious Relations in Israel.* Tel Aviv: Am Oved.

Eiran, Ehud, and Peter Krause. 2018. "Old (Molotov) Cocktails in New Bottles? 'Price-Tag' and Settler Violence in Israel and the West Bank." *Terrorism and Political Violence* 30 (4): 637–57.

Eisenstadt, S. N. 2000. "Multiple Modernities." *Daedalus* 129 (1): 1–29.

Ekim, Sinan, and Kemal Kirişci. 2017. "The Turkish Constitutional Referendum, Explained." Brookings, April 13. https://www.brookings.edu/blog/order-from-chaos/2017/04/13/the-turkish-constitutional-referendum-explained/.

El-Ghobashy, Mona. 2005. "The Metamorphosis of the Egyptian Muslim Brothers." *International Journal of Middle Eastern Studies* 37 (3): 373–95.

Eliash, Shulamit. 1985. "The Political Role of the Chief Rabbinate of Palestine during the Mandate: Its Character and Nature." *Jewish Social Studies* 47 (1): 33–50.

Elshtain, Jean B. 2009. "Religion and Democracy." *Journal of Democracy* 20 (2): 5–17.

Erdeniz, Gozde. 2016. "Challenges to the Religious-Political Establishment: The Cases of Anticapitalist Muslims and in Turkey and Women of the Wall in Israel." In *The Jarring Road to Democratic Inclusion: A Comparative assessment of State Society Engagements in Israel and Turkey,* edited by Aviad Rubin and Yusuf Sarfati, 83–111. Lanham, MD: Lexington Books.

Ergil, Doğu. 2000. "The Kurdish Question in Turkey." *Journal of Democracy* 11 (3): 122–35.

Esposito, John L., Tamara Sonn, and John Voll. 2015. *Islam and Democracy after the Arab Spring.* New York: Oxford University Press.

Evans, Peter, Dietrich Rueschemeyer, and Theda Skocpol, eds. 1985. *Bringing the State Back In.* New York: Cambridge University Press.

Ezrahi, Yaron. 1998. *Rubber Bullets: Power and Conscience in Modern Israel.* Berkeley: University of California Press.

Farhi, David. 1971. "The Şeriat as a Political Slogan: Or the 'Incident of the 31st Mart.'" *Middle Eastern Studies* 7 (3): 275–99.

Farooq, Umar. 2017. "Conservatives Turn against Turkish leader." *Los Angeles Times*, May 11. https://www.pressreader.com/usa/los-angeles-times/20170511/281556585745321.

Fererra, Allesandro. 2009. "The Separation of Religion and Politics in a Post-Secular Society." *Philosophy and Social Criticism* 35 (1–2): 77–91.

Filali-Ansary, Abdou. 2016. "Tunisia: Ennahda's New Course." *Journal of Democracy* 27 (4): 99–109.

Filkins, Dexter. 2012. "Turkey's Jailed Journalists." *New Yorker*, March 8. http://www.newyorker.com/online/blogs/comment/2012/03/turkeys-jailed-journalists.html.

———. 2016. "The Eleventh Hour for Turkish Democracy." *New Yorker*, May 6. http://www.newyorker.com/news/news-desk/the-eleventh-hour-for-turkish-democracy.

Findley, Carter V. 2008. "The Tanzimat II." In *The Cambridge History of Turkey: Turkey in the Modern World*, vol. 4, edited by Reşat Kasaba, 9–37. New York: Cambridge University Press.

Fish, Steven M. 2011. *Are Muslims Distinctive? A Look at the Evidence*. New York: Oxford University Press.

Fisher, Shlomo. 2004. "Ritual Artifacts and Political Liberalism: Organization of Reality and State Legitimacy According to Shas." In *Israel, Maelstrom of Identities: A Critical look at Religion and Secularity in Israel*, edited by Yossi Yonah and Yehuda Goodman, 249–76. Jerusalem: Van-Leer.

Fishman, Aryei. 1983. "Judaism and Modernization: The Case of the Religious Kibbutzim." *Social Forces* 62 (1): 9–31.

Fleet, Michael, and Brian Smith. 1997. *The Catholic Church and Democracy in Chile and Peru*. Notre Dame, IN: University of Notre Dame Press.

Fortna, Benjamin C. 2008. "The Reign of Abdülhamid II." In *The Cambridge History of Turkey: Turkey in the Modern World*, vol. 4, edited by Reşat Kasaba, 38–61. New York: Cambridge University Press.

Fox, Jonathan. 2008. *World Survey of Religion and the State*. New York: Cambridge University Press.

———. 2015. *Political Secularism, Religion, and the State*. New York: Cambridge University Press.

———. 2016. *The Unfree Exercise of Religion: A World Survey of Religious Discrimination against Religious Minorities*. New York: Cambridge University Press.

Fox, Jonathan, and Shmuel Sandler. 2004. *Bringing Religion into International Relations*. New York: Palgrave Macmillan.

Friedman, Menachem. 1972. "The Chief Rabbinate: Dilemma without Solution." *Medina U'Memshal* 1 (3): 118–22.

———. 1975. "Religious Zealotry in Israeli Society." In *On Ethnic and Religious Diversity in Israel*, edited by Solomon Poll and Ernest Krauzs, 91–111. Ramat Gan: Bar-Ilan University Institute for the Study of Ethnic and Religious Groups.

———. 1982. "The N.R.P. Transition—Behind the Party Decline." *Medina U'memshal Ve'Yahasim Bein-Le'umiim (State, Government and International Relations)* 19–20: 105–22.

———. 1984. "Relations between Religious and Non-Religious Jews Prior to the Establishment of the State of Israel." In *Chapters in the History of Zionism and the Yishuv*, edited by Anita Shapira, 69–86. Tel Aviv: Am-Oved.

———. 1991. *The Haredi (Ultra-Orthodox) Society: Sources, Trends and Processes*. Research Series no. 41. Jerusalem: Jerusalem Institute for Israel Studies. http://haredisociety.org/uploads/files/46498206618101313-haredcom.pdf.

———. 1994. "The Haredim and the Israeli Society." In *Whither Israel: The Domestic Challenges*, edited by Keith Kyle and Joel Peters, 177–201. London: Chatham House and I.B. Tauris.

———. 1999. "The Attitude of Religious Circles to the Establishment of Israel: A Clear Instance of 'The Return to History.'" In *Zionism and the Return to History, a Reevaluation*, edited by S. N. Eisenstadt and Moshe Lissak, 447–63. Jerusalem: Yad Yitzhak Ben-Zvi.

Friedman, Shimi. 2015. "Hilltop Youth: Political-Anthropological Research in the Hills of Judea and Samaria." *Israel Affairs* 21 (3): 391–407.

Frisch, Hillel. 2011. "Why Monarchies Persist: Balancing between Internal and External Vulnerability." *Review of International Studies* 37 (1): 167–84.

Fukuyama, Francis. 1996. *Trust: The Social Virtues and the Creation of Prosperity*. New York: Free Press.

———. 2002. "Social Capital and Development: The Coming Agenda." *SAIS Review* 22 (1): 23–37.

Gal-or, Naomi. 1986. *The Jewish Underground in the 1980s: Novelty or Continuity*. Tel Aviv: International Center for Peace in the Middle East.

Gat, Azar. 2012. *Nations: The Long History and Deep Roots of Political Ethnicity and Nationalism*. New York: Cambridge University Press.

Gause, Gregory F., III. 2011. "Why Middle East Studies Missed the Arab Spring: The Myth of Authoritarian Stability." *Foreign Affairs* 90 (4): 81–90.

Gazit, Shlomo. 1999. *Trapped*. Tel Aviv: Zmora Bitan.

Gerges, Fawaz A. 2014a. "ISIS and the Third Wave of Jihadism." *Current History* (December): 339–43.

———. 2014b. *The New Middle East: Protest and Revolution in the Arab World*. New York: Cambridge University Press.

Ghanem, As'ad. 2016. "Israel's Second-Class Citizens." *Foreign Affairs* (July/August).

Ghanem, As'ad, and Mohanad Mustafa. 2011. "Strategies of Electoral Participation by Islamic Movements: The Muslim Brotherhood and Parliamentary Elections in Egypt and Jordan, November 2010." *Contemporary Politics* 17 (4): 393–409.

Ghannouchi, Rached. 2016. "From Political Islam to Muslim Democracy: The Ennahda Party and the Future of Tunisia." *Foreign Affairs* 95 (5): 58–66. https://www.foreignaffairs.com/articles/tunisia/political-islam-muslim-democracy.

Gill, Anthony. 1998. *Rendering unto Caesar: The Catholic Church and the State in Latin America*. Chicago: University of Chicago Press.

———. 2001. "Religion and Comparative Politics." *Annual Review of Political Science* 4: 117–38.

Golan-Nadir, Niva. 2016. "Marriage Regulation in Israel and Turkey: The Interplay between Institutional Dynamics and Public Preferences." In *The Jarring Road to Democratic Inclusion*, edited by Aviad Rubin and Yusuf Sarfati, 193–215. Lanham, MD: Lexington Books.

Goldstein, Yosef. 1986. "Palastinocentrism among Russian Zionists." *Jewish History* 1 (2): 7–18.

Göle, Nilüfer. 1996. "Authoritarian Secularism and Isalmist Politics: The Case of Turkey." In *Civil Society in Middle East*, vol. 2, edited by Augustus Richard Norton, 17–43. Leiden: Brill.

———. 1997. "Secularism and Islamism in Turkey: The Making of Elites and Counter-Elites." *Middle East Journal* 51 (1): 46–58.

———. 2013. "Gezi—Anatomy of a Public Square Movement." *Insight Turkey* 15 (3): 7–14. http://file.insightturkey.com/Files/Pdf/it15_03_2013_gole.pdf.

Gordon, Evelyn. 1999. "The Creeping Delegitimization of Peaceful Protest." *Azure* 7: 27–37.

Gorski, Philip S., and Ates Altınordu. 2008. "After Secularization?" *Annual Review of Sociology* 34: 55–85.

Gorski, Philip, David Kyuman Kim, John Torpey, and Jonathan VanAntwerpen, eds. 2012. *The Post-Secular in Question: Religion in Contemporary Society*. New York: New York University Press.

Gourevitch, Peter. 1978. "The Second Image Reversed: The International Sources of Domestic Politics." *International Organization* 32 (4): 881–912.

Gözaydın, İştar B. 2009. "The Fethullah Gulen Movement and Politics in Turkey: A Chance for Democratization or a Trojan Horse?" *Democratization* 16 (6): 1214–36.

Graham, Elaine L. 2013. *Between a Rock and a Hard Place: Public Theology in a Post-Secular Age*. London: SCM Press.

Gravé-Lazi, Lidar. 2016. "Critics Say New Israeli Civics Textbook Whitewashes and Distorts Reality." *JPOST*, May 10. http://www.jpost.com/Israel-News/Critics-say-new-Israeli-civics-textbook-whitewashes-and-distorts-reality-453570.

Grosby, Steven. 2000. "The Verdict of History: The Inexpungeable Tie of Primordiality—A Response to Eller and Couhlan." In *Nationalism: Critical Concepts in Political Science*, vol. 1, edited by John Hutchinson and Anthony D. Smith, 180–86. London: Routledge.

Grzymala-Busse, Anna. 2012. "Why Comparative Politics Should Take Religion (More) Seriously." *Annual Review of Political Science* 15: 421–42.

———. 2015. *Nations under God: How Churches Use Moral Authority to Influence Policy*. Princeton, NJ: Princeton University Press.

———. 2016. "The Difficulty with Doctrine: How Religion Can Influence Politics." *Government and Opposition* 51 (2): 327–50.

Guida, Michelangelo. 2010. "The New Islamists' Understanding of Democracy in Turkey: The Examples of Ali Bulaç and Hayreddin Karaman." *Turkish Studies* 11 (3): 347–70.

Gülen, Fethullah. 2001. "A Comparative Approach to Islam and Democracy." *SAIS Review* 21 (2): 133–38.

Gunter, Michael M. 2015. "Iraq, Syria, Isis and the Kurds: Geostrategic Concerns for the U.S. and Turkey." *Middle East Policy* 22 (1): 102–11.

Gür, Bekir S. 2016. *What Erdoğan Really Wants for Education in Turkey: Islamization or Pluralisation?* Al Jazeera Centre for Studies. https://studies.aljazeera.net/en/reports/2016/03/160317094912447.html.

Gürcan, Efe C., and Efe Peker. 2015. *Challenging Neoliberalism at Turkey's Gezi Park: From Private Discontent to Collective Class Action.* New York: Palgrave Macmillan.

Gurses, Mehmet. 2014. "Islamists, Democracy and Turkey: A Test of the Inclusion-Moderation Hypothesis." *Party Politics* 20 (4): 646–53.

Gutwein, Daniel. 2007. "The Privatization Revolution and the Construction of Contrast between Judaism and Democracy in Israel." In *Dvarim ve'Shivrey Dvarim: On the Jewishness of a Democratic State*, edited by Aviezer Ravitzky and Yedidya Stern, 497–545. Jerusalem: Israeli Democracy Institute. https://www.idi.org.il/media/4944/gutvine.pdf.

Haas, Mark L., and David W. Lesch, eds. 2017. *The Arab Spring: The Hope and Reality of the Uprisings*, 2nd ed. Boulder, CO: Westview Press.

Habermas, Jurgen. 2008. "Notes on a Post-Secular Society." *New Perspectives Quarterly* 25 (4): 17–29.

Haklai, Oded. 2003. "Linking Ideas and Opportunities in Contentious Politics: The Israeli Nonparliamentary Opposition to the Peace Process." *Canadian Journal of Political Science* 36 (4): 791–812.

———. 2007. "Religious-Nationalist Mobilization and State Penetration: Lessons from Jewish Settlers' Activism in Israel and the West Bank." *Comparative Political Studies* 40 (6): 713–39.

———. 2009. "The Impact of Jewish Settlers in the West Bank on the Palestinian-Israeli Peace Process." Presented at the American Political Science Association Annual Meeting, Toronto. https://ssrn.com/abstract=1449067.

Hale, William. 2006. "Christian Democracy and the JDP: Parallels and Contrasts." In *The Emergence of A New Turkey: Democracy and the AK Party*, edited by Hakan M. Yavuz, 66–87. Salt Lake City: University of Utah Press.

Hamilton, Malcolm. 2001. *The Sociology of Religion: Theoretical and Comparative Perspectives*, 2nd ed. London: Routledge.

Hanafi, Hassan. 2002. "Alternative Conceptions of Civil Society: A Reflective Islamic Approach." In *Alternative Conceptions of Civil Society*, edited by Simon Chambers and Will Kymlicka, 171–89. Princeton, NJ: Princeton University Press.

Hanioğlu, Şükrü M. 1989. "Notes on the Young Turks and the Freemasons, 1875–1908." *Middle Eastern Studies* 25 (2): 186–97.

———. 1997. "Garbcılar: Their Attitudes toward Religion and Their Impact on the Official Ideology of the Turkish Republic." *Studia Islamica* 87: 133–58.

———. 2001. *Preparation for a Revolution: The Young Turks, 1902–1908*. New York: Oxford University Press.

———. 2008. "The Second Constitutional Period." In *The Cambridge History of Turkey: Turkey in the Modern World*, vol. 4, edited by Reşat Kasaba, 62–111. New York: Cambridge University Press.

Harel, Amos. 2014. "Settler Violence: No Longer a Few Bad Apples." *Haaretz*, April 9. http://www.haaretz.com/israel-news/.premium-1.584466.

Harkabi, Yehoshafat. 1988. *Israel's Fateful Decisions*. London: I.B. Tauris.

Harris, George S. 1970. "The Causes of the 1960 Revolution in Turkey." *Middle East Journal* 24 (4): 438–54.

Hashemi, Nader. 2009. *Islam Secularism and Liberal Democracy*. New York: Oxford University Press.

Hassner, Ron E. 2009. *War on Sacred Grounds*. Ithaca, NY: Cornell University Press.

Hasson, Nir. 2017. "Israel Arrests 33 in East Jerusalem over Temple Mount Riots." *Haaretz*, July 31. http://www.haaretz.com/israel-news/1.804317.

Hastings, Adrian. 1997. *The Construction of Nationhood: Ethnicity, Religion and Nationalism*. Cambridge: Cambridge University Press.

Haynes, Jeffrey. 1998. *Religion in Global Politics*. London: Longman.

Haynes, Jeffrey, and Anja Hennig. 2011. *Religious Actors in the Public Sphere: Means, Objectives, and Effects*. Abingdon: Routledge.

Hazan, Reuven. 1997. "Executive-Legislative Relations in an Era of Accelerated Reform: Reshaping Government in Israel." *Legislative Studies Quarterly* 22 (3): 329–50.

Hefner, Robert. 2001. "Public Islam and the Problem of Democratization." *Sociology of Religion* 62 (4): 491–514.

Hendrick, Joshua D. 2013. *Gülen: The Ambiguous Politics of Market Islam in Turkey and the World*. New York: New York Uniersity Press.

Heper, Metin. 1991. "The State, Religion and Pluralism: The Turkish Case in Comparative Perspective." *British Journal of Middle Eastern Studies* 18 (1): 38–51.

Heper, Metin, and Şule Toktaş. 2003. "Islam, Modernity, and Democracy in Contemporary Turkey: The Case of Recep Tayyip Erdoğan." *Muslim World* 93 (2): 157–85.

Hershlag, Z. Y. 1980. *Introduction to the Modern Economic History of the Middle East*. Leiden: Brill.

Hertzberg, Arthur. 1969. *The Zionist Idea: A Historical Analysis and Reader*. New York: Atheneum.

———. 1986. "The Religious Right in the State of Israel." *Annals of the American Academy of Political and Social Science* 483: 84–92.

———. 2003. *The Fate of Zionism: A Secular Future for Israel and Palestine*. New York: Harper Collins.

Hibbard, Scott. 2010. *Religious Politics and Secular States: Egypt, India, and the United States*. Baltimore: Johns Hopkins University Press.

Hinnebusch, Raymond. 1981. "Egypt under Sadat: Elites, Power Structure, and Political Change in a Post-Populist State." *Social Problems* 28 (4): 442–64.

———. 2006. "Authoritarian Persistence, Democratization Theory and the Middle East: An Overview and Critique." *Democratization* 13 (3): 373–95.

———. 2015a. "Globalization, Democratization, and the Arab Uprising: The International Factor in MENA's Failed Democratization." *Democratization* 22 (2): 335–57.

———. 2015b. "Introduction: Understanding the Consequences of the Arab Uprisings—Starting Points and Divergent Trajectories." *Democratization* 22 (2): 205–17.

Hobsbawm, Eric. 2000. "Introduction: Inventing Traditions." In *Nationalism: Critical Concepts in Political Science*, vol. 1, edited by John Hutchinson and Anthony D. Smith, 375–87. London: Routledge.

Horowitz, Dan, and Moshe Lissak. 1973. "Authority without Sovereignty: The Case of the National Centre of the Jewish Community in Palestine." *Government and Opposition* 8 (1): 48–71.

Horowitz, Donald L. 2013. *Constitutional Change and Democracy in Indonesia*. New York: Cambridge University Press.

Huber, Evelyne, Dietrich Rueschemeyer, and John D. Stephens. 1993. "The Impact of Economic Development on Democracy." *Journal of Economic Perspectives* 7 (3): 71–86.

Human Rights Watch. 2017. *Turkey: Events of 2016*. World Reports 2017, Human Rights Watch. https://www.hrw.org/world-report/2017/country-chapters/turkey.

Huntington, Samuel. 1965. "Political Development and Political Decay." *World Politics* 17 (3): 386–430.

———. 1991. *The Third Wave: Democratization in the Late Twentieth Century*. Norman: University of Oklahoma Press.

———. 1996. *The Clash of Civilizations and the Remaking of World Order*. New York: Simon & Schuster.

Hurriyet Daily News. 2014. "Turkish President Sends AKP-Linked Lawyers to Key Judges and Prosecutors Council." *Hurriyet Daily News*, October 27.

Ibrahim, Saad Eddin. 2007. "Toward Muslim Democracies." *Journal of Democracy* 18 (2): 5–13.

İnalcık, Halil. 1973. "Application of the Tanzimat and its Social Effects." *Archivum Ottomanicum* 5: 97–127.

Inbari, Motti. 2007a. "Fundamentalism in Crisis—The Response of the Gush Emunim Rabbinical Authorities to the Theological Dilemmas Raised by Israel's Disengagement Plan." *Journal of Church and State* 49 (4): 697–718.

———. 2007b. "Religious Zionism and the Temple Mount Dilemma." *Israel Studies* 12 (2): 29–47.

———. 2009. "When Prophecy Fails? The Theology of the Oslo Process—Rabbinical Responses to a Crisis of Faith." *Modern Judaism* 29 (3): 303–25.

———. 2012. *Messianic Religious Zionism Confronts Israeli Territorial Compromises*. New York: Cambridge University Press.

Inglehart, Ronald, and Pippa Norris. 2003. "The True Clash of Civilizations." *Foreign Policy* 135: 62–70.

Inglehart, Ronald, and Christian Welzel. 2005. *Modernization, Cultural Change, and Democracy: The Human Development Sequence*. New York: Cambridge University Press.

Israel Central Bureau of Statistics. 2016. *Prediction of Student Numbers in the Education System 2017–2021: Report on Methodology and Findings.* Israel Central Bureau of Statistics. https://old.cbs.gov.il/publications16/hinuh/educ_report_2017_21. pdf.

Jaber, Hala. 1997. *Hezbollah.* New York: Columbia University Press.

Jessop, Bob. 1977. "Recent Theories of the Capitalist State." *Cambridge Journal of Economics* 1 (4): 353–73.

Jobani, Yuval, and Nahshon Perez. 2014. "Women of the Wall: A Normative Analysis of the Place of Religion in the Public Sphere." *Oxford Journal of Law and Religion* 3 (3): 484–505.

———. 2017. *Women of the Wall: Navigating Religion in Sacred Sites.* New York: Oxford University Press.

Jones, Clive. 1999. "Ideo Theology and the Jewish State: From Conflict to Reconciliation?" *British Journal of Middle Eastern Studies* 26 (1): 9–26.

Joppke, Christian. 2013. "A Christian Identity for the Liberal State?" *British Journal of Sociology* 64 (4): 597–616.

Jordan, Bill. 1985. *The State: Authority and Autonomy.* Oxford: Blackwell.

Juergensmeyer, Mark. 1993. *The New Cold War?: Religious Nationalism Confronts the Secular State.* Berkeley: University of California Press.

———. 1995. "The New Religious State." *Comparative Politics* 27 (4): 379–91.

———. 2003. *Terror in the Mind of God: The Global Rise of Religious Violence.* Berkeley: University of California Press.

———. 2008. *Global Rebellion: Religious Challenges to the Secular State.* Berkeley: University of California Press.

Kadercan, Burak. 2017. "The Rise and Fall of Erdoganocracy: Why Victory May Defeat Turkey's President." War on the Rocks, April 26. https://warontherocks. com/2017/04/the-rise-and-fall-of-erdoganocracy-why-victory-may-defeat-turkeys-president/.

Kadioğlu, Ayşe. 1996. "The Paradox of Turkish Nationalism and the Construction of Official Identity." *Middle Eastern Studies* 32 (2): 177–93.

Kalaycıoğlu, Ersin. 2002. "The Motherland Party: The Challenge of Institutionalization in a Charismatic Leader Party." *Turkish Studies* 3 (1): 41–61.

Kandiyoti, Deniz. 1991. "End of Empire: Islam, Nationalism and Women in Turkey." In *Women, Islam and the State*, edited by Deniz Kandiyoti, 22–47. Basingstoke: Macmillan.

Kaplan, Kimi. 2007. *The Secret of Haredi Discourse.* Jerusalem: Zalman Shazar Center.

Kaplan, Kimi, and Nurit Stadler, eds. 2009. *Leadership and Authority in the Haredi Society in Israel: Challenges and Alternatives.* Jerusalem: Van Leer.

Kaplan, Zvi Jonathan. 2004. "Rabbi Joel Teitelbaum, Zionism, and Hunagrian Ultra-Orthodoxy." *Modern Judaism* 24 (2): 165–78.

Kaplan Sommer, Allison. 2017. "Explained: Israel's New Palestinian Land-Grab Law and Why It Matters." *Haaretz*, February 7. http://www.haaretz.com/israel-news/1.770102.

Karakas, Cemal. 2007. "Turkey: Islam and Laicism between the Interests of State, Politics and Society." Peace Research Institute Frankfurt.

Karasipahi, Sena. 2009. *Muslims in Modern Turkey: Kemalism, Modernism and the Revolt of the Islamic Intellectuals.* London: I.B. Tauris.

Karpat, Kemal. 1972. "Political Developments in Turkey, 1950–1970." *Middle Eastern Studies* 8 (3): 349–75.

Karpov, Vyacheslav. 2010. "Desecularization: A Conceptual Framework." *Journal of Church and State* 52 (2): 232–70.

Kasaba, Reşat. 1997. "Kemalist Certainties and Modern Ambiguities." In *Rethinking Modernity and National Identity in Turkey*, edited By Sibel Bozdoğan and Reşat Kasaba, 15–36. Seattle: University of Washington Press.

Kaufman, Stuart J. 2001. *Modern Hatreds: The Symbolic Politics of Ethnic War.* Ithaca, NY: Cornell University Press.

Kayali, Hasan. 2008. "The Struggle of Independence." In *The Cambridge History of Turkey: Turkey in the Modern World*, vol. 4, edited by Reşat Kasaba, 112–46. New York: Cambridge University Press.

Kedourie, Elie. 1968. "The End of the Ottoman Empire." *Journal of Contemporary History* 3 (4): 19–28.

Kehat, Hanna. 2002. "Talmud Torah in the Teaching of Rav Kook." In *Religious Zionism in Action Essays*, edited by Simcha Raz, 38–55. Jerusalem: Mizrahi—Hapoel Mizrahi—World Organization.

Kelly, Duncan. 2003. *The State of the Political: Conceptions of Politics and the State in the Thought of Max Weber, Carl Schmitt and Franz Neumann.* Oxford: Oxford University Press.

Keneş, Bülent. 2007. "No Need for 'Midnight Express' Anymore, We Have a Midnight Memorandum." *Today's Zaman*, April 30.

Kenig, Ofer, Michael Philippov, and Gideon Rahat. 2013. "Party Membership in Israel: An Overview." *Israel Studies Review* 28 (1): 8–32.

Kershner, Isabel. 2008. "Radical Settlers Take on Israel." *New York Times*, September 25. http://www.nytimes.com/2008/09/26/world/middleeast/26settlers.html.

Keyman, Fuat E. 2007. "Modernity, Secularism and Islam: The Case of Turkey." *Theory, Culture & Society* 24 (2): 215–34.

Kili, Suna. 1980. "Kemalism in Contemporary Turkey." *International Political Science Review* 1 (3): 381–404.

Kingsley, Patrick. 2017. "Turkey's Wars: Quelling Kurdish Uprisings, and Suffering from Terror Attacks." *New York Times*, March 31. https://www.nytimes.com/2017/03/31/world/europe/turkey-kurds-crackdown-terrorism.html.

Kiris, Hakan, M. 2012. "The CHP: From the Single Party to the Permanent Main Opposition Party." *Turkish Studies* 13 (3): 397–413.

Kitschelt, Herbert. 2003. "Accounting for Post Communist Regime Diversity: What Counts as a Good Cause?" In *Capitalism and Democracy in Central and Eastern Europe: Assessing the Legacy of Communist Rule*, edited by Grzegorz Ekiert and Stephen Hanson, 49–86. New York: Cambridge University Press.

Kook, Rebecca, Michael Harris, and Gideon Doron. 1998. "In the Name of G-d and Our Rabbi: The Politics of the Ultra-Orthodox in Israel." *Israel Affairs* 5 (1): 1–18.

Koplow, Michael J. 2017. "After Erdogan's Referendum Victory: Turkey's Polarization Will Only Deepen." *Foreign Affairs*, April 16. https://www.foreignaffairs.com/articles/turkey/2017-04-16/after-erdogans-referendum-victory.

Köprülü, Nur. 2017. "Is Jordan's Muslim Brotherhood Still the Loyal Opposition?" *Middle East Quarterly* 24 (2): 1–9. http://www.meforum.org/meq/pdfs/6560.pdf.

Kortweg, Anna C., and Gokce Yurdakul. 2014. *The Headscarf Debates: Conflicts of National Belonging*. Palo Alto, CA: Stanford university Press.

Krause, Peter, and Ehud Eiran. 2018. "How Human Boundaries Become State Borders: Radical Flanks and Territorial Control in the Modern Era." *Comparative Politics* 50 (4): 479–99.

Kubik, Jan. 2003. "Cultural Legacies of State Socialism: History-Making and Cultural-Political Entrepreneurship in Postcommunist Poland and Russia." In *Capitalism and Democracy in Central and Eastern Europe: Assessing the Legacy of Communist Rule*, edited by Ekiert Grzegorz and Stephen E. Hanson, 317–51. New York: Cambridge University Press.

Künkler, Mirjam, and Julia Leininger. 2009. "The Multi-Faceted Role of Religious Actors in Democratization Processes: Empirical Evidence from Five Young Democracies." *Democratization* 16 (6): 1058–92.

Künkler, Mirjam, Hanna Lerner, and Shylashri Shankar, eds. 2016. "Constitutionalism in Rough Seas: Balancing Religious Accommodation and Human Rights in, through, and despite, the Law." *American Behavioral Scientist* 60 (8): 911–18.

Kuru, Ahmet T. 2007. "Passive and Assertive Secularism: Historical Conditions, Ideological Struggles, and State Politics toward Religion." *World Politics* 59 (2): 568–94.

———. 2009. *Secularism and State Policies toward Religion: The United States, France, and Turkey*. Cambridge: Cambridge University Press.

Kushner, David. 2006. "Turkish Nationalism: Between Ethnicity and Civic Patriotism." In *Religion and State in the Middle East*, edited by David Menashri, 319–37. Tel Aviv: Hidekel.

Kutlay, Mustafa. 2015. "The Turkish Economy at a Crossroads: Unpacking Turkey's Current Account Challenge." Global Turkey in Europe Series, Working Paper 10 (April). https://www.iai.it/sites/default/files/gte_wp_10.pdf.

Lakatos, Imre. 1978. *The Methodology of Scientific Research Programmes: Vol. 1: Philosophical Papers*, edited by John Worrall and Gregory Currie. Cambridge: Cambridge University Press.

Landau, Jacob. 1976. "Politics and Islam: The National Salvation Party in Turkey." Research Monograph no. 5, Middle East Center, University of Utah.

———. 2004. *Exploring Ottoman and Turkish History*. London: Hurst.

Lapidot, Anat. 1995. "Islam and Nationalism: A Study of Contemporary Isamic Political Thought in Turkey (1980–1990)." PhD diss., Durham University. http://etheses.dur.ac.uk/1158/.

———. 1996. "Islamic Activism in Turkey since the 1980 Military Takeover." *Terrorism and Political Violence* 8 (2): 62–74.

Lasswell, Harold D. 1936. *Politics—Who Gets What, When, How?* New York: Meridian Press.

Lau, Binyamin. 2005. *MiMaran ad Maran: The Halakhic Perspective of Rabbi Ovadia Yosef.* Tel Aviv: Miskal.

Lazarus-Yafeh, Hava. 2003. *Islam-Judaism—Judaism-Islam.* Israel: Ministry of Defence.

Lehmann, David, and Batia Siebzehner. 2006. *Remaking Israeli Judaism: The Challenge of Shas.* London: Hurst.

———. 2008. "Self-Exclusion as a Strategy of Inclusion: The Case of Shas." *Citizenship Studies* 12 (3): 233–47.

Leiken, Robert S., and Steven Brooke. 2007. "The Moderate Muslim Brotherhood." *Foreign Affairs* 86 (2): 107–21.

Leon, Nissim. 2015. "Rabbi 'Ovadia Yosef, the Shas Party, and the Arab-Israeli Peace Process." *Middle East Journal* 69 (3): 379–95.

Lerner, Hanna. 2011. *Making Constitutions in Deeply Divided Societies.* New York: Cambridge University Press.

Letsch, Constanze. 2013. "Turkey Alcohol Laws Could Pull the Plug on Istanbul Nightlife." *Guardian*, May 31. https://www.theguardian.com/world/2013/may/31/turkey-alcohol-laws-istanbul-nightlife.

Levi, Avigdor. 1993. "The Foundation of the Hacham Bashi Institution in the Ottoman Empire and its Development between the Years 1835–1865." *Peamim* 55: 38–56.

Levinson, Chaim. 2012. "Israeli Settlers Make Up 30 Percent of New Likud Members." *Haaretz*, January 27. http://www.haaretz.com/israeli-settlers-make-up-30-percent-of-new-likud-members-1.409387.

Levy, Yagil. 2014. "The Theocratization of the Israeli MIlitary." *Armed Forces and Society* 4 (2): 269–94.

———. 2016. "Religious Authorities in the Military and Civilian Control: The Case of the Israeli Defense Forces." *Politics & Society* 44 (2): 305–32.

Lewis, Bernard. 1983. *The Emergence of Modern Turkey.* Jerusalem: Magnes.

———. 2000. *The Emergence of Modern Turkey.* New York: Oxford University Press.

———. 2002. *What Went Wrong? The Clash between Islam and Modernity in the Middle East.* New York: Oxford University Press.

Liebman, Charles. 1995. "Paradigms Sometimes Fit: The Haredi Response to the Yom Kippur War." *Israel Affairs* 1 (3): 171–84.

Liebman, Charles, and Eliezer Don-Yehiya. 1983. "The Dilemma of Reconciling Traditional Culture and Political Needs: Civil Religion in Israel." *Comparative Politics* 16 (1): 53–65.

Lijphart, Arend. 1969. "Consociational Democracy." *World Politics* 21 (2): 207–25.

———. 1999. *Patterns of Democracy: Government Forms and Performance in Thirty-Six Countries*. New Haven, CT: Yale University Press.

Linz, Juan J., and Alfred Stepan. 1996. *Problems of Democratic Transition and Consolidation*. Baltimore: Johns Hopkins University Press.

Lipset, Seymor Martin. 1959. *Political Man: The Social Bases of Politics*. Baltimore: Johns Hopkins University Press.

———. 1994. "The Social Requisites of Democracy Revisited." *American Sociological Review* 59 (1): 1–22.

Lis, Jonathan. 2017. "Israeli Lawmakers Back Contentious Jewish Nation-State Bill in Heated Preliminary Vote." *Haaretz*, May 10. http://www.haaretz.com/israel-news/1.788393.

Lupo, Jacob. 2004. *Can Shas Restore Past Glory?* Jerusalem: Floersheimer Institute.

———. 2006. "Shas: The Historical Depth." In *Shas: Cultural and Ideological Perspectives*, edited by Aviezer Ravitzky, 123–51. Tel Aviv: Am Oved.

Lustick, Ian S. 1987. "Israel's Dangerous Fundamentalists." *Foreign Policy* 68: 118–39.

Madan, T.N. 1997. "Secularism in Its Place." In *Politics in India*, edited by Sudipta Kaviraj, 342–49. Delhi: Oxford University Press.

Madeley, John. 2009. "Religion and the State." In *Routledge Handbook of Religion and Politics*, edited by Jeffrey Haynes, 174–91. Abingdon: Routledge.

Mahoney, James. 2000. "Path Dependence in Historical Sociology." *Theory and Society* 29 (4): 507–48.

Mandel, Neville J. 1974. "Ottoman Policy and Restrictions on Jewish Settlement in Palestine: 1881–1908: Part I." *Middle Eastern Studies* 10 (3): 312–32.

Mango, Andrew. 2008. "Atatürk." In *The Cambridge History of Turkey: Turkey in the Modern World*, vol. 4, edited by Reşat Kasaba, 147–72. New York: Cambridge University Press.

Maoz, Asher. 2006. "Religious Education in Israel." *University of Detroit Mercy Law Review* 83 (5): 679–728.

Mardin, Şerif. 1971. "Ideology and Religion in the Turkish Revolution." *International Journal of Middle East Studies* 2 (3): 197–211.

———. 1989. "The Influence of the French Revolution on the Ottoman Empire." *International Social Science Journal* 41: 17–31.

———. 1997. "Projects as Methodology: Some Thoughts on Modern Turkish Social Science." In *Rethinking Modernity and National Identity in Turkey*, edited by Sibel Bozdoğan and Reşat Kasaba, 64–77. Seattle: University of Washington Press.

———. 2006. "Turkish Islamic Exceptionalism Yesterday and Today: Continuity, Rapture and Reconstruction in Operational Codes." In *Religion and Politics in Turkey*, edited by Ali Çarkoğlu and Barry Rubin, 3–24. New York: Routledge.

Margui, Raphael, and Phillipe Simonnot. 1987. *Israel's Ayatollahs: Meir Kahane and the Far Right in Israel*. London: Saqi Books.

Margulies, Ronnie, and Ergin Yildizoğlu. 1988. "The Political Uses of Islam in Turkey." *Middle East Report* 18 (153): 12–17.

Martin, David. 1979. *A General Theory of Secularization.* New York: Harper Collins.

———. 2014. "Nationalism and Religion; Collective Identity and Choice: The 1989 Revolutions, Evangelical Revolution in the Global South, Revolution in the Arab World." *Nations and Nationalism* 20 (1): 1–17.

Marty, Martin, ed. 2015. *Hizmet Means Service: Perspectives on an Alternative Path within Islam.* Berkeley: University of California Press.

Marx, Anthony. 2003. *Faith in Nation: Exclusionary Origins of Nationalism.* New York: Oxford University Press.

Masmoudi, Radwan A. 2003. "The Silenced Majority." In *Islam and Democracy in the Middle East,* edited by Larry Diamond, Mark Plattner, and Daniel Brumberg, 258–62. Baltimore: Johns Hopkins University Press.

Masoud, Tarek. 2014. *Counting Islam: Religion, Class and Elections in Egypt.* New York: Cambridge University Press.

———. 2015. "Has the Door Closed on Arab Democracy?" *Journal of Democracy* 26 (1): 74–87.

McAdam, Doug, Sidney Tarrow, and Charles Tilly. 1997. "Toward an Integrated Perspective on Social Movements and Revolution." In *Comparative Politics: Rationality, Culture, and Structure,* edited by Mark I. Licbach and Alan S. Zuckerman, 142–73. New York: Cambridge University Press.

McCarthy, Rory. 2008. "Israeli Forces Evict Settlers from Disputed Hebron Home." *Guardian,* December 4. https://www.theguardian.com/world/2008/dec/04/israel-hebron-eviction.

Mecham, Quinn R. 2004. "From the Ashes of Virtue, a Promise of Light: The Transformation of Political Islam in Turkey." *Third World Quarterly* 25 (2): 339–58.

Menaldo, Victor. 2012. "The Middle East and North Africa's Resilient Monarchs." *Journal of Politics* 74 (3): 707–22.

Menchik, Jeremy. 2016. *Islam and Democracy in Indonesia: Tolerance without Liberalism.* New York: Cambridge University Press.

Migdal, Joel. 1988. *Strong Societies and Weak States: State-Society Relations and State Capabilities in the Third World.* Princeton, NJ: Princeton University Press.

———. 2001. *State in Society: Studying How States and Societies Transform and Constitute One Another.* Cambridge: Cambridge University Press.

———. 2009. "Researching the State." In *Comparative Politics: Rationality, Culture, and Structure,* edited by Mark Irving Lichbach and Alan S. Zuckerman, 162–92. New York: Cambridge University Press.

Miller, David. 2014. "Majorities and Minarets: Religious Freedom and Public Space." *British Journal of Political Science* 46: 437–56.

Monsma, Stephen V., and Christopher J. Soper. 2009. *The Challenge of Pluralism: Church and State in Five Democracies,* 2nd ed. Lanham, MD: Rowman and Littlefield.

Moore, Barrington. 1966. *Social Origins of Dictatorship and Democracy: Lord and Peasant in the Making of the Modern World*. London: Penguin Books.

Morris, Benny. 2009. *1948: A History of the First Arab-Israeli War*. New Haven, CT: Yale University Press.

Moses, Hanan. 2009. "Religious Zionism and the State—The State of Things." *Deot*.

Mosse, George. 1992. "Max Nordau, Liberalism and the New Jew." *Journal of Contemporary History* 27 (4): 565–81.

Najjar, Fauzi. 1958. "Islam and Modern Democracy." *Review of Politics* 20 (2): 164–80.

Nandy, Ashis. 1997. "A Critique of Modernist Secularism." In *Politics in India*, edited by Sudipta Kaviraj, 329–41. Delhi: Oxford University Press.

Navot, Doron, Aviad Rubin, and As'ad Ghanem. 2017. "The 2015 Israeli General Election: The Triumph of Jewish Skepticism, the Emergence of Arab Faith." *Middle East Journal* 71 (2): 248–68.

Negbi, Moshe. 1981. *Justice under Occupation*. Jerusalem: Cana Publishing House.

Neuberger, Benjamin. 1994. *Religion, State and Politics*. Tel Aviv: Open University Press.

———. 2002. "State-Religion Arrangements in Europe." In *The Conflict—Religion and State in Israel*, edited by Nahum Langental and Shuki Friedman, 336–53. Tel Aviv: Miskal.

———. 2006. "Splits and Parties in Israel." In *Israel and Modernity*, edited by Uri Cohen, Eliezer Ben-Rafael, Avi Bareli, and Ephraim Yaar, 169–210. Jerusalem: Yad Yitzhak Ben-Zvi.

Newman, David. 1986. "Gush Emunim between Fundamentalism and Pragmatism." *Jerusalem Quarterly* 39: 33–43.

———. 2005. "From Hitnachalut to Hitnatkut: The Impact of Gush Emunim and the Settlement Movement on Israeli Politics and Society." *Israel Studies* 10 (3): 192–224.

Norris, Pippa, and Ronald Inglehart. 2004. *Sacred and Secular: Religion and Politics Worldwide*. New York: Cambridge University Press.

Nynäs, Peter, Mika Lassander, and Terhi Utriainen, eds. 2012. *Post-Secular Society*. New Brunswick, NJ: Transaction Publishers.

O'Donnell, Guillermo, and Philip Schmitter. 1986. *Transitions from Authoritarian Rule: Tentative Conclusions about Uncertain Democracies*. Baltimore: Johns Hopkins University Press.

Öğret, Özgür. 2016. "Turkey Crackdown Chronicle: Week of December 18." Committee to Protect Journalists, December 23. https://cpj.org/blog/2016/12/turkey-crackdown-chronicle-week-of-december-18.php.

Okin, Susan M. 2002. " 'Mistresses of Their Own Destiny': Group Rights, Gender, and Realistic Rights of Exit." *Ethics* 112 (2): 205–30.

Öniş, Ziya. 2006a. "The Political Economy of Turkey's Justice and Development Party." In *The Emergence of a New Turkey: Democracy and the AK Parti*, edited by Hakan M. Yavuz, 207–34. Salt Lake City: University of Utah Press.

———. 2006b. "Turkey's Encounters with the New Europe: Multiple Transformations, Inherent Dilemmas and the Challenges Ahead." *Journal of Southern Europe and the Balkans* 8 (3): 279–98.

Oren, Michael. 2003. *Six Days of War: June 1967 and the Making of the Modern Middle East*. New York: Presidio Press.

Ottolenghi, Emanuele. 2001. "Why Direct Election Failed in Israel." *Journal of Democracy* 12 (4): 109–22.

Oxhorn, Philip. 1995. *Organizing Civil Society: The Popular Sector and the Struggle for Democracy in Chile*. University Park: Pennsylvania State University Press.

———. 2003. "Making Civil Society Relevant (Again)." *Focal Point: Spotlight on the Americas* 2 (1): 1–2.

———. 2006. "Conceptualizing Civil Society from the Bottom Up: A Political Economy Perspective." In *Civil Society and Democracy in Latin America*, edited by Richard Feinberg, Carlos H. Waisman, and Leon Zamosc, 59–84. New York: Palgrave Macmillan.

Oxhorn, Philip, and Graciela Ducatenzeiler, eds. 1998. *What Kind of Democracy? What Kind of Market? Latin America in the Age of Neo-Liberalism*. University Park: Pennsylvania State University Press.

Özbudun, Ergun. 1996. "Turkey: How Far from Consolidation?" *Journal of Democracy* 7 (3): 123–36.

———. 2014. "AKP at the Crossroads: Erdogan's Majoritarian Drift." *South European Society and Politics* 19 (2): 155–67.

Özçetin, Burak, Ulaş Tol, Ali M. Çalışkan, and Mustafa Özer. 2014. "Major Periods of Civil Society Sector Development in Turkey." Comparative Nonprofit Sector Working Paper no. 52, Johns Hopkins University Center for Civil Society Studies. http://ccss.jhu.edu/wp-content/uploads/downloads/2014/10/Turkey_CNP_WP52_FINAL_10.2014.pdf.

Özler, İlgü Ş. 2000. "Politics of the Gecekondu in Turkey: The Political Choice of Urban Squatters in National Elections." *Turkish Studies* 1 (2): 39–58.

PeaceNow. 2017. *Peace Now Data on Population in the Occupied Territories*. Peace-Now, August 18. http://peacenow.org.il/settlements-watch/matzav/population.

Pedahzur, Ami. 2000. *The Extreme Right-Wing Parties in Israel: Emergence and Decline?* Tel Aviv: Ramot.

Pedahzur, Ami, and Holly McCarthy. 2015. "Against All Odds—The Paradoxical Victory of the West Bank Settlers: Interest Groups and Policy Enforcement." *Israel Affairs* 21 (3): 443–61.

Pedahzur, Ami, and M. Ranstorp. 2001. "A Tertiary Model for Countering Terrorism in Liberal Democracies: The Case of Israel." *Terrorism and Political Violence* 13 (2): 1–26.

Peker, Emre. 2016. "Turkey's Recep Tayyip Erdogan Seeks to Consolidate Power with Overhaul of Constitution." *Wall Street Journal*, December 10. https://www.wsj.com/articles/turkeys-recep-tayyip-erdogan-seeks-to-consolidate-power-with-overhaul-of-constitution-1481384221.

Peled, Yoav. 1992. "Strangers in Utopia: The Civil Status of the Palestinians in Israel." *Theory and Criticism (Teorya U'Bikoret)* 3: 21–35.

———, ed. 2001. *Shas: The Challenge of Israeliness*. Tel Aviv: Miskal.

Peleg, Ilan, and Dov Waxman. 2007. "Losing Control? A Comparison of Majority-Minority Relations in Israel and Turkey." *Nationalism and Ethnic Politics* 13 (3): 431–63.

Peleg, Shmuel. 2002. *Zealotry and Vengeance: Quest of a Religious Identity Group: A Sociopolitical Account of the Rabin Assassination*. Lanham, MD: Lexington Books.

Pell, George. 2004. "Is There Only Secular Democracy? Imagining Other Possibilities for the Third Millennium." *Journal of Markets and Morality* 7 (2): 321–33.

Penner-Angrist, Michele. 2005. "Party Systems and Regime Foundation: Turkish Exceptionalism in Comparative Perspective." In *Authoritarianism in the Middle East: Regimes and Resistance*, edited by Marsha Pripstein-Posousny and Michele Penner-Angrist, 119–41. Boulder, CO: Lynne Rienner.

Perez, Nahshon, Jonathan Fox, and Jennifer M. McClure. 2017. "Unequal State Support of Religion: On Resentment, Equality, and the Separation of Religion and State." *Politics, Religion and Ideology* 18 (4): 431–48.

Peri, Yoram, ed. 2001. *The Assassination of Yitzhak Rabin*. Stanford, CA: Stanford University Press.

Perliger, Arie, and Eran Zaidise. 2015. "The Peculiar Victory of The National Camp in the 2013 Israeli Election." *Israel Affairs* 21 (2): 195–208.

Petras, James, and Stephen Vieux. 1994. "The Transition to Authoritarian Electoral Rule." *Latin American Perspective* 21 (4): 5–20.

Picard, Ariel. 2007. *The Philosophy of Rabbi Ovadia Yosef in an Age of Transition: Study of Halakha and Cultural Criticism*. Ramat Gan: Bar-Ilan University Press.

Pierret, Thomas. 2013. *Religion and State in Syria: The Sunni Ulama from Coup to Revolution*. New York: Cambridge University Press.

Pierson, Paul. 2004. *Politics in Time: History, Institutions, and Social Analysis*. Princeton, NJ: Princeton University Press.

Piketty, Thomas. 2014. *Capital in the Twenty-First Century*. Cambridge, MA: Harvard University Press.

Plattner, Marc. 1998. "Liberalism and Democracy: Can't Have One without the Other." *Foreign Affairs* (March/April).

Przeworski, Adam. 1986. "Some Problems in the Study of the Transition to Democracy." In *Transitions from Authoritarian Rule: Comparative Perspectives*, edited by Guillermo O'Donnell, Philip Schmitter, and Lawrence Whitehead, 47–63. Baltimore: Johns Hopkins University Press.

———. 2016. "Democracy: A Never-Ending Quest." *Annual Review of Political Science* 19: 1–12.

Przeworski, Adam, Michael E. Alvarez, Jose A. Cheibub, and Fernando Limongi. 2000. *Democracy and Development: Political Institutions and Well-Being in the World 1950–1990*. Cambridge: Cambridge University Press.

Przeworski, Adam, and Fernando Limongi. 1997. "Modernization: Theories and Facts." *World Politics* 49 (2): 155–83.

Putnam, Robert. 1993. *Making Democracy Work: Civic Traditions in Modern Italy.* Princeton, NJ: Princeton University Press.

Putnam, Robert D., and David E. Campbell. 2012. *American Grace: How Religion Divides and Unites Us.* New York: Simon & Schuster.

Ramadan, Tariq. 2011. "Democratic Turkey Is the Template for Egypt's Muslim Brotherhood." *Washington Report on Middle East Affairs* (April): 21–22.

Ravitzky, Aviezer. 1993. *Messianism, Zionism and Jewish Religious Radicalism.* Tel Aviv: Am Oved.

———. 2005. "Is a Halakhic State Possible? The Paradox of Jewish Theocracy." In *Religion and State in Twentieth-Century Jewish Thought*, edited by Aviezer Ravitzki, 9–42. Jerusalem: Israeli Democracy Institute.

———, ed. 2006. *Shas: Cultural and Ideological Perspectives.* Tel Aviv: Am Oved.

Reed, Howard A. 1954. "Revival of Islam in Secular Turkey." *Middle East Journal* 8 (3): 267–82.

Reich, Bernard. 2005. *A Brief History of Israel.* New York: Facts on File.

Reichner, Elyashiv. 2008. *Beemunato—The Story of HaRav Yehuda Amital.* Tel Aviv: Miskal.

Reinharz, Jehuda. 1993. "The Conflict between Zionism and Traditionalism before World War I." *Jewish History* 7 (2): 59–78.

———. 2000. "Zionism as a Jewish Identity." In *The Age of Zionism*, edited by Anita Shapira, Jehuda Reinharz, and Jay Harris, 37–44. Jerusalem: Zalman Shazar Center for Jewish History.

Repucci Sarah. 2007. "Turkey." In *Countries at the Crossroads: A Survey of Democratic Governanace*, edited by Sanja Kelli, Christopher Walker and Jake Dizard, 711–33. New York: Freedom House.

Rosefsky-Wickham, Carrie. 2013. *The Muslim Brotherhood: Evolution of an Islamist Movement.* Princeton, NJ: Princeton University Press.

Roth, Anat. 2013. " 'Something New Begins'—Religious Zionism in the 2013 Elections: From Decline to Political Recovery." *Israel Affairs* 21 (2): 209–29.

Rubin, Aviad. 2009. "Political-Elite Formation and Transition to Democracy in Pre-State Conditions: Comparing Israel and the Palestinian Authority." *Government and Opposition* 44 (3): 262–84.

———. 2012. "Can Turkey's State-Religion Relationship Serve as a Role Model for Emerging Arab Regimes? A Critical Assessment." *Contemporary Politics* 18 (4): 367–80.

———. 2013. "The Status of Religion in Emergent Political Regimes: Lessons from Turkey and Israel." *Nations and Nationalism* 19 (3): 493–512.

———. 2014. "Bifurcated Loyalty and Religious Actors' Behavior in Democratic Politics: The Case of Religious Zionism in Israel." *Religion, State and Society* 42 (1): 46–65.

———. 2015. "Book Review of Yusuf Sarfati's (2014), *Mobilizing Religion in the Middle East* (New York: Routledge)." *International Journal of Middle East Studies* 47 (1): 212–13.

———. 2016. "Dominant vs. Hegemonic Tendencies as Critical Features in Israel's and Turkey's Political Cultures." In *The Jarring Road to Inclusive Democracy: A Comparative Assessment of State-Society Engagements in Israel and Turkey*, edited by Aviad Rubin and Yusuf Sarfati, 143–71. Lanham, MD: Lexington Books.

———. 2017. "Turkish Citizenship: The Perils of Hegemonic Tendencies and the 'Shadow of Securitization.'" *Citizenship Studies* 21 (8): 872–88.

———. 2018. "The Palestinian Minority in the State of Israel: Challenging Jewish Hegemony in Difficult Times." In *Routledge Handbook of Minorities in the Middle East*, edited by Paul Rowe, 287–300. New York: Routledge.

Rubin, Aviad, Doron Navot, and As'ad Ghanem. 2014. "The 2013 Israeli General Election—Travails of the Former King." *Middle East Journal* 68 (2): 248–67.

Rubin, Lawrence. 2015. "Why Israel Outlawed the Northern Branch of the Islamic Movement." Brookings, December 7. https://www.brookings.edu/blog/markaz/2015/12/07/why-israel-outlawed-the-northern-branch-of-the-islamic-movement/.

Rubinstein, Amnon. 1984. *The Zionist Dream Revisited: From Herzl to Gush Emunim and Back*. New York: Schocken Books.

Rubinstein, Danny. 1982. *On the Lord's Side: Gush Emunim*. Tel Aviv: Hakibbutz Hameuchad.

Rustow, Dankwart A. 1959. "The Army and the Founding of the Turkish Republic." *World Politics* 11 (4): 513–52.

———. 1970. "Transitions to Democracy: Toward a Dynamic Model." *Comparative Politics* 2 (3): 337–63.

Rynhold, Jonathan, and Dov Waxman. 2008. "Ideological Change and Israel's Disengagement from Gaza." *Political Science Quarterly* 123 (1): 11–37.

Salloukh, Bassal. 2009. "Democracy in Lebanon: the Primacy of the Sectarian System." In *The Struggle over Democracy in the Middle East*, edited by Nathan Brown and Emad Shahin, 136–52. New York: Routledge.

Salmon, Yosef. 1990. *Religion and Zionism: First Encounters*. Jerusalem: Hassifria Haziyonit.

———. 2006. *Do Not Provoke Providence: Orthodoxy in the Grip of Nationalism*. Jerusalem: Zalman Shazar Center for Jewish History.

Sandler, Shmuel. 1996. "Religious Zionism and the State: Political Accommodation and Religious Radicalism in Israel." *Terrorism and Political Violence* 8 (2): 133–54.

Saracoğlu, Cenk. 2009. "'Exclusive Recognition': The New Dimensions of the Question of Ethnicity and Nationalism in Turkey." *Ethnic and Racial Studies* 32 (4): 640–58.

Sarfati, Yusuf. 2014. *Mobilizing Religion in Middle East Politics: A Comparative Study of Israel and Turkey*. New York: Routledge.

———. 2016. "The Politics of Religious Education in Turkey." In *Religion, Education and Governance in the Middle East: Between Tradition and Modernity*, edited by Sai Felicia Krishna-Hensel, 147–72. Abingdon: Routledge.

Sasson, Talya. 2005. "A (n Interim) Report about Illegal Outposts." Department of Justice, State of Israel, Jerusalem. http://www.pmo.gov.il/SiteCollection Documents/PMO/Communication/Spokesman/sason2.pdf.

Sasson, Theodore, Ephraim Tabory, and Dana Selinger-Abutbul. 2010. "Framing Religious Conflict: Popular Israeli Discourse on Religion and State." *Journal of Church and State* 52 (4): 662–85.

Sassoon, Joseph. 2016. *Anatomy of Authoritarianism in the Arab Republics*. Cambridge: Cambridge University Press.

Schiffer, Varda. 1999. *The Haredi Education System: Allocation, Regulation and Control*. Jerusalem: Floersheimer Institute. http://fips.huji.ac.il/sites/default/files/floersheimer/files/schiffer_the_haredi_education_system_english.pdf.

Schmitter, Philip, and Terry Lynn Karl. 1991. "What Democracy Is . . . And Is Not." *Journal of Democracy* 2 (3): 75–88.

Schwartz, Dov. 1999. *Religious Zionism between Logic and Messianism*. Tel Aviv: Am Oved.

Schwedler, Jillian. 2001. "Islamic Identity: Myth, Menace, or Mobilizer?" *SAIS Review* 21 (2): 1–17.

———. 2011. "Can Islamists Become Moderates? Rethinking the Inclusion-Moderation Hypothesis." *World Politics* 63 (2): 347–76.

Scott, James C. 1998. *Seeing Like a State: How Certain Schemes to Improve the Human Nature Have Failed*. New Haven, CT: Yale University Press.

Segev, Tom. 1991. *The Seventh Million: The Israelis and the Holocaust*. Jerusalem: Keter.

———. 2005. *1967: Israel, the War, and the Year that Transformed the Middle East*. Jerusalem: Keter.

Sezgin, Yüksel. 2017. "How a Constitutional Amendment Could End Turkey's Republic." *Washington Post*, January 24. https://www.washingtonpost.com/news/monkey-cage/wp/2017/01/24/how-a-constitutional-amendment-could-end-turkeys-republic/.

Shafat, Gershon. 1995. *Gush Emunim: The Story behind the Scenes*. Beit El: Beit El Library.

Shah, Timothy Samuel, and Monica Duffy Toft. 2006. "Why God Is Winning." *Foreign Policy* 155: 38–43.

Shapira, Anita. 1995. "Anti-Semitism and Zionism." *Modern Zionism* 15 (3): 215–32.

Shapiro, Yonatan. 1984. *Elite without Successors: Generations of Political Leaders in Israel*. Tel Aviv: Sifriat Poalim.

———. 1998. "Secular Politicians and the Status of Religion in the State of Israel." In *Multiculturalism in a Democratic and Jewish State: The Ariel Rosen-Zvi Memorial Book*, edited by Menachem Mautner, Avi Sagi, and Ronen Shamir, 663–74. Tel Aviv: Tel Aviv University Press.

Sharlo, Yuval. 2007. "The New Religious-Zionist Elites." In *New Elites in Israel*, edited by Eliezer Ben Refael and Yitzhak Sternberg, 334–54. Jerusalem: Bialik Institute.

Sharon, Jeremy. 2016. "Shaked: We Want to Annex Ma'ale Adumim." *JPOST*, December 31. http://www.jpost.com/Arab-Israeli-Conflict/Shaked-We-want-to-annex-Maale-Adumim-477064.

Shavit, Ari. 2005. *A Land Divided: Israelis Think about Disengagement*. Tel Aviv: Keter.

Shavit, Uriya, and Ofir Winter. 2016. *Zionism in Arab Discourses*. Manchester: Manchester University Press.

Shelef, Nadav. 2010. "Politicized Secularism in Israel: Secularists as a Party to Communal Conflict." *Contemporary Jewry* 30 (1): 87–104.

Sherwood, W. B. 1967. "The Rise of the Justice Party in Turkey." *World Politics* 20 (1): 54–65.

Shmuelevitz, Aryeh. 1996. "Urbanization and Voting for the Turkish Parliament." *Middle Eastern Studies* 32 (2): 162–76.

———. 2006. "Turkey: A Different Political Islam?" In *Religion and State in the Middle East*, edited by David Menashri, 184–91. Tel Aviv: Hidekel.

Shragai, Nadav. 1995. *The Temple Mount Conflict*. Jerusalem: Keter.

Simpson, Dwight J. 1965. "Development as a Process: The Menderes Phase in Turkey." *Middle East Journal* 19 (2): 141–52.

Skocpol, Theda. 1985. "Bringing the State Back In: Strategies of Analysis in Current Research." In *Bringing the State Back In*, edited by Peter Evans, Theda Skocpol, and Dietrich Rueschmeyer, 3–37. Cambridge: Cambridge University Press.

———. 1996. "Unraveling from Above." *American Prospect* 25: 20–25.

Skop, Yarden. 2016. "No One on Council of Higher Education Objected to Bennett Replacing Deputy." *Haaretz*, February 11. http://www.haaretz.com/israel-news/.premium-1.702680.

———. 2017. "Israeli University Heads Blast New Ethical Code as Undermining Academic Freedom." *Haaretz*, June 10. http://www.haaretz.com/israel-news/1.794953.

Smith, Anthony D. 1997. "The Golden Age and National Renewal." In *Myths and Nationhood*, edited by Geoffrey Hosking and George Schöpflin, 36–59. New York: Routledge.

———. 2000. "The Sacred Dimension of Nationalism." *Millenium: Journal of International Studies* 29 (3): 791–814.

———. 2008. *The Cultural Foundations of Nations: Hierarchy, Covenant, and Republic*. Malden, MA: Blackwell.

Smith, Donald Eugene. 1970. *Religion and Political Development*. Boston: Little, Brown.

Smooha, Sammi. 2002. "The Model of Ethnic Democracy: Israel as a Jewish and Democratic State." *Nations and Nationalism* 8 (4): 475–503.

Soper, J. Christopher, and Joel S. Fetzer. 2018. *Religion and Nationalism in Global Perspective*. New York: Cambridge University Press.

Sprinzak, Ehud. 1986. *Every Man Whatsoever Is Right in His Own Eyes: Illegalism in Israeli Society*. Tel Aviv: Sifriat Poalim.

———. 1989. "The Emergence of the Israeli Radical Right." *Comparative Politics* 21 (2): 171–92.

———. 1991. "Violence and Catastrophe in the Theology of Rabbi Meir Kahane: The Ideologization of Mimetic Desire." *Terrorism and Political Violence* 3 (3): 48–70.

———. 1995. *Political Violence in Israel*. Research Series no. 60. Jerusalem: Jerusalem Institute for Israel Studies.

———. 1998. "Extremism and Violence in Israel: The Crisis of Messianic Politics." *Annals of the American Academy of Political and Social Science* 555: 114–26.

———. 1999. *Brother against Brother: Violence and Extremism in Israeli Politics from Altelena to the Rabin Assassination*. New York: Free Press.

Stark, Rodney. 1999. "Secularization, R.I.P." *Sociology of Religion* 60 (3): 249–73.

———. 2015. *The Triumph of Faith: Why The World Is More Religious Than Ever*. Wilmington, DE: Intercollegiate Studies Institute.

Stepan, Alfred. 2000. "Religion, Democracy, and the Twin Tolerations." *Journal of Democracy* 11 (4): 37–57.

———. 2001. "The World Religious Systems and Democracy: Crafting the Twin Tolerations." In Alfred Stepan, *Arguing Comparative Politics*, 213–55. Oxford: Oxford University Press.

———. 2012. "Tunisia's Transition and the Twin Tolerations." *Journal of Democracy* 23 (2): 89–103.

———. 2016. "Multiple but Complementary, Not Conflictual, Leaderships: The Tunisian Democratic Transition in Comparative Perspective." *Daedalus* 145 (3): 95–108.

Stepan, Alfred, and Graeme B. Robertson. 2004. "Arab, Not Muslim, Exceptionalism." *Journal of Democracy* 15 (4): 140–46.

Stepan, Alfred, and Charles Taylor, eds. 2014. *Boundaries of Toleration*. New York: Columbia University Press.

Sumer, Beyza. 2003. "White vs. Black Turks: The Civilising Process in Turkey in the 1990's." Master's thesis, Middle East Technical University. http://etd.lib.metu.edu.tr/upload/1038777/index.pdf.

Sunar, Ilkay, and Binnaz Toprak. 1983. "Islam in Politics: The Case of Turkey." *Government and Opposition* 18 (4): 421–41.

Swatos, William H., Jr., and Kevin J. Christiano. 1999. "Secularization Theory: The Course of a Concept." *Sociology of Religion* 60 (3): 209–28.

Tabory, Ephrain, and Theodore Sasson. 2007. "A House Divided: Grassroots National Religious Perspectives on the Gaza Disengagement and Future of the West Bank." *Journal of Church and State* 49 (3): 423–43.

Tal, Israel. 1996. *National Security: The Few against the Many*. Tel Aviv: Dvir.

Tal, Uriel. 1987. *Myth and Reason in Contemporary Jewry*. Tel Aviv: Sifriyat Poalim.

Tamir, Yael. 1998. "Two Concepts of Multiculturalism." In *Multiculturalism in a Democratic Jewish State*, edited by Menachem Mautner, Avi Sagi, and Ronen Shamir, 79–93. Tel Aviv: Ramot.

Taub, Gadi. 2007. *The Settlers and the Struggle over the Meaning of Zionism*. Tel Aviv: Miskal.

Telhami, Shibley. 2013. *The World through Arab Eyes: Arab Public Opinion and the Reshaping of the Middle East*. New York: Basic Books.

Tepe, Sultan. 2006. "A Pro-Islamic Party?: Promises and Limits of Turkey's Justice and Development Party." In *The Emergence of A New Turkey: Democracy and the AK Party*, edited by Hakan M. Yavuz, 107–35. Salt Lake City: University of Utah Press.

———. 2008. *Beyond Sacred and Secular: Politics of Religion in Israel and Turkey*. Palo Alto, CA: Stanford University Press.

Tepperman, Jonathan. 2016. "Ministering Justice: A Conversation with Ayelet Shaked." *Foreign Affairs* 95: 2–8.

Tessler, Mark, and Eleanor Gao. 2005. "Gauging Arab Support for Democracy." *Journal of Democracy* 16 (3): 83–97.

Tezcür, Günes Murat. 2010. "The Moderation Theory Revisited: The Case of Islamic Political Actors." *Party Politics* 16 (1): 69–88.

Tilly, Charles. 1998. "Where Do Rights Come From?" In *Democracy, Revolution and History*, edited by Theda Skocpol, 55–72. Ithaca, NY: Cornell University Press.

———. 2004. *Contention and Democracy in Europe, 1650–2000*. New York: Cambridge University Press.

Timur, Safak, and Tim Arango. 2016. "Turkey Seizes Newspaper, Zaman, as Press Crackdown Continues." *New York Times*, March 4. http://www.nytimes.com/2016/03/05/world/middleeast/recep-tayyip-erdogan-government-seizes-zaman-newspaper.html.

Tirosh, Yossef, ed. 1974. *Religious Zionism, an Anthology*. Jerusalem: Daf-Hen.

Toft, Monica D., Daniel Philpott, and Timothy Samuel Shah. 2011. *God's Century: Resurgent Religion and Global Politics*. New York: Norton.

Toprak, Binnaz. 1981. *Islam and Political Development in Turkey*. Leiden: Brill.

———. 1996. "Civil Society in Turkey." In *Civil Society in Middle East*, vol. 2, edited by Augustus Richard Norton, 87–118. Leiden: Brill.

Tremblay, Pinar. 2013. "Erdogan Condemns Beer, Lauds Yogurt as National Drink." *Al Monitor*, April 28. http://www.al-monitor.com/pulse/originals/2013/04/erdogan-turkey-beer-yoghurt-national-drink.html.

Turam, Berna. 2007. *Between Islam and the State: The Politics of Engagement*. Palo Alto, CA: Stanford University Press.

Tzur, Eli. 2002. "The Attitude of Mapam to Religion during the Second Decade: From Militant Socialism to Liberal Secularism." In *On Both Sides of the Bridge: Religion and State in the Early Years of Israel*, edited by Mordechai Bar-On and Zvi Zameret, 246–72. Jerusalem: Yad Yitzhak Ben-Zvi.

Ülgen, Sinan. 2011. *From Inspiration to Aspiration: Turkey in the New Middle East*. Carnegie Papers. Washington, DC: Carnegie Endowment for International Peace.

Unger, Yaron. 2010. *The Limits of Disobeidience to Military Orders*. Jerusalem: Knesset Center for Research and Data. www.knesset.gov.il/mmm/data/pdf/m02408.pdf.

Uzer, Umut. 2016. *An Intellectual History of Turkish Nationalism: Between Turkish Ethnicity and Islamic Identity*. Salt Lake City: University of Utah Press.

Vasserman, Avraham. 2002. "Status Quo." In *The Conflict: Religion and State in Israel*, edited by Nahum Langental and Shuki Friedman, 287–301. Tel Aviv: Miskal.

Vital, David. 1998. "Zionism as Revolution? Zionism as Rebellion?" *Modern Judaism* 18 (3): 205–15.

Vonberg, Judith, Lauren Said-Moorhouse, and Kara Fox. 2017. "47,155 Arrests: Turkey's Post-Coup Crackdown by the Numbers." CNN, April 14. http://www.cnn.com/2017/04/14/europe/turkey-failed-coup-arrests-detained/.

Wald, Kenneth D., Dennis E. Owen, and Samuel S. Hill. 1988. "Churches as Political Communities." *American Political Science Review* 82 (2): 531–48.

Wald, Kenneth D., and Clyde Wilcox. 2006. "Getting Religion: Has Political Science Rediscovered the Faith Factor?" *American Political Science Review* 100 (4): 523–29.

Waldner, David. 1999. *State Building and Late Development*. Ithaca, NY: Cornell University Press.

Walzer, Michael. 1992. "The Civil Society Argument." In *Dimensions of Radical Democracy*, edited by Chantal Mouffe, 89–107. New York: Verso.

Weber, Max. 1905. *The Protestant Ethic and the Spirit of Capitalism*. London: Unwin Hyman.

———. 2009. *From Max Weber: Essays in Sociology*, edited by Charles Wright Mills and L. L. Gerth. Abingdon: Routledge.

Weiker, Walter F. 1963. *The Turkish Revolution 1960–61*. Washington, DC: Brookings Institute.

———. 1973. *Political Tutelage and Democracy in Turkey: The Free Party and Its Aftermath*. Leiden: Brill.

———. 1981. *The Modernization of Turkey: From Ataturk to the Present Day*. New York: Holmes and Meier.

Weiler, J. H. H. 2013. "Freedom of Religion and Freedom from Religion." *Maine Law Review* 65 (2): 759–68.

Weiss, Efrat. 2006. "Amona Evacuated; Hundreds Hurt." YNET, February 1. http://www.ynetnews.com/articles/0,7340,L-3209330,00.html.

Weissblau, Etti. 2005. *Data on Number of Students in the Hebreic Elementary Education System by Type of Supervision and Legal Status*. Jerusalem: Knesset Research and Information Center.

———. 2012. *Core Curriculum in the Haredi Education System*. Jerusalem: Knesset Research and Information Center. https://www.knesset.gov.il/mmm/data/pdf/m03113.pdf.

White, Jenny B. 2002. *Islamist Mobilization in Turkey: A Study in Vernacular Politics*. Seattle: University of Washington Press.

———. 2008. "Islam and Politics in Contemporary Turkey." In *The Cambridge History of Turkey: Turkey in the Modern World*, vol. 4, edited by Reşat Kasaba, 357–80. New York: Cambridge University Press.

Winters, Jeffrey A., and Benjamin I. Page. 2009. "Oligarchy in the United States?" *Perspectives on Politics* 7 (4): 731–51.

Yablonka, Hanna. 2001. *The State of Israel vs. Adolf Eichmann*. Tel Aviv: Miskal.

Yavuz, Hakan M. 1997. "Political Islam and the Welfare (Refah) Party in Turkey." *Comparative Politics* 30 (1): 63–82.

———. 1999. "Towards an Islamic Liberalism? The Nurcu Movement and Fethullah Gülen." *Middle East Journal* 53 (4): 584–605.

———, ed. 2006. *The Emergence of a New Turkey: Democracy and the AK Party*. Salt Lake City: University of Utah Press.

———. 2009. *Secularism and Muslim Democracy in Turkey*. New York: Cambridge University Press.

Yavuz, Hakan M., and John Esposito, eds. 2003. *Turkish Islam and the Secular State: The Gülen Movement*. Syracuse: Syracuse University Press.

Yavuz, Hakan, M., and Rasim Koç. 2016. "The Turkish Coup Attempt: The Gülen Movement vs. the State." *Middle East Policy* 23 (4): 136–48.

Yavuz, Hakan M., and Nihat A. Özcan. 2015. "Turkish Democracy and the Kurdish Question." *Middle East Policy* 22 (4): 73–87.

Yeginsu, Ceylan, and Tim Arango. 2014. "Turkey Greets Twitter Delegation with List of Demands." *New York Times*, April 16. http://www.nytimes.com/2014/04/17/world/europe/a-list-of-demands-greets-twitter-delegation-in-turkey.html.

Yeşilada, Birol Ali. 1988. "Problems of Political Development in the Third Turkish Republic." *Polity* 21 (2): 345–72.

———. 2002. "The Virtue Party." In *Political Parties in Turkey*, edited by Barry Rubin and Metin Heper, 62–81. London: Frank Cass.

———. 2016. "The Future of Erdoğan and the AKP." *Turkish Studies* 17 (1): 19–30.

Yildirim, A. Kadir. 2016. *Muslim Democratic Parties in the Middle East*. Bloomington: Indiana University Press.

Yildiz, Ahmet. 2003. "Politico-Religious Discourse of Political Islam in Turkey: The Parties of National Outlook." *Muslim World* 95: 187–208.

Yilmaz, Ihsan. 2005. "State, Law, Civil Society and Islam in Contemporary Turkey." *Muslim World* 95: 385–411.

Yom, Sean L., and Gregory F. Gause III. 2012. "Resilient Royals: How Arab Monarchies Hang On." *Journal of Democracy* 23 (4): 74–88.

Yuchtman-Yaar, Ephraim, and Tamar Hermann. 2000. "Shas: The Haredi-Dovish Image in a Changing Reality." *Israel Studies* 5 (2): 32–77.

Zakaria, Fareed. 1997. "The Rise of Illiberal Democracy." *Foreign Affairs* 76 (6): 22–43.

———. 2004. "Islam, Democracy and Constitutional Liberalism." *Political Science Quarterly* 119 (1): 1–20.

Zameret, Zvi. 2002. "Yes to a Jewish State, No to a Clericalist State: The Mapai Leadership and Its Attitude to Religion and Religious Jews." In *On Both Sides of the Bridge: Religion and State in the Early Years of Israel*, edited by Mordechai Bar-On and Zvi Zameret, 175–245. Jerusalem: Yad Yitzhak Ben-Zvi.

Zartman, William. 1992. "Democracy and Islam, the Cultural Dialectic." *Annals of the Academy of Political and Social Science* 524: 181–91.

Zertal, Idith. 2002. *Death and the Nation: History, Memory, Politics*. Or Yehuda: Dvir.

Zertal, Idith, and Akiva Eldar. 2004. *Lords of the Land: The Settlers and the State of Israel 1967–2004*. Or Yehuda: Kinneret, Zmora-Bitan, Dvir.

Zürcher, Erik J. 1991. *Political Opposition in the Early Turkish Republic, the Progressive Republican Party (1924–1925)*. Leiden: Brill.

———. 2005. *Turkey: A Modern History*. Tel Aviv: Tel Aviv University Press.

Index

Note: *Italicized* page numbers refer to figures,
bold page numbers refer to tables

www.ingramcontent.com/pod-product-compliance
Lightning Source LLC
Chambersburg PA
CBHW030640270326
41929CB00007B/146